SMALL
ARCHITECTURE

Philip Jodidio

SMALL
ARCHITECTURE

TASCHEN
Bibliotheca Universalis

CONTENTS

INTRODUCTION – Einleitung / Introduction **8**

2BY4-ARCHITECTS – Island House, *Breukelen, The Netherlands* **38**

WERNER AISSLINGER – Fincube, *Winterinn, Ritten, South Tyrol, Italy* **44**

ATELIER BOW-WOW – BMW Guggenheim LAB, *New York, USA; Berlin, Germany; Mumbai, India* **50**

Rendez-Vous, *Tokyo, Japan* **58**

SHIGERU BAN – Quinta Botanica, *Algarve, Portugal* **62**

Camper Pavilion, *Alicante, Spain; Sanya, China; Miami, USA; Lorient, France* **70**

Paper Temporary Shelters in Haiti, *Port-au-Prince, Haiti* **74**

BARKOW LEIBINGER ARCHITECTS – Marcus Prize Pavilion, *Menomonee Valley, Milwaukee, USA* **78**

BAUMRAUM – The Tree House, *Hechtel-Eksel, Belgium* **84**

Tree Whisper Tree-House Hotel, *Bad Zwischenahn, Germany* **92**

BCMF – Casa Cor Bar, *Belo Horizonte, Minas Gerais, Brazil* **98**

MARLON BLACKWELL – Saint Nicholas Eastern Orthodox Church, *Springdale, Arkansas, USA* **104**

JOSÉ CADILHE – House 77, *Póvoa de Varzim, Portugal* **108**

MANUEL CLAVEL-ROJO – Cloud Pantheon, *Espinardo, Murcia, Spain* **114**

COELACANTH AND ASSOCIATES – Sunken House, *Odawara, Kanagawa, Japan* **120**

JAVIER CORVALÁN – Hamaca House, *Luque, Paraguay* **126**

CROSSON CLARKE CARNACHAN – Hut on Sleds, *Whangapoua, New Zealand* **130**

DESIGN NEUOB – Shirakawa Public Toilet, *Kumamoto City, Japan* **140**

SHUHEI ENDO – Rooftecture OT2, *Osaka, Japan* **146**

MASAKI ENDOH – Natural Illuminance II, *Tokyo, Japan* **154**

ROBIN FALCK – Nido, *Sipoo, Finland* **158**

TERUNOBU FUJIMORI – Beetle's House, *Victoria and Albert Museum, London, UK* **162**

SOU FUJIMOTO – House K, *Nishinomiya-shi, Hyogo, Japan* **168**

Public Toilet in Ichihara, *Ichihara City, Chiba, Japan* **174**

GIJS VAN VAERENBERGH – Reading between the Lines, *Borgloon, Belgium* **178**

4

JORGE GRACIA GARCÍA – Endémico Resguardo Silvestre, *Valle de Guadalupe, Ensenada, Mexico* **186**

ZAHA HADID – Burnham Pavilion, *Chicago, USA* **194**

HAKUHODO – AND Market, *Kasumigaseki, Tokyo, Japan* **200**

HAUGEN/ZOHAR – Cave for Children, *Trondheim, Norway* **206**

Fireplace for Children, *Trondheim, Norway* **212**

HAWORTH TOMPKINS – Dovecote Studio, *Snape, Suffolk, UK* **216**

TIMOTHY HURSLEY – Alabama Silo, *Greensboro, Alabama, USA* **222**

CRISTINA IGLESIAS – Vegetation Room Inhotim, *Inhotim, Belo Horizonte, Brazil* **226**

JUNYA ISHIGAMI – Greenhouses, Japanese Pavilion, *Venice, Italy* **232**

ARATA ISOZAKI – Obscured Horizon, *Pioneertown, California, USA* **238**

TOYO ITO – Home-for-All in Rikuzentakata, *Rikuzentakata, Iwate, Japan* **246**

Inside In, *Tokyo, Japan* **252**

JAKOB+MACFARLANE – Pink Bar, *Centre Pompidou, Paris, France* **258**

ADAM KALKIN – illy Push Button House, *Venice, Italy* **264**

TETSUO KONDO – House in Chayagasaka, *Nagoya, Aichi, Japan* **268**

KENGO KUMA – Hojo-an, *Kyoto, Japan* **276**

Même Experimental House, *Hokkaido, Japan* **280**

LAAC – Top of Tyrol Mountain Platform, *Mount Isidor, Stubai Glacier, Tyrol, Austria* **286**

LOT-EK – Whitney Studio, *New York, USA* **292**

Van Alen Books, *New York, USA* **300**

KEISUKE MAEDA / UID ARCHITECTS – Peanuts, *Hiroshima, Japan* **304**

FUMIHIKO MAKI – Haus der Hoffnung, *Natori Performing Arts Center Multipurpose Hall, Natori, Miyagi, Japan* **312**

MARK+VIVI – The Tire Shop Project, *Verdun, Montreal, Canada* **318**

MARTE.MARTE – Mountain Cabin, *Laterns, Austria* **326**

MIRALLES TAGLIABUE EMBT – Camper Store, *Barcelona, Spain* **332**

KOTA MIZUISHI – Riverside House, *Suginami, Tokyo, Japan* **336**

TATZU NISHI – Discovering Columbus, *New York, USA* **344**

RYUE NISHIZAWA – Fukita Pavilion, *Shodoshima, Kagawa, Japan* **348**

OBRA ARCHITECTS – Red+Housing: Architecture on the Edge of Survival, *Beijing, China* **354**

OFFICE OF MOBILE DESIGN – OMD Prefab Show House, *Joshua Tree, California, USA* **360**

Taliesin Mod.Fab, *Taliesin West, Scottsdale, Arizona, USA* **366**

OLSON KUNDIG – Sol Duc Cabin, *Olympic Peninsula, Washington, USA* **368**

Gulf Islands Cabin, *Gulf Islands, British Columbia, Canada* **374**

Olson Cabin, *Longbranch, Washington, USA* **380**

JOHN PAWSON – House of Stone, *Milan, Italy* **384**

JIM POTEET – Container GuestHouse, *San Antonio, USA* **388**

RAAAF / ATELIER DE LYON – Bunker 599, *Zijderveld, The Netherlands* **392**

RAUMLABORBERLIN – Spacebuster, *New York, USA* **396**

RECETAS URBANAS – Aula Abierta / La Araña, *Seville, Spain* **402**

REX – Madison Avenue (Doll)House, *New York, USA* **408**

RINTALA EGGERTSSON – Hut to Hut, *Kagala, Karnataka, India* **414**

Seljord Watchtower, *Seljord, Telemark, Norway* **420**

Ark Booktower, *Victoria and Albert Museum, London, UK* **424**

ROJKIND ARQUITECTOS – Portal of Awareness, *Mexico City, Mexico* **428**

FERNANDO ROMERO – Children's Room, *Mexico City, Mexico* **432**

ROTOR – RDF181, *Brussels, Belgium* **438**

DAVID SALMELA – Yingst Pavilion and Sauna, *Traverse City, Michigan, USA* **444**

TODD SAUNDERS – Sogn og Fjordane Summer Cabin, *Rysjedalsvika, Norway* **450**

KAZUYO SEJIMA – Tsuchihashi House, *Tokyo, Japan* **454**

Inujima Art House Project, *Inujima, Okayama, Japan* **460**

SO – IL – Tri-Colonnade, *Shenzhen, China* **464**

JUAN AGUSTIN SOZA – Feuereisen House, *Santa Sofia de Lo Cañas, Santiago, Chile* **470**

Cozy Box, *Santa Sofia de Lo Cañas, Santiago, Chile* **476**

STUDIO MAKKINK & BEY – Brinta-House, *Vijversburg, Tytsjerk, The Netherlands* **482**

STUDIO MUMBAI – In-Between Architecture, *Victoria and Albert Museum, London, UK* **488**

STUDIO ROLF.FR AND ZECC ARCHITECTS – The Black Pearl, *Rotterdam, The Netherlands* **496**

STUDIO WG3 – Hypercubus, *Graz, Austria* **504**

TACKLEBOX – Saipua, *Brooklyn, New York, USA* **510**

KOJI TSUTSUI – Bent House, *Tokyo, Japan* **516**

TYIN TEGNESTUE ARCHITECTS – Boathouse, *Aure, Møre og Romsdal, Norway* **522**

UNSTUDIO – New Amsterdam Pavilion, *New York, USA* **528**

VAILLO + IRIGARAY ARCHITECTS – D Jewelry, *Pamplona, Spain* **534**

VO TRONG NGHIA – Low-Cost House, *Dongnai, Vietnam* **540**

JOHN WARDLE – Shearers Quarters, *North Bruny Island, Tasmania, Australia* **548**

HELENA WILLEMEIT – Airscape, *Berlin, Germany* **560**

INDEX – 566

CREDITS – 572

INTRODUCTION

SMALL, BUT PERFECTLY FORMED

What happens when economies falter and construction grinds nearly to a halt? Does architecture, often so deeply dependent on finances, also lose its inventiveness? In a time of excessive spending on construction, countries such as Spain produced a number of remarkable buildings, and brilliant new architects came to the fore. With young Spanish or Portuguese architects today seeking any work they can find elsewhere in Europe, does inventiveness evaporate, or is energy transferred elsewhere and into different types of projects? Despite what has been described as a global slowdown, some countries continue to develop at a rapid pace—thus the estimated GDP of China grew by 6.9% in 2015. Though it has fallen from a high of over 10% in 2010, India's economic growth in 2016 is estimated at about 7.1%. These countries and others are by no means in recession and their architecture reflects this fact.

SIZE DOES MATTER

Does size really matter in architecture? It may be interesting to note that many of today's outstanding architects, from Frank Gehry to Tadao Ando, started their careers with astonishing small projects—mostly houses. Their own transition to larger scale work was not always as successful as might have been hoped. So is bigger necessarily better? In fact, the larger a project is, the more bureaucratic and complex it tends to become, leaving the architect less and less say in the final result. Works like Frank Gehry's Guggenheim Bilbao (Spain, 1997) are basically the exceptions that prove the rule. Bigger is not automatically better and never has been. Works like Donato Bramante's Tempietto (San Pietro in Montorio, Rome, Italy, 1502–10), which is just 4.5 meters in diameter, have marked the history of architecture more than many larger buildings. It might be suggested that size does matter, but that small buildings often provide a degree of freedom to architects that cannot be obtained in gigantic public or corporate projects.

The advantages of small work also become apparent in a time of economic stress. Big budgets have become rare, but the desire or the need to build has not disappeared. Smaller is cheaper in most cases, so what happens when the money disappears—more small structures are created. This type of generalization is, of course, more or less true according to the parts of the world concerned. Some countries, like Japan, have a cultural preference for or bias toward small buildings. Due to the density of populations along Japan's eastern seaboard, in particular between Tokyo and Osaka, inhabitants have long since learned to make do with relatively little space. Real-estate prices in Tokyo and some other Japanese cities are such that even a tiny plot of land is very expensive to say the least. Thus, small homes, under 100 square meters, are more the rule than they are an exception, even when talented architects are called on to design them. Although Japan's economy has been in the doldrums since the 1990s, there is a continuous flow of new residential work that has given rise to more than one generation of very talented architects.

In Japan, but elsewhere as well, changes in lifestyle coupled with economic pressures seem to be reconfiguring many of the requirements of architecture. Where private houses, in postwar America for example, had a number of standard features such as distinct kitchen, dining, and living areas, more recent trends have, in a sense, broken down the walls between these spaces, or often eliminated them. An open living space that is contiguous with cooking or dining areas has become more frequent than enclosed volumes, which often implies a reduced space requirement. The Japanese, with their long tradition of sliding screens that can reconfigure interior space, or even the rapport between inside and outside, are presently leading the way in a new generation of houses that have practically no divisions in their spaces. Space that is sufficiently "flexible" to be used in many ways can allow a small building to satisfy more needs than larger ones did in the past.

SMALL IS SEXY

Bramante's Tempietto or much more recent works like Philip Johnson's Study (New Canaan, Connecticut, 1980) have long been erected at the very threshold between art and architecture. Johnson's odd Study has a floor area of just under 36 square meters. Though he did work in what he called this "monk's cell," Johnson's forms, like the later ones of Frank

Gehry, certainly approach sculpture. Small structures are clearly freer of extensive building requirements than their larger counterparts. This is one reason that artists who are interested in architecture sometimes indulge their fantasies by creating small buildings. The reverse is also true. For an architect, creating a veritable work of art can be more easily conceived at a small scale than in a huge building that must meet so many different demands. It is not always easy to create art when you have to park a thousand cars in the garage, or provide emergency egress for hundreds of panicked office workers.

This volume whose contents originated in the *Architecture Now!* series focuses on small buildings or spaces. This is no accident in terms of the inventiveness shown by the architects (and artists) selected, nor is this choice unrelated to larger events on the stage of the global economy. When there isn't enough money to conjure up huge convention centers and skyscrapers, small architecture starts to look very appealing indeed. Where excellent architects might well have declined small commissions a few years ago, a number of them are beginning to see the interest of downsizing in a positive way. No doubt about it, today, in architecture, small is sexy.

THE USEFUL AND THE USELESS

Where, precisely, does the line of demarcation between art and architecture lie? Several works published in this volume clearly pose this question. The American sculptor Richard Serra has stated that "the difference between art and architecture is that architecture serves a purpose." Though some architects may flirt (dangerously?) with structures that serve no discernable purpose, Serra's definition is a useful guideline that certainly does not keep us from including some of these "ambiguous" works in a volume essentially dedicated to architecture. Readers of the *Architecture Now!* series are by now familiar with these incursions into the domain of the "useless"—it being fairly obvious that artists are often ahead of their times and more in tune with the spirit of the moment than some of their more "concrete" architectural colleagues.

An interesting example of crossing the lines between art and architecture is offered by the Belgian team Gijs Van Vaerenberg. Pieterjan Gijs studied civil engineering and architecture at the Catholic University of Leuven (KUL, 2001–06) like his colleague Arnout Van Vaerenbergh, but he also obtained a Masters in Urbanism and Territorial Development. Their work Reading between the Lines (Borgloon, Belgium, 2011, page 180) has an area of just 28 square meters. It has a reinforced concrete foundation and was made with 30 tons of Corten steel and 2,000 columns. It is not a piece of architecture in the usual sense, but rather a "transparent object of art." It forms the outline of a church, but does not seek to serve that function, instead it is a commentary on absence on the dialogue between solidity and emptiness in architecture.

An interest in crossing the usual boundaries can be found in many disciplines, not only art and architecture per se. The Dutch designer Erik Rietveld is a case in point. He studied Economics & Business at the University Maastricht and graduated in 1993. He then studied Philosophy, Psychology, and Portuguese at the University of Sao Paolo (USP), graduating with a Master in Philosophy from the University of Amsterdam (UvA) in 2003. He works with his brother Ronald Rietveld (born in 1972) who is in fact an architect—the two of them worked on Bunker 599 (Diefdijklinie, Zijderveld, The Netherlands, 2010, page 394) involving a military bunker built by the New Dutch Waterline (NDW). The designers explain, "A seemingly indestructible bunker with monumental status is sliced open. The design thereby opens up the minuscule interior of one of NDW's 700 bunkers, the insides of which are normally cut off from view completely. In addition, a long wooden boardwalk cuts through the extremely heavy construction. It leads visitors to a flooded area and to the footpaths of the adjacent natural reserve." Cutting a concrete bunker in two and creating an open passage through it cannot be said to participate in a "useful" form of architecture, rather it is a philosophical and artistic interrogation about buildings themselves.

Ryue Nishizawa, half of the celebrated Pritzker Prize-winning duo SANAA has all the architectural credentials and yet is actively exploring the limits between what is built and what is simply willed into existence as a commentary on the art of building. His Fukita Pavilion in Shodoshima (Shodoshima-cho, Kagawa, Japan, 2013, page 350) covers an area of 185 square meters but is made up only of two overlapping, curved sheets of steel. The corners of the two sheets are welded together. The space thus created between the two sheets of metal provides seating for visitors, and also serves as a playground for children in the area leading to the temple. Despite its rather ephemeral appearance, this is a permanent structure without any foundation. The architect states, "It is a simple arrangement as if the pavilion had just brought and placed there." This type of reasoning is also applied to works of art of course, even if the "usefulness" of art can always be debated.

The Greenhouses created by another talented Japanese architect, Junya Ishigami, at the Japanese Pavilion of the *Venice Architecture Biennale* (Venice, Italy, 2008, page 234) were indeed tiny. Each of the greenhouses was conceived as an actual building, just barely able to stand up thanks to sophisticated calculations. His intention was to suggest "the future possibilities of architecture." Ishigami also refers to Joseph Paxton's Crystal Palace at the *Great Exhibition* in London (1851) which was in the form of a greenhouse. Ishigami worked with the botanist Hideaki Ohba who carefully selected varieties of plants that at first seemed to be native to the environment, but in fact represent a "slight disturbance in the landscape of the park." Wooden furniture was placed in the garden, suggesting the ambiguity or more precisely "simultaneity" of interior and exterior space, while the inside of the Pavilion itself was essentially empty except for delicate drawings on the white walls. Here, the usual definition of architecture may have been approached despite the very small size of the greenhouses, and yet, there was also a clearly artistic or thoughtful intention in these works.

The Spanish artist Cristina Iglesias, born in 1956, has a considerable reputation in the international gallery and exhibition circuit. She has also frequently branched out with her sculptures, into installations that occupy enough space to begin to be considered in architectural terms. Her Vegetation Room Inhotim (Inhotim, Belo Horizonte, Brazil, 2010–12, page 228) has a nine-by-nine-meter footprint. Located on the property of the Inhotim Contemporary Art Institute, the work alternates between polished stainless-steel surfaces that reflect surrounding plants and a carved vegetal design on the inner surfaces. Iglesias calls this a "plant room" and indeed its location on a property that includes 300 hectares of native forest and 110 botanical collections is appropriate. In this instance, the "usefulness" of the work is essentially artistic, but, as is the case with Olafur Eliasson, it surely makes visitors think again about the natural environment that surrounds them, and, perhaps, to respond to it in a different way.

TEAHOUSES AND TOWERS

Terunobu Fujimori is well known for his whimsical designs that are often deeply rooted in Japanese culture. His four-square-meter Beetle's House was one of the structures actually built for the exhibition *1:1 Architects Build Small Spaces 2010* held at the Victoria and Albert Museum in London from June 15 to August 30, 2010 (page 164). He points out that Japan is one of the few countries where there is a long history of top architects being involved in the design of tiny structures, often for the tea ceremony. His original plan to suspend the structure from the ceiling of the museum did not work out, but there is a part both of humor and of very serious thought involved in this project—it meets the criteria of Serra, because it was indeed designed to serve a purpose, but it is also very much at the threshold between an artistic installation and a tiny building.

Another participant in the 2010 exhibition at the Victoria and Albert Museum was the Oslo firm Rintala Eggertsson, established in 2007 by the Finnish architect Sami Rintala and the Icelandic architect Dagur Eggertsson. Their Ark Booktower (Victoria and Albert Museum, London, UK, 2010, page 424) measured a modest nine square meters in floor area, but their goal was no less than to allow an "escape from the physical space of the museum into the mental space of literature." By filling their tower with used books, the architects fulfilled something of their literary ambitions, but, as it happens, they also used the books as a "unified minimal wall surface." The debate about surface and content in architecture rages on, it would seem.

Rintala Eggertsson were also the architects of the Seljord Watchtower (Seljord, Telemark, Norway, 2011, page 420), part of a development program conceived by the municipality of Seljord. The Watchtower makes reference to a local legend that the lake of Seljord is home to a mysterious serpent. The tower doubles as a shelter for small exhibitions. With an area of 70 square meters, the structure demonstrates the interest of calling on talented architects in the context of efforts to attract tourists, a point also made in recent years elsewhere in Scandinavia in particular.

Much more subjected to the conditions of "real" construction and design in a more complex environment, their Hut to Hut (Kagala, Karnataka, India, 2012, page 416) is a 27-square-meter double structure built with locally produced supplies and renewable energy sources. The interesting aspect about this design is surely the combination of a regional aesthetic and materials with a real sense of Nordic invention and technical know-how.

THINKING ABOUT ARCHITECTURE

The young architects Florian Idenburg (born in 1975) and Jing Liu (born in 1980) have already made quite a name for themselves (So – II: Solid Objectives—Idenburg Liu) working in the United States and elsewhere. Their Tri-Colonnade (page 466), part of the exhibition *The Street* in the context of the *Shenzhen Hong Kong Bi-City Biennale*, curated by Terence Riley (2011), was very small (24 m²) but sought to pose some of the basic issues of architecture that are related to façades or surfaces. Noting that the façade has become "implicitly flat," they used a laminated marble print on columns with mirrors behind them, giving visitors the impression that the "marble" expands as visitors approach it. What appears to be flat is not. This concept, perhaps described as one of optical manipulation, is actually quite popular in contemporary architecture, where effects of light, transparency, and reflection are frequent. A pavilion like the Tri-Colonnade might again not be perceived as serving any real purpose, and thus characterized as being more like an art installation than architecture, and yet, its whole point is about architecture.

Another architect who is present in this volume with a work that might well be compared to art installations is the Mexican Michel Rojkind. Born in 1969 in Mexico City, Rojkind has worked frequently with the local offices of Nestlé, and, in 2012, he was the coordinator of an unusual project that involved Nescafé as the sponsor for work that included the participation of seven artists. Rojkind's own Portal of Awareness (page 430) was put in place, arcing over the sidewalks of the Paseo de la Reforma, one of the largest avenues of the Mexican capital. A structure made up of a weave of rebars supports 1500 metal coffee mugs. Given their quantity and the regularity of their placement, the mugs become a sort of decorative motif, although presumably the coffee-oriented nature of the work is lost on no one. With a low budget of just $11 000, Rojkind manages to put architecture, art, and commerce in the spotlight in a dignified and original way.

An unexpected case of transgression of the usual categories of photography, art, or architecture is that of Tim Hursley, a specialist in architectural images who has often seen his photos published in the *Architecture Now!* series. In the case of this book, Hursley proposed what is undoubtedly a small building, a 4.6-meter-diameter silo located in Greensboro, Alabama, in an area where he often works with Rural Studio. The 14-meter-high structure was badly damaged in about 1993 and remained in its curious bent form until Hursley noticed it, took pictures, and eventually acquired the object (page 224). In its twisted state, the silo would probably not meet Serra's definition of architectural usefulness, but its shape gives it an artistic aspect that Hursley has obviously noticed. Agricultural buildings, usually in a better state of repair, were catalogued in an almost scientific manner by the German couple Hilla and Bernd Becher. The Bechers are known for their influence on an entire generation of German "art" photographers, and, indeed, their focus on industrial buildings of various kinds did not only bring attention to a largely ignored form of architecture, but also suggested that photography can achieve a level of artistic quality with a subject that could be considered banal, but which reveals itself in pictures.

HOUSES WITH NO WALLS

It is interesting to note that the innovation seen in Japanese houses in recent years can, to some extent, be attributed to a kind of school of architecture, led by the generation of architects like Kazuyo Sejima (born in 1956). Half of the Pritzker Prize–winning team SANAA, Sejima continues to design some buildings on her own, such as the recent Tsuchihashi House published here (Tokyo, Japan, 2011, page 456). With a total floor area of just 72 square meters, the Tsuchihashi House emphasizes verticality with a full-height atrium. What is most striking in the design is, indeed, the openness of the interior and the sensitivity to light or even weather conditions on the roof terrace that is displayed. Sejima has ventured into territory also explored by Sou Fujimoto, where even floor levels seem to be distributed in a pattern that allows for intermediary levels and a very open use of space.

Born in 1975, Tetsuo Kondo worked for seven years in the office of Sejima (1999–2006), before creating his own firm. His House in Chayagasaka (Nagoya, Aichi, Japan, 2011–12, page 270) has a floor area of 90 square meters. His philosophical approach in the design is that the architecture should not have a dominant or "strong" system of organization but rather should "incorporate various meanings"—the organization is seen as a "soft order" rather than a more rigid, or "hard" one. As he explains, the use of space for a family with two small children evolves over time, and his "one-room house" allows for these changes.

(DOLL)HOUSE DREAMER

Joshua Prince-Ramus was the founding partner of OMA New York, the American affiliate of the Office for Metropolitan Architecture (OMA) / Rem Koolhaas in The Netherlands, and served as its Principal until he renamed the firm REX in 2006. His Madison Avenue (Doll)House (New York, USA, 2008, page 410) occupied an area of just four square meters in the Calvin Klein store on Madison Avenue. The architect was also asked to design a "concept house" for the "Calvin Klein woman," a 190-square-meter residence that remained an unbuilt scheme. This installation by Prince-Ramus might be seen as a commentary on architectural scale and purpose, but also on the minimalist environment of the store, which was the work of John Pawson. Not a freestanding structure in itself—though the concept house would have been—the Madison Avenue (Doll)House certainly deserves a place in a book about small buildings.

INTO THE WILD

From these very artistic incarnations of the small building, one might venture into the wild, or at least into nature, where small, ecologically sound structures allow some to spend time in a wilderness setting without having the impression of destroying the environment. An example of this approach is the Endémico Resguardo Silvestre (Valle de Guadalupe, Ensenada, Mexico, 2010–11, page 188) by the Mexican architect Jorge Gracia Garcia. This hotel features 20 rooms, each of which is a freestanding 20-square-meter structure. Using a steel skeleton that interferes as little as possible with the land on this 99-hectare site in the wine-producing area of Baja California, the architect employed COR-TEN steel for exterior surfaces in an effort to blend in with the tan or brown landscape. In this setting, guests can indeed enjoy nature, while also taking advantage of hotel services.

An example of a small individual structure placed in a natural setting is the Hut on Sleds (Whangapoua, New Zealand, 2011, page 132) by the Auckland firm Crosson Clarke Carnachan Architects. Placed on a white sand beach on the Coromandel Peninsula, the Hut is set on two wooden sleds that allow it to be moved onto the beach or onto a barge at will. "The aesthetic is natural and reminiscent of a beach artifact, perhaps a surf-life-saving or observation tower," according to the architects. Clad in wood, the Hut can be entirely closed when not in use, but large glass doors and a two-story front shutter, which serves as an awning when it is open, give this 35-square-meter holiday residence almost all the comforts of home.

Andreas Wenning (baumraum) is well known in Germany and other countries for his extensive work in designing and creating tree houses. Indeed, tree houses seem to have become quite fashionable in many parts of the world, perhaps because they offer adults a way to get away from urban stress, or to get closer to nature. One of Wenning's efforts at creating tree-house hotels is published here. His Tree Whisper Tree-House Hotel (Bad Zwischenahn, Germany, 2011, page 92) is formed by four tree-house "rooms" built at a total cost of 280 000 euros. Set 3.5 meters off the ground, the structures rest on steel columns but are suspended from their host trees with stainless-steel cables and textile straps. The tree house, like the Japanese teahouse, is almost by its very definition a type of small architecture. Neither tree houses, nor the tea ceremony, are comfortable with large spaces. In the case of the Bad Zwischenahn hotel, each tree-house cabin has a bedroom for two people, a bathroom, and a living area with a kitchen unit and two additional beds. Some might say that this degree of comfort goes beyond what can be expected when suspended from a tree, but the use of materials like untreated larch will surely calm such ecological doubts.

A talented American architect, Tom Kundig, based in Seattle, Washington, has made a name for himself in good part with small structures. His Sol Duc Cabin (Olympic Peninsula, Washington, United States, 2010–11, page 370), measures just 36 square meters in floor area. Clad in steel, the structure is lifted up on four steel columns to protect it from local flooding conditions. The client asked for "a compact, low-maintenance, virtually indestructible building to house himself and his wife during fishing expeditions" and there is something a bit war-like about this design. Above all, it shows just how much a talented architect can bring to the design of a very small temporary residence. Each element is used fully, thus for example the cantilevered roof provides not only shading but also storm protection.

ARCHITECTURE OF NEED

Small size is often a criterion for architecture that is meant to provide facilities for people who may be in distress due to natural catastrophe or simply left at the mercy of systems and cities that cannot adequately provide for everyone. The aptly named Home-for-All in Rikuzentakata (Iwate, Japan, 2012, page 248) is a 30-square-meter meeting place designed by Toyo Ito, Kumiko Inui, Sou Fujimoto, and Akihisa Hirata. The area was almost completely destroyed by the earthquake and subsequent tsunami of April 11, 2011. Designed with considerable input from local residents, the wooden building was the object of a display during the *13th Venice Architecture Biennale* (2012) in the Japan Pavilion in the Giardini, where it was awarded the Golden Lion for Best National Participant. The Venice jury stated: "The presentation and the storytelling in the pavilion are exceptional and highly accessible to a broad audience. The jury was impressed with the humanity of this project." It is of particular interest that top architects put this much energy into a scheme and a presentation that is, indeed, accessible to the public. Contemporary architecture (and even the *Venice Biennale*) have often been justifiably criticized for being elitist—the Japanese presence goes a long way to responding to that criticism. This is, indeed, what good architects should be doing.

Santiago Cirugeda, born in Seville, Spain, in 1971, has quite intentionally placed himself at the periphery of contemporary architecture, often operating in a legal gray zone where temporary construction and "squatting" are in any case dimly viewed. And yet, his actions in Spain are clearly associated with universities and people who are interested in testing the limits of urban rigidities, in terms of space, but also of materials used and methods. Given severe cutbacks in Spanish government spending in areas such as culture, Cirugeda's Recetas Urbanas seems ready to play an even more significant role. He states: "Since 1996, I have developed a critical practice through subversive projects in diverse urban environments, all of which ultimately demand the revision of city planning regulations and ordinances." His 80-square-meter Aula Abierta (Seville, Spain, 2011/12, page 404) was erected using materials that had been recuperated from a building slated for demolition in Granada in 2004, on an empty and essentially abandoned lot. Aula Abierta is part of a larger project called "Espacio Artístico—La Carpa" (Artistic Space—The Tent), which is the headquarters of the Varuma Theater and the future Circus School of Andalucía. In Europe, where government funding of culture has long been taken for granted, it may well be that Recetas Urbanas will become a role model for other such architecturally inclined organizations, trying to fill the gaps where government regulations and spending are inadequate.

The Vietnamese architect Vo Trong Nghia has been involved in the design of low-cost housing, a much needed contribution in his country, where many houses are actually smaller than 10 square meters. His Low-Cost Houses (Dongnai Province, Vietnam, 2012, page 542) are in the range of 20 square meters and cost just $3200 per house to build. Since they do not include bath and toilet facilities, assumed to be exterior and shared by several families, these one-room houses with curtains and floor level differentiation to provide some privacy, were designed to be flexible in terms of future expansions. Vo Trong Nghia has shown considerable expertise in the use of bamboo in architecture. Here louvers are in bamboo, but the walls are in polycarbonate panel, and corrugated FRP (Fiberglass Reinforced Plastic) is used for the roofing.

One of the real masters of temporary and relief architecture is of course the Japanese Pritkzer Prize winner Shigeru Ban who has designed a number of emergency buildings used after natural disasters such as the Paper Emergency Shelters for the UNHCR. More recently, he has worked in Haiti and L'Aquila, Italy, though bureaucratic and practical barriers make earthquake-victim relief in such circumstances rather complex. On January 12, 2010, a 7.0-magnitude earthquake struck near Port-au-Prince. Over a million people lost their homes and more than half a million took refuge in hastily made tents. Shigeru Ban collaborated with professors and students from the Universidad Iberoamericana and Pontificia Universidad Católica Madre y Maestra (Dominican Republic) to build the one hundred shelters made of paper tubes and local materials for Haitian earthquake victims (Paper Temporary Shelters, Port-au-Prince, Haiti, 2010/11, page 74).

PLAYTIME

It might seem logical that small structures are sometimes designed for children, precisely so that their own size is respected in the environment that surrounds them. The Norwegian firm Haugen/Zohar Arkitekter has been quite innovative in this area, as two of the projects published here can attest. Their Fireplace for Children (Trondheim, Norway, 2010, page 212) was commissioned by the city of Trondheim. With a very small budget the architects designed the 30-square-meter structure to be built with materials they managed to gather from a nearby construction site. With short pieces of wood assembled in 80 layered circles, each made with 28 pieces of pine, they were inspired by examples of some traditional regional structures. Their work was one of 25 in the last phase of the 2009 AR Emerging Architecture Awards. Their Cave for Children (Trondheim, Norway, 2012, page 208), also conceived for the city of Trondheim, is located next to a city kindergarten. Looking to natural caves for inspiration in this instance, the architects employed XP foam used for industrial packaging. By hollowing out this material and gluing it together, they managed to create a friendly 16-square-meter environment for small children, again with very limited means. A side benefit of their method was that the foam employed, destined to be disposed of, did not have to be burnt or otherwise pollute the environment.

Another, more substantial structure destined to children is the Peanuts nursery school (Hiroshima, Japan, 2011–12, page 306) designed by Keisuke Maeda (UID architects). The 119-square-meter timber structure is broadly glazed, giving ample natural light to the interior. With the omnipresence of curves in the design, the architect describes Peanuts as "not a completed form… like a plant bearing fruit in soil." This remark and some aspects of the design recall the statements of Tetsuo Kondo about his House in Chayagasaka, where the concept of a "soft order" is explored. Almost inevitably, the exterior of any building assumes a relatively "concrete" form, or at least one whose contours can be recognized. The "softness" employed by Maeda or by Kondo has to do in good part with the interior, where a gentle flexibility is conceived to allow for freedom of movement and perhaps to facilitate future changes. This approach might well seem to be diametrically opposed to the rigidity of the Modernist grid that has so long held the upper hand in contemporary architecture. For houses, ambiguities and overlapping functions (living, dining, cooking, etc.) are almost naturally conducive to a progressive abandonment of straight, hard walls. Privacy is naturally an issue, in particular in a house, but the Japanese seem to adapt well to the proximity imposed by small volumes, and to prefer fewer walls to a sense of strict separation.

A BLACK PEARL

The Japanese are, of course, not the only nation that tends to build small residences. The population density of a country such as The Netherlands has also encouraged over a long period the design and construction of small houses. One such building, dubbed The Black Pearl (Rotterdam, The Netherlands, 2008–10, page 498), was the home of the designer Rolf Bruggink. Bruggink was one of the founders in 2003 of Zecc Architects, a firm that gained some notoriety with projects such as their Stairway to Heaven house (Utrecht, The Netherlands, 2007), a converted church. Zecc worked on the 100-square-meter Black Pearl with Rolf Bruggink. A 100-year-old so-called *métier* house was the basis for the project, which involved the complete restructuring of the interior. Rather than the original series of small rooms, a continuous space was created on four floors. The architects explain: "This creates living spaces that are connected by voids, large stairwells, and long sightlines. All redundant banisters, railings, and doors are left out, causing a high degree of spatial abstraction. Floors, walls, stairs, and ceilings blend together and seem to recall an 'Escher-like' impossibility." Though aesthetics vary from country to country, it is interesting to note to what extent this description of open interior space might be applied to many of the recent Japanese houses published in this book.

CAST-IRON TREES AND A SYMBOL IN A PARK

Toilets are generally conceded to be relatively small spaces, but it is rare that talented architects take the time to design freestanding public facilities. This rule was broken in a conjuncture between the young firm design neuob and those responsible for the ongoing Kumamoto Artpolis project, which has scattered interesting pieces of architecture around the southern Japanese city since its creation in 1988. The Shirakawa Public Toilet (Kumamoto City, Japan, 2010–11, page 142) is an 11.6-square-meter structure that is marked by the presence of cast-iron trees. Given its location on the banks of the Shirakawa River, where Japanese regulations do not allow real trees to be planted, the gesture of planting artificial trees involves some commentary on the over-regulated and over-built environment that has developed over the years in relation to grand public spending intended to bring the country out of its economic doldrums. Design neuob wanted its Public Toilet to be in some harmony as well with an architectural environment that includes nearby works in the Artpolis project. In this case, the Richard Serra test of "usefulness" obviously applies, but the architects have also managed to give a little dignity, if not a touch of art, to a toilet.

The examples cited here and others in this book give some idea of the range of uses in contemporary architecture for small structures or spaces. They are useful, or useless, as Richard Serra defined the line of division between art and architecture. Well, almost: does a building that makes a comment about the state of architecture, but serves no other purpose, really qualify as architecture? Small architecture is often at the threshold between what might also be called being and non-being. To be or not to be? The New Amsterdam Pavilion (New York, USA, 2009, page 532) by UNStudio is a case in point: 37 square meters of polyurethane-coated wood, where inside and outside are blurred willfully by the Dutch architects. A purpose, of course, to celebrate the 400th anniversary of New Amsterdam, the original name of New York City. But otherwise, is it a shelter, an architectural statement, or, finally, a work of art? The same question of course arises for Zaha Hadid's 45-square-meter Burnham Pavilion (Chicago, Illinois, United States, 2009, page 196). It was one of a number of small structures commissioned to celebrate the 100th anniversary of the Burnham Plan for Chicago, another was by Ben van Berkel and UNStudio. Containing a video installation, such a structure could be said in a sense not to serve any real purpose. The architects stated, "The presence of the new structure triggers the visitor's intellectual curiosity whilst an intensification of public life around and within the pavilion supports the idea of public discourse." The usefulness of the architecture is then one of stimulating public awareness, much as would a work of art. Small is beautiful?

SIZE IS IN THE EYE OF THE BEHOLDER

The question of just what is "small" in architecture might also be posed. House 77 (Póvoa de Varzim, Portugal, 2009–10, page 110) by José Cadilhe has an area of 232 square meters, perhaps rather large for a book on small buildings? In fact, this house is extremely narrow, which means that the problem of small space is present throughout the design, even if the total floor area is relatively generous for a residence. A church by Marlon Blackwell (Saint Nicholas Eastern Orthodox Church, Springdale, Arkansas, USA, 2009, page 106) that is even larger figures here, but it may be argued that the definition of "small" is different according to the building types concerned. Churches are usually intended for relatively large congregations, as opposed to chapels that by definition are usually tiny. Most structures in this book have a floor area of less than 100 square meters, but in a country like Vietnam, where the architect Vo Trong Nghia points out that many houses measure less than 10 square meters, such a figure might seem palatial. What is small is relative to function and presence as well as to national cultures. How many wealthy Americans would ask a Pritzker Prize-winning architect to create a house with just 30 square meters of floor space (Kazuyo Sejima, Tsuchihashi House, Tokyo, Japan, 2011, page 456)? Probably none. Japanese architects such as Toyo Ito have long posited that their urban density and the solutions it engenders may well be a model for the future development of cities across the world. Today, 54 per cent of the world's population lives in urban areas, a proportion that is expected to increase to 66 per cent by 2050. The urban population of the world has grown from 746 million in 1950 to 3.9 billion in 2014. With rising urban density, and in any culture or country, space is more and more at a premium. It seems inevitable that small architecture will be a way of the future, particularly for residences. The trend to preserve and better use resources also points in the direction of smaller buidlings in the future, there will be less space for more people, hopefully in a more environmentally-oriented society. Perhaps, soon everyone will be happy to have just a few

der
...sparnis
..er Wande, ...t deren Hil.. sich ....c...e oder gar das
sind derzeit mit einer neuen Generation von Häusern wegweisend, die
...en. Raum, der ausreichend „flexibel" ist, um vielfach nutzbar zu sein,
...isse zu befriedigen als früher größere.

square meters of private space? It can be said that some of the most inspiring architectural spaces are "grand"—ample in size, almost too large for their use, in the spirit of Grand Central Station in New York for example. And yet in the right hands, even small buildings can have a grandeur and most significantly an intimate relation to the human scale. Indeed good design, good architecture is just as useful and significant for a small building as for a large one. There are of course great towers still rising in nearly every major city in the world, far from the realm of the Small Architecture featured in this book. And yet those buildings, destined often to wealth and powerful users for all their skyline-changing power, do not represent the world that most ordinary people live in. We are most definitely entering a time of small architecture, constrained by the conservation of resources, and rising populations. The future is small.

José Cadilhe, House 77, ►
Póvoa de Varzim, Portugal,
2009–10 (page 110).

EINLEITUNG

KLEIN, ABER PERFEKT GESTALTET

Was geschieht, wenn Staatshaushalte in Turbulenzen geraten und die Bauwirtschaft beinahe zum Erliegen kommt? Büßt die Architektur dann, oftmals ja so abhängig vom großen Geld, ebenfalls ihren Einfallsreichtum ein? In Zeiten exzessiver Bauinvestitionen entstand etwa in Spanien eine Vielzahl bemerkenswerter Gebäude, und brillante neue Architekten erschienen auf der Bildfläche. Verpufft nun jeder Einfallsreichtum, weil junge spanische oder portugiesische Architekten einfach nur irgendeine Arbeit suchen, egal, wo in Europa, oder fließt diese Energie nur woandershin, in andersartige Projekte? Trotz des sogenannten globalen Konjunkturrückgangs entwickeln sich einige Länder weiterhin in schnellem Tempo – so ist das geschätzte Bruttoinlandsprodukt Chinas 2015 um 6,9 Prozent gewachsen. Obgleich Indiens Wirtschaftswachstum vom Höhepunkt 2010 um über zehn Prozent zurückgegangen ist, wird es für 2016 auf etwa 7,1 Prozent geschätzt. Diese Länder und auch andere erleben keinerlei Rezession, und ihre Architektur ist ein Abbild dieser Tatsache.

ES KOMMT DOCH AUF GRÖSSE AN

Kommt es in der Architektur wirklich auf Größe an? Vielleicht ist der Hinweis interessant, dass viele der herausragenden Architekten von heute, von Frank Gehry bis Tadao Ando, ihre Karrieren mit erstaunlich kleinen Projekten begonnen haben – Wohnhäusern zumeist. Und dass der Übergang zu Projekten größeren Maßstabs nicht in allen Fällen so erfolgreich war wie erhofft. Ist größer also zwangsläufig besser? Tatsache ist, dass, je größer ein Projekt ist, es zumeist umso bürokratischer und komplizierter wird und dem Architekten immer weniger Mitsprache am Endresultat erlaubt. Arbeiten wie Frank Gehrys Guggenheim Bilbao (1997) sind die Ausnahmen, die das Regel bestätigen. Größer ist also nicht automatisch auch besser, und das war auch noch nie so. Bauwerke wie Donato Bramantes Tempietto (San Pietro in Montorio, Rom, 1502–10), dessen Durchmesser lediglich 4,5 m beträgt, haben die Architekturgeschichte stärker geprägt als viele große Gebäude. Vielleicht könnte man sagen, dass es zwar auf die Größe ankommt, aber dass kleine Gebäude Architekten häufig ein Maß an Freiheit verschaffen, das bei gigantischen staatlichen oder privatwirtschaftlichen Projekten schlicht nicht existiert.

In Zeiten ökonomischer Anspannung treten die Vorteile kleinerer Projekte natürlich deutlicher zutage. Große Budgets sind selten geworden, aber das Verlangen oder die Notwendigkeit zu bauen ist nicht verschwunden. Kleiner bedeutet in vielen Fällen auch kostengünstiger; was also geschieht, wenn das Geld verschwindet – es werden verstärkt kleinere Bauwerke entworfen. Diese Generalisierung ist natürlich nur mehr oder weniger zutreffend, je nachdem, über welchen Teil der Welt man spricht.

Einige Länder, wie etwa Japan, haben kulturell bedingte Präferenzen oder eine Vorliebe für kleine Gebäude. Aufgrund der Bevölkerungsdichte entlang der japanischen Ostküste, speziell zwischen Tokio und Osaka, sind die Menschen seit Jahren daran gewöhnt, mit relativ wenig Platz auszukommen. Die Immobilienpreise in Tokio und einigen anderen japanischen Städten sind derart hoch, dass bereits ein winziges Grundstück, gelinde gesagt, ziemlich teuer ist. Daher sind kleine Häuser unter 100 m² eher die Regel als die Ausnahme, auch wenn talentierte Architekten mit dem Entwurf beauftragt werden. Denn obwohl die Wirtschaft Japans seit den 1990er-Jahren in der Flaute ist, gibt es eine kontinuierliche Nachfrage nach neuen Wohnungsbauprojekten, was mehr als einer Generation sehr begabter Architekten den Aufstieg ermöglicht hat.

In Japan, aber genauso anderswo, sorgt ein veränderter Lebenswandel, gepaart mit ökonomischem Druck, offenkundig dafür, dass die Anforderungen an Architektur neu definiert werden. Waren in Privathäusern, beispielsweise in den USA der Nachkriegsjahre, abgetrennte Küchen-, Ess- und Wohnbereiche Standard, haben jüngere Trends die Wände zwischen den Räumen in gewisser Weise durchbrochen oder sie häufig ganz entfernt. Offene Wohnbereiche mit ineinander übergehenden Koch- und Essbereichen sind häufiger geworden als abgeschlossene Einheiten, was oftmals Platz bedeutet. Die Japaner mit ihrer langen Tradition verschiebbarer ████, m████ ██fte sich Innenräume ███ Verhältnis von innen und a████ ██ ███████ praktisch ohne A██

KLEIN IST SEXY

Bramantes Tempietto oder auch wesentlich jüngere Bauwerke wie etwa Philip Johnsons Glashaus (New Canaan, Connecticut, 1980) bewegen sich zweifelsohne just an der Schnittstelle zwischen Kunst und Architektur. Die Nutzfläche von Johnsons eigenwilligem Häuschen beträgt kaum mehr 36 m². Doch auch wenn er tatsächlich in der von ihm so genannten Mönchszelle arbeitete, so nähern sich seine Entwürfe, wie auch die späteren Frank Gehrys, doch dem Bereich Skulptur an. Kleinere Bauwerke sind eindeutig unabhängiger von umfangreichen baulichen Vorbedingungen als ihre größeren Pendants. Das ist ein Grund dafür, dass Künstler, die sich für Architektur interessieren, mitunter ihrer Fantasie freien Lauf lassen und kleine Gebäude entwerfen. Das Umgekehrte trifft ebenso zu. Auch für einen Architekten kann es leichter sein, ein veritables Kunstwerk in kleinem Maßstab zu schaffen statt eines riesigen Bauwerks, das endlos vielen Forderungen gerecht werden muss. Es ist nicht immer leicht Kunst zu machen, wenn es gleichzeitig gilt, 1000 Autos in der Garage unterzubringen oder Notausgänge für Hunderte panischer Büroarbeiter vorsehen zu müssen.

Dieser Band, dessen Inhalte aus der Reihe *Architecture Now!* stammen, widmet sich ausschließlich kleinen Gebäuden oder Räumen. Kein Wunder, möchte man meinen, bei dem Einfallsreichtum, den die ausgewählten Architekten (und Künstler) zeigen, gleichzeitig aber ist die Auswahl natürlich eng mit den größeren Umbrüchen auf der Bühne der Weltwirtschaft verbunden. Wenn es nicht genügend Geld gibt, um riesige Messezentren und Hochhäuser hervorzuzaubern, bekommt kleinformatige Architektur plötzlich einen ganz eigenen Reiz. Hätten hervorragende Architekten vor einigen Jahren kleinere Aufträge womöglich noch abgelehnt, so beginnt eine Reihe von ihnen nun, eine Verlockung darin zu erkennen, auf sinnvolle Weise zu verkleinern. Es besteht kein Zweifel, in der Architektur ist heutzutage klein sexy.

DAS NÜTZLICHE UND NUTZLOSE

Wo genau verläuft die Grenzlinie zwischen Kunst und Architektur? Mit dieser Frage beschäftigen sich mehrere Werke in diesem Band. Laut dem amerikanischen Bildhauer Richard Serra besteht der „Unterschied zwischen Kunst und Architektur darin (…), dass die Architektur einen Zweck verfolgt". Und auch wenn nun einige Architekten womöglich (riskanterweise?) mit Entwürfen ohne erkennbaren Zweck liebäugeln, so ist Serras Definition dennoch eine hilfreiche Richtlinie, die uns allerdings nicht davon abhält, einige dieser „zweideutigen" Arbeiten in einen Band aufzunehmen, der in erster Linie der Architektur gewidmet ist. Leser der Reihe *Architecture Now!* sind mit diesen Exkursionen in den Bereich des „Nutzlosen" längst vertraut – denn es ist ja offenkundig, dass Künstler oftmals ihrer Zeit voraus und mehr im Einklang mit dem momentanen Zeitgeist sind als einige ihrer eher „handfesten" Architekturkollegen.

Ein interessantes Beispiel für diese Grenzüberschreitung von Kunst und Architektur bietet das belgische Team Gijs Van Vaerenbergh. Pieterjan Gijs studierte, ebenso wie sein Kollege Arnout Van Vaerenbergh, Bauingenieurwesen und Architektur an der Katholischen Universität in Löwen (KUL, 2001–06), aber er erwarb auch einen Master in Städtebau und Regionalentwicklung. Ihr Bauwerk Reading between the Lines (Borgloon, Belgien, 2011, Seite 180) überdeckt eine Fläche von nur 28 m². Es hat ein Fundament aus Stahlbeton und wurde mit 30 Tonnen Corten-Stahl und 2 000 Stützen ausgeführt. Es handelt sich hier nicht um ein Werk der Architektur im herkömmlichen Sinne, vielmehr um ein „transparentes Kunstobjekt". Es hat die Außenform einer Kirche, soll aber nicht dieser Funktion dienen. Vielmehr ist es ein Kommentar über das Ausbleiben des Dialogs von Kompaktheit und Leere in der Architektur.

Ein Interesse an der Überschreitung gewohnter Grenzen ist in vielen Disziplinen erkennbar, nicht nur in der Kunst und Architektur per se. Der holländische Designer Erik Rietveld ist ein Beispiel dafür. Er studierte Wirtschaftswissenschaften an der Universität Maastricht mit Abschluss 1993. Danach studierte er Philosophie, Psychologie und Portugiesisch an der Universität São Paulo (USP) und erwarb 2003 einen Master in Philosophie an der Universität Amsterdam (UvA). Er arbeitet mit seinem Bruder Ronald Rietveld (*1972) zusammen, der wirklich Architekt ist – beide schufen gemeinsam das Werk Bunker 599 (Diefdijklinie, Niederlande, 2010, Seite 394), das einen Militärbunker der New Dutch Waterline (NDW) einbezieht. Die Gestalter erklären: „Ein scheinbar unzerstörbarer Bunker mit monumentaler Wirkung ist aufgeschlitzt. Dadurch wird das klitzekleine Innere eines der 700 NDW-Bunker sichtbar, deren Innenräume normalerweise total unsichtbar bleiben. Außerdem durchschneidet ein langer Bohlenweg das äußerst schwere Bauwerk und führt die Besucher zu einem überfluteten Bereich und zu den Fußwegen im anschließenden Naturschutzgebiet." Einen Betonbunker zu halbieren und einen freien

Durchgang zu schaffen heißt nicht unbedingt, eine „sinnvolle" Architekturform zu realisieren; es handelt sich vielmehr um eine philosophische und künstlerische Infragestellung von Bauten per se.

Ryue Nishizawa, einer aus dem berühmten Duo Sanaa der Pritzker-Prize-Gewinner, besitzt alle architektonischen Referenzen und erforscht dennoch aktiv die Grenzen zwischen dem, was gebaut wird, und dem, was einfach nur geschaffen wird als Beitrag zur Kunst des Bauens. Sein Pavillon Fukita in Shodoshima (Shodoshima-ko, Kagawa, Japan, 2013, Seite 350) hat eine Fläche von 185 m². Er besteht aus nur zwei sich überschneidenden, gekrümmten Stahlplatten, die an den Ecken zusammengeschweißt sind. Der so entstandene Raum bietet Sitzplätze für Besucher und dient auch zum Spielen für Kinder im Vorbereich zum Tempel. Trotz seines eher vergänglichen Erscheinungsbilds ist dies ein dauerhaftes Bauwerk, wenn auch ohne Fundament. „Es ist ein schlichtes Arrangement, als wäre der Pavillon gerade erst angeliefert und dort hingestellt worden", sagen die Architekten. Diese Art der Begründung lässt sich natürlich auch auf Kunstwerke übertragen, auch wenn der „Nutzen" von Kunst stets infrage gestellt werden kann.

Die von einem anderen begabten japanischen Architekten, Junya Ishigami, geschaffenen Gewächshäuser beim Japanischen Pavillon auf der Architekturbiennale in Venedig (Venedig, Italien, 2008, Seite 234) waren wirklich klein. Jedes dieser Treibhäuser wurde als eigenständiger Bau geplant und war nur aufgrund ausgeklügelter Berechnungen standfest. Ishigamis Absicht war die Andeutung „künftiger Möglichkeiten der Architektur". Er erwähnt u. a. Paxtons Kristallpalast auf der Weltausstellung in London (1851), der auch die Form eines Gewächshauses hatte. Ishigami arbeitete gemeinsam mit dem Botaniker Hideaki Ohba, der sorgfältig eine Vielfalt von Pflanzen auswählte, die zuerst wie der Umgebung zugehörig wirkten, aber tatsächlich einen „leichten Eingriff in die Landschaft des Parks" darstellten. In dem Garten wurden hölzerne Möbel aufgestellt, um die Ambivalenz oder, genauer gesagt, die „Gleichzeitigkeit" von Innen- und Außenraum anzudeuten, während der Pavillon selbst immer fast leer war, abgesehen von den zarten Zeichnungen an den weißen Wänden. Hier ist man vielleicht der üblichen Definition von Architektur sehr nahe gekommen, trotz der geringen Größe der Treibhäuser – und doch war in diesen Bauten auch eine künstlerische oder bewusste Absicht deutlich spürbar.

Die spanische Künstlerin Cristina Iglesias, geboren 1956, genießt in internationalen Galerie- und Museumskreisen einen exzellenten Ruf. Mit ihren skulpturalen Arbeiten beschreitet sie ständig neue Wege, bis hin zu Werken, die genügend Raum einnehmen, um sie als Architektur begreifen zu können. Ihr Vegetation Room Inhotim (Inhotim, Belo Horizonte, Brasilien, 2010–12, Seite 228) hat eine Grundfläche von 9 x 9 m. Die Arbeit, gelegen auf dem Gelände des Zentrums für Gegenwartskunst Inhotim, changiert zwischen polierten Flächen aus rostfreiem Stahl, die die umgebenden Pflanzen spiegeln, und den gefrästen pflanzenartigen Reliefs der Innenseiten. Iglesias nennt die Arbeit einen „Pflanzenraum", und dazu passt natürlich der Standort auf einem Gelände, zu dem mehr als 300 ha Urwald und 110 botanische Sammlungen gehören. Hier ist die „Nützlichkeit" der Arbeit eine rein künstlerische, aber wie im Fall von Eliasson wird auch hier der Besucher dazu angehalten, erneut über seine natürliche Umgebung nachzudenken und womöglich auf andere Weise auf sie zu reagieren.

TEEHÄUSER UND TÜRME

Terunobu Fujimori ist weithin für seine skurrilen Entwürfe bekannt, die oftmals tief in der japanischen Kultur verwurzelt sind. Sein 4 m² großes Beetle's House gehört zu den realisierten Entwürfen für die Ausstellung „1:1 Architects Build Small Spaces", die vom 15. Juni bis 30. August 2010 im Londoner Victoria and Albert Museum stattfand (Seite 164). Er betont, Japan gehöre zu den wenigen Ländern, in denen die Beteiligung von Toparchitekten am Entwurf kleinerer Bauwerke, oftmals für die Teezeremonie genutzt, bereits eine lange Tradition hat. Sein ursprünglicher Plan, das Haus von der Decke des Museums hängen zu lassen, ließ sich nicht realisieren, aber neben Humor steckt auch eine Menge Ernsthaftigkeit in dem Projekt – einerseits entspricht es den Kriterien Richard Serras, weil der Entwurf tatsächlich zweckdienlich ist, gleichzeitig bewegt es sich exakt an der Schnittstelle zwischen künstlerischer Installation und winzigem Gebäude.

Ein weiterer Teilnehmer der Ausstellung im Victoria and Albert Museum 2010 war das in Oslo ansässige Büro Rintala Eggertsson, 2007 von den Architekten Samt Rintala aus Finnland und Dagur Eggertsson aus Island gegründet. Die Nutzfläche ihres Ark Booktower (Victoria and Albert Museum, 2010, Seite 424) maß bescheidene 9 m², ihr eigentliches Anliegen bestand darin, eine „Fluchtmöglichkeit aus dem physikalischen Raum des Museums hinein in den mentalen Raum der

Literatur" zu kreieren. Indem sie ihren Turm mit gebrauchten Büchern füllten, kamen die Architekten zum einen ihren literarischen Ambitionen nach, schufen darüber hinaus aber, gleichsam zufällig, eine „einheitliche, minimale Wandoberfläche". Die Debatte über Oberfläche und Inhalt in der Architektur tobt also weiter, so mag es scheinen.

Rintala Eggertsson sind auch die Architekten des Seljord-Aussichtsturms (Seljord, Telemark, Norwegen, 2011, Seite 420), Bestandteil eines von der Stadtverwaltung Seljord initiierten regionalen Entwicklungsprogramms. Der Aussichtsturm nimmt Bezug auf eine lokale Legende, laut der im See von Seljord eine mysteriöse Schlange wohne. Zum Turm gehört außerdem ein Nebengebäude für kleine Ausstellungen. Der Bau mit einer Gesamtfläche von 70 m² demonstriert das Bestreben, unter Einbeziehung talentierter Architekten Touristen anzulocken, ein Vorhaben, das in den letzten Jahren besonders in Skandinavien vorangetrieben wurde.

Ihr Projekt Hut to Hut (Kagala, Karnataka, Indien, 2012, Seite 416) ist sehr viel stärker den Bedingungen „realen" Bauens und Entwerfens in einer schwierigeren Umgebung unterworfen. Die 27 m² große Doppelstruktur wurde mit lokal produzierten Baustoffen errichtet und verfügt über erneuerbare Energiequellen. Der interessanteste Aspekt ist sicherlich die Verbindung regionaler Ästhetik und Materialien mit echtem nordeuropäischen Erfindungsgeist und technischem Know-how.

NACHDENKEN ÜBER ARCHITEKTUR

Die beiden jungen Architekten Florian Idenburg (geboren 1975) und Jing Liu (geboren 1980) genießen aufgrund ihrer Arbeit (So – Il: Solid Objectives – Idenburg Liu) in den USA und anderswo ebenfalls einen beachtlichen Ruf. Ihre Tri-Colonnade (Seite 466), Teil der Ausstellung „The Street" im Rahmen der Shenzhen Hongkong Bi-City Biennale, kuratiert von Terence Riley (2011), war äußerst klein (24 m²), stellte aber eine Reihe architektonischer Grundfragen in Bezug auf Fassaden und Oberflächen. Weil sie feststellten, dass die Fassade mittlerweile stillschweigend als flach vorausgesetzt wird, nutzten die Architekten mit einem Marmordruck verkleidete Säulen und dahinter Spiegel, um bei den Besuchern den Eindruck zu vermitteln, der „Marmor" dehne sich aus, wenn der Betrachter sich nähert. Was flach wirkt, ist es in Wirklichkeit nicht. Dieses Konzept, das man als „optische Manipulation" beschreiben könnte, ist in der zeitgenössischen Architektur ziemlich gängig, wo häufig mit Licht, Transparenz und Reflexion gearbeitet wird. Auch Iri-Colonnade erfüllt keinen reellen Zweck und kann daher eher als Kunstinstallation denn als Architektur charakterisiert werden, und dennoch geht es ausschließlich um Architektur.

Ein anderer Architekt, der in diesem Band mit einer Arbeit vertreten ist, die stark an Kunstinstallationen erinnert, ist der Mexikaner Michel Rojkind. Rojkind wurde 1969 in Mexiko-Stadt geboren und hat häufig für die lokale Nestlé-Vertretung gearbeitet, 2012 war er etwa Koordinator eines ungewöhnlichen, u. a. von Nescafé gesponserten Projekts, an dem sieben Künstler beteiligt waren. Rojkinds eigenes Projekt Portal of Awareness (Seite 430) wurde so platziert, dass es den Gehsteig des Paseo de la Reforma überspannte, eine der größten Straßen der mexikanischen Metropole: eine Gitterkonstruktion aus Bewehrungsstahl, an der 1500 Kaffeebecher aus Metall hängen. Aufgrund der Menge und der Regelmäßigkeit ihrer Platzierung werden die Becher zu einer Art dekorativem Motiv, auch wenn wahrscheinlich niemandem der kaffeeorientierte Charakter der Arbeit entgeht. Mit einem kleinen Budget von nur 11 000 Dollar gelingt es Rojkind hier, Architektur, Kunst und Kommerz auf erhabene und originelle Weise in den Blick zu rücken.

Einen überraschenden Fall der Überschreitung der üblichen Grenzen zwischen Fotografie, Kunst und Architektur stellt Tim Hursley dar, ein Spezialist für Architekturfotografie, von dem schon zahlreiche Aufnahmen in der Serie *Architecture Now!* veröffentlicht worden sind. In diesem Band ist Hursley mit einem zweifellos kleinen Gebäude vertreten, einem Silo von nur 4,6 m Durchmesser in Greensboro, Alabama, einer Gegend, in der er häufig für Rural Studio arbeitet. Die 14 m hohe Konstruktion wurde um 1993 schwer beschädigt und behielt ihre eigenartig abgeknickte Form, bis Hursley das Objekt entdeckte, Aufnahmen davon machte und es schließlich erwarb (Seite 224). In seinem verdrehten Zustand entspräche das Silo wohl nicht Richard Serras Definition architektonischer Nützlichkeit, aber seine Form verleiht ihm einen künstlerischen Aspekt, den Tim Hursley offenkundig bemerkt hat. Bernd und Hilla Becher haben ja ihrerseits landwirtschaftliche Gebäude, meist in besserem Zustand, auf beinahe wissenschaftliche Weise katalogisiert. Ihr Einfluss auf eine ganze Generation von deutschen „Kunst"-Fotografen ist bekannt, ihre Bilder von Industriegebäuden verschiedener Art haben nicht nur die

Aufmerksamkeit auf einen weitgehend ignorierten Architekturtyp gelenkt, sondern gleichzeitig gezeigt, dass die Fotografie mit der Abbildung von vermeintlich banalen Objekten eine künstlerische Qualität erreichen kann, die sich aber erst in den Bildern offenbart.

HÄUSER OHNE WÄNDE

Es ist bemerkenswert, dass die Innovationen, die bei japanischen Häusern in den letzten Jahren zu beobachten waren, zu einem gewissen Teil einer Art Schule zugerechnet werden können, angeführt von der Generation von Architekten, zu der auch Kazuyo Sejima gehört (geboren 1956). Sejima, die eine Hälfte des Teams SANAA, das den Pritzker-Preis erhielt, entwirft weiterhin auch einige Gebäude allein, etwa das jüngst realisierte Haus Tsuchihashi, das hier vorgestellt wird (Tokio, 2011, Seite 456). Mit einer Gesamtnutzfläche von lediglich 72 m² setzt das Haus mit einem Atrium über die gesamte Höhe ganz auf das Vertikale. Das wohl Beeindruckendste an dem Entwurf sind allerdings die Offenheit der Räume und die Sensitivität gegenüber dem Licht oder gar den Wetterbedingungen auf der Dachterrasse. Sejima ist hier in einem Terrain unterwegs, das auch von Sou Fujimoto erforscht wird, der durch die Verteilung der Stockwerke Zwischenebenen und einen offenen Umgang mit dem Raum ermöglicht.

Tetsuo Kondo, geboren 1975, hat sieben Jahre lang in Sejimas Büro gearbeitet (1999–2006), bevor er seine eigene Firma gründete. Sein Haus in Chayagasaka (Nagoya, Aichi, Japan, 2011/12, Seite 270) verfügt über eine Nutzfläche von 90 m². Die Philosophie dieses Entwurfs ist, dass die Architektur kein dominantes oder „strenges" Ordnungssystem vorgeben, sondern eher „verschiedene Bedeutungen einfließen lassen sollte" – das Ordnungsprinzip begreift er mehr als ein „weiches" denn als ein rigides, „strenges". Die Raumnutzung einer Familie mit zwei kleinen Kindern, so erklärt er, verändere sich im Lauf der Zeit, und sein „Ein-Raum-Haus" mache diese Wechsel möglich.

(DOLL)HOUSE DREAMER

Joshua Prince-Ramus war Mitgründer von OMA New York, dem amerikanischen Ableger des Office for Metropolitan Architecture (OMA)/Rem Koolhaas in den Niederlanden und fungierte als dessen Leiter, bis er das Büro 2006 in REX umbenannte. Sein Madison Avenue (Doll)House (New York, 2008, Seite 410) im dortigen Calvin-Klein-Geschäft umfasste eine Fläche von lediglich 4 m². Der Architekt war außerdem beauftragt worden, ein „Konzepthaus" für die „Calvin-Klein-Frau" zu entwerfen, ein 190 m² großes Anwesen, das jedoch ein unverwirklichter Entwurf blieb. Prince-Ramus' Installation kann als Kommentar zu Größenverhältnissen und Zweckmäßigkeit in der Architektur gesehen werden, gleichzeitig aber auch zur minimalistischen Gestaltung des Ladens selbst, die das Werk von John Pawson ist. Auch wenn es keine frei stehende Konstruktion ist – das Konzepthaus wäre das gewesen –, verdient das Madison Avenue (Doll)House zweifellos einen Platz in einem Buch über kleine Gebäude.

AUF IN DIE WILDNIS

Von diesen sehr künstlerischen Inkarnationen kleiner Gebäude könnte man sich in Richtung Wildnis aufmachen oder zumindest in die Natur, wo kleine, ökologisch korrekte Behausungen es möglich machen, inmitten unberührter Landschaft Zeit zu verbringen, ohne die Sorge, die Umwelt zu zerstören. Ein Beispiel für diesen Zugang ist das Endémico Resguardo Silvestre (Valle de Guadalupe, Ensenada, Mexiko, 2010/11, Seite 188) des mexikanischen Architekten Jorge Gracia Garcia. Das Hotel verfügt über 20 Zimmer, wobei jedes ein frei stehendes Gebäude von 20 m² darstellt. Für die Außenflächen der Stahlkonstruktion, die so wenig wie möglich in die Landschaft des 99 ha großen Grundstücks im Weinanbaugebiet der Baja California eingreift, verwendete der Architekt Cor-Ten-Stahl in dem Versuch, sich den Dunkelgelb- bis Brauntönen der Landschaft anzupassen. In dieser Umgebung können die Gäste die Natur genießen und die Vorzüge eines Hotels nutzen.

Ein weiteres Beispiel für ein kleines, individuelles Bauwerk in natürlicher Umgebung ist die Hut on Sleds des Büros Crosson Clarke Carnachan Architects aus Auckland (Whangapoua, Neuseeland, 2011, Seite 132). Das Haus, das an einem weißen Sandstrand der Coromandel-Halbinsel steht, ruht auf zwei hölzernen Kufen, wodurch es je nach Belieben am Strand bewegt oder auf einen Frachtkahn geladen werden kann. „Die Ästhetik ist natürlich und erinnert an eine Strandeinrichtung, eine Rettungsstation vielleicht oder einen Aussichtsturm", so die Architekten. Die Hütte ist holzverkleidet und kann vollständig verschlossen werden, wenn sie nicht in Gebrauch ist, aber große Glastüren und ein über zwei Geschosse reichender Fensterladen, der im geöffneten Zustand als Sonnendach dient, machen dieses 35 m² große Ferienhaus beinahe so komfortabel wie das eigene Zuhause.

Andreas Wenning (baumraum) ist in Deutschland und vielen anderen Ländern für seine langjährige Arbeit als Planer und Gestalter von Baumhäusern bekannt. Tatsächlich sind Baumhäuser offenbar in vielen Teilen der Welt ziemlich in Mode gekommen, womöglich weil sie Erwachsenen eine Möglichkeit eröffnen, dem Stress der Großstadt zu entfliehen oder der Natur näher zu kommen. Eines der von Wenning entworfenen Baumhaushotels wird hier vorgestellt. Sein Baumhaushotel Baumgeflüster (Bad Zwischenahn, 2011, Seite 92) besteht aus vier Baumhaussuiten, deren Bau insgesamt nur 280 000 Euro gekostet hat. Die Häuser in einer Höhe von 3,5 m ruhen zwar auf Stahlpfeilern, sind aber zusätzlich an den Bäumen mit rostfreien Stahlseilen und Gewebegurten befestigt. Das Baumhaus, ähnlich wie das japanische Teehaus, ist beinahe per Definition ein Archetyp kleinformatiger Architektur. Weder Baumhäuser noch die Teezeremonie brauchen viel Raum, damit man sich wohlfühlt. Im Fall des Hotels in Bad Zwischenahn verfügt jede Baumhaussuite über ein Schlafzimmer für zwei Personen, ein Bad, einen Wohnbereich mit Kücheneinheit und zwei zusätzlichen Betten. Man könnte meinen, dieser Komfort gehe weit über das hinaus, was man an einem Baum hängend erwarten kann, aber die Verwendung von Materialien wie unbehandeltem Lärchenholz wird solche ökologischen Bedenken sicher entkräften.

Tom Kundig, ein talentierter Architekt aus Seattle, Washington, hat sich vor allem mit kleinen Bauten einen Namen gemacht. Seine Sol Duc Cabin (Olympic Peninsula, Washington, D.C., USA, 2010/11, Seite 370) hat gerade mal 30 m² Grundfläche. Das mit Stahl verkleidete Gebäude ist auf vier Stahlstützen gestellt, um es vor lokalen Überflutungen zu schützen. Der Bauherr forderte „ein kompaktes, pflegeleichtes, praktisch unverwüstliches Gebäude als Herberge für ihn und seine Frau auf ihren Ausflügen zum Fischen", und dieser Entwurf hat wirklich etwas Provisorisches an sich. Vor allem zeigt er, was ein begabter Architektur auch bei der Planung eines sehr kleinen, temporären Wohnhauses leisten kann. Jedes Element wird voll ausgenutzt, so bietet zum Beispiel das überstehende Dach nicht nur Schatten, sondern auch Schutz vor Stürmen.

NOTARCHITEKTUR

Geringe Größe ist auch häufig Kriterium einer Architektur, die Menschen mit Einrichtungen versorgen soll, die wegen Naturkatastrophen in Not geraten oder einfach auf Gedeih und Verderb staatlichen Systemen oder Städten ausgeliefert sind, die nicht jeden angemessen unterstützen können. Das treffend benannte Home-for-All in Rikuzentakata (Iwate, Japan, 2012, Seite 248) ist ein 30 m² großer Ort der Begegnung, entworfen von Toyo Ito, Kumiko Inui, Sou Fujimoto und Akihisa Hirata. Die Gegend wurde am 11. April 2011 vom Erdbeben und vom folgenden Tsunami beinahe vollständig verwüstet. Eine Studie des hölzernen Gebäudes, an dessen Entwurf in der Region Ansässige maßgeblich beteiligt waren, war während der XIII. Biennale in Venedig 2012 im Japanischen Pavillon in den Giardini zu sehen, wo es mit dem Goldenen Löwen für den besten nationalen Beitrag ausgezeichnet wurde. Die Jury dazu: „Die Präsentation und die Vermittlung von Geschichten im Pavillon sind außergewöhnlich und einem breiten Publikum leicht zugänglich. Die Jury war von der Humanität des Projekt beeindruckt." Es ist bemerkenswert, dass Toparchitekten derart viel Energie in einen Entwurf und eine Präsentation stecken, die für das Publikum tatsächlich nachvollziehbar sind. Zeitgenössische Architektur (und selbst die Biennale als solche) ist oft zu Recht dafür kritisiert worden, elitär zu sein – der Auftritt der Japaner hilft sehr, auf diese Kritik zu reagieren. Denn das ist es, was gute Architekten tun sollten.

Santiago Cirugeda, 1971 in Sevilla geboren, hat sich ganz bewusst an der Peripherie zeitgenössischer Architektur angesiedelt. Häufig operiert er in einer juristischen Grauzone, in der temporäres Bebauen und „Besetzen" jedenfalls mit Missbilligung betrachtet werden. Und doch sind an seinen Aktivitäten eindeutig auch Universitäten und Menschen beteiligt, die daran interessiert sind, die Grenzen städtischer Rigidität in Bezug auf Raum, aber auch Materialien und Methoden auszuloten. Vor dem Hintergrund drastischer Kürzungen der spanischen Regierung, etwa im Bereich der Kulturförderung, könnten Cirugedas Recetas Urbanas bald eine noch wichtigere Rolle spielen. Er selbst dazu: „Seit 1996 habe ich in verschiedenen städtischen Zusammenhängen eine kritische Praxis entwickelt anhand subversiver Projekte, die letztendlich die Revision stadtplanerischer Regularien und Bestimmungen verlangen." Seine 80 m² große Aula Abierta Sevilla (Sevilla, 2011/12, Seite 404), bei der u.a. aus einem 2004 in Granada zum Abriss freigegebenen Gebäude gerettete Materialien Verwendung fanden, wurde auf einem leeren und praktisch verlassenen Grundstück errichtet. Die Aula Abierta gehört zu dem größeren Projekt „Espacio Artístico – La Carpa" (Kunstraum – Zelt), in dem das Varuma-Theater und die zukünftige Zirkusschule von Andalusien untergebracht sind. Es mag gut sein, dass Recetas Urbanas in Europa, wo staatliche Kulturförderung lange als selbstverständlich galt, ein Vorbild für andere architektonisch interessierte Organisationen wird, die versuchen, die Lücken zu füllen, wo staatliche Regulationen und Hilfen ungenügend sind.

Der vietnamesische Architekt Vo Trong Nghia hat sich mit der Entwicklung von Niedrigpreishäusern beschäftigt, die in seiner Heimat dringend benötigt werden, wo viele Häuser kleiner als 10 m² sind. Seine Niedrigpreishäuser (Provinz Dongnai, Vietnam, 2012, Seite 542) bewegen sich im Spektrum von 20 m² und kosten im Bau lediglich 3200 US-Dollar. Auf den Einbau von Bad und Toilette, die außen liegen und von mehreren Familien geteilt werden, wurde verzichtet, um die Ein-Raum-Häuser, in denen Vorhänge und verschiedene Bodenniveaus für etwas Privatsphäre sorgen, mit Blick auf zukünftige Erweiterungen flexibel zu halten. Vo Trong Nghia hat beachtliches Know-how bei der Verwendung von Bambus in der Architektur unter Beweis gestellt. In diesem Fall besteht die Innenverkleidung daraus, die Wände sind aus Polycarbonatplatten, für das Dach wurde GFK (glasfaserverstärkter Kunststoff) verwendet.

Einer der wahren Meister der temporären und der Katastrophenarchitektur ist natürlich der japanische Pritzker-Preisträger Shigeru Ban, der eine Anzahl von Notunterkünften nach Naturkatastrophen, wie die Paper Emergency Shelters für das Flüchtlingshilfswerk der Vereinten Nationen UNHCR, geplant hat. In letzter Zeit hat er in Haiti und L'Aquila, Italien, gearbeitet, obgleich bürokratische und praktische Beschränkungen die Hilfe nach Erdbeben unter diesen Umständen erheblich erschweren. Am 12.Januar 2010 gab es ein Erdbeben der Stärke 7,0 bei Port-au-Prince. Über eine Million Menschen verloren ihre Wohnungen, und mehr als eine halbe Million suchten Zuflucht in eilig aufgestellten Zelten. Shigeru Ban arbeitete gemeinsam mit Professoren und Studenten von der Universidad Iberoamericana und der Pontificia Universidad Católica Madre y Maestra (Dominikanische Republik) am Bau von einhundert Unterkünften aus Pappröhren und örtlichen Materialien für die Erdbebenopfer aus Haiti (Paper Temporary Shelters, Port-au-Prince, Haiti, 2010/11, Seite 74).

PLAYTIME

Es mag logisch erscheinen, dass kleine Bauwerke auch manchmal für Kinder entworfen werden, nämlich dann, wenn man ihre Größe im Vergleich zu ihrer Umgebung tatsächlich ernst nimmt. Das norwegische Büro Haugen/Zohar Arkitekter hat sich in diesem Bereich als innovativ hervorgetan, wie zwei der hier vorgestellten Projekte belegen. Ihre Feuerstelle für Kinder (Trondheim, 2010, Seite 212) war ein Auftrag der Stadt Trondheim. Mit einem recht kleinen Budget entwarfen sie das 30 m² große Gebäude, das aus Materialien gebaut wurde, die sie bei einer nahe gelegenen Baustelle geschenkt bekamen. Bei ihrer Konstruktion aus kurzen Holzstücken, angeordnet in 80 übereinandergeschichteten Kreisen aus je 28 Pinienhölzern, ließen sie sich von traditionellen regionalen Bauten inspirieren. Ihre Arbeit war unter den letzten 25 der AR Emerging Architecture Awards 2009.

Ihre Höhle für Kinder (Trondheim, 2012, Seite 208), ebenfalls ein Auftrag der Stadt Trondheim, steht gleich neben einem Kindergarten. Diesmal ließen sich die Architekten von natürlichen Höhlen anregen und verwendeten XP-Kunststoff, ein industrielles Verpackungsmaterial. Indem sie das Material aushöhlten und verklebten, schufen sie eine freundliche 16 m² große Landschaft für die Kleinen, wiederum mit sehr limitierten Mitteln. Ein positiver Nebeneffekt der Methode war, dass der verwendete Schaumstoff eigentlich hätte entsorgt werden sollen, nun aber weder verbrannt werden musste noch auf andere Weise die Umwelt verschmutzte.

Ein anderes, allerdings wesentlich komplexeres Gebäude für Kinder ist die Peanuts Nursery School (Hiroshima, Japan, 2011/12, Seite 306), entworfen von Keisuke Maeda (UID architects). Die 119 m² große Holzkonstruktion ist rundum verglast, wodurch das Innere von natürlichem Licht durchflutet wird. Vor dem Hintergrund der im Entwurf omnipräsenten Rundungen versteht der Architekt Peanuts nicht „als fertige Form", sondern „mehr wie eine Pflanze, deren Früchte in der Erde verborgen liegen". Diese Bemerkung und einige Details im Entwurf erinnern an die Äußerungen Tetsuo Kondos hinsichtlich seines Hauses in Chayagasaka, wo mit dem Konzept einer „sanften Ordnung" experimentiert wird. Nun ist es unvermeidlich, dass das Äußere jedes Gebäudes eine relativ „konkrete" Form annimmt, zumindest aber eine, deren Konturen erkennbar sind. Die „Sanftheit", mit der Maeda oder Kondo arbeiten, bezieht sich daher zum großen Teil auf das Innere, wo eine dezente Flexibilität angestrebt wird, um Bewegungsfreiheit zu gewährleisten und unter Umständen künftige Veränderungen zu vereinfachen. Es liegt der Eindruck nahe, dieser Ansatz stünde der Starrheit des modernistischen Rasters diametral entgegen, das in der zeitgenössischen Architektur so lange die Oberhand gehabt hat. Dabei sorgen Zweideutigkeiten und einander überschneidende Funktionen innerhalb eines Hauses (Wohnen, Essen, Kochen etc.) beinahe wie von selbst für eine sukzessive Abschaffung starrer, unverrückbarer Wände. Natürlich ist die Privatsphäre ein Thema, insbesondere in einem Haus, aber die Japaner scheinen sich an die erzwungene Nähe innerhalb kleiner Einheiten gut anpassen zu können und weniger Wände einer strikten Aufteilung vorzuziehen.

EINE SCHWARZE PERLE

Die Japaner sind natürlich nicht die einzige Nation, die zum Bau kleiner Wohneinheiten neigt. Die Bevölkerungsdichte eines Landes wie die Niederlande leistet bereits seit Längerem dem Entwerfen und Errichten kleiner Häuser Vorschub. Eines dieser Gebäude, genannt The Black Pearl (Rotterdam, 2008–10, Seite 498), ist das Wohnhaus des Designers Rolf Bruggink. Bruggink war 2003 an der Gründung von Zecc Architecten beteiligt, eines Büros, das es aufgrund von Projekten wie des Hauses Stairway to Heaven (Utrecht, 2007), einer umgebauten Kirche, zu einiger Bekanntheit gebracht hat. Zecc arbeitete gemeinsam mit Rolf Bruggink an dem 100 m² großen Haus Black Pearl. Ein rund 100 Jahre altes Ständehaus bildete den Ausgangspunkt des Projekts, zu dem auch der vollständige Neuaufbau des Hausinneren gehörte. Die ursprüngliche Abfolge kleiner Räume wurde durch die Schaffung eines durchgehenden Raums über vier Stockwerke abgelöst. „So entstehen Lebensbereiche, die durch Leerstellen, lange Treppen und weite Sichtachsen verbunden sind", erklären die Architekten. „Überflüssige Geländer, Brüstungen und Türen werden weggelassen, was für ein hohes Maß an räumlicher Abstraktion sorgt. Böden, Wände, Treppen und Decken gehen ineinander über und evozieren ein Gefühl der Unmöglichkeit à la Escher." Und auch wenn die Ästhetik sich von Land zu Land unterscheidet, so ist es doch interessant festzuhalten, wie sehr die Beschreibung eines offenen Innenraums sich auf viele der neuen in diesem Buch vorgestellten japanischen Häuser anwenden ließe.

BÄUME AUS GUSSEISEN UND EIN SYMBOL IN EINEM PARK

Dass Toiletten grundsätzlich eher kleine Räumlichkeiten sind, ist ein Gemeinplatz, selten jedoch ist es, dass talentierte Architekten sich die Zeit nehmen, solche frei stehenden öffentlichen Örtlichkeiten zu entwerfen. Diese Regel wurde durch das Zusammentreffen des jungen Büros design neoob mit den Verantwortlichen des laufenden Kumamoto-Artpolis-Projekts gebrochen, das seit seiner Initiierung 1988 über die Stadt im Süden Japans verstreut bereits einige interessante architektonische Arbeiten hinterlassen hat. Die öffentliche Toilette am Shirakawa-Fluss (Kumamoto, Japan, 2010/11, Seite 142) ist ein 11,6 m² großes Gebäude, dessen Hauptmerkmal umstehende gusseiserne Bäume sind. Mit Blick auf den Standort am Flussufer des Shirakawa, wo nach japanischer Bauordnung keine echten Bäume gepflanzt werden dürfen, ist die Geste, künstliche Bäume zu pflanzen sicher auch ein Kommentar zur überregulierten und verbauten Umgebung, die sich im Lauf der Jahre mithilfe hoher öffentlicher Investitionen entwickelt hat, die das Land aus seiner ökonomischen Flaute herausholen sollten. Design neoob wünschte sich für die Toilette ein gewisses Maß an Harmonie auch mit dem architektonischen Umfeld, zu dem einige nahe gelegene Bauten des Artpolis-Projekts gehören. In diesem Fall ist die Frage Richard Serras nach „Nützlichkeit" eindeutig zu beantworten, den Architekten ist es aber auch gelungen, einer Toilette eine gewisse Würde, wenn nicht gar etwas Künstlerisches zu verleihen.

Die hier erwähnten Beispiele und die anderen in diesem Buch vermitteln einen Eindruck von dem doch sehr breit gefächerten Umgang der zeitgenössischen Architektur mit kleinen Bauwerken oder Räumen. Mal sind sie nützlich, mal ohne Nutzen, wo Richard Serra ja die Trennlinie zwischen Kunst und Architektur verortete – zumindest ungefähr: Denn ist ein Gebäude, das zwar Architektur kommentiert, sonst aber keinen anderen Zweck verfolgt, wirklich selbst Architektur

Crosson Clarke Carnachan, ▶
Hut on Sleds, Whangapoua,
New Zealand, 2011 (page 132)

zu nennen? Kleinformatige Architektur bewegt sich häufig an der Schwelle zwischen etwas, das man auch als Sein oder Nichtsein beschreiben könnte. Sein oder Nichtsein? Der New Amsterdam Pavilion (New York, 2009, Seite 532) von UN-Studio mag da als Paradebeispiel dienen: 37 m² mit Polyurethan beschichtetes Holz, wobei die Grenzen zwischen innen und außen von den niederländischen Architekten ganz bewusst verwischt wurden. Eine Zweckbestimmung gibt es, sicher: Gefeiert wird damit der 400. Geburtstag New Amsterdams, wie New York City ursprünglich hieß. Aber was ist es darüber hinaus, ein Schutzraum, ein architektonisches Statement oder letztlich doch ein Kunstwerk? Unberechtigt ist die Frage nicht. Ein kleines Haus kann sehr wohl eine willkommene Unterkunft sein, für eine Familie, die in einer Naturkatastrophe alles verloren hat, oder für eine, die an einem Ort lebt, wo sich nicht jeder ein richtiges Haus leisten kann.

Die gleiche Frage erhebt sich natürlich auch bei Zaha Hadids 45 m² großem Burnham Pavilion (Chicago, Illinois, USA, 2009, siehe Seite 196). Er war eines der kleinen Gebäude, die zur 100-Jahr-Feier des Burnham-Plans für Chicago in Auftrag gegeben wurden, ein weiterer stammte von Ben van Berkel und UNStudio. Er enthielt eine Video-Installation, aber ansonsten könnte man sagen, dass ein derartiges Bauwerk keiner wirklichen Funktion dienen kann. Die Architekten erklärten: „Die Anwesenheit des neuen Gebäudes regt die intellektuelle Neugier des Besuchers an, während die Intensivierung des öffentlichen Lebens um und im Pavillon die Idee der öffentlichen Diskussion unterstützt." Die Zweckmäßigkeit der Architektur stimuliert dann, ebenso wie ein Kunstwerk, die öffentliche Wahrnehmung. Ist klein auch schön?

DIE GRÖSSE LIEGT IM AUGE DES BETRACHTERS

Man kann sich die Frage stellen, was in der Architektur überhaupt unter „klein" zu verstehen ist. Haus 77 (Póvoa de Varzim, Portugal, 2009/10, Seite 110) von José Cadilhe erstreckt sich über eine Fläche von 232 m² – vielleicht etwas zu groß für ein Buch über kleine Gebäude? Tatsächlich aber ist das Haus extrem schmal, das Raumproblem also im ganzen Entwurf präsent, auch wenn die Nutzfläche für ein Wohnhaus relativ großzügig bemessen ist. Die Kirche von Marlon Blackwell (Saint Nicholas Eastern Orthodox Church, Springdale, Arkansas, 2009, Seite 106) ist sogar noch größer, aber man könnte sagen, dass die Definition von „klein" natürlich auch davon abhängt, um welche Art Gebäude es geht. Kirchen sind üblicherweise für große Menschenmengen angelegt, im Gegensatz zu Kapellen, die qua Definition meist winzig sind. Die meisten Gebäude in diesem Buch haben eine Grundfläche von weniger als 100 m², aber in einem Land wie Vietnam, wo viele Häuser weniger als 10 m² messen, worauf der Architekt Vo Trong Nghia hinweist, mag eine solche Zahl luxuriös anmuten. Was klein ist, hängt also immer von der Funktion, dem Erscheinungsbild wie auch der jeweiligen nationalen Kultur ab. Wie viele wohlhabende Amerikaner würden einen Pritzker-Preisträger bitten, ein Haus mit nur 30 m² Grundfläche zu entwerfen (Kazuyo Sejima: Haus Tsuchihashi, Tokio, 2011, Seite 456)? Wahrscheinlich kein einziger. Architekten wie Toyo Ito haben hingegen postuliert, dass die städtische Verdichtung in Japan und die Lösungen, die dafür gefunden werden, sehr wohl ein Modell für zukünftige Stadtentwicklung weltweit sein könnten.

Heute leben 54 Prozent der Weltbevölkerung in städtischen Bereichen, und diese Zahl wird sich vermutlich bis 2050 auf 66 Prozent erhöhen. Die Stadtbevölkerung der Welt ist von 746 Millionen im Jahr 1950 auf 3,9 Billionen im Jahr 2014 angestiegen. Mit Zunahme der städtebaulichen Dichte wird, wie auch in allen Kulturen und Ländern, der Wohnraumbedarf immer größer. Es erscheint unvermeidlich, dass kleine Architektur ein Weg in die Zukunft sein wird, besonders im Bereich des Wohnungsbaus. Der Trend, Ressourcen zu bewahren und besser zu nutzen, weist auch künftig in die Richtung kleinerer Bauten. Dann wird es weniger Raum für mehr Menschen geben, hoffentlich in einer umweltbewussteren Gesellschaft. Wird es vielleicht schon sehr bald so sein, dass man sich darüber freut, auch nur ein paar Quadratmeter Privatsphäre zu haben?

Man kann durchaus sagen, dass einige der interessantesten Bauwerke „großartig" sind – von eindrucksvoller Größe, fast zu groß für ihre Funktion, zum Beispiel die Grand Central Station in New York. Und doch können sogar kleine Bauten, wenn sie von den richtigen Architekten stammen, eine Größe und ein ebenso gutes Verhältnis zum menschlichen Maßstab haben wie ein großes Gebäude. Natürlich entstehen in fast jeder großen Stadt der Welt weiterhin Hochhäuser, die sehr weit weg sind von der in diesem Buch vorgestellten kleinen Architektur. Und dennoch repräsentieren auch diese für reiche und mächtige Nutzer bestimmten Bauten trotz ihrer die Skyline verändernden Wirkung nicht die Welt, in der die meisten Normalbürger leben. Wir stehen mit Sicherheit vor einer Zeit der kleinen Architektur, bestimmt von der Bewahrung unserer Ressourcen und dem Wachstum der Bevölkerung. Die Zukunft ist klein.

INTRODUCTION

PETIT, MAIS PARFAIT

Que se passe-t-il lorsque les économies chancellent et que le bâtiment ralentit au point de presque s'immobiliser ? L'architecture, souvent très dépendante des financements, perd-elle alors toute inventivité ? À notre époque de dépenses de construction somptuaires, des pays comme l'Espagne ont produit nombre de bâtiments remarquables, tandis que de jeunes architectes brillants attiraient l'attention. Mais l'inventivité se volatilise-t-elle avec ces jeunes architectes espagnols ou portugais qui courent aujourd'hui après les commandes hors d'Europe ? Ou s'agit-il d'un simple transfert d'énergie ailleurs, vers différents types de projets ? Malgré ce qu'on a décrit comme un ralentissement mondial, certains pays continuent de se développer à un rythme rapide – le PIB estimé de la Chine a cru de 6,9 % en 2015, et même si elle a baissé après avoir culminé à plus de 10 % en 2010, la croissance économique indienne est estimée à 7,1 % environ. Ces pays, et d'autres, ne sont en aucun cas en récession, ce dont leur architecture témoigne.

L'IMPORTANCE DE LA TAILLE

Mais la taille importe-t-elle vraiment en architecture ? On peut noter avec intérêt que maints grands architectes d'aujourd'hui, de Frank Gehry à Tadao Ando, ont commencé leur carrière avec des projets d'une taille singulièrement réduite – pour la plupart des maisons –, et leur passage à des travaux de plus grande envergure n'a pas toujours connu le succès escompté. Alors, plus grand veut-il forcément dire mieux ? En fait, plus un projet est ambitieux, plus il a tendance à devenir complexe et bureaucratique, avec un résultat final qui laisse de moins en moins la parole à l'architecte. Les réalisations comme le musée Guggenheim de Bilbao (Espagne, 1997) par Frank Gehry restent les exceptions qui confirment la règle. La taille n'est pas forcément synonyme de qualité et ne l'a jamais été. Des objets comme le Tempietto de Bramante (San Pietro in Montorio, Rome, 1502–10), dont le diamètre n'excède pas 4,5 mètres, ont plus marqué l'histoire de l'architecture que bien des bâtiments plus imposants. On pourrait donc penser que, si la taille importe bel et bien, les petites constructions donnent aux architectes une liberté impensable dans des projets gigantesques pour des États ou des entreprises.

Les avantages des petites réalisations deviennent également visibles en périodes de tensions économiques. En effet, si les gros budgets sont aujourd'hui rares, le désir ou le besoin de bâtir existe toujours. Et dans la plupart des cas, il revient moins cher de construire plus petit. Donc, logiquement, lorsqu'il n'y a plus d'argent, un plus grand nombre de petites structures voient le jour. Bien sûr, cette généralisation rapide est plus ou moins vraie selon la région du monde concernée. Certains pays, comme le Japon, ont une préférence culturelle pour une tendance à construire petit. Du fait de la densité de population sur le littoral oriental du pays, surtout entre Tokyo et Osaka, les habitants sont appris depuis longtemps à s'accommoder d'espaces relativement réduits. De plus, les prix de l'immobilier à Tokyo et dans d'autres villes japonaises ont atteint un tel niveau que même la plus minuscule des parcelles revient pour le moins très cher. Par conséquent, les petites maisons de moins de 100 mètres carrés sont plus la règle que l'exception, même lorsque des architectes de talent sont recrutés pour les créer. Et même si l'économie japonaise est en crise depuis les années 1990, le flux de commandes résidentielles ne s'est pas interrompu et a donné naissance à plus d'une génération d'architectes de grand talent.

Au Japon, mais aussi ailleurs, les changements du mode de vie couplés aux tensions économiques semblent redéfinir nombre des exigences autrefois imposées à l'architecture. Ainsi, alors que les maisons individuelles, notamment dans l'Amérique de l'après-guerre, devaient correspondre à un certain nombre de critères standard tels qu'une cuisine séparée ou des espaces distincts destinés aux repas et au séjour, les tendances plus récentes ont pour ainsi dire brisé les murs entre ces différents espaces, les éliminant souvent purement et simplement. Les salons ouverts contigus aux coins repas et cuisine sont aujourd'hui plus courants que les volumes fermés qui exigent souvent de réduire les surfaces. Les Japonais et leur longue tradition de panneaux coulissants qui redessinent à volonté l'espace intérieur et redéfinissent le rapport entre intérieur et extérieur ouvrent aujourd'hui la voie vers une nouvelle génération de maisons dont les divisions entre les différentes parties sont quasiment absentes. Une surface suffisamment « flexible » pour permettre des usages multiples peut aider un petit bâtiment à répondre à plus de besoins que ne le pouvaient autrefois de plus grands.

CE QUI EST PETIT SÉDUIT

Le Tempietto de Bramante, mais aussi des œuvres plus récentes comme le bureau de Philip Johnson (New Canaan, Connecticut, 1980), occupent depuis longtemps la frontière entre art et architecture. L'étrange bâtiment de Johnson occupe une surface au sol d'à peine 36 mètres carrés. Bien qu'il ait travaillé dans ce qu'il appelait sa « cellule monastique », les formes de Johnson, comme celles plus tardives de Frank Gehry, se rapprochent incontestablement de la sculpture. Il faut dire que les petites structures ne sont bien évidemment pas soumises aux mêmes exigences de construction que les plus grandes. C'est l'une des raisons pour lesquelles des artistes qui s'intéressent à l'architecture cèdent parfois à leurs désirs et créent de petits bâtiments. Mais l'inverse est également vrai : pour un architecte, il est parfois plus facile de concevoir une véritable œuvre d'art à petite échelle que dans une immense structure qui doit répondre à de multiples contraintes. En effet, il n'est pas toujours évident de se montrer créatif lorsqu'il s'agit de garer mille voitures dans un garage ou de pratiquer une sortie de secours pour des centaines d'employés de bureau affolés.

Ce volume, dont le contenu est tiré de la série *Architecture Now!* est entièrement consacré aux petits bâtiments ou espaces. Ce choix n'est pas dû au hasard, si l'on se réfère à l'inventivité dont font preuve les architectes (et artistes) sélectionnés, il n'est pas non plus sans lien avec des événements de plus grande portée sur la scène économique mondiale. Lorsque l'argent ne suffit plus pour faire sortir de terre d'immenses palais des congrès et gratte-ciel, la petite architecture commence véritablement à dévoiler ses charmes. Et, alors que d'excellents architectes auraient sans doute décliné de trop petites commandes il y a quelques années, ils sont aussi nombreux à voir désormais d'un œil positif l'intérêt de l'encombrement réduit. Cela ne fait aujourd'hui plus aucun doute : en architecture, ce qui est petit séduit.

L'UTILE ET L'INUTILE

Mais où la ligne de démarcation entre art et architecture passe-t-elle exactement ? Plusieurs des œuvres publiées ici posent ouvertement la question. Pour le sculpteur américain Richard Serra : « La différence entre art et architecture est que l'architecture est utile. » Bien que certains architectes flirtent (dangereusement ?) avec des structures sans utilité apparente, la définition de Serra est une ligne directrice précieuse, même si elle ne nous a pas empêchés d'inclure certaines de ces œuvres « ambiguës » dans ce volume essentiellement consacré à l'architecture. Mais les lecteurs de la série *Architecture Now* sont désormais familiers de ces incursions dans l'« inutile » – tant il est évident que les artistes sont souvent en avance sur leur époque et plus en accord avec l'état d'esprit du moment que leurs collègues architectes plus « réalistes ».

L'équipe d'architectes belges Gijs Van Vaerenberg nous offre un exemple intéressant de franchissement des frontières entre art et architecture. Comme son collègue Gijs Van Vaerenbergh, Pieterjan Gijs a fait des études de génie civil et d'architecture à l'Université catholique de Louvain (KUL, 2001–06), mais il est aussi titulaire d'un master en urbanisme et développement territorial. Leur construction Reading Between the Lines (Borgloon, Belgique, 2011, page 180) faite de 30 tonnes d'acier Corten et de 2000 colonnes, dont la superficie ne dépasse pas 28 mètres carrés, repose sur des fondations en béton armé. Ce n'est pas une réalisation architecturale au sens où on l'entend généralement, plutôt un « objet artistique transparent ». Sa silhouette est celle d'une église, mais elle ne cherche pas à exercer la fonction correspondante, c'est bien plus un commentaire sur l'absence de dialogue entre solidité et vide en architecture.

Cet intérêt pour le franchissement des frontières coutumières est présent dans de nombreuses disciplines, pas seulement l'art et l'architecture. Le designer néerlandais Erik Rietveld en est un parfait exemple. Après des études d'économie & business à l'université de Maastricht (1993), il a étudié la philosophie, la psychologie et le portugais à l'université de São Paulo (USP) et a obtenu un master de philosophie à l'université d'Amsterdam (UvA) en 2003. Il travaille avec son frère Ronald Rietveld (1972) qui est, lui, architecte – ils ont notamment collaboré à Bunker 599 (Diefdijklinie, Pays-Bas, 2010, page 394) dans un ancien bunker de la Nouvelle ligne d'eau de Hollande (NDW). Selon les designers, « un bunker en apparence indestructible, véritable monument, est ouvert par une tranchée. La conception dévoile l'intérieur exigu de l'un des 700 bunkers de la NDW, normalement fermé aux regards. Une promenade en bois traverse aussi la construction d'une lourdeur extrême. Elle mène les visiteurs à une zone inondée et aux sentiers de la réserve naturelle voisine ». Couper un bunker en deux et créer un passage découvert à travers n'est pas vraiment une contribution à une forme d'architecture « utile », mais plutôt une interrogation philosophique et artistique sur le bâtiment lui-même.

Ryue Nishizawa, l'un des membres du duo Sanaa lauréat du fameux prix Pritzker, possède toutes les références architecturales voulues, mais continue néanmoins d'explorer activement les limites entre ce qui est construit et ce qui a été simplement voulu, dans le but de commenter l'art de la construction. Son pavillon Fukita à Shodoshima (Shodoshima-cho, Kagawa, Japon, 2013, page 350) a une surface de 185 mètres carrés, mais est uniquement fait de deux feuilles d'acier courbes qui se chevauchent. Elles sont soudées l'une à l'autre aux angles. L'espace créé entre les deux permet aux visiteurs de s'asseoir et tient lieu de terrain de jeux pour les enfants sur le chemin vers le temple. Malgré son apparence éphémère, il s'agit d'une structure destinée à durer, sans la moindre fondation. Pour les architectes, « c'est une composition simple, comme si le pavillon avait simplement été apporté et disposé ici ». Ce genre de raisonnement s'applique aussi, bien sûr, aux œuvres d'art même si l'« utilité » de l'art peut toujours faire débat.

Les serres créées par un autre architecte japonais de talent, Junya Ishigami, au pavillon japonais de la Biennale d'architecture de Venise (2008, page 234) étaient quant à elles véritablement minuscules. Chacune a été conçue comme un bâtiment en soi, auquel des calculs savants permettaient de tout juste tenir debout. L'intention de l'architecte était de suggérer « les futures possibilités de l'architecture ». Ishigami évoque aussi le Crystal Palace construit par Paxton pour la grande exposition de Londres (1851) et qui avait la forme d'une serre. Il a travaillé avec le botaniste Hideaki Ohba qui a choisi avec soin des variétés de plantes qui semblent à première vue indigènes, mais incarnent en réalité une « une légère perturbation de l'environnement du parc ». Des meubles en bois ont été placés dans le jardin, évoquant l'ambiguïté, ou plus exactement la « simultanéité » entre l'espace intérieur et extérieur, tandis que le pavillon lui-même était presque totalement vide, à l'exception de fins dessins sur les murs blancs. On a peut-être approché ici la définition habituelle de l'architecture malgré la taille très réduite des serres, et pourtant elles témoignaient aussi d'une intention clairement artistique ou réfléchie.

L'artiste espagnole Cristina Iglesias, née en 1956, jouit elle aussi d'une grande réputation sur la scène internationale des galeries et expositions. Elle a souvent étendu ses sculptures à des installations qui occupent un espace suffisant pour qu'on puisse commencer à les considérer comme des œuvres architecturales. Sa *Vegetation Room Inhotim* (Inhotim, Belo Horizonte, Brésil, 2010–12, page 228) occupe une surface de neuf mètres sur neuf. Situé sur le terrain du centre d'art contemporain Inhotim, l'ensemble fait alterner les surfaces d'acier inoxydable polies qui reflètent les plantes environnantes et un motif végétal sculpté à l'intérieur. Iglesias lui donne le nom de *plant room* et elle est parfaitement à sa place dans un domaine qui comporte 300 hectares de forêt naturelle et 110 collections botaniques. Dans cet exemple, l'« utilité » de l'œuvre est essentiellement d'ordre artistique, mais comme pour celle d'Eliasson, elle incite les visiteurs à repenser le décor naturel qui les entoure et, peut-être, à y répondre différemment.

DES MAISONS DE THÉ AUX TOURS

Terunobu Fujimori est célèbre pour ses créations originales souvent profondément enracinées dans la culture japonaise. Sa « Maison du scarabée » (*Beetle's House*, page 164) de 4 mètres carrés a été construite pour l'exposition « 1:1 Architects Build Small Spaces 2010 » au Victoria and Albert Museum de Londres du 15 juin au 30 août 2010. Il explique que le Japon est l'un des rares pays à posséder une longue tradition de structures minuscules créées par des architectes de renom, notamment pour la cérémonie du thé. Sa première idée de suspendre la construction au plafond du musée n'a pas pu être réalisée, mais le projet comporte néanmoins à la fois une part d'humour et une réflexion très sérieuse – il correspond à la définition de Richard Serra, car il a été conçu dans un but utile, mais se situe vraiment à la frontière entre installation artistique et construction miniature.

Parmi les autres participants à l'exposition de 2010 au Victoria and Albert Museum, on compte l'agence d'Oslo Rintala Eggertsson fondée en 2007 par les architectes finlandais Sami Rintala et islandais Dagur Eggertsson. Leur *Ark Booktower* (page 424) n'occupe que neuf modestes mètres carrés au sol, mais a bel et bien pour objectif de permettre d'« échapper à l'espace physique du musée vers l'espace mental de la littérature ». En remplissant la tour de livres usagés, les architectes ont réalisé certaines de leurs ambitions littéraires, mais ils ont aussi fini par utiliser les livres en tant que « surface murale minimale unifiée ». On le voit donc, en architecture, le débat fait rage entre surface et contenu.

Rintala Eggertsson a également réalisé la tour d'observation de Seljord (Seljord, Telemark, Norvège, 2011, page 420) dans le cadre d'un programme de développement mis au point par la municipalité. La tour évoque une légende locale selon laquelle le lac de Seljord serait habité par un mystérieux serpent. Elle abrite également de petites expositions. Avec sa surface de 70 mètres carrés, elle montre l'intérêt de faire appel à des architectes de renom pour attirer les touristes, ce que l'on a constaté ailleurs en Scandinavie ces dernières années.

Leur Hut to Hut (Kagala, Karnataka, Inde, 2012, page 416) relève plus de la « véritable » construction et de la conception dans un environnement plus complexe. Cette structure double de 27 mètres carrés a été construite avec des matériaux produits localement et des sources d'énergie renouvelables. L'aspect le plus intéressant de ce projet est sans doute l'association d'une esthétique et de matériaux régionaux avec un sens réel de l'invention et d'un savoir-faire technique nordiques.

UNE RÉFLEXION SUR L'ARCHITECTURE

Les deux architectes jeunes Florian Idenburg (né en 1975) et Jing Liu (née en 1980) se sont déjà fait une solide réputation (So – Il: Solid Objectives – Idenburg Liu) aux États-Unis ou ailleurs. Leur Tri-Colonnade (page 466), qui faisait partie de l'exposition « The Street » à la Biennale d'urbanisme et d'architecture de Shenzhen et Hong Kong (2011, commissaire Terence Riley), cherchait, malgré sa taille très réduite (24 m²), à poser quelques-unes des questions fondamentales de l'architecture relatives aux façades ou surfaces. Ayant remarqué que la façade était devenue « implicitement plane », les architectes ont posé un imprimé plastifié marbré sur des colonnes, puis des miroirs par derrière, afin de donner l'impression aux visiteurs que le « marbre » se dilatait au fur et à mesure qu'ils s'en approchaient. Ce qui semble plat ne l'est pas. L'idée, parfois décrite comme une illusion d'optique, est aujourd'hui très populaire parmi les architectes contemporains qui multiplient les effets de lumière, de transparence et de reflets. Là encore, un pavillon comme Tri-Colonnade peut ne pas être perçu comme réellement utile, et donc classé plutôt parmi les installations artistiques que parmi les réalisations architecturales. Pourtant, son intérêt est purement architectural.

Un autre architecte présent dans ce volume crée des œuvres susceptibles d'être comparées à des installations artistiques, le Mexicain Michel Rojkind. Né en 1969 à Mexico, il a beaucoup travaillé avec les agences locales de Nestlé et a coordonné en 2012 un projet inédit sponsorisé par Nescafé auquel ont participé sept artistes. Son « Portail de la conscience » (page 430) a été posé en arceau sur le trottoir du Paseo de la Reforma, l'une des principales avenues de la capitale mexicaine. La structure faite d'un treillis de barres d'armature porte près de 1500 tasses de café en métal. Du fait de leur quantité et de la régularité de leur disposition, les tasses forment un motif décoratif, tandis que la nature « caféinée » de l'œuvre n'échappe à personne. Avec un petit budget de seulement 11 000 dollars, Rojkind est parvenu à mettre en vedette l'architecture, l'art et le commerce de manière aussi digne qu'originale.

Tim Hursley, spécialiste des représentations architecturales qui a souvent vu ses photos publiées dans la série Architecture Now, est un cas inattendu de transgression des catégories habituelles de photographie, art ou architecture. Pour ce livre, il a proposé un bâtiment de taille incontestablement réduite, un silo de 4,6 mètres de diamètre à Greensboro, dans l'Alabama, une région où il travaille souvent avec Rural Studio. Haut de 14 mètres, l'édifice (page 224) fortement endommagé en 1993 avait conservé sa curieuse forme tordue jusqu'à ce qu'Hursley le remarque, le photographie et finalement l'achète. Dans son état, le silo ne correspond sans doute pas à la définition de l'utilité architecturale de Richard Serra, mais sa forme lui confère un aspect artistique qui n'a visiblement pas échappé à Tim Hursley. Les bâtiments agricoles, souvent en meilleur état, ont fait l'objet d'un inventaire presque scientifique par le couple allemand Hilla et Bernd Becher, connus pour avoir influé sur toute une génération de photographes d'« art » allemands. L'attention exclusive qu'ils portent aux divers bâtiments industriels a non seulement mis en lumière une forme d'architecture très largement méconnue, mais a aussi suggéré que la photographie peut atteindre un niveau de qualité artistique élevé avec un sujet que l'on pourrait considérer comme banal mais qui se révèle sur les photos.

DES MAISONS SANS MURS

On notera avec intérêt que l'innovation constatée dans les maisons japonaises depuis quelques années peut, dans une certaine mesure, être attribuée à une école d'architecture sous la houlette d'une génération d'architectes tels que Kazuyo Sejima (née en 1956). Membre de l'équipe SANAA lauréate du prix Pritzker, Sejima crée aussi ses propres bâtiments, comme la maison Tsuchihashi achevée récemment et publiée ici (Tokyo, 2011, page 456). Avec sa surface au sol de seulement 72 mètres carrés et l'atrium sur toute la hauteur de la maison, elle met clairement l'accent sur la verticalité. Mais le plus frappant reste l'ouverture de l'intérieur et la sensibilité à la lumière ou aux conditions météorologiques affichée sur la terrasse du toit. Sejima s'est ici aventurée sur les traces de Sou Fujimoto dans un territoire où les sols des différents étages semblent être disposés selon un schéma qui crée des niveaux intermédiaires et permet une exploitation de l'espace très ouverte.

Né en 1975, Tetsuo Kondo a travaillé sept ans dans l'agence de Sejima (1999–2006) avant de créer la sienne. Sa maison à Chayagasaka (Nagoya, Aichi, Japon, 2011–12, page 270) possède une surface au sol de 90 mètres carrés. Sa philosophie de la conception est que l'architecture ne doit pas obéir à un système et à une organisation dominants ou « forts », mais qu'elle doit plutôt « intégrer des significations diverses » – l'organisation est alors vue comme un « ordre souple », et non rigide ou « dur ». Il explique en effet que l'utilisation de l'espace par une famille de deux petits enfants change avec le temps et que sa « maison à pièce unique » permet ces changements.

LE RÊVEUR DE MAISON (DE POUPÉES)

Joshua Prince-Ramus est l'un des partenaires fondateurs d'OMA New York, la branche américaine de l'Office for Metropolitan Architecture (OMA)/Rem Koolhaas aux Pays-Bas, qu'il a dirigée avant de la rebaptiser REX en 2006. Sa « Maison (de poupées) de Madison Avenue » (*Madison Avenue (Doll)House*, New York, 2008, page 410) a occupé une surface de seulement 4 mètres carrés dans le magasin Calvin Klein de Madison Avenue. L'architecte avait également été chargé de créer une *concept house* pour « Calvin Klein Woman », une résidence de 190 mètres carrés non réalisée. L'installation de Prince-Ramus pourrait être interprétée comme un commentaire sur l'échelle et le but de l'architecture, mais aussi sur le décor minimaliste du magasin, œuvre de John Pawson. Sans être une structure autonome – ce qu'aurait été la *concept house* –, la *Madison Avenue (Doll)House* a parfaitement sa place dans un livre consacré aux constructions de petite taille.

RETOUR À LA VIE SAUVAGE

Après ces représentants hautement artistiques de la petite construction, aventurons-nous dans des contrées plus retirées, ou du moins dans la nature, où de petites structures écologiques permettent de passer un moment dans un décor naturel sauvage sans avoir l'impression de détruire la planète. Le projet Endémico Resguardo Silvestre (Valle de Guadalupe, Ensenada, Mexique, 2010–11, page 188) par l'architecte mexicain Jorge Gracia Garcia est un exemple de cette approche. L'hôtel comporte vingt chambres, chacune dans une construction distincte de 20 mètres carrés. L'architecte a utilisé un squelette en acier pour un impact minimal sur le sol de ce site de 99 hectares situé dans la région viticole de Basse-Californie, il a choisi de l'acier Corten pour les surfaces extérieures afin qu'elles se fondent le plus possible dans le brun ou l'ocre du paysage. Dans ce décor, les clients peuvent véritablement profiter de la nature tout en bénéficiant des services de l'hôtel.

La Cabane-traîneau (Hut on Sleds, Whangapoua, Nouvelle-Zélande, 2011, page 132) de l'agence d'Auckland Crosson Clarke Carnachan Architects est un autre exemple de petite structure individuelle dans un décor naturel. Installée sur une plage de sable blanc de la péninsule de Coromandel, la petite maison repose sur deux patins de bois qui permettent de la déplacer à volonté sur la plage ou sur une péniche. Les architectes expliquent que « l'esthétique est naturelle et rappelle un autre bâtiment de plage, peut-être un point de sauvetage pour surfeurs ou une tour d'observation ». Revêtue de bois, la cabane peut être entièrement fermée lorsqu'elle n'est pas habitée, tandis que de grandes portes vitrées et un volet de la hauteur de deux étages qui sert d'auvent lorsqu'il est ouvert confèrent à cette maison de vacances de 35 mètres carrés presque tout le confort d'une vraie maison.

Andreas Wenning (baumraum) est célèbre en Allemagne et ailleurs pour ses nombreuses maisons dans les arbres. Le concept semble aujourd'hui très à la mode dans de nombreuses régions du monde – peut-être les maisons dans les arbres offrent-elles aux adultes un moyen d'échapper au stress des grandes villes, ou de se rapprocher de la nature ? Nous publions l'une des tentatives de Wenning de créer des hôtels dans les arbres. L'établissement Baumgeflüster (Murmure des arbres, Bad Zwischenahn, Allemagne, 2011, page 92) est constitué de quatre « chambres », dont la construction a coûté au total 280 000 euros. À 3,5 mètres au-dessus du sol, elles sont posées sur des poteaux en acier, mais sont aussi suspendues aux arbres par des câbles en acier inoxydable et des sangles textiles. À l'instar des maisons de thé japonaises, les maisons dans les arbres appartiennent pour ainsi dire par définition à la petite architecture. Ni les unes, ni les autres ne s'accommodent confortablement de grands espaces. Dans le cas de l'hôtel de Bad Zwischenahn, chaque maison dispose d'une chambre pour deux personnes, d'une salle de bains et d'un espace séjour avec un coin cuisine et deux lits supplémentaires. D'aucuns diront qu'un tel niveau de confort est très supérieur à ce que l'on est en droit d'attendre lorsque l'on dort suspendu dans un arbre, mais le choix de matériaux tels que du mélèze non traité devrait apaiser leurs doutes écologiques.

Un autre architecte américain de talent, Tom Kundig, basé à Seattle, doit sa réputation en grande partie à de petites structures. La surface au sol de sa cabane Sol Duc (péninsule Olympique, Washington, 2010–11, page 370) mesure tout juste 36 mètres carrés. Revêtue d'acier, elle est perchée sur quatre colonnes également en acier pour la protéger des crues occasionnelles dans la région. Le client voulait « un bâtiment compact, nécessitant peu d'entretien et quasiment indestructible pour l'abriter lui et sa femme pendant leurs expéditions de pêche », et le design n'est pas sans rappeler ce qui se faisait en temps de guerre. Mais il montre surtout ce qu'un architecte de talent peut apporter à la conception d'une toute petite résidence temporaire. Chacun des éléments en est utilisé au maximum de ses possibilités, le toit en encorbellement par exemple, ombrage la cabane, mais la protège aussi des tempêtes.

L'ARCHITECTURE D'URGENCE

La taille réduite est souvent un critère en architecture lorsqu'il s'agit d'abriter des populations dans le besoin après une catastrophe naturelle, ou tout simplement à la merci des systèmes et des villes qui ne peuvent les loger tous de manière adéquate. La bien nommée Maison pour tous de Rikuzentakata (Iwate, Japon, 2012, page 248) est un espace de réunion de 30 mètres carrés créé par Toyo Ito, Kumiko Inui, Sou Fujimoto et Akihisa Hirata dans une ville presque entièrement détruite par le tremblement de terre et le tsunami du 11 mars 2011. Conçue avec une forte participation des habitants, la construction en bois a été présentée à la XIIIe Biennale d'architecture de Venise (2012) dans le pavillon du Japon des Giardini et a reçu le Lion d'or de la meilleure participation nationale. Selon les termes du jury : « La présentation et l'histoire du pavillon sont exceptionnelles et parfaitement accessibles à un large public. Le jury a été impressionné par l'humanité du projet. » Il est particulièrement intéressant de voir des architectes parmi les plus grands investir tant d'énergie dans une entreprise et une présentation qui restent néanmoins à la portée de tous. En effet, l'architecture contemporaine (et notamment la Biennale de Venise) a souvent été critiquée à juste titre pour son élitisme – la présence japonaise fournit en grande partie la réponse à ce reproche, et c'est bien là ce que tout bon architecte devrait faire.

Santiago Cirugeda, né à Séville en 1971, a délibérément choisi une position en périphérie de l'architecture contemporaine et opère souvent dans une zone grise légale où la construction temporaire et l'occupation des lieux ne sont pas clairement perçues. Ses actions en Espagne n'en sont pas moins explicitement associées à des universités et personnes qui cherchent à tester les limites de la rigidité urbaine en termes d'espace, mais aussi de matériaux utilisés et de méthodes. Avec les coupes claires opérées par le gouvernement espagnol dans les dépenses allouées à la culture, Recetas Urbanas de Cirugeda semble aujourd'hui disposé à jouer un rôle plus important que jamais. Il déclare : « Depuis 1996, j'ai développé une pratique critique à travers des projets subversifs dans divers environnements urbains qui exigent tous en fin de compte la révision des règlements et décrets en matière d'urbanisme. » Son Aula Abierta Sevilla (2011–12, page 404) de 80 mètres carrés a été construite à Grenade sur un terrain vide et presque à l'abandon à partir de matériaux récupérés sur un édifice voisin destiné à être démoli en 2004. L'ensemble fait aujourd'hui partie d'un projet plus vaste appelé « Espacio Artístico – La Carpa » (Espace artistique – Le Chapiteau), siège de la troupe de théâtre Varuma et de la future école du cirque d'Andalousie. Dans tous les pays d'Europe où le financement de la culture a longtemps été tenu pour acquis, Recetas Urbanas pourrait bien devenir un modèle pour d'autres organisations architecturales qui tentent de combler le fossé lorsque la réglementation et les subventions publiques ne sont pas adaptées.

L'architecte vietnamien Vo Trong Nghia a lui aussi participé à la conception de logements à faible coût, une contribution essentielle dans un pays où la surface des maisons n'excède souvent pas 10 mètres carrés. Ses Maisons à bas prix (province de Dong Nai, Viêtnam, 2012, page 542) comptent une vingtaine de mètres carrés chacune, et leur construction coûte seulement 3200 $ par maison. Sans salles de bains ni toilettes – extérieures et communes à plusieurs familles – ces maisons à pièce unique, où des rideaux et des différences de niveau du sol apportent un peu d'intimité, ont été conçues pour être ouvertes à de futures extensions. Vo Trong Nghia est connu pour sa grande maîtrise du bambou en architecture. Ici, seules les persiennes sont en bambou, les murs sont des panneaux polycarbonates, et la toiture est en FRP (plastique renforcé de fibre de verre) ondulé.

L'un des grands maîtres de l'architecture temporaire et humanitaire est, bien sûr, le lauréat japonais du prix Pritkzer Shigeru Ban, qui a souvent conçu des habitations de secours pour venir en aide aux victimes de catastrophes naturelles, comme les abris d'urgence en papier pour le HCR. Plus récemment, il a aussi travaillé à Haïti et à L'Aquila, en Italie, mais les barrières bureaucratiques et techniques entravent considérablement l'aide aux victimes des tremblements de terre. Le 12 janvier 2010, un tremblement de terre d'une magnitude de 7,0 a frappé Port-au-Prince. Plus d'un million d'habitants ont perdu leur logis et plus d'un demi-million a trouvé refuge sous des tentes de fortune. Shigeru Ban a travaillé avec les professeurs et les étudiants de l'Université ibéro-américaine et de l'Université pontificale catholique Madre y Maestra (République dominicaine) pour construire une centaine d'abris en tubes de carton et matériaux locaux destinés aux victimes (Paper Temporary Shelters, Port-au-Prince, Haïti, 2010/11, page 74).

L'HEURE DE LA RÉCRÉATION

Il paraît logique que les petits structures soient souvent conçues pour les enfants afin de tenir compte de leur petite taille dans leur environnement. L'agence norvégienne Haugen/Zohar Arkitekter a fait preuve de beaucoup d'innovation dans ce domaine, comme en témoignent deux des projets publiés ici. Leur Foyer pour enfants (Trondheim, Norvège, 2010, page 212) a été commandé par la ville de Trondheim. Avec un budget extrêmement réduit, les architectes ont imaginé une structure de 30 mètres carrés construite avec des matériaux récupérés sur un chantier voisin. De petits morceaux de bois assemblés en 80 cercles superposés de chacun 28 pièces de pin s'inspirent de structures traditionnelles régionales. L'ouvrage était l'un des 25 en phase finale pour le prix AR+D pour l'architecture naissante en 2009. Leur Caverne pour enfants (Trondheim, Norvège, 2012, page 208), également réalisée pour la ville de Trondheim, est placée à proximité d'un jardin d'enfants municipal. S'inspirant cette fois des grottes naturelles, les architectes ont utilisé de la mousse PIR utilisée pour l'emballage industriel : en évidant et collant le matériau, ils sont parvenus à créer un lieu accueillant de 16 mètres carrés pour les jeunes enfants et, là encore, avec des moyens très limités. Cette méthode présente par ailleurs l'avantage supplémentaire que la mousse utilisée, au départ destinée à être jetée, n'a pas dû être brûlée et n'a donc produit aucune pollution.

L'école maternelle Peanuts (Hiroshima, Japon, 2011–12, page 306) par Keisuke Maeda (UID architects) est une autre structure de plus grande envergure destinée aux enfants. L'ensemble en bois d'œuvre de 119 mètres carrés est très largement vitré, ce qui permet à la lumière naturelle de pénétrer abondamment à l'intérieur. Du fait de l'omniprésence des courbes dans le dessin, l'architecte décrit Peanuts comme « une forme inachevée… telle une plante portant un fruit encore dans le sol ». Cette description et certains aspects du design rappellent les explications de Tetsuo Kondo sur sa maison de Chayagasaka avec laquelle il explore le concept d'« ordre souple ». Inévitablement cependant, l'extérieur d'un bâtiment doit présenter une forme « concrète », ou au moins une forme dont les contours sont reconnaissables. La « souplesse » de Maeda ou de Kondo concerne essentiellement l'intérieur où une agréable flexibilité a été introduite pour permettre une grande liberté de mouvement et peut-être faciliter de futurs changements. Cette approche semblera à certains diamétralement opposée à la rigidité de la grille moderniste qui a si longtemps eu la préférence de l'architecture contemporaine. Or, dans une maison, l'ambivalence et le chevauchement des différentes fonctions (séjour, repas, cuisine, etc.) favorisent presque naturellement l'abandon progressif des murs droits et durs. L'intimité reste importante, surtout dans une habitation, mais les Japonais semblent s'accommoder de la proximité imposée par les petits volumes et préférer moins de murs à une séparation trop stricte.

UNE PERLE NOIRE

Bien sûr, les Japonais ne sont pas la seule nation à construire plutôt des petites maisons. La densité de population d'un pays comme les Pays-Bas y a également favorisé pendant longtemps la conception et la construction de petites résidences. Le designer Rolf Bruggink a habité l'une d'entre elles, appelée The Black Pearl (Rotterdam, 2008–10, page 498). Bruggink est l'un des fondateurs en 2003 de Zecc Architects, une agence qui doit notamment sa notoriété à des projets tels que l'église reconvertie en maison Stairway to Heaven (Utrecht, Pays-Bas, 2007) et avec laquelle il a collaboré aux 100 mètres carrés de la Black Pearl. Une maison de métier vieille d'une centaine d'années a constitué la base du projet qui prévoyait la restructuration complète de l'intérieur. Au lieu des petites pièces d'origine, un espace continu a été créé sur quatre étages. Les architectes expliquent : « Cela ouvre des espaces à vivre reliés par des vides, de larges escaliers et d'immenses panoramas. Toutes les rampes, balustrades et portes superflues ont été mises à l'écart, ce qui crée un degré élevé d'abstraction spatiale. Les sols, murs, escaliers et plafonds fusionnent comme pour évoquer une impossibilité de « type Escher ». » Même si l'esthétique est différente selon les pays, on ne manquera pas de trouver intéressant dans quelle mesure cette description d'un espace intérieur ouvert s'applique à bon nombre des maisons japonaises récentes publiées ici.

DES ARBRES DE FONTE ET UN SYMBOLE DANS UN PARC

Les toilettes sont généralement des espaces nécessairement réduits, mais il est rare que des architectes de talent prennent le temps d'imaginer des édicules publics. La règle a connu une première infraction, née de la rencontre entre la jeune agence design neuob et les responsables du projet en cours Kumamoto Artpolis, qui sème des réalisations architecturales dignes d'intérêt à travers cette ville du sud du Japon depuis son lancement en 1988. Les toilettes publiques Shirakawa (Kumamoto, Japon, 2010–11, page 142) sont un édifice de 11,6 mètres carrés, marqué surtout par la présence d'arbres en fonte sur son toit. Il est situé sur les berges de la rivière Shirakawa où les lois japonaises interdisent la plantation de vrais arbres. Ainsi, le geste de planter des arbres artificiels constitue en soi un commentaire de l'environnement excessivement contrôlé et construit qui a vu le jour parallèlement aux généreuses dépenses publiques visant à sortir le pays du marasme économique. Design neuob voulait aussi des toilettes publiques en accord avec l'architecture environnante et notamment les réalisations voisines du projet Artpolis. La question de l'« utilité » selon Richard Serra se pose bien évidemment ici, mais les architectes sont aussi parvenus à conférer une certaine dignité, pour ne pas dire une note artistique, à leurs toilettes.

Les exemples cités ici, et d'autres dans le livre, donnent une idée des multiples usages des petites structures ou des petits espaces en architecture contemporaine. Ils sont utiles ou inutiles, selon la ligne de démarcation entre art et architecture tracée par Richard Serra – ou presque, car un bâtiment qui n'a d'autre objectif que d'émettre un commentaire sur l'état de l'architecture peut-il vraiment être qualifié lui-même d'architecture ? La petite architecture est souvent située au seuil de ce que l'on pourrait aussi appeler l'être et le non-être. Être ou ne pas être ? Le pavillon de la Nouvelle-Amsterdam (New York, 2009, page 532) par UNStudio est un exemple typique : 37 mètres carrés de bois recouvert de polyuréthane, les limites entre intérieur et extérieur délibérément effacées par les architectes néerlandais. L'objectif est, bien sûr, de célébrer le 400ᵉ anniversaire de la Nouvelle-Amsterdam, le premier nom de New York. Mais de quoi s'agit-il sinon ? Un abri, une affirmation architecturale ou en fin de compte une œuvre d'art ? La question est parfaitement justifiée : une petite maison peut être un abri bienvenu pour une famille qui a tout perdu dans une catastrophe naturelle, ou qui habite un endroit où tout le monde ne peut pas se loger convenablement. La même question se pose naturellement pour le pavillon Burnham (Chicago, 2009, voir page 196) de 45 mètres carrés, construit par Zaha Hadid et qui faisait partie des nombreuses autres petites structures commandées pour célébrer le 100ᵉ anniversaire du plan Burnham de

36

Shuhei Endo, Rooftecture OT2, ▶
Osaka, Japan, 2012 (page 148)

restructuration urbaine de Chicago, parmi lesquelles l'une a été réalisée par Ben van Berkel et UNStudio. Le bâtiment abrite une installation vidéo, mais on ne peut pas vraiment dire qu'il réponde à un réel objectif. Les architectes déclarent : « La présence de cette nouvelle structure suscite la curiosité intellectuelle du visiteur, tandis qu'un développement de la vie publique autour et dans le pavillon renforce l'idée de discours public. » L'utilité de l'architecture serait alors de stimuler la prise de conscience du public, comme beaucoup d'œuvres d'art. Alors, le petit, c'est beau ?

LA TAILLE EST SUBJECTIVE

On pourrait aussi poser la question de ce que signifie « petit » en architecture ? La Maison 77 (Póvoa de Varzim, Portugal, 2009–10, page 110) par José Cadilhe occupe une surface de 232 mètres carrés – un peu beaucoup pour un livre consacré aux petits édifices ? Mais avec son étroitesse extrême, le problème de la petitesse est présent dans le design, même si la surface totale au sol est plutôt généreuse. De même, une église par Marlon Blackwell (église orthodoxe d'Orient Saint-Nicolas, Springdale, Arkansas, 2009, page 106), plus grande encore, figure dans le livre, mais on dira que la définition de « petit » est différente selon le type de bâtiment. Les églises sont généralement destinées à accueillir de grandes congrégations, contrairement aux chapelles qui sont par définition plutôt petites. La plupart des réalisations publiées ici ont une surface au sol inférieure à 100 mètres carrés, mais dans un pays comme le Viêtnam où l'architecte Vo Trong Nghia fait remarquer que de nombreuses maisons ont moins de 10 mètres carrés, ce chiffre peut paraître énorme. Ce qui est petit l'est par rapport à sa fonction, sa présence et aux cultures nationales. Combien de riches Américains demanderaient à un architecte lauréat du prix Pritzker de construire une maison dont la surface au sol n'excède pas 30 mètres carrés (Kazuyo Sejima : maison Tsuchihashi, Tokyo, 2011, page 456) ? Sans doute aucun. Les architectes japonais comme Toyo Ito ont postulé que la densité urbaine dans leur pays et les solutions qui en résultent pourraient bien être un modèle pour le futur développement des villes dans le monde entier.

Aujourd'hui, 54 % de la population mondiale vit en ville, et cette proportion devrait atteindre 66 % en 2050. La population urbaine est passée de 746 millions en 1950 à 3,9 milliards en 2014. Avec cette densité croissante quels que soient la culture ou le pays, l'espace fait de plus en plus prime. L'avenir passera par l'architecture de petite taille, cela paraît inévitable, surtout pour les logements. De même, la tendance à la préservation et la meilleure utilisation des ressources va aussi dans le sens de constructions plus petites, puisqu'il y aura moins d'espace pour plus de gens, dans une société que nous espérons plus respectueuse de l'environnement. Peut-être que, bientôt, nous serons tous heureux de disposer de seulement quelques mètres carrés d'intimité ?

On peut dire sans se tromper que certains des espaces architecturaux les plus stimulants sont « grands » – de grande taille, presque trop pour l'usage qui en est fait, dans l'esprit de la gare new-yorkaise Grand Central Station par exemple. Car oui, placés entre de bonnes mains, même les plus petits des bâtiments ne manquent pas de grandeur et entretiennent surtout une relation intime significative avec l'échelle humaine. Il faut dire que le design de qualité, et l'architecture de qualité sont aussi utiles et significatifs dans un petit bâtiment que dans un grand. Bien sûr, d'immenses tours continuent de s'élever dans presque toutes les grandes villes du monde, loin de la petite architecture célébrée dans ce livre. Mais ces constructions, souvent destinées aux riches et puissants et malgré leur capacité à transformer la ligne d'horizon, ne représentent pas le monde dans lequel la plupart des gens ordinaires vivent. Nous entrons incontestablement dans une ère de petite architecture, limitée par les impératifs de préservation des ressources et l'accroissement de la population. L'avenir sera petit.

38

2BY4-ARCHITECTS

REMKO REMIJNSE was born in 1974 in Epsom, UK. He studied at the School of Architecture of Michigan State University (MSU, 1998–99) and graduated in Architecture from the Technical University (TU) of Delft (1997–2001). After working in the office of Claus & Kaan (Rotterdam, 2001–02), he founded Remijnse Architectuur (Rotterdam, 2002) and was then a cofounder of 2by4-architects (Rotterdam, 2005). **ROCCO REUKEMA** was born in 1972 in Assen, The Netherlands. He also attended MSU (1999–2000), and graduated in Architecture from the TU of Delft (1998–2002), also cofounding 2by4 in 2005. Their work includes a Spa and Wellness Resort (Dordrecht, 2008–11); the Island House (Breukelen, 2011–12, published here); and a public square in Glashaven (Rotterdam, 2011–13). Current work includes Eltheto Healthcare Housing (Rijssen, 2008–14); and a Water Ski Track and Facilities (Sneek, 2013–14), all in The Netherlands.

REMKO REMIJNSE wurde 1974 in Epsom, England, geboren. Er studierte an der School of Architecture der Michigan State University (MSU, 1998–99) und machte sein Diplom in Architektur an der Technischen Universität (TU) Delft (1997–2001). Nachdem er im Büro Claus & Kaan (Rotterdam, 2001–02) gearbeitet hatte, gründete er 2002 seine eigene Firma Remijnse Architectuur in Rotterdam und war danach Mitbegründer von 2by4-architects (Rotterdam, 2005). **ROCCO REUKEMA** wurde 1972 in Assen, Niederlande, geboren. Auch er studierte an der MSU (1999–2000), machte seinen Abschluss in Architektur an der TU Delft (1998–2002) und war ebenfalls Mitbegründer von 2by4-architects. Zu ihren Werken zählen ein Spa und Wellness Resort (Dordrecht, 2008–11); das Island House (Breukelen, 2011–12), hier veröffentlicht) und die Gestaltung eines öffentlichen Platzes in Glashaven (Rotterdam, 2011–13). Aktuelle Arbeiten sind Eltheto Healthcare Housing (Rissen, 2008–14) und eine Anlage für Wasserski (Sneek, 2013–14), alle in den Niederlanden.

REMKO REMIJNSE est né en 1974 à Epsom (GB). Il a fait ses études à l'École d'architecture de l'université du Michigan (MSU, 1998–99) et possède également un diplôme en architecture de l'Université technique (TU) de Delft (1997–2001). Il a d'abord travaillé dans l'agence Claus & Kaan (Rotterdam, 2001–02), puis a fondé Remijnse Architectuur (Rotterdam, 2002) avant de cofonder 2by4-architects (Rotterdam, 2005). ROCCO REUKEMA est né en 1972 à Assen (Pays-Bas). Il a également suivi les cours de la MSU (1999–2000) et il est également diplômé en architecture de la TU de Delft (1998–2002). Il est l'autre cofondateur de 2by4. Leurs réalisations comprennent un centre de spa et bien-être (Dordrecht, 2008–11); Island House (Breukelen, 2011–12, publiée ici) et une place à Glashaven (Rotterdam, 2011–13). Ils travaillent actuellement aux logements médicalisés d'Eltheto (Rijssen, 2008–14) et à une piste et centre de ski nautique (Sneek, 2013–14), tous aux Pays-Bas.

ISLAND HOUSE
Breukelen, The Netherlands, 2011–12

*Area: 21 m². Collaboration: Jille Koop,
Isabel Rivas, Loenor Coutinho.*

Located on a narrow island in the lake district of Loosdrechtse Plas, this cabin is intended to "customize the interaction with the surrounding natural setting." One glass façade and a dark-wood surface can be completely opened onto an outdoor wooden terrace. The folded wooden façade "becomes an abstract perpendicular element that floats above the water." Despite its very small size, the house includes a shower, toilet, kitchen, closets, storage, and other functions that are integrated into a double wall. A black, metal fireplace, which can be rotated, hangs from the ceiling. An east-west orientation allows the house to take in both sunrise and sunset. The steel-frame structure has wood and structural glass façades, wooden furniture, and a white epoxy floor.

Loosdrechtse Plas heißt die Seengegend, in der sich auf einem schmalen Inselgrundstück dieses Haus befindet, das „die Interaktion mit der natürlichen Umgebung je nach Bedürfnislage ermöglichen soll". Eine Glasfassade und eine dunkle Fläche aus Holz können vollständig auf eine Holzterrasse geöffnet werden. Die faltbare Holzfassade „wird zum abstrakten Element, das lotrecht über dem Wasser hängt". Trotz der geringen Größe verfügt das Haus über eine Dusche, ein WC, eine Küche, Schränke, Stauraum und weitere in eine zweischalige Wand integrierte Funktionen. Eine schwarze, drehbare Feuerstelle aus Metall hängt von der Decke. Die Ost-West-Ausrichtung ermöglicht es, Sonnenaufgang und Sonnenuntergang zu betrachten. Die Stahlrahmenkonstruktion verfügt über Holz- und tragende Glasfassaden, Holzmobiliar und einen weißen Boden aus Epoxid.

Située sur une île étroite dans la région lacustre de Loosdrechtse Plas, cette petite maison vise à «créer une interaction sur commande avec le décor naturel environnant». Une façade vitrée et une autre face de bois sombre peuvent être entièrement ouvertes sur une terrasse en bois, la façade en bois repliée «devient alors un élément perpendiculaire abstrait qui flotte sur l'eau». Malgré sa taille très réduite, la maison comporte une douche, des toilettes, une cuisine, des placards, des rangements et d'autres fonctions intégrées à un double mur. Une cheminée rotative de métal noir est suspendue au plafond. L'orientation est-ouest permet à la maison d'être éclairée à la fois par le lever et par le coucher du soleil. La structure à ossature d'acier est équipée de façades porteuses en bois et en verre, de mobilier en bois et d'un sol en époxy blanc.

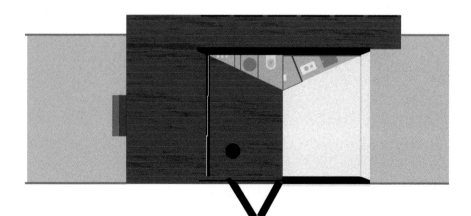

The orientation of the house is based on the directions of the rising and setting sun. The steel-frame structure has two structural glass façades, and two Plato wood façades.

Das Haus ist nach der aufgehenden bzw. untergehenden Sonne ausgerichtet. Die Stahlrahmenkonstruktion verfügt über zwei tragende Außenwände aus Glas und zwei Außenwände aus Plato-Holz.

L'orientation de la maison suit les directions du soleil levant et couchant. La structure à ossature d'acier présente deux façades porteuses en verre et deux en bois Plato.

With one glass side and part of the wooden façade open, the entire house becomes a covered exterior space by the water.

Eine Glas- und ein Teil der Holzwand können geöffnet werden, sodass das gesamte Haus zu einem überdachten Freiluftareal am Wasser wird.

Une façade vitrée et une partie de la façade en bois peuvent être ouvertes pour transformer la maison en un espace extérieur couvert au bord de l'eau.

The architects explain that the wooden floor of the living area is directly adjacent to the water, so when the wooden façade is folded open, it "enables the inhabitants to access the lake from the living room."

Den Architekten zufolge grenzt der Holzboden des Wohnbereichs bei aufgeklappter Holzwand direkt ans Wasser und „ermöglicht Bewohnern den Zugang zum See vom Wohnraum aus".

Les architectes expliquent que, lorsque la façade de bois est repliée et ouverte, le sol en bois du séjour se trouve en contact direct avec l'eau, « ce qui permet à ses occupants d'accéder directement au lac depuis le salon ».

WERNER AISSLINGER

WERNER AISSLINGER was born in Nördlingen, Germany, in 1964. He studied design at the University of Arts (Hochschule der Künste, 1987–91), Berlin. From 1989 to 1992, he freelanced with the offices of Jasper Morrison and Ron Arad in London and at the Studio de Lucchi in Milan. In 1993, he founded Studio Aisslinger in Berlin, focusing on product design, design concepts, and brand architecture. From 1998 to 2005, he was a Professor of Product Design at the Design College (Hochschule für Gestaltung) in Karlsruhe (Department of Product Design). He has developed furniture with Italian brands such as Cappellini and Zanotta and office furniture with Vitra in Switzerland. He works on product designs and architectural projects with brands like Interlübke, Mercedes-Benz, Adidas, and Hugo Boss. In 2003, he designed the Loftcube, a temporary residence intended for rooftop installation (Berlin), which would appear to have a conceptual relation to the Fincube (Ritten, Italy, 2010) published here.

WERNER AISSLINGER wurde 1964 in Nördlingen geboren und studierte Design an der Hochschule der Künste Berlin (1987–91). Zwischen 1989 und 1992 arbeitete er als freier Mitarbeiter für die Büros von Jasper Morrison und Ron Arad in London sowie für das Studio de Lucchi in Mailand. 1993 gründete er das Studio Aisslinger in Berlin, das sich auf Produktdesign, Designkonzepte und Markenarchitektur spezialisiert hat. Von 1998 bis 2005 war Aisslinger Professor für Produktdesign an der Hochschule für Gestaltung in Karlsruhe. Er entwickelte Möbel für italienische Hersteller wie Cappellini und Zanotta sowie Büromöbel für Vitra in der Schweiz. Aisslinger arbeitet an Produktentwürfen für Firmen wie Interlübke, Mercedes-Benz, Adidas und Hugo Boss. 2003 entwarf er den Loftcube, eine temporäre Wohneinheit, die sich auf Dächern installieren lässt (Berlin) und vom Konzept her erkennbar mit dem hier vorgestellten Fincube (Ritten, Italien, 2010) verwandt ist.

WERNER AISSLINGER, né à Nördlingen (Allemagne) en 1964, a étudié le design à l'Université des arts de Berlin (Hochschule der Künste,1987–91). De 1989 à 1992, il collabore en free-lance avec les agences de Jasper Morrison et Ron Arad à Londres et le Studio de Lucchi à Milan. En 1993, il fonde le Studio Aisslinger à Berlin, qui se consacre au design produit, aux concepts de design et à l'architecture de marques. De 1998 à 2005, il a été professeur de design produit à l'École supérieure de Design de Karlsruhe (Hochschule für Gestaltung). Il a créé des meubles pour des marques italiennes comme Cappellini et Zanotta, et du mobilier de bureau pour Vitra en Suisse. Il travaille aussi bien sur des projets de design que d'architecture pour des marques comme Interlübke, Mercedes-Benz, Adidas ou Hugo Boss. En 2003, il a conçu le Loftcube, résidence temporaire destinée à une toiture berlinoise, projet non sans lien conceptuel avec son Fincube (Ritten, Italie, 2010), publié ici.

FINCUBE

Winterinn, Ritten, South Tyrol, Italy, 2010

Area: 47 m². Client: Josef Innerhofter, Fincube. Cost: €150 000 (basic version).
Collaboration: Tina Bunyaprasit (Studio Aisslinger, Interior Design),
Markus Lobis (Interior Wood Structure), Matthias Prast (Finishes).

The extensive use of locally harvested larch and a double skin assures that this easily transportable house is also ecologically sound.

Dank der Nutzung lokaler Lärchenholzbestände und einer doppelten Außenhaut ist das transportable Haus auch ökologisch nachhaltig.

Le recours intensif au mélèze local et à la double peau assurent à cette maison facilement transportable de réelles qualités écologiques.

According to the designer: "Natural high tech is the concept of this new modular, sustainable, and transportable low-energy house." The structure was installed at an altitude of 1200 meters above sea level in South Tyrol and made with local collaboration. Built with locally harvested larch, the structure employs "long-lasting and recyclable materials," and so the Fincube can be dismantled and reassembled on another site. Triple glazing and a double façade are formed into a "unique overall mushroom-like monoshape." The client has envisaged placing a group of these residences in temporary locations, given that minimum preparation of the site is required.

Der Designer erklärt: „Das Konzept dieses neuen modularen, nachhaltigen und transportablen Niedrigenergiehauses ist naturverbundenes Hightech." Der Bau wurde in Tirol auf einer Höhe von 1200 m über N.N. errichtet und in Zusammenarbeit mit lokalen Firmen realisiert. Die Konstruktion aus regional geschlagenem Lärchenholz nutzt „langlebige und recycelbare Materialien", weshalb sich der Fincube demontieren und an anderen Standorten wiedererrichten lässt. Dreifachverglasung und Doppelfassade sind zu einem „außergewöhnlichen, pilzähnlichen fließenden Gesamtkörper" geformt. Da der Baugrund nur minimal vorbereitet werden muss, plant der Auftraggeber, eine ganze Gruppe dieser Wohnbauten vor Ort zu errichten.

Selon le designer : « Le concept de cette nouvelle maison modulaire, durable, transportable, à faible consommation d'énergie est le high-tech naturel. » Cette structure en « cube » a été installée à une altitude de 1200 m dans le Tyrol du Sud en collaboration avec des entreprises locales. Réalisé en mélèze de la région, il fait appel à « des matériaux de longue durabilité et recyclables ». Le Fincube peut être démonté et réassemblé ailleurs. Sa double façade à triple vitrage présente une « forme monocoque originale de champignon ». Intéressé par le faible coût de préparation du terrain, le client a envisagé de réaliser un groupe de ces résidences destinées à la location temporaire.

Despite its double skin, the house remains quite open to its environment, as seen in the image above.

Trotz seiner doppelten Außenhaut öffnet sich das Haus zur Umgebung, wie die Aufnahme oben belegt.

Malgré sa double peau, la maison reste ouverte sur son environnement, comme le montre l'image ci-dessus.

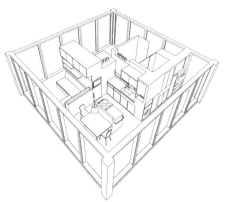

A rendering shows the way the volume of the house sits above the site. An axonometric of the interior renders explicit the compact, square design. Above, an interior view.

Ein Rendering verdeutlicht die minimale Bodenversiegelung durch den Baukörper. Eine Axonometrie des Innenraums bietet Einblicke in den kompakten Entwurf auf quadratischem Grundriss. Oben eine Innenaufnahme.

L'image de synthèse montre comment la maison repose sur son terrain. La vue axonométrique de l'intérieur précise la compacité des aménagements à l'intérieur de la forme carrée. En haut, une vue de l'intérieur.

ATELIER BOW-WOW

Atelier Bow-Wow was established in 1992 by Yoshiharu Tsukamoto and Momoyo Kaijima. **YOSHIHARU TSUKAMOTO** was born in 1965 in Tokyo and studied amongst others at the École d'architecture de Paris-Belleville (1987–88), before graduating from the Tokyo Institute of Technology (Doctorate in Engineering, 1994). He was a Visiting Associate Professor at UCLA (2007–08). **MOMOYO KAIJIMA** was born in 1969 in Tokyo, and graduated from Japan Women's University (1991), the Graduate School of the Tokyo Institute of Technology (1994), and studied at the ETH (Zurich, 1996–97). Their work includes the Hanamidori Cultural Center (Tokyo, Japan, 2005); the House and Atelier Bow-Wow (Tokyo, Japan, 2005); Mado Building (Tokyo, Japan, 2006); Pony Garden (Kanagawa, Japan, 2008); Machiya Guesthouse (Kanazawa, Japan, 2008); Mountain House (Nevada, USA, 2008); Four Boxes Gallery (Skive, Denmark; 2009); Machiya Tower (Tokyo, Japan, 2010); the BMW Guggenheim Lab (New York, USA, 2010; Berlin, Germany, 2012, published here; Mumbai, India, 2012–13); and housing on Rue Rebière (Paris, France, 2012).

1992 gründeten Yoshiharu Tsukamoto und Momoyo Kaijima ihr Büro Atelier Bow-Wow. **YOSHIHARU TSUKAMOTO**, 1965 in Tokio geboren, studierte u. a. an der École d'Architecture (Paris, Belleville, UP8, 1987–88) und promovierte 1994 am Tokyo Institute of Technology in Bauingenieurwesen. 2007/08 war er Gastprofessor an der UCLA. **MOMOYO KAIJIMA** wurde 1969 in Tokio geboren und absolvierte ihr Studium an der Japan Women's University (1991), der Graduiertenfakultät des Tokyo Institute of Technology (1994) sowie der ETH Zürich (1996–97). Zu ihren Projekten zählen das Kulturzentrum Hanamidori (Tokio, 2005), Haus und Atelier Bow-Wow (Tokio, 2005), das Mado-Gebäude (Tokio, 2006), der Pony Garden (Kanagawa, Japan, 2008), das Gästehaus Machiya (Kanazawa, Japan, 2008), das Mountain House (Nevada, USA, 2008), die Four Boxes Gallery (Skive, Dänemark, 2009), der Machiya Tower (Tokio, 2010), das BMW Guggenheim Lab (New York, 2010; Berlin, 2012, hier vorgestellt; Mumbai, 2012–13) und ein Wohnbauprojekt an der Rue Rebière (Paris, 2012).

Atelier Bow-Wow a été créé en 1992 par Yoshiharu Tsukamoto et Momoyo Kaijima. Yoshiharu. Né en 1965 à Tokyo, **YOSHIHARU TSUKAMOTO** est diplômé de l'Institut de technologie de Tokyo (doctorat en ingénierie, 1994). Il a également étudié à l'École d'architecture de Paris-Belleville (Paris, 1987–88). Il a été professeur associé à UCLA (2007–08). Née en 1969 à Tokyo et diplômée de l'Université pour les femmes du Japon (1991) et de la faculté d'études supérieure de l'Institut de technologie de Tokyo (1994), **MOMOYO KAIJIMA** a étudié à l'ETH (Zurich, 1996–97). Leurs réalisations comprennent le Centre culturel Hanamidori (Tokyo, 2005); la maison et atelier Bow-Wow (Tokyo, 2005); l'immeuble Mado (Tokyo, 2006); le Pony Garden (Kanagawa, Japon, 2008); la pension Machiya (Kanazawa, Japon, 2008); la Mountain House (Nevada, 2008); la galerie Four Boxes (Skive, Danemark, 2009); la tour Machiya (Tokyo, 2010); le BMW Guggenheim Lab (New York, 2010; Berlin, 2012, présenté ici; Bombay, 2012–13) et des logements, rue Rebière (Paris, 2012).

BMW GUGGENHEIM LAB

New York, USA, 2011; Berlin, Germany, 2012; Mumbai, India, 2012–13

Area: 184 m². Client: The Solomon R. Guggenheim Foundation.
Collaboration: Mirai Morita, Masatoshi Hirai, Fiedler Marciano Architecture (New York),
Magma Architecture (Berlin).

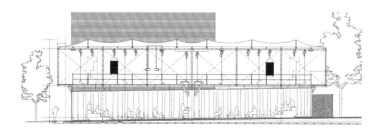

This project is the result of collaboration between the automobile manufacturer BMW and the Guggenheim Museum in New York. Part urban think tank, part community center and public gathering space, the BMW Guggenheim Lab is a global initiative aimed at raising awareness of urban challenges. The curators of the museum were looking for a "non-iconic" design that can be readily disassembled for transport. Air-conditioning was eliminated through plans to mount the project in "moderate" seasons. The architects explain: "We envisioned a super-light structure that hovers above ground in between buildings. The super-light structural frame was created with carbon-fiber reinforced plastic, which has the same strength as steel with one sixth of the weight. Steel was used in combination for columns to overcome safety and fire regulations. The space under the structure is lit uniformly with light filtering through polyester roof membrane. Sides of the top half of the structure are clad with double-layer polyester mesh creating a moiré effect. At ground level, there are just six columns and curtains, resulting in architecture without a floor or walls." The structure was recreated in Prenzlauer Berg, Berlin, and in Mumbai, India.

Das Projekt entstand als Kooperation zwischen BMW und dem Guggenheim Museum, New York. Das BMW Guggenheim Lab ist urbaner Thinktank, Kommunikationszentrum sowie Versammlungsort und versteht sich als eine globale Initiative, die ein Bewusstsein für drängende urbane Fragen schaffen will. Die Kuratoren wollten einen Entwurf, der nicht als „Highlight" auftritt und zu Transportzwecken leicht demontierbar ist. Eine Klimatisierung des Baus ist nicht nötig, da das Projekt bei „moderater" Witterung realisiert wird. Die Architekten erklären: „Unser Konzept ist eine ultraleichte Konstruktion, die zwischen Gebäuden über dem Boden zu schweben scheint. Das ultraleichte Tragwerk wurde mit kohlenstofffaserverstärktem Kunststoff realisiert und ist so belastbar wie Stahl bei nur einem Sechstel des Gewichts. Aufgrund von Sicherheits- und Brandschutzvorschriften kommt auch Stahl zum Einsatz, etwa bei den Stützen. Der Innenraum wird durch ein Dach aus Polyestermembran gleichmäßig belichtet. Seitlich ist der Aufbau mit einem doppellagigen Polyesternetz umhüllt, wodurch Moiréeffekte entstehen. Die untere Zone der Konstruktion besteht lediglich aus sechs Stützen und Vorhängen – eine Architektur ohne Boden und Wände." Der Bau stand ebenfalls im Berliner Stadtteil Prenzlauer Berg und war in Mumbai, Indien, zu sehen.

Ce projet est le fruit d'une collaboration entre le constructeur BMW et le musée Guggenheim de New York. Cellule de réflexion sur l'urbanisme et lieu de réunions publiques, le BMW Guggenheim Lab est une initiative mondiale de sensibilisation aux défis urbains. Les curateurs voulaient une structure « non emblématique » et facilement démontable. Pour éliminer la climatisation, le projet sera monté en saison « tempérée ». Les architectes ont imaginé « un bâtiment ultra-léger, flottant au-dessus du sol entre les immeubles. La structure ultra-légère est en plastique renforcé de fibre de carbone, d'une résistance équivalente à l'acier pour un sixième de son poids. L'acier a été utilisé dans les colonnes pour répondre aux normes de sécurité et anti-incendie. L'espace sous la structure est éclairé par la lumière filtrée par la membrane en polyester du toit. Les façades latérales de la moitié supérieure du bâtiment sont habillées d'un treillis en polyester double-couche, créant un effet moiré. Au sol, six piliers isolés et des rideaux créent une architecture sans plancher ni murs ». Le bâtiment a été remonté à Berlin et à Bombay.

The simple, essentially industrial vocabulary employed by the architects is evident in the image above, where openness is also obvious. Left, a section drawing shows materials used and a careful attention to individual objects and spaces.

Die schlichte, eher industrielle Formensprache der Architekten zeigt sich oben im Bild; hier wird auch die Offenheit des Entwurfs deutlich. Ein Aufriss links illustriert Materialien und durchdachte Planung der einzelnen Objekte und Bereiche.

Le vocabulaire simple et essentiellement industriel, utilisé par les architectes, et l'ouverture de l'espace sont évidents dans la photo ci-dessus. Ci-contre, un coupe montre les matériaux utilisés et l'attention portée aux objets et espaces individuels.

Left, an interior view of the New York installation of the Lab. Below, an overall site plan of the structure and its surrounding space.

Links eine Innenansicht des Labs am New Yorker Standort. Der Überblicksplan unten zeigt den Bau in seinem Umfeld.

Ci-contre, une vue intérieure de l'installation du Lab à New York. Ci-dessous, un plan de situation du bâtiment dans son espace environnant.

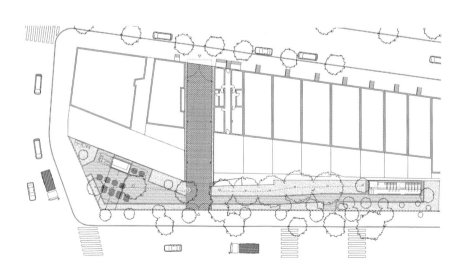

The Lab, as seen from Houston Street, offers outdoor space that is partially beneath the building.

Das Lab von der Houston Street aus gesehen; Freiflächen liegen teilweise unterhalb der Konstruktion.

Le Lab, vu depuis Houston Street, offre un espace en extérieur situé en partie sous le bâtiment.

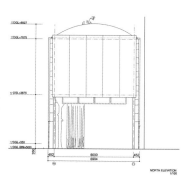

NORTH ELEVATION
1/100

In the Berlin location, an elevation
drawing showing the PVC materials
employed. Also on this page, two
interior views showing the open
space beneath the main volume.

Ein Aufriss des Baus am Berliner
Standort illustriert den Einsatz
verschiedener PVC-Stoffe. Ebenfalls
auf dieser Seite: zwei Ansichten
der offenen Zone unterhalb der
Konstruktion.

Sur le site de Berlin, une élévation
montrant les matériaux PVC employés. Sur cette même page, deux
vues intérieures montrant l'espace
ouvert sous le volume principal.

An exterior view of the Berlin location shows how the polyester curtains allow for space to be closed off while still remaining open to the exterior.

Eine Ansicht am Berliner Standort zeigt die Möglichkeit, den Raum mit Polyestervorhängen abzuschirmen und dennoch durchlässig zum Außenraum zu halten.

Une vue extérieure du site de Berlin montre comment les rideaux en polyester permettent de fermer l'espace tout en le maintenant ouvert sur l'extérieur.

RENDEZ-VOUS

National Museum of Modern Art, Tokyo, Japan, 2010

Area: 52 m². Client: The National Museum of Modern Art Tokyo.
Collaboration: Yuki Chida, Reika Tatekawa.

Designed between November 2009 and March 2010, this installation was placed in the forecourt of Yoshiro Taniguchi's National Museum of Modern Art Tokyo from April 29 to August 8, 2010. It was made of bamboo, steel, and reinforced concrete. Sensing the reticence of visitors to step onto the lawn of this rather strict space, Atelier Bow-Wow attempted "to ease this austere mood, while not letting go of the dignity of the place, but instead just slightly loosening up the atmosphere to turn it into a gentler space." Inspiring themselves from the name of the closest subway station (Takebashi, meaning "bamboo bridge"), they decided to work with bamboo. "Placing so-called architecture in the face of an architectural work by Yoshiro Taniguchi is not a good idea, as our construction is an ephemeral one after all and would therefore pale before the permanent structure." They imagined "some gigantic animal striding across" the wooded gardens of the nearby Imperial Palace. "The result," they wrote, "would be a mixing of human and animal, almost as if the two were meeting up in the forecourt of the museum." They conclude: "The main interest of Atelier Bow-Wow is to create spaces imbued with tolerance and generosity, fully aware of the interactive nature of architecture as a form of common cultural capital, or creative commons in public and shared platforms. This focus remains unchanged, whether the architecture in question is housing, a public space, or an installation for an art exhibition."

Die zwischen November 2009 und März 2010 entworfene Installation war vom 29. April bis 8. August 2010 im Vorhof des National Museum of Modern Art in Tokio zu sehen, einem Bau von Yoshiro Taniguchi. Die Konstruktion bestand aus Bambus, Stahl und Stahlbeton. Atelier Bow-Wow hatte den Eindruck, dass die Besucher zögerten, den Rasen des eher strengen Museumsgeländes zu betreten, und versuchten, „die strenge Atmosphäre aufzuhellen, ohne die Würde des Ortes anzutasten, vielmehr die Atmosphäre aufzulockern und dem Ort sanftere Seiten abzugewinnen". Angeregt durch den Namen der nächstgelegenen U-Bahnstation (Takebashi, „Bambusbrücke"), beschlossen sie, mit Bambus zu arbeiten. „Es schien keine gute Idee, etwas Architektonisches direkt neben einer Architektur von Yoshiro Taniguchi zu platzieren; schließlich wirkt unsere Konstruktion eher ephemer und wäre neben dem permanenten Bau verblasst." So erfanden sie ein „riesiges Tier", das sich durch die waldigen Gärten des nahe gelegenen Kaiserlichen Palastes „heranpirscht". „Das Resultat", schreiben sie, „war eine Kreuzung aus Mensch und Tier, fast so, als würden sich die beiden im Vorhof des Museums begegnen." Das Team fasst zusammen: „Das zentrale Interesse von Atelier Bow-Wow ist es, Räume zu schaffen, die von Toleranz und Großzügigkeit geprägt sind. Dabei sind wir uns zutiefst bewusst, dass Architektur interaktiv ist – im Sinne eines gemeinschaftlichen kulturellen Kapitals beziehungsweise eines Creative Commons (CC, dt. gemeinfreie Werke), das auf öffentlichen und gemeinschaftlich genutzten Plattformen präsent ist. Dieses zentrale Anliegen bleibt unverändert, ob es sich bei der fraglichen Architektur nun um Wohnbauten, öffentlichen Raum oder eine Installation für eine Kunstausstellung handelt."

Conçue entre novembre 2009 et mars 2010, cette installation en bambou, acier et béton armé a été mise en place dans l'avant-cour du Musée national d'art moderne de Tokyo (Yoshiro Taniguchi architecte) du 29 avril au 8 août 2010. Conscient des réticences des visiteurs à marcher sur la pelouse de cet espace très formel, l'Atelier Bow-Wow a tenté « d'adoucir l'austérité de cette ambiance, sans rien perdre pour autant de la dignité du lieu, juste en détendant légèrement l'atmosphère pour en faire un espace plus aimable ». S'inspirant du nom d'une station de métro proche, Takebashi (« pont de bambou » en japonais), les architectes ont décidé d'opter pour le bambou. « Faire ce que l'on appelle de l'architecture face à une œuvre architecturale de Yoshiro Taniguchi n'est pas une bonne idée, mais notre projet qui pourrait faire pâle figure devant cette structure permanente n'est après tout qu'éphémère. » Ils ont imaginé « une sorte de gigantesque animal se déplaçant par grandes enjambées » dans les jardins boisés du palais impérial tout proche. « Il en résulte un mélange d'humain et d'animal, un peu comme si les deux se rencontraient dans cette avant-cour du musée… La principale préoccupation de l'Atelier Bow-Wow est de créer des espaces pénétrés de tolérance et de générosité, pleinement conscients de la nature interactive de l'architecture qui appartient au patrimoine culturel commun, des espaces communautaires créatifs dans des lieux publics et de partage. Cet objectif reste inchangé, que l'architecture en question soit des logements, un lieu public ou une installation pour une exposition artistique. »

The curious animal forms chosen
for the installation by the architects
clearly attracted passersby and others to explore the structures.

Ganz offensichtlich wirkt die
ungewöhnliche Formgebung der
Installation, die an ein Tier erinnert,
einladend auf Passanten und Besucher und regt zum Entdecken an.

Les formes animalières voulues par
les architectes attirent visiblement
les passants et invitent à
l'exploration.

Visitors are picnicking under the arching forms of the Rendez-Vous installation, fully justifying its title.

Besucher beim Picknick unter den Bögen der Installation, die ihrem Titel Rendez-Vous alle Ehre macht.

Des visiteurs piqueniquent sous les arches de l'installation Rendez-Vous, qui justifie ainsi son titre.

SHIGERU BAN

Born in 1957 in Tokyo, **SHIGERU BAN** studied at SCI-Arc from 1977 to 1980. He then attended the Cooper Union School of Architecture, where he studied under John Hejduk (1980–82). He worked in the office of Arata Isozaki (1982–83), before founding his own firm in Tokyo in 1985. His work includes the Hanegi Forest Annex (Setagaya, Tokyo, Japan, 2004); Mul(ti) houses (Mulhouse, France, 2001–05); the Takatori Church (Kobe, Hyogo, Japan, 2005); the disaster relief Post-Tsunami Rehabilitation Houses (Kirinda, Hambantota, Sri Lanka, 2005); the Papertainer Museum (Seoul Olympic Park, Songpa-Gu, South Korea, 2006); the Nicolas G. Hayek Center (Tokyo, Japan, 2007); the Paper Teahouse (London, UK, 2008); Quinta Botanica (Algarve, Portugal, 1999/2004–09, published here); Haesley Nine Bridges Golf Clubhouse (Yeoju, South Korea, 2009); the Paper Tube Tower (London, UK, 2009); and the Metal Shutter Houses on West 19th Street in New York (New York, USA, 2010). Recent work includes the Camper Pavilion (Alicante, Spain; Sanya, China; Miami, Florida, USA; Lorient, France, prefabrication June to September 2011); Kobe Kushinoya (Osaka, Japan, 2011); L'Aquila Temporary Concert Hall (L'Aquila, Italy, 2011); the Camper NY SoHo store (New York, USA, 2012); and Tamedia (Zurich, Switzerland, 2011–13).

Geboren 1957 in Tokio, studierte **SHIGERU BAN** von 1977 bis 1980 an der SCI-Arc. Dann besuchte er die Cooper Union School of Architecture, wo er bei John Hejduk studierte (1980–82). Er arbeitete im Büro von Arata Isozaki (1982–83), bevor 1985 sein eigenes Büro in Tokio gründete. Zu seinen Arbeiten gehören außerdem der Hanegi Forest Annex (Setagaya, Tokio, 2004), die Mul(ti)houses (Mulhouse, Frankreich, 2001–05), die Takatori-Kirche (Kobe, Hyogo, Japan, 2005), das Tsunami-Wiederaufbauprojekt (Kirinda, Hambantota, Sri Lanka, 2005), das Papertainer Museum (Seoul Olympic Park, Songpa-Gu, Südkorea, 2006), das Nicolas G. Hayek Center (Tokio, 2007), das Paper Teahouse (London, 2008), die Quinta Botanica (Algarve, Portugal, 1999/2004–09, hier vorgestellt), das Heasley Nine Bridges Golf Clubhouse (Yeoju, Südkorea, 2009), der Paper Tube Tower (London, 2009) und die Metal Shutter Houses West 19th Street in New York (2010). Zu den jüngeren Arbeiten zählen der Camper Pavillon (Alicante, Spanien; Sanya, China; Miami, Florida; Lorient, Frankreich; Vorfabrikation Juni bis September 2011), Kobe Kushinoya (Osaka, Japan, 2011), die temporäre Konzerthalle in L'Aquila (Italien, 2011), der Camper NY SoHo Store (New York, 2012) und der Tamedia-Hauptsitz (Zürich, 2011–13).

Né en 1957 à Tokyo, **SHIGERU BAN** a fait ses études au SCI-Arc de 1977 à 1980, puis à l'École d'architecture de la Cooper Union auprès de John Hejduk (1980–82). Avant d'ouvrir son agence à Tokyo en 1985, il a travaillé pour Arata Isozaki (1982–83). Parmi ses réalisations : l'immeuble Hanegi Forest Annex (Setagaya, Tokyo, 2004) ; le lotissement Mul(ti)houses (Mulhouse, 2001-05) ; l'église de Takatori (Kobe, Hyogo, Japon, 2005) ; les maisons de réhabilitation dans le cadre des secours aux victimes du tsunami (Kirinda, Hambantota, Sri Lanka, 2005) ; le musée Papertainer (parc Olympique de Séoul, Songpa-Gu, Corée-du-Sud, 2006) ; le Centre Nicolas G. Hayek (Tokyo, 2007) ; la Paper Teahouse (Londres, 2008) ; Quinta Botanica (Algarve, Portugal, 1999/2004–09, publié ici) ; le clubhouse du golf de Haesley Nine Bridges (Yeoju, Corée du Sud, 2009) ; la Paper Tube Tower (Londres, 2009) et les immeubles Metal Shutter Houses de la 19ᵉ Rue Ouest à New York (2010). Ses réalisations récentes comprennent le pavillon Camper (Alicante, Espagne ; Sanya, Chine ; Miami ; Lorient, préfabrication de juin à septembre 2011) ; le restaurant Kobe Kushinoya (Osaka, 2011) ; la salle de concerts temporaire de L'Aquila (Italie, 2011) ; le magasin Camper NY de SoHo (New York, 2012) et le siège de Tamedia (Zurich, 2011–13).

QUINTA BOTANICA

Algarve, Portugal, 1999/2004–09

Area: 92 m². Client: Quinta Botanica S.A.
Collaboration: Minoru Tezuka (Engineer), Bereket Mitiku Gebre.

With his trademark paper tube design and the extreme simplicity often achieved in his smaller buildings, Shigeru Ban innovates with his use of space and form.

Mit seinen Bauten aus Pappröhren, seinem Markenzeichen, und der extremen Schlichtheit gerade seiner kleineren Werke beschreitet Shigeru Ban in Sachen Raumgestaltung und Formensprache ganz neue Wege.

Avec le design en tubes de carton, sa marque de fabrique, et l'extrême simplicité qui caractérise souvent ses petits bâtiments, Shigeru Ban innove dans l'utilisation qu'il fait de l'espace et de la forme.

Quinta Botanica is located on a cliff above the ocean in the southernmost area of Portugal. The four-hectare property it is built on is owned by an art and plant collector. The structure serves as an artistic installation and residence for visiting artists and botanists. The Quinta Botanica is structurally identical to Ban's Paper House (1995), the first permanent paper structure that was granted approval under Article 38 of the Japanese Building Standards Act. Wooden joints and paper tubes fixed with lag bolts comprise the foundation. It has been demonstrated that this system is capable of withstanding vertical loads and lateral force. To avoid cutting down trees, its plan was designed to weave through them in an S-shaped layout that gradually decreases in width from 7.5 meters to 3 meters over its 25-meter length. Local doubts about the safety and stability of the structure led the owner to order the materials himself, piece by piece, and to complete the project over a 10-year time span.

Die Quinta Botanica liegt am südlichsten Zipfel Portugals auf einem Felsen über dem Meer. Das 4 ha große Grundstück gehört einem Kunst- und Pflanzensammler. Das Gebäude ist sowohl Kunstinstallation als auch Unterkunft für Künstler und Botaniker, die hier zu Gast sind. Von der Konstruktion her ist die Quinta Botanica mit Bans Paper House (1995) identisch, dem ersten permanenten Bauwerk aus Pappe, das gemäß Artikel 38 des japanischen Baugesetzes genehmigt wurde. Mit hölzernen Verbindungselementen verschraubte Papphröhren bilden das Grundgerüst – ein System, das erwiesenermaßen Vertikal- und Seitenlasten aushält. Um keinen der Bäume fällen zu müssen, sah der Entwurf vor, sich s-förmig zwischen ihnen hindurch zu fädeln, wobei sich das Gebäude auf seiner Gesamtlänge von 25 m fortlaufend von 7,5 auf 3 m verjüngt. Bedenken lokaler Autoritäten hinsichtlich Stabilität und Sicherheit der Konstruktion bewogen den Besitzer schließlich dazu, die Materialien nach und nach selbst zu bestellen und das Projekt über einen Zeitraum von zehn Jahren hinweg fertigzustellen.

Quinta Botanica est placée sur une falaise qui surplombe l'océan à l'extrême sud du Portugal. La propriété de quatre hectares sur laquelle elle est bâtie appartient à un collectionneur d'art et de plantes. La structure tient lieu d'installation artistique et de résidence pour des artistes et botanistes en visite. Quinta Botanica est structurellement identique à la Maison en papier de Ban (1995), la première construction permanente en papier à avoir été approuvée selon l'article 38 de la loi japonaise relative aux normes de construction. Les fondations sont faites de joints en bois et de tubes en carton fixés par des tire-fonds : il a été prouvé que ce système pouvait résister à des charges verticales et à des forces latérales. Pour éviter de couper des arbres, le plan a été conçu pour que la maison serpente entre eux avec sa disposition en forme de S dont la largeur diminue progressivement, de 7,5 m à 3 m, pour une longueur de 25 m. En raison de doutes émis localement sur la sûreté et la stabilité de l'ensemble, le propriétaire a commandé lui-même le matériel, élément après élément, et a mis 10 ans à achever le projet.

As seen in the drawing below and the photos (left and above), the structure opens out to a long rectangular pool.

Der Bau öffnet sich zu einem langen rechteckigen Pool hin, wie auf der Zeichnung unten und den Fotos (linke Seite und oben) zu sehen ist.

Comme on le voit sur le schéma ci-dessous et les photos (à gauche et ci-dessus), le bâtiment ouvre sur une piscine rectangulaire et allongée.

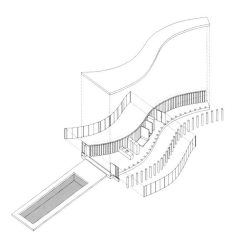

To the right, an image with the double-colonnade design at the narrowest point of the building visible—an almost classical air for an unusual structure.

Rechts ein Bild der doppelten Kolonnaden an der schmalsten Stelle des Gebäudes – eine nahezu klassische Anmutung für ein derart ungewöhnliches Bauwerk.

À droite, vue de la double colonnade au point le plus étroit du bâtiment visible – une allure presque classique pour une structure inédite.

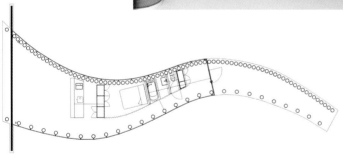

The curving walls made of paper tubes admit daylight while providing a sense of protection for the modern interior spaces.

Die geschwungenen Wände aus Pappröhren lassen Tageslicht hinein, vermitteln in den modern gestalteten Innenräumen jedoch gleichzeitig ein Gefühl von Geborgenheit.

Les courbes des murs en tubes de carton laissent pénétrer la lumière du jour tout en donnant un caractère protecteur aux espaces intérieurs modernes.

Above, the plan shows how unexpected the actual design is, with its curves and columns that are denser on one side than on the other.

Die Zeichnung oben zeigt, wie ungewöhnlich der Entwurf tatsächlich ist mit seinen Kurven und Säulen, die auf einer Seite dichter stehen als auf der anderen.

Ci-dessus, le plan montre la grande originalité du design avec ses courbes et ses colonnes plus serrées d'un côté que de l'autre.

CAMPER PAVILION

Alicante, Spain; Sanya, China; Miami, USA;
Lorient, France: prefabrication June to September 2011

Area: 250 m². Client: Camper.
Collaboration: Jean de Gastines, Marc Ferrand.

This is a paper tube structure, like others that Shigeru Ban has created in the past. It is designed to be assembled and dismantled easily in order to travel to marinas around the world where the yacht ports are located. There are four different diameters of paper tubes, which can be nested inside each other to minimize the bulk of the materials when they are shipped. The pavilion has a round floor plan and a membrane roof, assuring protection from the elements. With its Camper flag and basic form, the structure might recall military tents of another era although, clearly, the architect's intent and design are very much of this time. The ephemeral nature of the structure imposes certain constraints but also liberates the architecture from the requirements of more permanent designs.

Der Bau ist eine Konstruktion aus Pappröhren, wie Shigeru Ban sie bereits in der Vergangenheit realisierte. Der Entwurf ist leicht auf- und abbaubar, um in Jachthäfen in aller Welt errichtet werden zu können. Die Pappröhren mit vier unterschiedlichen Durchmessern lassen sich zur Minimierung des Transportvolumens ineinanderschieben. Der Pavillon mit rundem Grundriss hat ein Membrandach, das vor den Elementen schützt. Mit der Camper-Flagge und seiner schlichten Grundform erinnert der Pavillon an historische Militärzelte, obwohl Motivation und Entwurf des Architekten deutlich zeitgenössisch sind. Die temporäre Natur des Baus bringt gewisse Einschränkungen mit sich, befreit die Architektur jedoch auch von vielen Anforderungen, denen dauerhaftere Bauprojekte unterliegen.

Il s'agit d'une structure en tubes de carton, similaire à d'autres déjà créées par Shigeru Ban et conçue de façon à être facilement montée et démontée, pour son transport dans des ports de plaisance à travers le monde. Les tubes emboîtables, de quatre diamètres différents, permettent de réduire le volume à transporter. Le pavillon, d'un plan circulaire, est protégé contre les éléments par un toit en membrane. Avec son drapeau Camper et sa forme simple, la structure peut rappeler les tentes militaires d'une autre époque, mais le propos et le design sont clairement actuels. La nature éphémère de la structure impose des contraintes, mais libère aussi les architectes des impératifs dictés par des projets plus pérennes.

The structure is open on all sides, which certainly encourages visitors to enter. Irregular spacing of the columns indicates the preferred entry points.

Der Bau ist zu allen Seiten offen, was Besucher zum Eintreten einlädt. Der unregelmäßige Säulenabstand deutet Haupteingangszonen an.

La structure est ouverte sur tous les côtés, encourageant assurément les visiteurs à entrer. L'espacement irrégulier des colonnes indique les points d'entrée privilégiés.

The gently sloping membrane roof of the pavilion and its paper tube columns provide shelter for the Camper installation in its Alicante setting.

Das sanft geneigte Membrandach des Baus und Säulen aus Pappröhren definieren einen schützenden Raum für den Camper-Pavillon an seinem Standort in Alicante.

La toiture en membrane légèrement en pente du pavillon et ses colonnes de carton fournissent un abri pour l'installation de Camper sur son site d'Alicante.

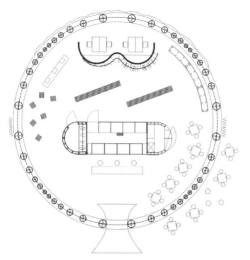

To the left, a plan of the circular
structure. Below, retail space is
partially defined by an undulating
paper tube wall. To the right, the
café area looking out on the sea.

Links ein Grundriss des Rundbaus.
Der Verkaufsraum (unten) wird
teilweise von einer geschwungenen
Wand aus Pappröhren definiert.
Rechts das Café mit Blick aufs
Meer.

Ci-contre, un plan de la structure
circulaire. Ci-dessous, l'espace
commercial est en partie délimité
par un mur ondulant en tubes de
carton. Page de droite, l'espace
du café face à la mer.

PAPER TEMPORARY SHELTERS IN HAITI

Port-au-Prince, Haiti, 2010–11

Area: 16 m² per shelter. Client: Voluntary Architects' Network (VAN).
Cost: $300 per unit; total cost $30,000 for 50 units.
Collaboration: Universidad Iberoamericana (UNIBE), Santo Domingo, Dominican Republic.

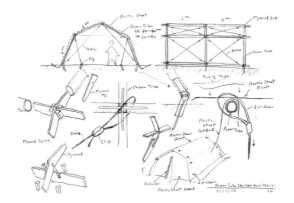

Shigeru Ban has worked on numerous structures destined to relief projects in earthquake or disaster zones, including his native Japan, Turkey, Sri Lanka, Sichuan, or L'Aquila, Italy. He has created a personal NGO called Voluntary Architects' Network for these projects. Subsequent to the earthquake that struck Haiti on January 12, 2010, he began an effort to provide temporary housing for some of the 500,000 people left without homes. He arrived in Port-au-Prince on February 14, 2010 with students and professors from the Universidad Iberoamericana (UNIBE) located in Santo Domingo. Working on a site near the U.S. Embassy, and working with the local population, he erected 37 hand-built shelters using polyurethane coated paper tubes, plywood joints, and plastic tarps.

Shigeru Ban realisierte bereits zahlreiche Bauvorhaben für Flüchtlingsprojekte in Erdbeben- oder anderen Katastrophengebieten – in seinem Heimatland Japan ebenso wie in der Türkei, in Sri Lanka, Sichuan oder im italienischen L'Aquila. Zu diesem Zweck gründete er eigens eine NGO, das sogenannte Voluntary Architects' Network. Nach dem Erdbeben in Haiti vom 12. Januar 2010 machte er sich daran, Notunterkünfte für einige der rund 500 000 obdachlos gewordenen Menschen zu planen. Am 14. Februar 2010 erreichte er Port-au-Prince, zusammen mit Studierenden und Professoren der Universidad Iberoamericana (UNIBE) aus Santo Domingo. Auf einem Gelände unweit der US-amerikanischen Botschaft errichtete er gemeinsam mit Anwohnern 37 Notunterkünfte von Hand, die aus polyurethanbeschichteten Pappröhren, Sperrholzsteckverbindungen und Plastikplanen bestanden.

Shigeru Ban a travaillé sur de nombreux projets de structures de secours temporaires utilisables lors de tremblements de terre ou de désastres naturels, pour son pays natal, le Japon, mais aussi pour la Turquie, le Sri Lanka, le Sichuan et la ville de L'Aquila en Italie. Il a fondé une ONG, Voluntary Architects' Network, pour mettre en œuvre ces projets. Arrivé à Port-au-Prince le 14 février 2010 en compagnie d'étudiants et de professeurs de l'Université Ibéro-américaine (UNIBE) de Saint-Domingue, il a lancé un programme de logements temporaires pour 500 000 personnes victimes du tremblement de terre qui avait frappé Haïti le 12 janvier. Travaillant sur un terrain proche de l'ambassade américaine et à l'aide de la population locale, il a érigé 37 abris montés à la main en tubes de carton enduits de polyuréthane, d'articulations en contreplaqué et de bâches en plastique.

Images showing local residents participating in the construction of the Paper Shelters designed by Shigeru Ban for Haiti after the earthquake.

Anwohner beteiligen sich am Aufbau der Paper Shelters, die Shigeru Ban nach dem Erdbeben in Haiti entworfen hatte.

Images montrant des habitants participant à la construction des abris en carton conçus par Shigeru Ban pour Haïti après le séisme.

Tents using a simple paper tube structure and plastic sheeting are erected in Haiti.

Aufbau der Zelte mit einer einfachen Konstruktion aus Pappröhren und Plastikplanen in Haiti.

Montage de tentes faites d'une simple ossature en tubes de carton et d'une bâche de plastique.

Below, shelters being assembled
with an easy-to-install system that
provides some protection from the
elements and privacy.

Notunterkünfte werden errichtet
(unten). Das einfache, von Hand
montierbare System bietet
zumindest etwas Schutz vor
der Witterung und ein gewisses
Maß an Privatsphäre.

Ci-dessous, construction des
abris faciles à monter. Ils offrent
un certain niveau d'intimité et de
protection contre les éléments.

BARKOW LEIBINGER ARCHITECTS

REGINE LEIBINGER was born in 1963 in Stuttgart, Germany. She studied Architecture in Berlin (Diploma, Technical University, 1989) and at Harvard University (M.Arch, 1990). She created a joint office with Frank Barkow in 1993. She has been a Visiting Professor at the Architectural Association (AA) in London (Unit Master, 1997–98), Cornell University, and Harvard University, and, since 2006, a Professor for Building Construction and Design at the Technische Universität Berlin. **FRANK BARKOW** was born in 1957 in Kansas City, USA, and studied Architecture at Montana State University (B.Arch, 1982) and at Harvard University (M.Arch, 1990). He has been working with Regine Leibinger in Berlin since 1993. Barkow has been a Visiting Professor at the AA in London (Unit Master, 1995–98), Cornell University, Harvard University, and at the State Academy of Art and Design in Stuttgart. Their recent work includes Pavilions for Research and Production (Grüsch, Switzerland, 2001; 2004); a house in Berlin-Karlshorst (2007); a Gatehouse (Stuttgart, Ditzingen, 2007); Campus Restaurant (Ditzingen, 2006–08); and the Marcus Prize Pavilion (Menomonee Valley, Milwaukee, Wisconsin, USA, 2008, published here), all in Germany unless stated otherwise.

REGINE LEIBINGER, geboren 1963 in Stuttgart, studierte Architektur an der Techischen Universität Berlin (Diplom 1989) und der Harvard University (M. Arch. 1990). 1993 gründete sie mit Frank Barkow ein Gemeinschaftsbüro in Berlin. Leibinger war Gastprofessorin an der Architectural Association (AA) in London (Unit Master, 1997–98) sowie an den Universitäten Cornell und Harvard, seit 2006 ist sie Professorin für Baukonstruktion und Entwerfen an der TU Berlin. **FRANK BARKOW**, geboren 1957 in Kansas City in den USA, erwarb 1982 seinen B.Arch an der Montana State University und 1990 seinen M. Arch. an der Harvard University. Wie Leibinger war Barkow Gastprofessor an der AA in London (Unit Master, 1995–98) und den Universitäten Cornell und Harvard, außerdem lehrte er an der Staatlichen Akademie der Bildenden Künste Stuttgart. Zu den jüngeren Arbeiten des Gespanns gehören zwei Forschungs- und Produktionspavillons für eine Maschinenfabrik im schweizerischen Grüsch (2001; 2004), ein Wohnhaus in Berlin-Karlshorst (2007), die Hauptpforte der Firma Trumpf (2007) und ihr Betriebsrestaurant (2006–08) in Ditzingen bei Stuttgart und der Marcus Prize Pavilion (Menomonee Valley, Milwaukee, Wisconsin, USA, 2008, hier vorstellt).

REGINE LEIBINGER, née en 1963 à Stuttgart (Allemagne) a étudié l'architecture à Berlin (diplômée de la Technische Universität, 1989) et à Harvard University (M. Arch, 1990). Elle a créé son agence en association avec Frank Barkow en 1993. Elle a été professeure invitée à l'Architectural Association (AA) de Londres (Unit Master, 1997–98), Cornell University et Harvard University, et, depuis 2006, est professeure de conception et de construction à la Technische Universität de Berlin. **FRANK BARKOW**, né in 1957 à Kansas City (États-Unis), a étudié l'architecture à la Montana State University (B. Arch, 1982) et Harvard University (M. Arch, 1990). Il travaille depuis 1993 avec Regine Leibinger à Berlin. Barkow a été professeur invité à l'AA de Londres (Unit Master, 1995–98), Cornell University, Harvard University et l'Académie d'État d'art et de design à Stuttgart. Parmi leurs récents travaux : des pavillons pour la recherche et la production (Grüsch, Suisse, 2001–04) ; une maison à Berlin-Karlshorst (2007) ; un pavillon d'entrée (Ditzingen, Stuttgart, 2007), un restaurant de campus (également à Ditzingen, Stuttgart, 2007) et le pavillon du prix Marcus (Menomonee Valley, Milwaukee, Wisconsin, États-Unis, 2008, publié ici).

MARCUS PRIZE PAVILION

Menomonee Valley, Milwaukee, USA, 2008

Area: 23 m². Client: Menomonee Valley Partners. Cost: $35 000.
Collaboration: Professor Kyle Talbott and 16 students from the University of Wisconsin—
Milwaukee's School of Architecture and Urban Planning.

The Marcus Prize is given for "emerging talent in architecture." Barkow Leibinger won the award in 2007, and taught for a semester at the University of Wisconsin-Milwaukee's School of Architecture and Urban Planning. Working with Professor Kyle Talbott, Frank Barkow and Regine Leibinger participated in a community design-build project in a studio with 16 students. The project was carried out with the nonprofit organization Menomonee Valley Partners, which focuses on revitalizing an industrial area near downtown Milwaukee, with the intention of providing a meeting place, a location for informal classes, and storage for landscaping equipment. Students were asked to study local leaves, flowers, and ferns to identify possible roof structures. The group was divided into four sections concerning skin, materials, site, and structure. Their study resulted in "a leaf-shaped roof structure made of plywood and glued-laminated beams that is supported by a system of V-shaped steel column clusters" that was erected beneath the 35th Street viaduct. The group used a digital model followed by digital shop drawings and templates to make a series of unique elements for the design. Transparent corrugated polycarbonate was used for the rooftop. Recycled stones and black locust wood were employed in the structure as well.

Im Jahr 2007 erhielten Barkow Leibinger den in regelmäßiger Folge an „verheißungsvolle Talente auf dem Gebiet der Architektur" verliehenen Marcus Prize und unterrichteten ein Semester lang an der Winconsin-Milwaukee School of Architecture and Urban Planning. Gemeinsam mit dem dort lehrenden Kyle Talbott und 16 studentischen Teilnehmern eines Werkstattprojekts erarbeiteten Frank Barkow und Regine Leibinger einen Entwurf, der anschließend realisiert werden sollte. Ausgeführt wurde das Projekt mit Unterstützung der gemeinnützigen Organisation Menomonee Valley Partners, die sich der Wiederbelebung eines in Stadtzentrumsnähe gelegenen Industriegebiets widmet, in dem ein Kommunikations-zentrum mit Räumlichkeiten für freien Unterricht und zur Unterbringung von Equipment zur Landschaftsgestaltung entstehen soll. Die Studenten waren aufgerufen, auf dem betreffenden Areal wachsende Blätter, Blumen und Farne unter die Lupe zu nehmen und auf Strukturen hin zu untersuchen, die sich zum Bau eines Daches eignen könnten. Anschließend wurden vier Gruppen eingeteilt, die sich mit der Gebäudeverkleidung, Baumaterialien, dem Standort und der Konstruktion auseinander-setzen sollten. Aus diesen Untersuchungen ergab sich der Entwurf für „eine blattförmige Dachstruktur aus Sperrholz und Brettschichtträgern, die von einem System aus v-förmig angeordneten Pfeilergruppen getragen wird". Ausgehend von einem Computermodell entstanden digitale Fertigungszeichnungen und Templates zur Anfertigung der einzelnen Spezialbauteile. Neben einer Dachabdeckung aus durchsichtigem gewellten Polykarbonat kamen auch natürliche Materialen – wiederverwer-tete Steine und Robinienholz – zum Einsatz. Der fertige Pavillon wurde unterhalb der Überführung der 35th Street aufgestellt.

Le prix Marcus est destiné à des « talents émergents en architecture ». Barkow Leibinger l'a remporté en 2007 et tous deux ont enseigné pendant un semestre à l'École d'architecture et d'urbanisme de l'Université de Wisconsin-Milwaukee. En collaboration avec le professeur Kyle Talbott, Frank Barkow et Regine Leibinger ont travaillé sur ce projet dans le cadre d'un atelier de conception collective avec seize étudiants. Il a été mené à bien grâce au soutien d'une association à but non lucratif, les Menomonee Valley Partners, qui a pour objectif de revitaliser une zone industrielle proche du centre de Milwaukee, et souhaitait créer un lieu de réunions où pourraient être donnés des cours et stocké du matériel d'entretien paysager. Les participants ont été chargés d'étudier les feuillages, les fleurs et les fougères locales dans le cadre d'une recherche sur la structure de la toiture. Le groupe a été divisé en quatre sous-groupes : peau, matériau, site, structure. Leur étude a abouti à « une structure de toit en forme de feuilles, faite de poutres en lamellé-collé et contreplaqué, soutenue par un ensemble de colonnes d'acier en forme de V » qui a été mise en place sous le viaduc de la 35ᵉ Rue. L'atelier a réalisé une maquette en images de synthèse, puis a conçu des plans et des modèles sur ordinateur pour préparer la fabrication des éléments spéci-fiques du projet. Le toit utilise aussi des panneaux de polycarbonate ondulé transparent. On remarque dans la structure des pierres et du bois de caroubier noir de récupération.

Seen above in its situation below the 35th Street viaduct, the Marcus Prize Pavilion is a lightweight, largely wooden structure.

Der Marcus Prize Pavilion, oben eine Fotografie seines Standortes unter der Überführung der 35. Straße, ist eine leichte, vornehmlich aus Holz bestehende Konstruktion.

Vu ci-dessus en situation, sous le viaduc de la 35e Rue, le pavillon Marcus Prize est une construction légère, en grande partie en bois.

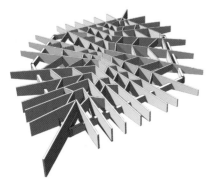

Plans and drawings on this page
reveal its full forms.

*Die Konstruktionszeichnungen
auf dieser Seite zeigen den
Gesamtaufbau.*

*Les plans et les dessins de cette
page explicitent sa forme.*

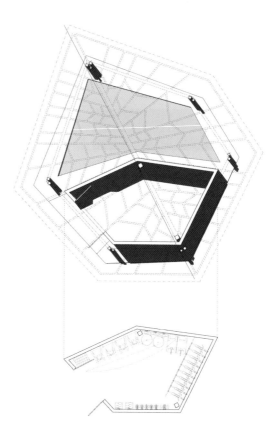

BAUMRAUM

ANDREAS WENNING was born in 1965 in Mönchengladbach, Germany. He trained as a cabinetmaker in Weinheim (1982–85), and studied Architecture at the Technical University of Bremen, where he obtained his degree in 1995. He worked in the office of José Garcia Negette in Sydney, Australia (2000–01), and he created his own office, baumraum, in Bremen in 2003. His completed work includes the Lookout Tree House (Seeboden, Austria, 2005); Casa Girafa (Curitiba, Brazil, 2006); Meditation Tree House (Rome, Italy, 2007); Cliff Tree House (New York State, USA, 2007); Copper Cube Tree House (near Berlin, Germany, 2009); Belvedere Tree House (Bremen, Germany, 2011); Tree Whisper Tree-House Hotel (Bad Zwischenahn, Germany, 2011, published here); House on Stilts (Mendoza, Argentina, 2012); and the Tree House (Hechtel-Eksel, Belgium, 2012, also published here). He has also worked on weblike "grabnet" rope structures for trees (Lower Saxony Horticultural Show, Wolfsburg, Germany, 2004), and organized seminars on "The Body Language of Trees," and "Building a Tree House without Impairing the Tree." His firm offers to build unique tree houses for clients. In 2009, he published a book on his work entitled *Baumhäuser – Neue Architektur in den Bäumen*.

ANDREAS WENNING wurde 1965 in Mönchengladbach geboren. Nach einer Lehre als Möbeltischler in Weinheim (1982–85) studierte er Architektur an der Technischen Universität Bremen, wo er 1995 seinen Abschluss machte. Er arbeitete im Büro von José Garcia Negette in Sydney (2000–01) und machte sich 2003 mit seiner eigenen Firma baumraum in Bremen selbstständig. Zu seinen realisierten Arbeiten gehören die se(e)(h)station (Seeboden, Österreich, 2005), die Casa Girafa (Curitiba, Brasilien, 2006), das Meditations-Baumhaus (Rom, 2007), das Cliff House (New York State, 2007), der Kupfer Kubus (nahe Berlin, 2009), das Baumhaus Belvedere (Bremen, 2011), das Baumhaushotel Baumgeflüster (Bad Zwischenahn, 2011, hier vorgestellt), eine Hotelerweiterung in Mendoza (Argentinien, 2012) und The Tree House (Hechtel-Eksel, Belgien, 2012, ebenfalls hier vorgestellt). Er beschäftigte sich auch mit netzartigen Seilkonstruktionen für Bäume (Niedersächsische Landesgartenschau, Wolfsburg, 2004) und organisierte Seminare über die „Körpersprache von Bäumen" und „Wie man ein Baumhaus baut, ohne den Baum zu beschädigen". Seine Firma realisiert auch individuelle Baumhäuser für Kunden. Unter dem Titel *Baumhäuser – Neue Architektur in den Bäumen* hat er 2009 ein Buch über seine Arbeit veröffentlicht.

ANDREAS WENNING est né en 1965 à Mönchengladbach, en Allemagne. Il a fait des études d'ébénisterie à Weinheim (1982–85) et d'architecture à l'Université technique de Brême dont il est diplômé (1995). Il a travaillé dans l'agence de José Garcia Negette à Sydney, en Australie (2000–01) et a créé sa société, baumraum, à Brême en 2003. Ses projets construits comprennent : l'Observatoire (Seeboden, Autriche, 2005) ; la Casa Girafa (Curitiba, Brésil, 2006) ; la Maison de méditation dans les arbres (Rome, 2007) ; la Cliff Tree House (État de New York, 2007) ; le Cube de cuivre dans les arbres (près de Berlin, 2009) ; la maison Belvedere dans les arbres (Brême, 2011) ; l'hôtel dans les arbres Murmure des arbres (Bad Zwischenahn, Allemagne, 2011, publié ici) ; la Maison sur pilotis (Mendoza, Argentine, 2012) et la Maison dans les arbres (Hechtel-Eksel, Belgique, 2012, également publiée ici). Il a aussi travaillé à des structures en corde « filet » de type toile d'araignée dans les arbres (Exposition horticole de Basse-Saxe, Wolfsburg, Allemagne, 2004) et a organisé des séminaires sur « le langage corporel des arbres » ou « comment construire une maison dans un arbre sans l'abîmer ». Son agence construit des maisons dans les arbres personnalisées pour ses clients. En 2009, il a publié un livre sur son travail intitulé *Baumhäuser – Neue Architektur in den Bäumen* (Maisons dans les arbres, une nouvelle architecture dans les arbres).

THE TREE HOUSE

Hechtel-Eksel, Belgium, 2012

*Area: 50 m². Client: Sappi, Flemish Forest and Nature Agency,
Hechtel-Eksel, and Proximity BBDO. Cost: €220 000.*

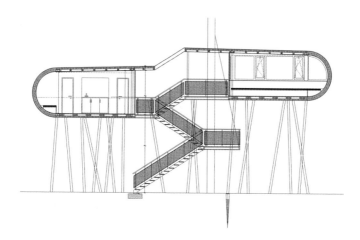

The association of the paper manufacturer Sappi, the Flemish Forest and Nature Agency, the town of Hechtel-Eksel, and the advertising agency Proximity BBDO is intended to stimulate companies, politicians, and organizations to "embrace sustainability in their daily activities." Located in the forests of Hechtel-Eksel, the Tree House includes two cabins on different levels, connecting terraces, a staircase, and a connecting roof. The lower cabin includes a coffee lounge, pantry, restroom, and technology room. The upper area is dedicated to meetings and other events that are appropriate for this space in the trees. Benches covered with pillows surround the space. The cabins and upper terraces are perched on 19 angled steel stilts. A heat pump and water purification from a nearby museum guarantee a high degree of self-sufficiency.

Der Papierhersteller Sappi, die Agentur für Wald und Natur Flandern, die Stadt Hechtel-Eksel und Proximity BBDO, eine Werbeagentur, wollen mit ihrem Zusammenschluss Firmen, Politiker und Organisationen dazu anregen, „das Thema Nachhaltigkeit in ihren Alltag zu integrieren". Ihr gemeinsames Tree House, gelegen in den Wäldern von Hechtel-Eksel, verfügt über zwei Räume auf unterschiedlichen Ebenen, verbindende Terrassen, eine Treppe und ein gemeinsames Dach. Im unteren Raum befinden sich eine Coffee Lounge, eine Vorratskammer, Toiletten und ein Technikraum. Der obere Bereich ist für Versammlungen und andere Anlässe gedacht, zu denen dieser Ort in den Bäumen passt. Der Raum ist rundherum von gepolsterten Bänken flankiert. Die Räume und Terrassen lasten auf 19 schräg stehenden Stahlstelzen. Eine Wärmepumpe und die Wasseraufbereitungsanlage eines nahe gelegenen Museums garantieren ein hohes Maß an Unabhängigkeit.

Le papetier Sappi, l'Agence flamande de la forêt et de la nature, la ville de Hechtel-Eksel et l'agence de publicité Proximity BBDO se sont associés pour inciter les entreprises, les politiques et les associations à « inclure la durabilité dans leurs activités au quotidien ». Située dans la forêt d'Hechtel-Eksel, la Maison dans les arbres comprend deux cabines à deux niveaux différents reliées par des terrasses, une cage d'escalier et un toit commun. La cabine du bas contient un salon, un office, des toilettes et un espace technique. La cabine supérieure est consacrée aux réunions et autres manifestations convenant à une telle situation dans les arbres. La pièce est entourée de banquettes matelassées. Les deux cabines et leurs terrasses sont perchées sur 19 pilotis d'acier inclinés. Une pompe à chaleur et le système d'épuration des eaux d'un musée voisin garantissent un degré élevé d'autosuffisance.

Though supported on metal struts as opposed to being suspended from trees, the structure is indeed lifted up in its forest setting, as seen in the image above and the section drawing. The interior is cheerfully modern.

Auch wenn es auf Metallstreben ruht, anstatt zwischen Bäumen zu hängen, so schwebt das Gebäude trotzdem hoch oben an seinem Platz im Wald, wie auf dem Bild oben und dem Querschnitt zu sehen ist. Das Innere ist fröhlich-modern gestaltet.

Bien que porté par des pieux métalliques et non suspendu dans les arbres, l'ensemble est surélevé haut dans le décor forestier, comme on le voit sur la photo ci-dessus et le schéma en coupe. L'intérieur moderne est très gai.

A tree branch pattern enlivens the
curved ceiling, while wood details
recall the forest setting. Right,
a plan of the entire structure.

*Ein Zweigmuster belebt die
geschwungene Decke; Details aus
Holz rufen den Standort Wald in
Erinnerung. Rechts ein Grundriss
des ganzen Gebäudes.*

*Un motif de branchages égaie le
plafond arrondi, tandis que des
détails en bois rappellent la forêt.
À droite, un plan de la structure
dans son ensemble.*

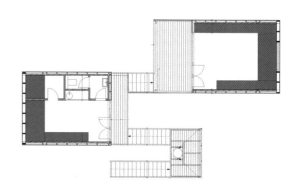

Providing a good deal more space
and more amenities than most tree
houses, the structure appears to
open new perspectives for those
who are not satisfied with living
on the ground.

Mit sehr viel mehr Platz und
Annehmlichkeiten, als die meisten
Baumhäuser zu bieten haben,
eröffnet der Bau offenkundig
denjenigen ganz neue Perspektiven,
die das ebenerdige Wohnen nicht
zufriedenstellt.

Avec nettement plus d'espace et de
confort que la plupart des maisons
dans les arbres, le projet pourrait
ouvrir de nouvelles perspectives à
tous ceux que la vie à ras de terre
ne satisfait pas.

TREE WHISPER
TREE-HOUSE HOTEL

Bad Zwischenahn, Germany, 2011

Area: 36 m². Client: Insa Otteken. Cost: €280 000 (four tree houses).

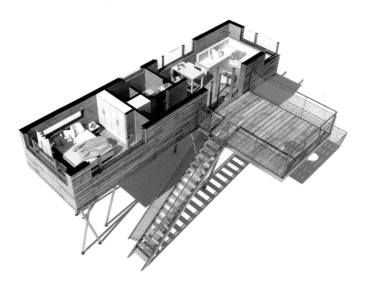

Built on the site of a former farm, four tree houses complement restored farm buildings to form a hotel. Ongoing work will include the construction of additional tree houses to accommodate extra guests. Each of the cabins is nearly 13 meters long, and they rest on 14 irregularly arranged steel columns and are suspended using stainless-steel cables and textile straps. A steel stairway provides access to the tree houses, which are built 3.5 meters above ground level. Façades and interiors are made of untreated larch wood. Each tree-house cabin has a bedroom for two people, a bathroom, and a living area with a kitchen unit and two additional beds.

Wo einst ein Bauernhof stand, dienen nun restaurierte Altgebäude, ergänzt um vier Baumhäuser, als Hotel. Im Zuge der noch andauernden Bauarbeiten werden weitere Baumhäuser entstehen, um noch mehr Gäste unterbringen zu können. Jede der Hütten ist fast 13 m lang und ruht auf 14 unregelmäßig angeordneten Stahlstützen, ist aber zusätzlich an rostfreien Stahlseilen und Textilgurten aufgehängt. Über eine Stahltreppe gelangt man zu den Baumhäusern, die sich 3,5 m über dem Boden befinden. Verkleidungen und Ausbauten sind aus unbehandeltem Lärchenholz. Jedes Baumhaus verfügt über ein Zwei-bettzimmer, ein Bad und einen Wohnbereich mit Kücheneinheit und zwei zusätzlichen Betten.

Quatre maisons dans les arbres complètent les bâtiments restaurés d'une ferme ancienne pour former un hôtel. D'autres sont prévues. Chacune est longue de 13 m, posée sur 14 poteaux en acier disposés irrégulièrement et suspendue aux arbres par des câbles en acier inoxydable et des sangles textiles. Elles sont construites à 3,5 m au-dessus du sol et accessibles par un escalier en acier. Les façades et les intérieurs sont en mélèze non traité. Chaque maison dispose d'une chambre pour deux personnes, d'une salle de bains et d'un espace séjour avec un coin cuisine et deux lits supplémentaires.

Again, lifting the structure off the ground on inclined metal struts, Andreas Wenning provides a combination of comfort and tree-house-type living. Left, a drawing shows the entire interior.

Auch hier lässt Andreas Wenning das Gebäude auf schrägen Metall-pfeilern über der Erde schweben und sorgt für eine Mischung aus Komfort und typischem Baumhaus-leben. Links zeigt eine Zeichnung das Innere.

Là encore, en surélevant la structure sur des pieux métalliques inclinés, Andreas Wenning associe confort et habitat de type maison dans les arbres. À gauche, schéma de l'intérieur.

The all-wood interior and generous windows augment the impression of really living among the trees. The décor is modern and functional.

Die Innere aus Holz und die großen Fenster verstärken den Eindruck, tatsächlich inmitten der Bäume zu leben. Die Ausstattung ist modern und funktional.

L'intérieur tout en bois et le généreux vitrage donnent encore plus l'impression de vivre parmi les arbres. Le décor est moderne et fonctionnel.

A wooden deck is wrapped around
a tree in the image above. Right,
a bathroom again provides more
comfort than most tree houses.

Eine hölzerne Plattform umschließt
auf dem Bild oben einen Baum.
Das Bad rechts bietet mehr Komfort
als sonst in Baumhäusern üblich.

Ci-dessus, la terrasse en bois
entoure un arbre. À droite, une salle
de bains elle aussi plus confortable
que celles de la plupart des maisons
dans les arbres.

BCMF

BCMF is an association created in 2001 by Bruno Campos, with Marcelo Fontes and Sílvio Todeschi as partners. **BRUNO CAMPOS**, born in 1970, graduated from the Federal University of Minas Gerais (UFMG, Belo Horizonte, 1989–94), and received an M.A. in Housing and Urbanism at the Architectural Association School (London, 1997–98). He worked in the office of Weiss/Manfredi Architects, before establishing his own practice. Born in 1971, **MARCELO FONTES** also graduated from the UFMG (1990–95). **SÍLVIO TODESCHI** was born in 1968 and graduated from the UFMG in 1992. He has had his own practice since 1992, and was a collaborator of BCMF Arquitetos on several projects, before joining them as a partner in 2010. Their work includes MOCAO (Montes Claros Stadium, 2001–03); the Deodoro Sports Complex (Shooting, Equestrian, Modern Pentathlon, Grass Hockey, and Archery) built for the Rio 2007 Pan American Games (2005–07); and they were hired by the Brazilian Olympic Committee (COB) to develop various concept studies for the Rio 2016 Candidature Bid (2008–09). More recently they have worked on the Casa Cor Bar (Belo Horizonte, 2010, published here); and they have been responsible for the execution of the Mineirão Stadium for the 2014 FIFA World Cup (Pampulha, Belo Horizonte, 2011–12), all in Brazil.

BCMF wurde 2001 als Bürogemeinschaft von Bruno Campos gegründet, Partner sind Marcelo Fontes und Sílvio Todeschi. **BRUNO CAMPOS**, geboren 1970, schloss sein Studium an der Universidade Federal de Minas Gerais (UFMG, Belo Horizonte, 1989–94) ab und erlangte einen Master in Wohnungsbau und Stadtplanung an der Architectural Association in London (1997–98). Vor Gründung der Bürogemeinschaft war er für Weiss/Manfredi Architects tätig. Auch **MARCELO FONTES**, Jahrgang 1971, studierte an der UFMG (1990–95). **SÍLVIO TODESCHI**, 1968 geboren, schloss sein Studium 1992 ebenfalls an der UFMG ab. Ab 1992 praktizierte er zunächst selbstständig und kooperierte bei mehreren Projekten mit BCMF Arquitetos, bevor er sich dem Team 2010 als Partner anschloss. Zu ihren Projekten zählen das MOCAO (Stadion Montes Claros, 2001–03), der Sportkomplex Deodoro (Schießen, Reiten, moderner Fünfkampf, Feldhockey und Bogenschießen) für die Panamerikanischen Spiele 2007 in Rio (2005–07). Im Auftrag des Brasilianischen Olympischen Komitees (COB) erarbeitete das Team verschiedene Konzeptstudien für die Bewerbung Rios für die Sommerspiele 2016 (2008–09). Jüngere Projekte sind die Casa Cor Bar (Belo Horizonte, 2010, hier vorgestellt) sowie die Bauleitung des Mineirão-Stadions für die Fußball-Weltmeisterschaft 2014 (Pampulha, Belo Horizonte, 2011–12), alle in Brasilien.

BCMF est une association créée en 2001 par Bruno Campos et ses partenaires Marcelo Fontes et Sílvio Todeschi. **BRUNO CAMPOS**, né en 1970, est diplômé de l'université fédérale de Minas Gerais (UFMG, Belo Horizonte, Brésil, 1989–94) et possède un M.A. en habitat et urbanisme de l'Architectural Association (Londres, 1997–98). Il a travaillé dans le cabinet d'architectes Weiss/Manfredi avant d'ouvrir le sien. Né en 1971, **MARCELO FONTES** est également diplômé de l'UFMG (1990–95). **SÍLVIO TODESCHI** est né en 1968 et a obtenu son diplôme à l'UFMG en 1992. Il a possédé son propre cabinet à partir de 1992 et a collaboré avec BCMF Arquitetos à plusieurs projets avant d'en devenir un partenaire en 2010. Leurs réalisations comprennent notamment le MOCAO (stade de Montes Claros, Brésil, 2001–03) et le complexe sportif de Deodoro (tir sportif, équitation, pentathlon moderne, hockey sur gazon et tir à l'arc) construit pour les Jeux panaméricains de Rio en 2007 (2005–07) ; ils ont par ailleurs été chargés par le Comité olympique brésilien (COB) de développer plusieurs études de projets pour la candidature de Rio aux Jeux olympiques de 2016 (2008–09). Plus récemment, ils ont travaillé au bar Casa Cor (Belo Horizonte, 2010, publié ici) et ils ont été responsables des travaux du stade Mineirão pour la Coupe du monde de la FIFA 2014 (Pampulha, Belo Horizonte, 2011–12), tous au Brésil.

CASA COR BAR

Belo Horizonte, Minas Gerais, Brazil, 2010

*Area: 69m². Client: Casa Cor / Stella Artois /
Arcelor Mittal. Cost: $70 000.*

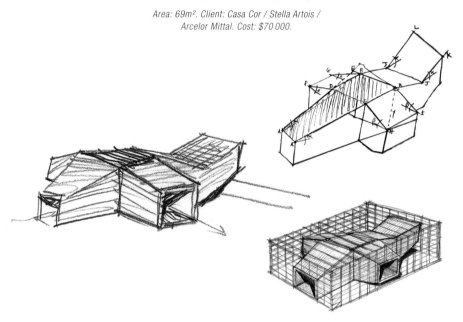

This unusual project, built in only three weeks, was implemented using a steel-frame design, and stainless-steel plate with a mirror finish inside and a matte finish on the exterior. The structure is intended to be "non-site specific," portable, and usable in different ways, but essentially it is "an informal lounge and retreat space." The architect states: "With dim lighting and some cork benches distributed at strategic points, the orange carpet floor unfolds into bleachers and stepped platforms where people can relax and admire the landscape from inside or outside. This unusual and irregular 'bolide' landed on a rooftop, in this case, but can be moved later anywhere else without losing its visual impact: a park, a plaza, a garden, or even the roof of another building."

Das ungewöhnliche Projekt wurde mit einem Stahlrahmenskelett und einer Edelstahlblechhülle realisiert, die innen verspiegelt und außen mattiert ist. Konzipiert wurde der Bau als „nicht ortsspezifisch", als transportabel und variabel nutzbar, ist im Grunde jedoch eine „entspannte Lounge, ein Ort zum Abschalten". Die Architekten erklären: „Gedämpftes Licht und eine Reihe von Korkbänken wurden an strategischen Punkten platziert; der Boden mit orangefarbener Auslegeware ist zu Tribünen und wie Treppen gestalteten Podesten ausgeformt. Hier können Gäste sitzen und die Landschaft von drinnen und draußen genießen. Der ungewöhnliche, asymmetrische ‚Bolid' ist hier auf einem Dach gelandet, lässt sich jedoch an einen beliebigen Ort versetzen, ohne an Wirkung einzubüßen: in einen Park, einen Garten oder auf das Dach eines anderen Gebäudes."

Ce projet original, construit en seulement trois semaines, a été conçu à l'aide d'une charpente en acier et de plaques en acier inoxydable au fini miroir à l'intérieur et mat à l'extérieur. La structure se veut « non rattachée à un lieu », transportable et utilisable de diverses manières, mais reste avant tout « un espace informel de détente et de retraite ». Pour l'architecte : « Avec le faible éclairage et quelques bancs en liège dispersés aux endroits stratégiques, la moquette orange se déploie sur des gradins où se détendre en admirant le paysage de l'intérieur ou de l'extérieur. Le "bolide" original et irrégulier s'est ici posé sur un toit, mais il peut être transféré n'importe où sans perdre de son impact visuel : dans un parc, sur une place, dans un jardin, ou même sur le toit d'un autre bâtiment. »

Angled but essentially tubular, the
bar opens in four directions as seen
in the sketches to the left, while
the interior gives an impression of
almost hermetic continuity.

Die schiefwinklige, schlauchförmige
Bar öffnet sich in vier Richtungen,
wie auf den Skizzen links zu sehen
ist. Das Interieur wirkt geradezu
hermetisch geschlossen.

De forme anguleuse, mais surtout
tubulaire, le bar s'ouvre dans quatre
directions comme on le voit sur les
croquis, tandis que l'intérieur donne
une impression de continuité quasi
hermétique.

At the end of a rooftop, the bar
seems to be part of the garden
design with its almost organic
skin patterns.

Die Bar am Ende des Daches fügt
sich mit ihrer fast organischen
Oberflächenstruktur harmonisch
in das Gartenkonzept ein.

À l'extrémité du toit, le bar semble
faire partie de l'architecture du
jardin avec les motifs presque organiques de son revêtement extérieur.

MARLON BLACKWELL

MARLON BLACKWELL was born in Munich, Germany, in 1956. He received his undergraduate degree from Auburn University (1980) and an M.Arch. II degree from Syracuse University in Florence, Italy, in 1991. In 1994, he cofounded the University of Arkansas "Mexico Summer Urban Studio," and has coordinated and taught in the program at the Casa Luis Barragán in Mexico City since 1996. He is a Professor and Department Head in the School of Architecture at the University of Arkansas. Recent and current work includes Saint Nicholas Eastern Orthodox Church (Springdale, Arkansas, 2009, published here); the Ruth Lilly Visitors Pavilion (Indianapolis, Indiana, 2009–10); Fallingwater Cottages (Mill Run, Pennsylvania, 2010); Burnett Cabin and Bunkhouse (Caddo Gap, Arkansas, 2010); Crystal Bridges Museum of American Art Store (Bentonville, Arkansas, 2011); the renovation and expansion of the University of Arkansas School of Architecture, Steven L. Anderson Design Center (Fayetteville, Arkansas, 2012); and the expansion of the Bella Vista Library (Bella Vista, Arkansas, 2012), all in the USA.

MARLON BLACKWELL wurde 1956 in München geboren. Nach dem Grundstudium an der Auburn University (1980) absolvierte er 1991 einen M. Arch. II an der Syracuse University in Florenz, Italien. 1994 war er Mitbegründer des Mexico Summer Urban Studio an der University of Arkansas und ist seit 1996 in der Casa Luis Barragán in Mexiko-Stadt als Programmkoordinator und Lehrer tätig. Außerdem ist er Professor und Fachbereichsleiter Architektur an der University of Arkansas. Zu seinen jüngeren und laufenden Projekten gehören die Saint Nicholas Eastern Orthodox Church (Springdale, Arkansas, 2009, hier vorgestellt), der Ruth Lilly Visitors Pavilion (Indianapolis, Indiana, 2009–10), die Fallingwater Cottages (Mill Run, Pennsylvania, 2010), Burnett Cabin and Bunkhouse (Caddo Gap, Arkansas, 2010), der Crystal Bridges Museum of American Art Store (Bentonville, Arkansas, 2011), die Renovierung und Erweiterung der Architekturfakultät der University of Arkansas, das Steven L. Anderson Design Center (Fayetteville, Arkansas, 2012) und die Erweiterung der Bella Vista Library (Bella Vista, Arkansas), alle in den USA.

MARLON BLACKWELL est né à Munich en 1956. Il est titulaire d'un diplôme de premier cycle de l'université d'Auburn (1980) et d'un M. Arch II de l'université Syracuse de Florence, en Italie (1991). Il a participé en 1994 à la fondation du « Mexico Summer Urban Studio » à l'université de l'Arkansas, il coordonne le programme et y enseigne à la Casa Luis Barragán de Mexico depuis 1996. Il est professeur et directeur de département à l'École d'architecture de l'université de l'Arkansas. Ses travaux récents et en cours comprennent l'église orthodoxe d'Orient Saint-Nicolas (Springdale, Arkansas, 2009, publiée ici) ; le centre d'accueil des visiteurs Ruth Lilly (Indianapolis, Indiana, 2009–10) ; les Fallingwater Cottages (Mill Run, Pennsylvanie, 2010) ; la cabane et le dortoir Burnett (Caddo Gap, Arkansas, 2010) ; la boutique du musée de l'Art américain Crystal Bridges (Bentonville, Arkansas, 2011) ; la rénovation et extension de l'École d'architecture de l'université de l'Arkansas, le centre de design Steven L. Anderson (Fayetteville, Arkansas, 2012) et l'extension de la bibliothèque de Bella Vista (Bella Vista, Arkansas, 2012), tous aux États-Unis.

SAINT NICHOLAS EASTERN ORTHODOX CHURCH

Springdale, Arkansas, USA, 2009

Area: 334 m². Client: Saint Nicholas Eastern Orthodox Church.
Cost: $405 000.

Built on a 1.2-hectare site near a public park and a major highway, this church project is based on an existing steel-framed shop building. A new skin of box ribbed metal panels and colored glass openings were added. The architects "folded" the narthex 90° to the axis of the sanctuary to respect the fact that Eastern Orthodox churches usually face east. The narthex is marked by a long piece of white oak that is used for lighting prayer candles and paying respects to saints. A tower was added to the original structure. Lit by a skylight, it houses a red glass cross that faces west and is backlit by the rising sun. Artificially lit at night, it is visible from the nearby highway. The eastern end of the sanctuary features a nine-meter-wide glass transom. The iconostasis, separating the sanctuary and the altar area, symbolizing the separation between heaven and earth, has hand-painted and gilt icons. A dome made of a reused satellite dish that was plastered and inverted is inscribed with an image of Christ Pantocrator. Though larger than many structures in this book, the sanctuary is small by the standards of churches and obviously calls on limited means, while updating the idea of sacred space.

Grundlage dieses Kirchenbauprojekts, das auf einem 1,2 ha großen Grundstück unweit eines städtischen Parks und einer Hauptverkehrsstraße steht, war ein bereits vorhandenes Gewerbegebäude mit Stahlskelett. Eine neue Verkleidung aus Trapezblech wurde angebracht und Öffnungen für farbige Glasfenster geschaffen. Die Architekten „klappten" den Narthex 90 Grad von der Achse des Chorraums ab, um der Tatsache Respekt zu zollen, dass orthodoxe Kirchen üblicherweise nach Osten ausgerichtet sind. Der Narthex wird von einer langen Tafel aus Weißeiche geprägt, auf der Gebetskerzen entzündet werden und den Heiligen Reverenz erwiesen wird. Dem Originalgebäude wurde ein Turm hinzugefügt und in diesen ein rotes Glaskreuz eingelassen, das nach Westen zeigt und sowohl durch ein Oberlicht als auch von hinten von der aufgehenden Sonne erhellt wird. Nachts wird es künstlich beleuchtet und ist vom nahe gelegenen Highway aus zu sehen. Am östlichen Ende des Chorraums befindet sich ein 9 m langes schmales Querfenster. Die Ikonostase, die Chorraum und Altarbereich voneinander abgrenzt und symbolisch die Trennung zwischen Himmel und Erde nachempfindet, schmücken handgemalte und vergoldete Heiligenbilder. Eine Kuppel, hergestellt aus einer recycelten Satellitenschüssel, mit Gips verputzt und umgedreht, ziert ein Christus Pantokrator. Obwohl größer als viele Bauten in diesem Buch, ist der Chorraum für eine Kirche klein und muss ganz offenkundig mit begrenzten Mitteln auskommen, während er zugleich das Konzept eines heiligen Ortes erneuert.

Construite sur un site de 1,2 hectare à proximité d'un jardin public et d'une grande autoroute, l'église a pour base un bâtiment commercial existant à charpente métallique. Une nouvelle enveloppe de panneaux métalliques à nervures-caissons et des ouvertures garnies de verre coloré ont été ajoutées. Les architectes ont « replié » le narthex à 90° par rapport à l'axe du sanctuaire afin de tenir compte du fait que les églises orthodoxes d'Orient sont généralement construites face à l'est. Il est marqué par une longue planche de chêne blanc pour allumer les bougies de prière et honorer les saints. Une tour a été ajoutée à la structure d'origine. Éclairée par une lucarne, elle abrite une croix de verre rouge qui fait face à l'ouest et se trouve donc rétroéclairée par le soleil levant. Elle est également éclairée artificiellement la nuit et visible de l'autoroute voisine. L'extrémité est du sanctuaire présente une imposte vitrée large de 9 m. L'iconostase qui sépare le sanctuaire de la nef et symbolise la séparation entre le ciel et la terre est ornée d'icônes peintes à la main et dorées. Un dôme fait d'une antenne parabolique récupérée, plâtrée et posée à l'envers, porte une représentation du Christ pantocrator. Bien que plus grand que la plupart des objets présentés ici, le sanctuaire est petit pour une église et a dû manifestement se contenter de moyens limités, tout en renouvelant l'idée d'espace sacré.

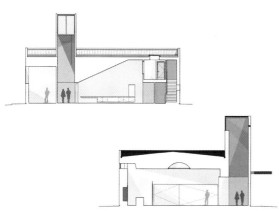

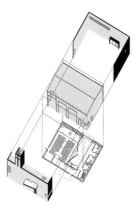

Above, drawings make the simple design of the church clear. Interior spaces are simple and yet the architect successfully plays on light as well as color.

Die Zeichnungen oben verdeutlichen den einfachen Entwurf der Kirche. Die Innenräume sind schlicht gehalten, doch der Architekt spielt effektvoll mit Licht und auch Farbe.

Ci-dessus, les plans mettent en évidence la simplicité du design. Les espaces intérieurs sont sobres, et pourtant l'architecte a réussi à y jouer avec la lumière et la couleur.

JOSÉ CADILHE

JOSÉ CADILHE was born in Póvoa de Varzim, Portugal, in 1980. He graduated as an architect from the Escola Superior Artística do Porto (Portugal, 2005). He created his own firm, dIONISO LAB, in 2009, but went on to complete a Master's degree in Architecture and Urbanism at the Architectural Association in London (2012). He has engaged in collaboration with Zaha Hadid Architects in London among others. Given the very recent creation of the firm and the studies of José Cadilhe, the firm has relatively few completed buildings. dIONISO LAB has worked on House 77 (2010, published here); Building L7 (2010); Apartment RT (2011); and House L27 (2012), all in Póvoa de Varzim. "Modulo L400" is a 2012 exhibition installation designed by the firm in Porto.

JOSÉ CADILHE wurde 1980 in Póvoa de Varzim, Portugal, geboren. Sein Architekturstudium absolvierte er an der kunstwissenschaftlichen Fakultät der Universität Porto (2005). Mit dIONISO LAB gründete er 2009 sein eigenes Büro, machte aber gleichzeitig noch einen Master in Architektur und Stadtplanung bei der Architectural Association in London (2012). Dort arbeitete er neben anderen auch mit Zaha Hadid Architects zusammen. Da die Gründung noch nicht sehr lange zurückliegt und aufgrund von José Cadilhes Studium, hat das Büro bislang erst relativ wenige Bauvorhaben realisiert. Zu den Arbeiten von dIONISO LAB gehören Haus 77 (2011, hier vorgestellt), Gebäude L7 (2010), Apartment RT (2011) und Haus L27 (2012), alle in Póvoa de Varzim. „Modulo L400" ist eine Installation für einen Messestand, die das Büro in Porto entworfen hat.

JOSÉ CADILHE est né à Póvoa de Varzim, au Portugal, en 1980. Il a obtenu son diplôme d'architecte à l'Escola Superior Artística do Porto (Portugal, 2005). Il a ouvert son agence, dIONISO LAB, en 2009, mais a ensuite poursuivi ses études et obtenu un master en architecture et urbanisme à l'Architectural Association de Londres (2012) où il a entamé des collabora-tions avec, notamment, Zaha Hadid Architects. Du fait de la création très récente de l'agence et des études de José Cadilhe, il n'a encore que relativement peu de bâtiments déjà achevés à son actif mais dIONISO LAB a travaillé à la Maison 77 (2010, publiée ici) ; au bâtiment L7 (2010) ; à l'appartement RT (2011) et à la Maison L27 (2012), tous à Póvoa de Varzim. *Modulo L400* est une installation pour exposition conçue en 2012 par l'agence à Porto.

HOUSE 77

Póvoa de Varzim, Portugal, 2009–10

Area: 232 m².

This house, which is described as "simple" by its architect, has the public areas on the lower floors and private spaces above, the whole structured in half-floors. A stairway is the "heart of the house" and a wall painted in the blue used by the French artist Yves Klein is also very present. The west façade has aluminum venetian blinds that open toward a small garden. Stainless-steel panels mark the main façade. They are perforated with *siglas poveiras*, a "proto-writing" system used locally for communication or also to mark personal belongings or fishing equipment. These symbols were hereditary and were often used for several generations. The architect writes: "In this way, the house, in the very center of Bairro Norte, shares some of the city's memories and references with the population and revitalizes a legacy that has been progressively forgotten and abandoned. Quietly, the house confesses its pride in the city…"

In dem Haus, das der Architekt selbst als „schlicht" beschreibt, befinden sich die gemeinsamen Bereiche auf den unteren Stockwerken und die Privaträume darüber, wobei das komplette Gebäude in Halbetagen aufgeteilt ist. Eine Treppe bildet das „Herz des Hauses", starke Präsenz hat zudem eine Wand, die in jenem Blauton gehalten ist, den der französische Künstler Yves Klein verwendete. An der Westseite öffnen sich Jalousien aus Aluminium zu einem kleinen Garten hin. Die Hauptfassade ist mit Platten aus rostfreiem Stahl verkleidet. Sie sind von *siglas poveiras* durchbrochen, einem lokalen „Zeichensystem", das zur Kommunikation und zur Kennzeichnung persönlichen Eigentums oder der Fischerei-Ausrüstung dient. Diese Symbole waren vererbbar und wurden oftmals über Generationen hinweg verwendet. Der Architekt schreibt dazu: „Auf diese Weise teilt das Haus, mitten im Zentrum des Bairro Norte gelegen, einige der stadtgeschichtlichen Erinnerungen und Anspielungen mit der Bevölkerung und belebt eine Tradition, die nach und nach vergessen und aufgegeben wurde. Stillschweigend bringt das Haus so den Stolz auf die Stadt zum Ausdruck…"

La maison, qualifiée de « simple » par l'architecte, comporte des pièces communes dans les étages inférieurs et des parties privées plus haut, le tout étant structuré par demi-niveaux. La cage d'escalier forme le « cœur de la maison », tandis qu'une paroi peinte dans le bleu créé par l'artiste français Yves Klein apporte aussi une forte présence. La façade ouest est dotée de stores vénitiens en aluminium qui donnent sur un petit jardin. La façade principale est caractérisée par ses panneaux d'acier inoxydable perforés de *siglas poveiras*, un système de « proto-écriture » utilisé localement pour communiquer ou pour marquer ses possessions ou son matériel de pêche. Les symboles en sont héréditaires et ont souvent servi à plusieurs géné-rations. L'architecte a écrit à ce sujet : « La maison en plein centre de Bairro Norte partage ainsi avec la population un peu de la mémoire et des références de la ville, tout en redonnant vie à un héritage en passe d'être oublié et abandonné. Elle affirme ainsi, en toute discrétion, sa fierté d'appartenir à cette ville… »

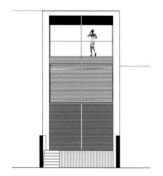
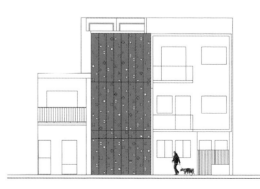

The architect successfully plays on the very narrow design, enlivening the façade with cut-out forms and folding metal shutters.

Der Architekt spielt gekonnt mit dem äußerst schmalen Entwurf und verleiht der Fassade durch ausgestanzte Ornamente und faltbare Metallfensterläden etwas Heiteres.

L'architecte joue avec l'étroitesse extrême de la maison pour un résultat très réussi, enjolivant la façade de formes découpées et de volets pliants métalliques.

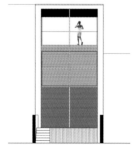
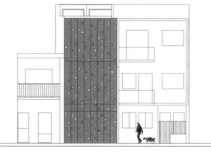

The tapered floor plan is seen for each level (right). Using light and an alternation of openings and opaque surfaces, the design is both lively and innovative.

Rechts wird der sich verjüngende Grundriss für jedes Stockwerk ersichtlich. Durch die Art, wie der Entwurf mit Licht und dem Wechsel von Öffnungen und blickdichten Oberflächen arbeitet, bekommt er etwas Lebhaftes und Innovatives.

À droite, le plan fuselé de chaque niveau. Avec la lumière et une alternance d'ouvertures et de surfaces opaques, le design est à la fois plein de vie et innovant.

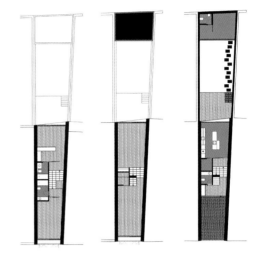

MANUEL CLAVEL-ROJO

MANUEL CLAVEL-ROJO was born in Murcia in 1976. He received his degree in Architecture from the Polytechnic University of Madrid. He served as head of Culture for the Murcia Architects Association (2007–10). He has been a Visiting Professor at Miami University (Florida) since 2012. His work includes the Las Salinas Marina (San Pedro del Pinatar, Murcia, 2002); Mesa del Castillo Hospital (Murcia, 2004); Portman Bay Regeneration Project (Portman, La Unión, 2007); Café del Arco (Murcia, 2009); Cloud Pantheon (Murcia, 2010, published here); Avenida Libertad Parking Lot (Murcia, 2010); Casanueva Pharmacy (Murcia, 2010); Centrifugal Ultralight Pavilion (Shenzhen, China, 2011); rehabilitation of a penthouse for art collectors (Murcia, 2011); Liuye Lake Civic Center (Changde, Hunan, China, 2012); and the 4 in 1 House (Guadalupe, Murcia, 2013), all in Spain unless otherwise indicated.

MANUEL CLAVEL-ROJO wurde 1976 in Murcia geboren. Er erwarb sein Diplom in Architektur an der Polytechnischen Universität Madrid. 2007–10 war er Kulturchef des Architektenverbands von Murcia. Seit 2012 ist er Gastprofessor an der Miami University (Florida). Zu seinen Werken zählen die Marina Las Salinas (San Pedro del Pinatar, Murcia, 2012); das Hospital Mesa del Castillo (Murcia, 2004); das Sanierungsprojekt Portman Bay (Portman, La Unión, 2007); das Café del Arco (Murcia, 2009); Cloud Pantheon (Murcia, 2010, hier veröffentlicht); Parking Avenida Libertad (Murcia, 2010); die Apotheke Casanueva (Murcia, 2011); der Pavillon Centrifugal Ultralight (Shenzen, China, 2011); die Sanierung eines Penthouse für Kunstsammler (Murcia, 2011); das Liuye Lake Civic Center (Changde, Hunan, China, 2012) und das 4 in 1 House (Guadalupe, Murcia, 2013), alle in Spanien, sofern nicht anders angegeben.

MANUEL CLAVEL-ROJO est né à Murcie en 1976. Il est diplômé en architecture de l'Université polytechnique de Madrid. Il a été directeur culturel de la Murcia Architects Association (2007–10), puis professeur associé à l'université de Miami (Floride) où il travaille depuis 2012. Ses réalisations comprennent la marina Las Salinas (San Pedro del Pinatar, Murcie, 2002) ; l'hôpital Mesa del Castillo (Murcie, 2004) ; le projet de restauration du milieu dans la baie de Portman (Portman, La Unión, 2007) ; le Café del Arco (Murcie, 2009) ; Panteón Nube (Murcie, 2010, publié ici) ; le parking Avenida Libertad (Murcie, 2010) ; la pharmacie Casanueva (Murcie, 2010) ; le Centrifugal Ultralight Pavilion (Shenzhen, Chine, 2011) ; la rénovation d'un appartement de standing pour des collectionneurs d'art (Murcie, 2011) ; le centre administratif du lac Liuye (Changde, Hunan, Chine, 2012) et la maison 4 en 1 (Guadalupe, Murcie, 2013), toutes en Espagne sauf mention contraire.

CLOUD PANTHEON

Espinardo, Murcia, Spain, 2010

Area: 53 m². Collaboration: Robin Harloff,
Mauricio Méndez-Bustos, David Hernández-Conesa.

The project concerned "a stage setting for a burial, taking into account the spatial and temporal situations" with the interior inspired by "a cloud that is crossed by beams of sun." The large abstract cloud was made with triangulated steel plates coated in white polyurethane paint. The rear wall is translucent allowing in minimal natural light, while three irregular skylights admit more daylight and give the "cloud" a "weightless and enigmatic" appearance. Five trapezoidal doors made of tinted glass are framed in satin-finished stainless steel; revolving on hidden metallic rods, they appear to be permanently closed.

Das Projekt betraf „die Szenerie für eine Grabstätte unter Berücksichtigung der räumlichen und zeitlichen Situation", mit einem Innenraum, der „an eine von Sonnenstrahlen durchdrungene Wolke" erinnert. Diese große, abstrakte Wolke besteht aus dreieckigen, mit weißer Polyurethanfarbe gestrichenen Stahlplatten. Die Rückwand, durch die minimales natürliches Licht einfällt, ist durchscheinend, während drei ungleichmäßige Oberlichter zusätzliches Tageslicht einlassen und der „Wolke" eine schwerelose und geheimnisvolle Wirkung verleihen. Fünf trapezförmige Türen aus Buntglas sind mit Rahmen aus satiniertem Edelstahl versehen; sie drehen sich um verborgene Metallstäbe und wirken wie ständig geschlossen.

Le projet faisait partie du «décor d'un enterrement, prenant en compte les situations spatiales et temporelles» et l'intérieur a été inspiré par «un nuage que traversent des rayons de soleil». L'immense nuage abstrait est fait de plaques d'acier triangulaires recouvertes de peinture polyuréthane blanche. Le mur du fond est translucide et laisse entrer une lumière naturelle minimale, trois lucarnes aux formes irrégulières éclairent plus et donnent au «nuage» un aspect «énigmatique et comme en apesanteur». Cinq portes trapézoïdales en verre teint sont encadrées d'acier inoxydable aux finitions satinées et tournent sur des tiges métalliques invisibles selon un mécanisme qui les fait paraître toujours fermées.

The translucent wall of the memorial, as well as its modern design that stands apart amongst other more traditional graves gives an ethereal splendor to this very small structure. Its pivoting doors open broadly as seen on the following pages.

Die lichtdurchlässige Wand der Gedenkstätte und ihre moderne Gestaltung unterscheiden sie von traditionelleren Grabstätten und verleihen diesem sehr kleinen Bauwerk eine geistige Größe. Die Drehtüren lassen sich weit öffnen.

Le mur translucide du mémorial et la modernité de son design, qui le distingue des autres tombeaux plus traditionnels, donne à cette structure très réduite une splendeur éthérée. Les portes pivotantes s'ouvrent largement.

COELACANTH AND ASSOCIATES

KAZUKO AKAMATSU, the President of CAt, was born in Tokyo in 1968. She graduated with a B.Arch. degree from Japan Women's University (Tokyo, 1990), and joined Coelacanth Architects in the same year. In 2002, she became a partner in the firm that was reorganized in 2005 as Coelacanth and Associates (C+A). The Tokyo office is called CAt (C+A Tokyo). She is currently an Associate Professor at Hosei University. **KAZUHIRO KOJIMA**, also President of CAt, was born in Osaka in 1958. He obtained his B.Arch. degree from Kyoto University (1982) and his M.Arch. from the University of Tokyo (Hiroshi Hara Laboratory, 1984). He is currently a Professor at Y-GSA (Yokohama Graduate School of Architecture). The firm has worked on the Liberal ˙Arts and Science College at Education City (Doha, Qatar, 2004; master plan Arata Isozaki, i-Net); and again with Isozaki on the Naryn Campus of the University of Central Asia (Aga Khan Development Network, Kyrgyzstan, 2009). They have engaged in numerous other educational projects such as the Makuhari International School (Chiba, Japan, 2009); the Uto Elementary School (Uto, Kumamoto, Japan, 2011); and the Ho Chi Minh University of Architecture (Ho Chi Minh City, Vietnam, 2005–). They have also completed the Sunken House (Odawara, Kanagawa, Japan, 2010, published here).

KAZUKO AKAMATSU, Chefin von CAt, wurde 1968 in Tokio geboren. Sie schloss ihr Studium an der japanischen Frauenuniversität mit einem B. Arch. ab (Tokio, 1990) und ging noch im gleichen Jahr zu Coelacanth Architects. 2002 wurde sie Teilhaberin des Büros, aus dem nach einer Umstrukturierung 2005 Coelacanth and Associates (C+A) wurde. Das Büro in Tokio heißt CAt (C+A Tokyo). Sie hat an verschiedenen Universitäten in Japan gelehrt und ist derzeit Privatdozentin an der Hosei University. **KAZUHIRO KOJIMA**, ebenfalls Chef von CAt, wurde 1958 in Osaka geboren. Er absolvierte seinen B. Arch. an der Universität Kioto (1982) und seinen M. Arch. an der Universität Tokio (Hiroshi Hara Laboratory, 1984). Derzeit ist er Professor an der Y-GSA (Yokohama Graduate School of Architecture). Das Büro hat an der Planung des Liberal Art and Science College in Education City (Doha, Katar, 2004; Gesamtkonzept: Arata Isozaki, i-Net) mitgearbeitet und, ebenfalls mit Isozaki, an der des Naryn-Campus der Universität von Zentralasien (Aga Khan Development Network, Kirgisistan, 2009). Die beiden waren an zahlreichen anderen Bildungsprojekten beteiligt, wie der Makuhari International School (Chiba, Japan, 2009), der Grundschule Uto (Uto, Kumamoto, Japan, 2011) und der Ho-Chi-Minh-Universität für Architektur (Ho-Chi-Minh-Stadt, Vietnam, seit 2005). Sie haben zudem das Sunken House fertiggestellt (Odawara, Kanagawa, Japan, 2010, hier vorgestellt).

KAZUKO AKAMATSU, présidente de CAt, est née à Tokyo en 1968. Elle est titulaire d'un B.Arch de l'Université féminine du Japon (Tokyo, 1990) et a rejoint Coelacanth Architects la même année. En 2002, elle est devenue partenaire de la société qui a été restructurée pour devenir Coelacanth and Associates (C+A) en 2005. L'agence de Tokyo est aussi appelée CAt (C+A Tokyo). Elle a enseigné dans plusieurs universités japonaises et est actuellement maître de conférences à l'université Hosei. **KAZUHIRO KOJIMA**, l'autre président de CAt, est né à Osaka en 1958. Il est titulaire d'un B.Arch de l'université de Kyoto (1982) et d'un M.Arch de l'université de Tokyo (laboratoire de Hiroshi Hara, 1984). Il est professeur à la Y-GSA (Yokohama Graduate School of Architecture). L'agence a participé au bâtiment des arts libéraux et des sciences de la Cité de l'éducation (Doha, Qatar, 2004 ; plan directeur d'Arata Isozaki, i-Net) et, de nouveau avec Isozaki, au campus de Naryn de l'université d'Asie centrale (Réseau Aga Khan de développement, Kirghizistan, 2009). Elle est engagée dans de nombreux autres projets éducatifs comme la Makuhari International School (Chiba, Japon, 2009) ; l'école élémentaire d'Uto (Uto, Kumamoto, Japon, 2011) et l'université d'architecture Ho Chi Minh (Ho Chi Minh-Ville, Viêtnam, 2005–). Elle a également réalisé la Maison engloutie (Odawara, Kanagawa, Japon, 2010, publiée ici).

SUNKEN HOUSE

Odawara, Kanagawa, Japan, 2010

Area: 87 m².

This unusual design combines a completely glazed ground level with a thin roof and a sunken living space.

Dieser ungewöhnliche Entwurf kombiniert ein rundum verglastes Erdgeschoss mit einem flachen Dach und einem abgesenkten Wohnbereich.

Cette création inédite associe un étage au niveau du sol entièrement vitré à une toiture fine et un séjour enfoncé dans le sol.

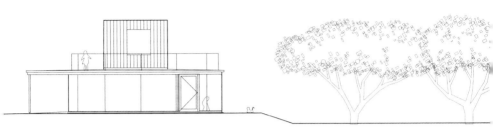

Built on a 270-square-meter site in an area where farms and residences are in close proximity, this small house is a two-story wooden structure. Floor-to-ceiling glazing gives a decidedly modern appearance. The residence is surrounded by fields planted with kaki (persimmon) trees. The architects explain: "We created a house in which it feels as if the room is connected to the bottom of the trees. Living in this space makes you relate to the outside rather than the inside. The house is sunken by 70 centimeters (below grade) but, as it is surrounded by lawn on all four sides, you can see the sky above the green. The interior is black so that the outside appears to be closer." The interior of the house has 16 movable partitions that can be fully opened to create a one-room studio. With all the partitions closed, the house has nine rooms. The technical aspects of the house are grouped in a central core, leaving the surrounding living space completely free. Although the idea of movable partitions is traditional in Japan, this use has a particularly modern result.

Dieses kleine Haus, ein zweistöckiges Gebäude aus Holz, steht dicht umgeben von Bauernhöfen und Wohnhäusern auf einem 270 m² großen Areal. Bodentiefe Verglasung verleiht ihm ein dezidiert modernes Erscheinungsbild. Auf den das Haus umgebenden Feldern stehen Kaki-Bäume. Die Architekten dazu: „Wir haben ein Haus geschaffen, in dem es sich anfühlt, als reichten die Räume bis unten an die Bäume heran. Hier zu leben bedeutet, wesentlich stärker mit dem Außen verbunden zu sein als mit dem Innen. Das Haus wurde 70 cm in die Erde abgesenkt, weil es aber rundum von Rasen umgeben ist, kann man oberhalb des Grüns den Himmel sehen. Die Innenräume sind in Schwarz gehalten, so erscheint einem das Außen näher." Im Inneren des Hauses gibt es 16 bewegbare Wandelemente, die sich aber vollständig öffnen lassen, um ein Ein-Raum-Studio zu schaffen. Werden alle Wandelemente geschlossen, hat das Haus neun Räume. Die technischen Notwendigkeiten sind alle in einem zentralen Kern angeordnet, sodass der umgebende Raum frei bleibt. Obgleich die Idee beweglicher Raumelemente in Japan Tradition hat, wirkt ihre Anwendung hier außerordentlich modern.

Construite sur un terrain de 270 m² dans une zone où les fermes voisinent avec les bâtiments résidentiels, cette petite maison est une structure en bois à deux niveaux. Le vitrage du sol au plafond lui confère une apparence résolument moderne. Elle est entourée de champs de kakis (plaqueminiers). Les architectes expliquent avoir « créé une maison dans laquelle la pièce semble prolongée par la cime des arbres. En vivant dans cet espace, un rapport plus intense s'instaure avec l'extérieur qu'avec l'intérieur. La maison est enfoncée de 70 cm (en dessous du niveau du sol), mais elle est entourée de gazon sur les quatre côtés, de sorte qu'on voit le ciel au-dessus du vert. L'intérieur est noir, ce qui fait paraître l'extérieur plus proche ». L'espace intérieur est doté de 16 cloisons mobiles qui peuvent être toutes ouvertes pour créer un studio. Lorsqu'elles sont toutes fermées, la maison a neuf pièces. Les équipements techniques sont groupés dans un noyau central, tandis que l'espace à vivre tout autour est entièrement libre. Les cloisons mobiles sont traditionnelles au Japon, mais l'utilisation qui en est faite ici donne un résultat particulièrement moderne.

The basic plan is quite simple, with an enclosed, more private core and a glazed periphery. The interior design verges on the industrial in terms of its strict, functional appearance.

Der Grundriss ist relativ simpel mit einem abgeschlossenen, eher privaten Kern und einem verglasten Äußeren. Die Innenarchitektur grenzt aufgrund ihres strengen, funktionalen Erscheinungsbilds ans Industrielle.

Le plan est plutôt simple avec un noyau clos plus intime et un périmètre vitré. Le décor intérieur est presque industriel avec son apparence sévère et fonctionnelle.

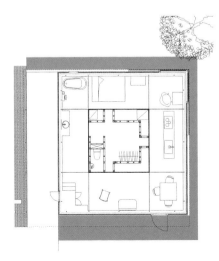

JAVIER CORVALÁN

JAVIER CORVALÁN was born in Asunción, Paraguay, in 1962. He obtained his degree as an architect from the Faculty of Science and Technology of the UCA (Universidad Católica Nuestra Señora de la Asunción, 1981–87). He created his own studio in 1990. He is Visiting Professor at the IUAV University in Venice (Italy). His work includes the Sotoportego House (2009); Hamaca House (2009, published here), the Subeldía House (2010); the APG Public Golf Driving Range (2013); and the Sports Center of the Paraguayan Olympic Committee (2014–), all in the area of Luque, Paraguay.

JAVIER CORVALÁN wurde 1962 in Asunción, Paraguay, geboren. Er erwarb sein Diplom in Architektur an der Fakultät für Naturwissenschaften und Technik der UCA (Universidad Católica Nuestra Señora de la Asunción, 1981–87). Sein eigenes Büro gründete er 1990. Er ist Gastprofessor an der Universität IUAV in Venedig (Italien). Zu seinen Werken zählen das Sotoportego House (2009); das Hamaca House (2009, hier veröffentlicht); das Subeldía House (2010); AGP Public Golf Driving Range (2013) und das Sportzentrum des Paraguayischen Olympischen Komitees, 2014–), alle im Bereich von Luque, Paraguay.

JAVIER CORVALÁN est né à Asunción, au Paraguay en 1962. Il est titulaire d'un diplôme d'architecte de la faculté des sciences et technologies de l'UCA (Universidad Católica Nuestra Señora de la Asunción, 1981–87). Il a créé son agence en 1990. Il est aujourd'hui professeur associé à l'université IUAV de Venise. Ses réalisations comprennent la maison Sotoportego (2009) ; la maison Hamaca (2009, publiée ici) ; la maison Subeldía (2010) ; le practice du golf public APG (2013) et le centre sportif du Comité olympique paraguayen (2014–), toutes autour de Luque, au Paraguay.

HAMACA HOUSE

Luque, Paraguay, 2009

Area: 80 m². Client: Francisco Oddone. Cost: $25 000.

Hamaca House is named after the form of the hammock that inspired it. Built on a 360-square-meter site, two brick-clad blocks at either end "counterbalance" the galvanized-steel roof. These massive tilted blocks forming opposite ends of the structure are mirrored inside where the central space is essentially open, with the steel roof connecting and protecting this intermediate space. A closed area is contrasted with this large open, or "intermediate," space with a kitchen and barbecue.

Das Hamaca House erhielt seinen Namen von *hammock*, dem englischen Wort für Hängematte, von deren Form es inspiriert wurde. Auf einem 360 m² großen Gelände bilden zwei mit Backstein verkleidete Blöcke auf beiden Seiten ein „Gegengewicht" zum Dach aus feuerverzinktem Stahl. Diese stark geneigten Blöcke an den gegenüberliegenden Enden des Bauwerks spiegeln sich im Inneren. Dort ist der zentrale Raum überwiegend offen gelassen, und das Stahldach verbindet und schützt diesen Zwischenbereich. Als Kontrast zu diesem großen, offenen oder „dazwischen liegenden" Raum gibt es einen geschlossenen Bereich mit Küche und Barbecue.

La maison Hamaca doit son nom au hamac dont elle s'est inspirée de la forme. Construite sur un terrain de 360 mètres carrés, deux blocs revêtus de briques « contrebalancent » de chaque côté le toit en acier galvanisé. Massifs et inclinés, ils forment les extrémités de la structure et se reflètent à l'intérieur où l'espace central est fondamentalement ouvert, uni et protégé par le toit. Un espace clos contraste avec cette vaste zone ouverte ou « intermédiaire » qui comprend une cuisine et un coin barbecue.

A floor plan of the house shows the central kitchen area and the barbecue space to the right. A patio continues outdoors to the right of the barbecue.

Ein Grundriss des Hauses zeigt rechter Hand den zentralen Küchen- und Grillbereich. Ein Innenhof rechts vom Barbecue führt direkt nach draußen.

Le plan de la maison montre la cuisine centrale et l'espace barbecue à droite. Un patio la prolonge à l'extérieur, à droite du barbecue.

CROSSON CLARKE CARNACHAN

KEN CROSSON was born in 1957. He studied at the Auckland University School of Architecture (1976–80), receiving his B.Arch. degree in 1981. He created his own firm in Auckland in 1982, before working with Covell Matthews Wheatley in London (1984–86) and again creating his own offices in New Zealand beginning in 1987, founding his present firm in 2004, which he directs together with Paul Clarke and Anna-Marie Chin. Their work includes the Tutukaka House (Tutukaka, Northland, 2007); Omaha Beach House (Omaha Beach, 2007); Wanaka House (Wanaka, Otago, 2007); Opito Bay House (Opito, Whitianga, 2008); Birkenhead House (Birkenhead, 2010); Mount Iron House (Mount Iron, 2011); the Hut on Sleds (Whangapoua, 2011, published here); and Peka Peka House (Peka Peka, 2013), all in New Zealand.

KEN CROSSON wurde 1957 geboren. Er studierte an der Auckland University School of Architecture (1976–80) und machte 1981 seinen B. Arch. Er gründete 1982 sein eigenes Büro in Auckland, bevor er mit Covell Matthews Wheatley in London kooperierte (1984–86) und von 1987 an erneut eigene Büros in Neuseeland eröffnete, 2004 dann sein jetziges, das er gemeinsam mit Paul Clarke und Anna-Marie Chin leitet. Zu ihren Arbeiten zählen das Tutukaka House (Tutukaka, Northland, 2007), das Omaha Beach House (Omaha Beach, 2007), das Wanaka House (Wanaka, Otago, 2007), das Opito Bay House (Opito, Whitianga, 2008), das Birkenhead House (Birkenhead, 2010), das Mount Iron House (Mount Iron 2011), die Hut on Sleds (Whangapoua, 2011, hier vorgestellt) und das Peka Peka House (Peka Peka, 2013), alle in Neuseeland.

KEN CROSSON est né en 1957. Il a fait ses études à l'École d'architecture de l'université d'Auckland (1976–80) et a obtenu son B.Arch en 1981. Il a créé sa société à Auckland en 1982, avant de travailler avec Covell Matthews Wheatley à Londres (1984–86) et de créer de nouveau des bureaux en Nouvelle-Zélande en 1987, puis l'entreprise actuelle en 2004, qu'il dirige avec Paul Clarke et Anna-Marie Chin. Leurs réalisations comprennent la Tutukaka House (Tutukaka, Northland, 2007) ; l'Omaha Beach House (Omaha Beach, 2007) ; la Wanaka House (Wanaka, Otago, 2007) ; l'Opito Bay House (Opito, Whitianga, 2008) ; la Birkenhead House (Birkenhead, 2010) ; la Mount Iron House (Mount Iron, 2011) ; la Hut on Sleds (Whangapoua, 2011, publiée ici) et la Peka Peka House (Peka Peka, 2013), toutes en Nouvelle-Zélande.

HUT ON SLEDS

Whangapoua, New Zealand, 2011

Area: 35 m².

The Hut on Sleds combines what might appear to be an austere exterior with dramatic glazed openings that allow the entire interior to be opened up.

Bei der Hut on Sleds verbindet eine vermeintlich herbe Außenwelt mit spektakulären Glasfenstern, mit denen sich das Innere vollständig öffnen lässt.

La cabane-traîneau combine un extérieur d'apparence plutôt austère et de spectaculaires baies vitrées qui permettent d'ouvrir entièrement l'espace intérieur.

Next to the beach, the building has a somewhat industrial appearance in the view above. Right, a section showing the sleeping and bath area at the rear and the more public areas near the large opening shutters and doors.

Am Strand stehend, hat das Gebäude auf der Ansicht oben etwas Industrielles. Rechts zeigt ein Querschnitt den Schlafbereich sowie das Bad im hinteren Teil und die öffentlicheren Bereiche in der Nähe der großen Flügeltüren.

À proximité de la plage, le bâtiment a un caractère presque industriel sur la photo ci-dessus. À droite, vue en coupe avec l'espace couchage et salle de bains à l'arrière et les parties plus communes du côté des volets et des portes à large ouverture.

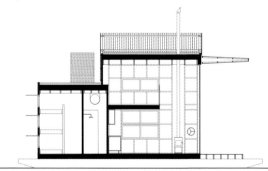

*Right, plans show the division of
space and the void in front. Set up
on the beach, the Hut allows for
great proximity to its natural setting.*

*Die Pläne rechts zeigen die
Raumaufteilung und den offenen
Bereich vorne. Am Strand aufge-
stellt, bietet das Haus eine große
Nähe zur natürlichen Umgebung.*

*À droite, les plans montrent les
divisions de l'espace et le vide
à l'avant. Posée sur une plage,
la cabane permet une vie très
proche de la nature.*

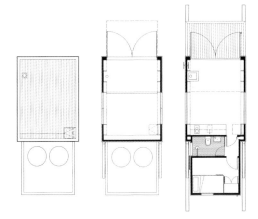

This hut was placed on a white sand beach on the Coromandel Peninsula. Since it is located in a coastal erosion zone, it is required that the structure should be removable. Set on two wooden sleds, it can be moved across the beach and onto a barge without considerable difficulty. The architects state: "The aesthetic is natural and reminiscent of a beach artifact/ perhaps a surf-life-saving or observation tower. The fittings and mechanics are industrial and obvious, the structure is gutsy and exposed." Although it measures less than 40 square meters, the structure can accommodate a family of five in a living area, two sleeping zones, and a three-tiered bunk for children. Clad in front in macrocarpa wood (*Cupressus macrocarpa*), it can be entirely closed to protect it from the elements, with the two-story front shutter serving as an awning when it is open. Double-height steel-framed glass doors can be opened behind the shutter. The rear of the structure is covered in "flat sheet"—described as "a cheap building material found in many traditional New Zealand holiday homes." A "worm tank" waste system and the extensive use of wood, together with the temporary nature of the design make the entire project highly sustainable and respectful of its sensitive dune environment.

Das Häuschen steht an einem weißen Sandstrand auf der Coromandel-Halbinsel. Da es sich hierbei um Küstenerosionsgebiet handelt, ist es unabdingbar, dass das Gebäude beweglich ist. Dank zweier hölzerner Kufen kann es ohne größere Schwierigkeiten am Strand verschoben oder auf einen Frachtkahn verladen werden. Die Architekten dazu: „Die Ästhetik ist natürlich und erinnert an eine Strandeinrichtung, eine Rettungsstation vielleicht oder einen Aussichtsturm. Die Beschläge und Mechanik sind industriell und einfach, die Konstruktion verwegen und offen." Obgleich das Haus weniger als 40 m² misst, bietet es im Wohnbereich, in zwei Schlafzonen und einer Dreierkoje für Kinder Platz für eine fünfköpfige Familie. Das Haus ist vorne mit Monterey-Zypresse *(Cupressus marcrocarpa)* verkleidet und kann mittels der über beide Geschosse reichenden Blende, die in geöffnetem Zustand als Sonnendach dient, vollständig verschlossen und vor den Elementen geschützt werden. Die stahlgerahmten Glastüren in der gleichen Höhe hinter der Blende können ebenfalls geöffnet werden. Die Gebäuderückseite ist mit *flat sheet* verkleidet – einem „preiswerten, bei vielen traditionellen Ferienhäusern in Neuseeland verwendeten Baumaterial". Dank eines „Wurm-Tank"-Abwassersystems und der extensiven Nutzung von Holz als Baustoff erweist sich das Projekt als in hohem Maß nachhaltig und nimmt Rücksicht auf die empfindliche Dünenlandschaft, in der es steht.

La cabane a été installée sur une plage de sable blanc de la péninsule de Coromandel. Comme la zone est soumise à l'érosion du littoral, la structure devait pouvoir être déplacée. Posée sur deux patins de bois, elle peut être transportée sur la plage ou sur une péniche sans grande difficulté. Les architectes expliquent que « l'esthétique est naturelle et rappelle un autre bâtiment de plage, peut-être un point de sauvetage pour surfeurs ou une tour d'observation. Les installations et éléments mécaniques sont courants et peu chers, la structure est audacieuse et aérienne ». Malgré sa surface inférieure à 40 m², elle peut loger une famille de cinq personnes avec un espace salon, deux parties couchage et trois couchettes superposées pour les enfants. L'avant est recouvert de cyprès de Lambert (*Cupressus macrocarpa*) et peut être entièrement fermé pour protéger la maison des intempéries, le volet de la hauteur de deux niveaux servant d'auvent lorsqu'il est ouvert. Derrière le volet, des baies vitrées double hauteur à cadre en acier peuvent elles aussi être ouvertes. L'arrière est revêtu de tôles lisses – « un matériau de construction bon marché présent dans de nombreuses maisons de vacances traditionnelles en Nouvelle-Zélande ». Un système d'élimination des déchets à vers et l'usage du bois à grande échelle, en même temps que la nature temporaire du concept, en font un projet extrêmement durable et respectueux de son environnement sensible de dunes.

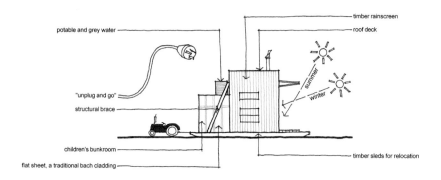

timber rainscreen

potable and grey water

roof deck

summer

winter

"unplug and go"

structural brace

children's bunkroom

timber sleds for relocation

flat sheet, a traditional bach cladding

Above, a tractor hauls the structure into place. Left, an elevation drawing describes the attention to ecological concerns.

Ein Traktor schleppt das Bauwerk an seinen Standort (oben). Links verdeutlicht ein Aufriss die ökologischen Gesichtspunkte.

En haut, un tracteur tire la cabane pour la mettre en place. À gauche, un schéma en élévation montre l'attention portée aux questions écologiques.

Above, the narrow shower space has a full-height glazed opening, with the water heater suspended above.

Der schmale Duschraum oben hat über die volle Höhe eine Glasöffnung; der Boiler ist unter der Decke aufgehängt.

Ci-dessus, la douche étroite présente une ouverture vitrée sur toute sa hauteur et le chauffe-eau suspendu au plafond.

Below, the kitchen and living
spaces; right, looking from the mezzanine out to the upper part
of the front void of the Hut.
Wood interiors give a warm
feeling to the spaces.

Unten Küche und Wohnbereich,
rechts der Blick vom Zwischen-
geschoss über den offenen
Bereich im vorderen Teil hinweg.
Einbauten aus Holz verleihen den
Räumen etwas Warmes.

Ci-dessous, la cuisine et les
espaces à vivre. À droite, vue de
la mezzanine sur la partie haute
du vide devant la cabane. Le bois
à l'intérieur crée une atmosphère
chaleureuse.

DESIGN NEUOB

Born in 1968 in Tokyo, **HIROSHI OTA** studied at the Department of Architecture, University of Tokyo (1987–91), before attending the Master's program in the same institution (1991–93). He was a research associate in the Campus Planning Office of the University of Tokyo (1993–98), before founding the firm design neuob in 2000. **TORU KASHIHARA** was born in 1972 in Hyogo Prefecture. He is the President and Chief design architect for the firm. He graduated from Kyoto University, Department of Architecture (1996), before completing a doctorate at the University of Tokyo, Graduate School of Engineering (2001). He worked with design neuob, before creating his own firm Toru Kashihara Architects (2004–09)—then returning to design neuob. Both partners studied in the laboratory of Hiroshi Hara at the University of Tokyo. Their work includes the Ouchiyama Bird Observatory (Mie, 2000); Tokoname Daiwa Kindergarten (Aichi, 2001); Kugahara Guest House (Tokyo, 2003); and Shirakawa Public Toilet (Kumamoto, 2010–11, published here), all in Japan.

Geboren 1968 in Tokio, studierte **HIROSHI OTA** an der Architekturfakultät der Universität Tokio (1987–91), bevor er ebendort das Masterprogramm absolvierte (1991–93). Er arbeitete zunächst als wissenschaftlicher Mitarbeiter im Campus-Planungsbüro der Universität (1993–98), bevor er 2000 design neuob gründete. **TORU KASHIHARA** wurde 1972 in der Präfektur Hyogo geboren. Er ist Leiter und Chefarchitekt des Büros. Seinen Universitätsabschluss machte er an der Architekturfakultät der Universität Kioto (1996) und promovierte an der Graduate School of Engineering der Universität Tokio (2001). Er arbeitete bei design neuob und betrieb dann mit Toru Kashihara Architects ein eigenes Büro (2004–09), bevor er zu design neuob zurückkehrte. Beide Partner haben an der Universität Tokio in Hiroshi Haras Labor studiert. Zu ihren Arbeiten gehören die Vogelbeobachtungsstation Ouchiyama (Mie, 2000), der Kindergarten Tokoname Daiwa (Aichi, 2011), das Kugahara Guest House (Tokio, 2003) und die öffentliche Toilette am Shirakawa-Fluss (Kumamoto, 2010–11, hier vorgestellt), alle in Japan.

Né en 1968 à Tokyo, **HIROSHI OTA** a fait ses études au département d'architecture de l'université de Tokyo (1987–91) et a ensuite suivi un programme de master dans la même institution (1991–93). Il a été chercheur au service de planification du campus de l'université de Tokyo (1993–98) et a fondé la société design neuob en 2000. **TORU KASHIHARA** est né en 1972 dans la préfecture de Hyogo. Il est le président et architecte concepteur en chef de l'agence. Il est diplômé du département d'architecture de l'université de Kyoto (1996) et a ensuite fait un doctorat à la Graduate School of Engineering de l'université de Tokyo (2001). Il a travaillé avec design neuob, puis a créé sa propre agence Toru Kashihara Architects (2004–09) avant de revenir à design neuob. Ils ont tous les deux été étudiants au laboratoire de Hiroshi Hara à l'université de Tokyo. Leurs réalisations comprennent l'observatoire d'oiseaux Ouchiyama (Mie, 2000) ; le jardin d'enfants Tokoname Daiwa (Aichi, 2001) ; la maison d'hôtes Kugahara (Tokyo, 2003) et les toilettes publiques Shirakawa (Kumamoto, 2010–11, publié ici), toutes au Japon.

SHIRAKAWA PUBLIC TOILET

Kumamoto City, Japan, 2010–11

Area: 11.6 m². Client: Kumamoto City. Cost: ¥13.5 million.

The architects call this Public Toilet a "small landmark on the riverbank." It is located five minutes from the Kumamoto Station and faces the Shirakawa River. The development of this area is part of the ongoing Kumamoto Artpolis project. Design neuob sought to create a link between their small work and two entrances to Kumamoto Station designed by Mitsuhiko Sato and Ryue Nishizawa in 2012, and an earlier art project by Kazuko Fujie on the Shirakawa Bridge (1992). The tree-shaped parts of the design are made of cast iron. The architects state: "We did not want it to be serious, but tried to be charming enough to welcome visitors from the station, and friendly enough to greet the residents who pass over the bridge. Another reason for the tree-shape is that we wanted to add softened and humanized atmosphere in the landscape of river area, which seemed us too oversized and too engineer-designed." Japanese regulations do not allow the planting of trees on riverbanks for reasons of flood control—so the architects planted their iron trees there nonetheless.

Die Architekten bezeichnen diese öffentliche Toilette als „kleines Wahrzeichen am Flussufer". Es ist fünf Minuten vom Bahnhof Kumamoto entfernt und zum Shirakawa-Fluss hin ausgerichtet. Die Entwicklung des Gebiets ist Teil des laufenden Kumamoto-Artpolis-Projekts. Design neuob wollte eine Verbindung zwischen dem kleinen Gebäude, den zwei Eingängen des von Mitsuhiko Sato und Ryue Nishizawa 2012 entworfenen Bahnhofs von Kumamoto und einer etwas älteren Installation von Kazuko Fujie auf der Shirakawa-Brücke (1992) herstellen. Die baumartigen Teile des Gebäudes sind aus Gusseisen. Dazu die Architekten: „Wir wollen es nicht zu ernst, sondern charmant genug, um Besucher aus Richtung Bahnhof anzulocken, und freundlich genug, um so die Bewohner zu begrüßen, die über die Brücke kommen. Durch die Baumform wollten wir der Uferlandschaft, die uns viel zu überdimensioniert und -technisiert erschien, außerdem etwas atmosphärisch Weiches und Menschliches hinzufügen." Aus Gründen des Hochwasserschutzes verbietet es die japanische Gesetzgebung, an Flussufern Bäume zu pflanzen – die Architekten setzten ihre eisernen Bäume einfach trotzdem dort hin.

Les architectes décrivent ces toilettes publiques comme « un petit jalon sur les berges » – elles sont situées à 5 minutes de la gare de Kumamoto, face à la rivière Shirakawa. Le développement de cette zone fait partie du projet en cours Kumamoto Artpolis. Design neuob a cherché à créer en lien entre leur petite construction et deux entrées de la gare de Kumamoto, créées par Mitsuhiko Sato et Ryue Nishizawa en 2012, ainsi qu'un projet artistique plus ancien de Kazuko Fujie sur le pont de la Shirakawa (1992). Les formes d'arbres sont en fonte. Les architectes ont expliqué : « Nous ne voulions pas en faire un lieu sérieux, nous avons essayé de le rendre assez charmant pour accueillir les voyageurs venant de la gare et assez sympathique pour saluer les habitants de la ville qui passent sur le pont. L'autre raison des formes d'arbres est que nous souhaitions adoucir et humaniser l'atmosphère dans ce paysage fluvial qui nous semblait trop démesuré et conçu trop industriellement. » Les lois japonaises interdisent de planter des arbres sur les berges pour des raisons de contrôle des crues – mais les architectes y ont quand même placé leurs arbres de fer.

The architects have created an
unusual mixture between angled
modern forms and willfully organic
metal "trees" in this quite visible
setting.

Für diesen recht exponierten
Standort haben die Architekten
eine ungewöhnliche Mixtur aus
modernen, schrägen Formen und
betont organischen „Metallbäumen"
geschaffen.

Les architectes ont créé un mélange
inhabituel de formes modernes
anguleuses et d'«arbres» métalliques délibérément organiques
dans un décor apparent.

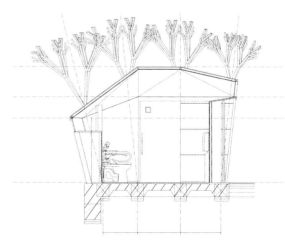

2

144

For the Japanese, toilets must be both modern and clean. Here, bright colors are added to the high ceilings and daylight to make the space as agreeable as possible.

Japanern ist es wichtig, dass Toiletten sowohl modern als auch sauber sind. Hier wurden helle Farben, hohe Decken und Tageslicht kombiniert, um den Ort so angenehm wie möglich zu machen.

Pour les Japonais, les toilettes se doivent d'être à la fois modernes et propres. Ici, des couleurs vives sont associées à une grande hauteur de plafond et à la lumière naturelle pour rendre l'endroit aussi agréable que possible.

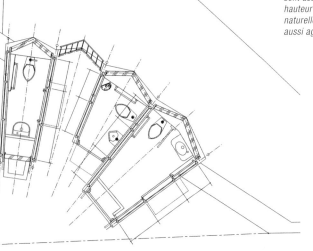

The structure has an almost alien presence at night, as seen in the image below, but the organic aspect somehow escapes from the "postmodern" connotation that such tree-like additions might have elicited.

Das Gebäude sieht nachts fast außerirdisch aus, wie im Bild unten erkennbar; der Aspekt des Organischen, den solche „postmodernen" baumartigen Zusätze hätten hervorrufen können, geht eher verloren.

Le bâtiment dégage une présence presque extraterrestre la nuit, comme ci-dessous, mais l'aspect organique échappe pour ainsi dire à la connotation « postmoderne » que ce type d'ajout arboré pourrait suggérer.

SHUHEI ENDO

Born in Shiga Prefecture, Japan, in 1960, **SHUHEI ENDO** obtained his Master's degree from the Kyoto City University of Art in 1986. He worked after that with the architect Osamu Ishii and established his own firm, the Endo Shuhei Architect Institute, in 1988. His work has been widely published and he has received numerous prizes including the Andrea Palladio International Prize in Italy (1993). He is currently Professor at the Graduate School of Architecture, Kobe University. His work includes Slowtecture S (Maihara, Shiga, 2002); Growtecture S (Osaka, 2002); Springtecture B (Biwa-cho, Shiga, 2002); Bubbletecture M (Maihara, Shiga, 2003); Rooftecture C (Taishi, Hyogo, 2003); Rooftecture H (Kamigori, Hyogo, 2004); and Bubbletecture O (Maruoka, Fukui, 2004). Along with Bubbletecture H (Sayo-cho, Hyogo, 2006–07), he completed Slowtecture M (Miki, Hyogo) and Rooftecture M (Habikino, Osaka) in 2007, all in Japan. He continues to use the same system of names for his projects, completing Rooftecture OT2 in 2012 (Osaka, published here).

SHUHEI ENDO, geboren 1960 in der japanischen Präfektur Shiga, machte 1986 an der Kunstuniversität der Stadt Kyoto seinen Master. Danach arbeitete er mit dem Architekten Osamu Ishii zusammen und gründete 1988 sein eigenes Büro, das Endo Shuhei Architect Institute. Über seine Arbeit ist viel geschrieben worden, und er hat zahlreiche Preise erhalten, u. a. den Andrea Palladio International Prize in Italien (1993). Derzeit ist er Professor an der Graduate School of Architecture an der Universität Kobe. Zu seinen Arbeiten gehören Slowtecture S (Maihara, Shiga, 2002), Growtecture S (Osaka, 2002), Springtecture B (Biwa-cho, Shiga, 2002), Bubbletecture M (Maihara, Shiga, 2003), Rooftecture C (Taishi, Hyogo, 2003), Rooftecture H (Kamigori, Hyogo, 2004) und Bubbletecture O (Maruoka, Fukui, 2004). Zeitgleich mit Bubbletecture H (Sayo-cho, Hyogo, 2006–07) stellte er 2007 Slowtecture M (Miki, Hyogo) und Rooftecture M (Habikino, Osaka), alle in Japan, fertig. Auch weiterhin verwendet er bei seinen Projekten dieselbe Systematik der Namensgebung. Rooftecture OT2 (Osaka, hier vorgestellt) wurde 2012 realisiert.

Né dans la préfecture de Shiga, au Japon, en 1960, **SHUHEI ENDO** a obtenu son master de l'Université des arts de Kyoto en 1986. Il a ensuite travaillé pour l'architecte Osamu Ishii et fondé sa propre agence, Endo Shuhei Architect Institute, en 1988. Son œuvre a été largement publié et a reçu de nombreuses distinctions, dont le prix Andrea Palladio International en Italie (1993). Il enseigne actuellement à l'École supérieure d'architecture de l'université de Kôbe. Parmi ses réalisations : Slowtecture S (Maihara, Shiga, 2002) ; Growtecture S (Osaka, 2002) ; Springtecture B (Biwa-cho, Shiga, 2002) ; Bubbletecture M (Maihara, 2003) ; Rooftecture C (Taishi, Hyogo, 2003) ; Rooftecture H (Kamigori, Hyogo, 2004) et Bubbletecture O (Maruoka, Fukui, 2004). Parallèlement à Bubbletecture H (Sayo-cho, Hyogo, 2006–07), il a achevé Slowtecture M (Miki, Hyogo) et Rooftecture M (Habikino, Osaka) en 2007, toujours au Japon. En utilisant toujours le même système de noms, il a terminé Rooftecture OT2 en 2012 (Osaka, publié ici).

ROOFTECTURE OT2

Osaka, Japan, 2012

Area: 128 m².
Collaboration: Aoi Endo, Aya Houri.

Although its total floor area is a respectable 128 square meters, this house for a couple and their three children in the heart of Osaka has a footprint of just 44 square meters and a site that is only 55 square meters in area. Set on a busy street, the house has a relatively closed perforated metal façade that nonetheless provides the necessary light and ventilation. An operable skylight, set above the central stairway, encourages airflow through the home. The perforation of the façade gives it a particular presence at night. The structure is three stories in height and has an inner atrium. A "Harvest Panel" system is used for inside walls and ceilings, creating a warm contrast to the metallic appearance of the exterior of the house.

Obgleich sich die Gesamtnutzfläche auf respektable 128 m² beläuft, hat dieses von zwei Erwachsenen und drei Kindern bewohnte Haus im Zentrum von Osaka eine Grundfläche von lediglich 44 m² und eine Grundstücksgröße von gerade einmal 55 m². Das Gebäude, an einer geschäftigen Straße gelegen, verfügt über eine relativ geschlossene Fassade aus perforierten Metallplatten, die für die nötige Licht- und Luftzufuhr sorgen. Ein steuerbares Oberlicht fördert die Luftzirkulation im Haus zusätzlich. Die Perforierung der Fassade verleiht ihr bei Dunkelheit eine besondere Präsenz. Das Gebäude verfügt über drei Geschosse, im Innern befindet sich ein Atrium. Innenwände und Decken wurden mit Grobspanplatten verkleidet, was einen warmen Kontrast zum metallischen Äußeren des Hauses schafft.

Malgré une respectable superficie totale de 128 m², l'empreinte au sol de cette maison conçue pour un couple et ses trois enfants au centre d'Osaka ne dépasse pas 44 m² sur un terrain de seulement 55 m². Située dans une rue animée, elle présente une façade métallique perforée assez fermée qui laisse néanmoins pénétrer l'air et la lumière nécessaires. Une lucarne au-dessus de l'escalier central peut être ouverte et favorise la circulation d'air dans toute la maison. La perforation de la façade lui confère une présence insolite la nuit. La construction s'élève sur trois niveaux et a un patio intérieur. Les murs et plafonds intérieurs sont recouverts de panneaux «Harvest» qui créent un contraste chaleureux avec l'aspect métallique de la maison à l'extérieur.

Working in the extremely dense urban fabric of Osaka where small structures are very common, the architect combines a continuous exterior appearance with an intriguing, translucent aspect.

Inmitten des extrem dichten urbanen Gewebes von Osaka, wo kleine Bauten üblich sind, verbindet der Architekt ein geschlossenes äußeres Erscheinungsbild mit faszinierender Transluzenz.

L'architecte a installé sa maison dans le tissu urbain extrêmement dense d'Osaka où les petites structures sont très courantes. Il associe un aspect extérieur continu à une fascinante translucidité.

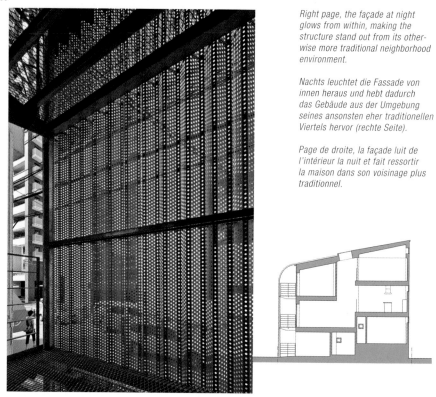

Right page, the façade at night glows from within, making the structure stand out from its otherwise more traditional neighborhood environment.

Nachts leuchtet die Fassade von innen heraus und hebt dadurch das Gebäude aus der Umgebung seines ansonsten eher traditionellen Viertels hervor (rechte Seite).

Page de droite, la façade luit de l'intérieur la nuit et fait ressortir la maison dans son voisinage plus traditionnel.

Details show the perforated metal façade from different angles—either quite opaque or rather transparent depending on the angle of view and the light.

Detailaufnahmen zeigen aus verschiedenen Perspektiven die perforierte Metallfassade, die sich je nach Blickwinkel und Lichteinfall beinahe dicht oder ziemlich transparent zeigt.

Les détails montrent la façade métallique perforée sous différents angles – plutôt opaque ou transparente, selon le point de vue et la lumière.

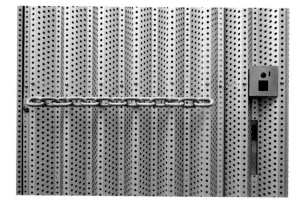

Wood or particle-board interiors and a stairway that appears to hang in space give liveliness and a certain degree of warmth to the enclosed spaces.

Einbauten aus Holz oder Spanplatten und eine Treppe, die im Raum zu schweben scheint, verleihen den geschlossenen Räumen Lebendigkeit und eine gewisse Wärme.

Avec l'escalier qui semble suspendu, le bois et les panneaux de particules de l'intérieur donnent de la vie et une certaine chaleur aux espaces clos.

Quite different in feeling as compared to the metallic façade, the interior is both open and bright thanks to skylights.

Im deutlichen Kontrast zur metallenen Fassade erweist sich das Innere dank der Oberlichter als offen und hell.

Grâce aux lucarnes, l'intérieur est à la fois ouvert et clair, il produit un sentiment très différent de la façade métallique.

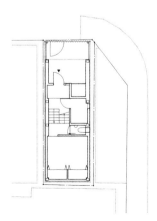

MASAKI ENDOH

MASAKI ENDOH was born in Tokyo, Japan, in 1963. He graduated from the Science University of Tokyo in 1987 and completed an M.Arch. in 1989, at the same university. He worked for the KAI-Workshop (1989–94), and established his firm EDH Endoh Design House in 1994. He has been a Professor at Chiba Institute of Technology since 2008. He was awarded the Tokyo House Prize for Natural Shelter in 2000; the Yoshioka Award for Natural Shelter in 2000; and the JIA "Rookie of the Year 2003" for Natural Ellipse in 2003. His works include Natural Shelter (Tokyo, 1999); Natural Illuminance (Tokyo, 2001); Natural Slats (Tokyo, 2002); Natural Ellipse (Tokyo, 2002); Natural Wedge (Tokyo, 2003); Natural Strata (Kawasaki, 2003); and, more recently, Natural Illuminance II (Tokyo, 2010–11, published here); and Natural Strip IV (Tokyo, 2010–11), all in Japan.

MASAKI ENDOH wurde 1963 in Tokio geboren. Er schloss sein Studium 1987 an der Naturwissenschaftlichen Universität Tokio ab und absolvierte dort 1989 seinen M. Arch. Nach seiner Tätigkeit für den KAI-Workshop (1989–94) gründete er 1994 sein Büro EDH Endoh Design House. Endoh ist seit 2008 Professor am Chiba Institute of Technology. 2000 wurde er für sein Projekt Natural Shelter mit dem Tokyo House Prize und dem Yoshioka Award ausgezeichnet sowie 2003 mit dem „Rookie of the Year 2003" der JIA für das Projekt Natural Ellipse. Zu seinen Projekten zählen Natural Shelter (Tokio, 1999), Natural Illuminance (Tokio, 2001), Natural Slats (Tokio, 2002), Natural Ellipse (Tokio, 2002), Natural Wedge (Tokio, 2003), Natural Strata (Kawasaki, 2003) sowie in jüngerer Zeit Natural Illuminance II (Tokio, 2010–11, hier vorgestellt) und Natural Strip IV (Tokio, 2010–11).

MASAKI ENDOH, né à Tokyo en 1963, est diplômé de l'Université des sciences de Tokyo (1987) et a obtenu son M.Arch. de la même institution en 1989. Il a travaillé pour l'agence KAI-Workshop (1989-94) et fondé sa propre structure EDH, Endoh Design House, en 1994. Il est professeur à l'Institut de technologie de Chiba depuis 2008. En 2000, il a reçu le prix de la maison de Tokyo et le prix Yoshioka pour son Natural Shelter et le « Rookie of the Year 2003 » de la JIA pour Natural Ellipse en 2003. Ses réalisations récentes, toutes au Japon, comprennent les maisons Natural Shelter (Tokyo, 1999) ; Natural Illuminance (Tokyo, 2001) ; Natural Slats (Tokyo, 2002) ; Natural Ellipse (Tokyo, 2002) ; Natural Wedge (Tokyo, 2003) ; Natural Strata (Kawasaki, 2003) et, plus récemment, Natural Illuminance II (Tokyo, 2010–11, publiée ici) et Natural Strip IV (Tokyo, 2010-11).

NATURAL ILLUMINANCE II

Tokyo, Japan, 2010–11

Area: 37.50 m².

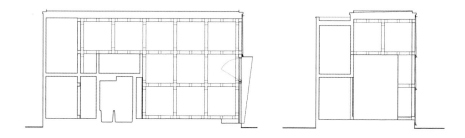

This small house was designed with a wood-beam frame clad on the exterior with translucent glass. A grid of wooden squares forms the interior walls, with the gaps between the squares covered with translucent plastic that allow daylight in from all angles. Masaki Endoh explains that these strips form a surface equivalent to a single large window and yet they provide light from every side. The architect explains that the design actually consists of two structures—one being the high-ceilinged living room and the other a wood-framed loft with steel walls containing the kitchen, master bedroom, and children's bedroom. The architects explain: "This is the smallest house ever designed by EDH, built for Mr. Endoh's brother. The land plot and volume (cubic meters) are of an average size for central Tokyo. Building area is limited by law, so space must be used efficiently. The house is just as small as any other in the neighborhood but the high-ceilinged living room, loft, and smaller bedrooms allocate more room to areas used by the entire family and give a sense of spaciousness."

Das kleine Haus ist im Prinzip eine transluzent verschalte Holzrahmenkonstruktion. Markantes Merkmal des Innenraums ist ein Raster aus Holzquadraten, durch dessen Zwischenräume aus transluzentem Kunststoff allseitig Tageslicht einfällt. Masaki Endoh zufolge entspricht die Gesamtfläche der Lichtstreifen einem großen Einzelfenster, erlaubt jedoch Lichteinfall von allen Seiten. Der Architekt verweist auf die Gliederung des Entwurfs in zwei Volumina – einen hohen Wohnraum sowie einen Holzrahmenanbau mit Stahlwänden für Küche, Elternschlafzimmer und Kinderzimmer. Den Architekten zufolge ist „das Haus der kleinste bis dato von EDH entworfene Wohnbau, geplant für den Bruder von Masaki Endoh. Grundstücksgröße und -volumen (in m³) sind für Tokioter Verhältnisse durchschnittlich. Die Bebauungsfläche ist gesetzlich vorgeschrieben, weshalb eine effiziente Raumnutzung unverzichtbar ist. Das Haus ist ebenso klein wie seine Nachbarbauten, doch der hohe Wohnbereich, der Anbau und die kleinen Schlafzimmer bieten eine bessere Raumnutzung für die gemeinschaftlich von der Familie genutzten Bereiche und vermitteln Großzügigkeit."

Cette petite maison à ossature en bois, construite pour le frère de Masaki Endoh, est en grande partie habillée de verre translucide. À l'intérieur, l'ossature en bois montée sur une trame carrée reste visible, les vides étant remplis par des panneaux de plastique translucide. Masaki Endoh explique que ces bandeaux de lumière forment une surface équivalente à une grande baie, mais éclairent en même temps de tous les côtés. Le projet se compose, en fait, de deux éléments : le premier est un séjour sous grande hauteur de plafond, et le second un loft à ossature de bois également mais à murs d'acier, contenant la cuisine, la chambre principale et la chambre des enfants. « C'est la plus petite maison jamais conçue par EDH, explique l'architecte, la taille de la parcelle et le volume disponible sont de dimensions normales pour le centre de Tokyo. La constructibilité des terrains est limitée par la réglementation, et l'espace doit donc être utilisé de manière efficace. Si la maison est aussi petite que ses voisines, le séjour à hauts plafonds, le loft, et les petites chambres accordent à la famille davantage de place que d'habitude et donnent le sentiment de volumes spacieux. »

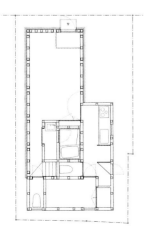

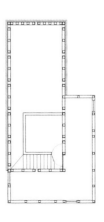

The plan of the house and its eleva-
tions do not fully prepare the viewer
for its unusual pattern of openings
and its essentially closed nature.

*Grund- und Aufrisse bereiten
den Besucher nicht wirklich auf
die Wirkung der ungewöhnlichen
Öffnungen und die prinzipielle
Geschlossenheit des Hauses vor.*

Le plan et les élévations de la
maison ne préparent pas vraiment le
visiteur à l'aspect très fermé de la
maison et au rythme surprenant des
ouvertures.

ROBIN FALCK

ROBIN FALCK was born in 1990. He received his B.A. degree in Industrial Design from the Aalto University of Art, Design, and Architecture (Helsinki) in 2011. He has been the Creative Director of his own firm, Falck Helsinki, since 2012. Before that, he worked as a photographer. As he is quite young, his project list is not long, but it is clear that Robin Falck has numerous talents, including those required to design Nido (published here), when he was just 19.

ROBIN FALCK wurde 1990 geboren und erwarb 2011 seinen Bachelor in Industriedesign an der Aalto University of Art, Design and Architecture (Helsinki). Seit 2012 ist er Kreativdirektor seiner eigenen Firma, Falck Helsinki. Davor arbeitete er als Fotograf. Angesichts seines jugendlichen Alters ist seine Projektliste nicht lang, aber es ist klar, dass Robin Falck vielerlei Begabungen hat, darunter solche, die ihn für die Planung von Nido (hier veröffentlicht) befähigten, als er erst 19 Jahre alt war.

ROBIN FALCK est né en 1990. il a obtenu son B.A. de design industriel à l'université Aalto d'art, design et architecture (Helsinki) en 2011. il a d'abord travaillé comme photographe, puis est devenu directeur de la création de sa propre agence, Falck Helsinki, en 2012. Il est encore très jeune, de sorte que sa liste de réalisations n'est pas longue, mais il est évident qu'il possède de nombreux talents, parmi lesquels ceux qu'il a déployés pour créer Nido (publié ici) alors qu'il avait seulement 19 ans.

NIDO

Sipoo, Finland

Area: 9 m². Cost: €10 000.

Nido was designed by Robin Falck in 2009 and built after his military service (2009–10), completed in 2011. This cabin was designed to be built without a permit. The designer states that he "wanted to maximize the use of this space, just having the essentials and stripping away all the unnecessary parts," a philosophy that he now follows as a designer. The top level has a bed and space to keep clothes and books. A table was made with left-over materials. Falck used locally sourced wood and enlisted the help of a local carpenter to build the window frame and door. The cabin is insulated with flax and is warmed during the winter with a small heat fan. Colors were chosen to "mimic a large boulder and let it melt into the surroundings easily." He called the cabin "Nido" (meaning "bird's nest" in Italian) because his own name, Falck, means "falcon" in Swedish.

Robin Falck entwarf Nido im Jahr 2009 und stellte das Projekt 2011 nach seinem Armeedienst (2009–10) fertig. Es sollte ohne Baugenehmigung errichtet werden können. Der Designer wollte die „maximale Ausnutzung eines Raums, der nur mit dem Notwendigsten ausgestattet und von allem Überflüssigen befreit ist" – eine Philosophie, der er auch weiterhin folgt. Im Obergeschoss befinden sich ein Bett sowie Stauraum für Kleidung und Bücher. Der Tisch wurde aus Ausschussmaterialien angefertigt. Robin Falck griff auf Holz aus der Region zurück und ließ sich von einem Tischler aus der Gegend beim Bau der Holzrahmen für Fenster und Türen helfen. Das Projekt verfügt über eine Flachsdämmung und wird im Winter mit einem kleinen Lüfter beheizt. Die Farbgebung sollte „einen großen Felsen nachahmen" und das Gebäude „mit der Umgebung verschmelzen". Falck nannte sein Projekt „Nido" (nach dem italienischen Wort für „Vogelnest"). Sein Nachname bedeutet auf Deutsch „Falke".

Robin Falck a dessiné Nido en 2009 et l'a construit après son service militaire (2009–10), puis achevé en 2011. La cabane devait pouvoir être bâtie sans permis de construire. Le designer explique qu'il « a voulu optimiser l'usage de l'espace, se contenter de l'essentiel et se débarrasser de tout ce qui n'est pas nécessaire », une philosophie qui est encore la sienne aujourd'hui. Le lit se trouve à l'étage, avec un espace de rangement pour des vêtements et des livres. Une table a été fabriquée avec des matériaux de récupération. Robin Falck a uniquement utilisé du bois d'origine locale et s'est assuré le concours d'un menuisier de la région pour l'encadrement de la fenêtre et la porte. La cabane est isolée avec du lin et chauffée par un petit radiateur soufflant en hiver. Les couleurs ont été choisies pour « imiter un gros rocher et permettre à la maison de se fondre facilement dans le décor ». L'architecte l'a appelée « Nido » (« nid » en italien) parce que son nom à lui, Falck, signifie « faucon » en suédois.

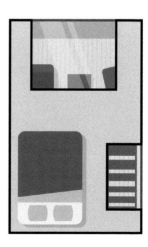

Although the design appears to be quite simple, it has a number of unexpected features, such as the very large inclined window.

Trotz seiner Einfachheit besitzt der Entwurf eine Reihe überraschender Merkmale, darunter das große Dachschrägenfenster.

Malgré une conception d'apparence plutôt simple, la construction possède de nombreux éléments inattendus, comme la très grande fenêtre.

TERUNOBU FUJIMORI

Born in Chino City, Nagano, Japan, in 1946, **TERUNOBU FUJIMORI** attended Tohoku University (1965–71) in Sendai, before receiving his Ph.D. in Architecture from the University of Tokyo (1971–78). He is a Professor Emeritus at the University of Tokyo's Institute of Industrial Science. Although research on Western-style buildings in Japan from the Meiji period onwards remains his main activity, he is also a practicing architect. His first built work was the Jinchokan Moriya Historical Museum (Chino City, Nagano, 1990–91), which won mixed praise for the use of local materials over a reinforced-concrete structure. Other completed projects include the Akino Fuku Art Museum (Hamamatsu, Shizuoka, 1995–97); Nira House (Leek House, Machida City, Tokyo, 1995–97); Student Dormitory for Kumamoto Agricultural College (Koshi City, Kumamoto, 1998–2000); Ichiya-tei (One Night Tea House, Ashigarashimo, Kanagawa, 2003); Chashitsu Tetsu (Tea House Tetsu, Musée Kiyoharu Shi-rakaba, Nakamaru, Hokuto City, Yamanashi, 2005); and Charred Cedar House (Nagano City, Nagano, 2006–07). Recent work includes the Beetle's House (Victoria and Albert Museum, London, UK, 2010, published here); the Walking Café (Munich, Germany, 2012); Hamamatsu House (Shizuoka, 2012); and the Stork House (Vienna, Austria, 2013), all in Japan unless stated otherwise.

TERUNOBU FUJIMORI, geboren 1949 in Chino, im japanischen Nagano, studierte zunächst an der Tohoku-Universität in Sendai (1965–71), bevor er an der Universität Tokio (1971–78) in Architektur promovierte. Er ist emeritierter Professor am dortigen Institute of Industrial Science. Auch wenn er sich hauptsächlich seiner Forschung zu westlich beeinflussten Gebäuden in Japan seit der Meiji-Zeit widmet, ist er als Architekt tätig. Sein erster realisierter Entwurf war das Historische Museum Jinchokan Moriya (Chino, Nagano, 1990–91), wobei das Zusammenspiel lokaler Materialien mit einem Stahlbetonrohbau gemischte Reaktionen hervorrief. Weitere realisierte Projekte sind das Kunstmuseum Akino Fuku (Hamamatsu, Shizuoka, 1995–97), Nira-Haus (Lauchhaus, Machida, Tokio, 1995–97), das Studentenwohnheim des Kumamoto Agricultural College (Koshi, Kumamoto, 1998–2000), Ichiya-tei (Eine-Nacht-Teehaus, Ashigarashimo, Kanagawa, 2003), das Chashitsu Tetsu (Tee-haus Tetsu, Kiyoharu Shirakaba Museum, Nakamaru, Hokuto, Yamanashi, 2005) und das Haus aus versengter Zeder (Nagano, Nagano, 2006–07). Zu seinen jüngeren Arbeiten zählen das Beetle's House (Victoria and Albert Museum, London, 2010, hier vorgestellt), das Walking Café (München, 2012), das Haus Hamamatsu (Shizuoka, 2012) und das Storchenhaus (Wien, 2013).

Né à Chino City, Nagano (Japon) en 1946, **TERUNOBU FUJIMORI** a suivi les cours de l'université Tohoku (1965-71) à Sendai avant d'obtenir son doctorat en architecture à l'université de Tokyo (1971–78). Il est aujourd'hui professeur émérite à l'Institut de science industrielle de l'université de Tokyo. Il continue de pratiquer l'architecture, même si la recherche sur les bâtiments de style occidental au Japon à partir de la période Meiji reste son activité principale. Son premier projet construit a été le Musée historique Jinchokan Moriya (Chino City, Nagano, 1990–91) qui a reçu un accueil mitigé en raison du choix de matériaux locaux sur une structure en béton armé. Ses autres réalisations achevées comprennent le Musée d'art Akino Fuku (Hamamatsu, Shizuoka, 1995–97) ; la maison Nira (Leek House, Machida City, Tokyo, 1995–97) ; le dortoir des étudiants du collège agricole de Kumamoto (Koshi City, Kumamoto, 1998–2000) ; Ichiya-tei (One Night Tea House, Ashigarashimo, Kana-gawa, 2003) ; Chashitsu Tetsu (maison de thé Tetsu, musée Kiyoharu Shirakaba, Nakamaru, Hokuto City, Yamanashi, 2005) et la Maison de cèdre brûlé (Nagano City, Nagano, 2006–07). Parmi ses projets récents : *Beetle's House* (Victoria and Albert Museum, Londres, 2010, publiée ici) ; le Walking Café (Munich, 2012) ; la Maison Hamamatsu (Shizuoka, 2012) et la Maison de la cigogne (Vienne, Autriche, 2013), tous au Japon sauf mention contraire.

BEETLE'S HOUSE

Victoria and Albert Museum, London, UK, 2010

Area: 4 m².
Client: Victoria and Albert Museum.

This was part of the exhibition *1:1 Architects Build Small Spaces 2010* held at the Victoria and Albert Museum in London from June 15 to August 30, 2010. For this exhibition, the museum invited 19 architects to submit proposals for small structures that examine notions of refuge and retreat. Seven of these proposals were selected for construction—including those by Sou Fujimoto, and Rintala Eggertsson with their Ark Booktower (see page 424). Another selected architect was Terunobu Fujimori. He writes: "In the architectural history of the world, the Japanese teahouse is the one and only example of small building acknowledged as a building type. For adults, first-class Japanese architects made very small, independent buildings. Given this history, I made a teahouse for drinking tea in the United Kingdom. After the black tea, charcoal was used for inside and outside finishes." The architect emphasizes the fact that people throughout history have been partial to small comfortable spaces—though his elevated teahouse may not have inspired a sense of security for all who entered it. "My first plan," says Fujimori "was to suspend it, but that was not feasible and it finally had legs."

Das Haus war Teil der Ausstellung „1:1 Architects Build Small Spaces 2010", die vom 15. Juni bis 30. August im Victoria and Albert Museum in London zu sehen war. Für die Ausstellung hatte das Museum 19 Architekten um Vorschläge für kleine Bauwerke gebeten, die sich mit den Themen Zuflucht und Rückzug auseinandersetzen. Sieben Vorschläge wurden ausgewählt und realisiert – einschließlich jener von Sou Fujimoto und Rintala Eggertsson mit ihrem Ark Booktower (siehe Seite 424). Auch Terunobu Fujimori zählte zu den Ausgewählten. Er schreibt: „In der Architekturgeschichte der Welt ist das japanische Teehaus das einzige Beispiel eines kleinen Bauwerks, das als eigener Gebäudetypus anerkannt ist. Erstklassige japanische Architekten haben sehr kleine, freistehende Gebäude für Erwachsene gestaltet. Vor diesem Hintergrund habe ich ein eigenes Teehaus für Großbritannien entworfen. Die für Innen- und Außenflächen verwendete Holzkohle spielt auf den Schwarztee an." Der Architekt betont, dass es zu allen Zeiten Menschen gegeben habe, die eine spezielle Vorliebe für kleine, heimelige Räume gehegt haben – obwohl sein aufgeständertes Teehaus vielleicht nicht allen, die es betreten haben, ein Gefühl von Sicherheit vermittelte. „Meine erste Idee war", so Fujimori, „es aufzuhängen, aber das war nicht realisierbar, und am Ende hatte es dann Beine."

Le projet faisait partie de l'exposition « 1:1 Architects Build Small Spaces 2010 » au Victoria and Albert Museum de Londres du 15 juin au 30 août 2010. Le musée avait invité 19 architectes à faire des propositions de petites structures étudiant la notion de refuge et de retraite. Sept des propositions ont ensuite été sélectionnées pour être construites – dont celle de Sou Fujimoto et l'Ark Booktower de Rintala Eggertsson (p. 424). Terunobu Fujimori était l'un des autres architectes sélectionnés. Il écrit : « Dans l'histoire de l'architecture mondiale, la maison de thé japonaise est le seul et unique exemple de petite construction reconnue comme un type de bâtiment en soi. De remarquables architectes japonais ont ainsi réalisé de toutes petites maisons indépendantes pour adultes. Je me suis basé sur ce passé et j'ai créé une maison pour boire du thé au Royaume-Uni. Après le thé noir, j'ai utilisé du charbon de bois pour les finitions intérieures et extérieures. » L'architecte souligne par ailleurs qu'à travers l'histoire les hommes ont toujours aimé les petits espaces confortables – même si cette maison de thé surélevée n'inspire pas forcément un sentiment de sécurité à ceux qui y entrent. « Ma première idée, dit-il, était de suspendre la construction, mais cela n'a pas pu être réalisé, et elle a donc des pattes. »

Fujimori has designed a number of tree houses or suspended tea ceremony spaces. Drawings show the limited space and the unexpected, almost humorous design.

Fujimori hat bereits eine Reihe von Baumhäusern oder hängenden Räumlichkeiten für die Teezeremonie konzipiert. Die Zeichnungen zeigen die limitierten Raumverhältnisse und den überraschenden, beinahe humorvollen Entwurf.

Fujimori a déjà créé de nombreuses maisons dans les arbres et maisons de thé suspendues. Les dessins montrent l'étroitesse de l'espace et le design totalement inattendu et presque humoristique.

Interiors have an artistic patterning, heightened by the irregular forms. As his drawings show, the house can either be suspended or set up on legs.

Der Innenraum hat ein künstlerisches Muster, das durch unregelmäßige Formen betont wird. Wie Fujimoris Zeichnungen zeigen, kann das Haus sowohl aufgehängt als auch auf Ständer gestellt werden.

Un motif artistique orne l'intérieur, rehaussé par l'irrégularité des formes. Comme le montrent les schémas, la maison peut être suspendue ou posée sur des pieds.

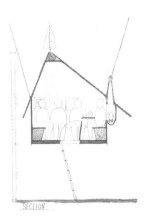

SECTION

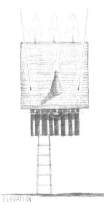

ELEVATION

If not suspended, legs are needed.

The Japanese are, of course, used to small spaces and also place importance in the precise locations of significant objects, such as the teapot seen in this image taken from the high point of the structure.

Die Japaner sind natürlich an kleine Räume gewöhnt und legen zudem Wert auf die präzise Anordnung wichtiger Objekte wie etwa die Teekanne auf diesem Bild, das vom höchsten Punkt des Gebäudes aus aufgenommen wurde.

Naturellement, les Japonais sont habitués aux petits espaces et accordent de l'importance aux emplacements précis des objets importants, comme la théière qu'on voit sur cette photo prise depuis le point le plus haut de la construction.

SOU FUJIMOTO

SOU FUJIMOTO was born in 1971. He received a B.Arch. degree from the University of Tokyo, Faculty of Engineering, Department of Architecture (1990–94). He established his own firm, Sou Fujimoto Architects, in 2000. He is considered one of the most interesting rising Japanese architects, and his forms usually evade easy classification. His work includes the Industrial Training Facilities for the Mentally Handicapped (Hokkaido, 2003); Environment Art Forum, Annaka (Gunma, 2003–06); Treatment Center for Mentally Disturbed Children (Hokkaido, 2006); House O (Chiba, 2007); N House (Oita Prefecture, 2007–08); and the Final Wooden House (Kumamura, Kumamoto, 2007–08). Other recent work includes his participation in Toyo Ito's Sumika Project (House Before House, Utsunomiya, Tochigi, 2008); Musashino Art University Museum and Library (Tokyo, 2007–09); House H (Tokyo, 2008–09); Tokyo Apartment (Itabashiku, Tokyo, 2009–10); the Uniqlo Store in Shinsaibashi (Osaka, 2010); House NA (Tokyo, 2010); House K (Nishinomiya-shi, Hyogo, 2011–12, published here); and the 2013 Serpentine Summer Pavilion (Kensington Gardens, London, UK, 2013), all in Japan unless stated otherwise.

SOU FUJIMOTO wurde 1971 geboren. Sein Architekturstudium an der Fakultät für Bauingenieurwesen der Universität Tokio schloss er mit einem B. Arch. ab (1990–94). Sein eigenes Büro, Sou Fujimoto Architects, gründete er 2000. Er gilt als einer der interessantesten jungen Architekten Japans, seine Formensprache entzieht sich einfachen Zuordnungen. Zu seinen Projekten zählen Ausbildungsstätten für Menschen mit geistiger Behinderung (Hokkaido, 2003), das Umwelt-Kunst-Forum in Annaka (Gunma, 2003–06), ein Behandlungszentrum für psychisch kranke Kinder (Hokkaido, 2006), Haus O (Chiba, 2007), Haus N (Präfektur Oita, 2007–08) und das Final Wooden House (Kumamura, Kumamoto, 2007–08). Zu den jüngeren Projekten zählen außerdem seine Beteiligung an Toyo Itos Sumika-Projekt (House Before House, Utsunomiya, Tochigi, 2008), Museum und Bibliothek der Kunstuniversität Musashino (Tokio, 2007–09), Haus H (Tokio, 2008–09), das Tokio-Apartment (Itabashiku, Tokio, 2009–10), der Uniqlo-Store in Shinsaibashi (Osaka, 2010), das Haus NA (Tokio, 2010), das Haus K (Nishinomiya-shi, Hyogo, 2011–12, hier vorgestellt) und der Serpentine Summer Pavilion 2013 (Kensington Gardens, London, 2013).

SOU FUJIMOTO, né en 1971, a obtenu son B.Arch à l'université de Tokyo (faculté d'ingénierie, département d'architecture, 1990–94). Il crée sa propre agence, Sou Fujimoto Architects, en 2000. On le considère comme l'un des plus intéressants jeunes architectes japonais apparus récemment, et son vocabulaire formel échappe à toute classification aisée. Parmi ses réalisations : des installations de formation pour handicapés mentaux (Hokkaido, 2003) ; l'Environment Art Forum d'Annaka (Gunma, 2003–06) ; un centre de traitement pour les enfants souffrant de troubles mentaux (Hokkaido, 2006) ; la Maison O (Chiba, 2007) ; la Maison N (préfecture d'Oita, 2007–08) et la Maison de bois « définitive » (Kumamura, Kumamoto, 2007–08). Plus récemment, il a participé au projet Sumika de Toyo Ito (Maison d'avant la maison, Utsunomiya, Tochigi, 2008) et a réalisé le musée et la bibliothèque de l'Université d'art Musashino (Tokyo, 2007–09) ; la Maison H (Tokyo, 2008–09) ; l'appartement Tokyo (Itabashiku, 2009–10) ; le magasin Uniqlo à Shinsaibashi (Osaka, 2010) ; la Maison NA (Tokyo, 2010) ; la Maison K (Nishinomiya-shi, Hyogo, 2011–12, publiée ici) et le pavillon d'été 2013 de la Serpentine Gallery (Kensington Gardens, Londres, 2013), tous au Japon sauf mention contraire.

HOUSE K

Nishinomiya-shi, Hyogo, Japan, 2011–12

Area: 118 m².

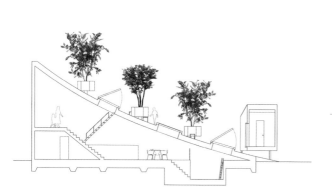

Drawings and images show how the architect has made use of the roof of House K to add an unexpected amount of extra living space to the design.

Zeichnungen und Bilder zeigen, wie der Architekt sich das Dach von Haus K zunutze gemacht hat, um unerwarteten, zusätzlichen Lebensraum zu gewinnen.

Les plans et les photos montrent comment l'architecte a tiré profit du toit de la Maison K pour ajouter à sa création un espace à vivre supplémentaire d'une taille inattendue.

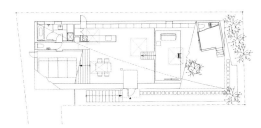
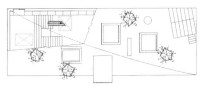

Located in a calm residential area of Nishinomiya-shi, between Osaka and Kobe, this house was conceived with an open line of sight toward woods located to the west. The concept of roof garden was extended here in a diagonal form. Dotted with potted trees that look as though they are "floating" on the roof, the garden is described alternatively as "semi-natural" or "semi-artificial." There are three interior floor levels, with kitchen and living space on the ground level. Windows were created in a random pattern, creating a variety of different views, accentuated by the diagonal rise of the house. An important part of the design involved creating connections between the interior and the roof garden at all levels so that the residence assumed a kind of natural "topography." A hut or shed was placed on the roof, like a "small villa."

Orientierungspunkt bei der Planung des Hauses, das in einer ruhigen Wohngegend von Nishinomiya-shi zwischen Osaka und Kobe liegt, war eine unverstellte Sichtachse auf ein westlich gelegenes Waldgebiet. Das Konzept Dachgarten wurde in die Diagonale ausgedehnt. Punktuell mit Bäumen in Kübeln bestanden, die aussehen, als „schwebten" sie auf dem Dach, kann der Garten entweder als „halb natürlich" oder „halb künstlich" beschrieben werden. Im Inneren gibt es drei Ebenen, Küche und Wohnbereich befinden sich im Erdgeschoss. Die Fenster sind unregelmäßig angeordnet, bieten eine Vielzahl verschiedener Perspektiven, was durch den diagonalen Anstieg des Hauses noch akzentuiert wird. Ein zentrales Anliegen des Entwurfs war, auf allen Ebenen Verbindungen zwischen Innenraum und Dachgarten zu schaffen, sodass das Haus eine Art natürliche „Topografie" bekam. Eine Hütte oder Schuppen wurde auf dem Dach platziert wie eine „kleine Villa".

Située dans un quartier résidentiel calme de Nishinomiya-shi, entre Osaka et Kōbe, cette maison a été conçue pour avoir une vue dégagée sur les bois situés à l'ouest. Le concept de jardin sur le toit prend ici une forme diagonale. Ponctué par des arbres en pots qui semblent « flotter » sur le toit, le jardin est décrit alternativement comme « semi-naturel » ou « semi-artificiel ». L'intérieur compte trois niveaux, la cuisine et le salon occupant celui du bas. Les fenêtres ont été créées de manière aléatoire et ouvrent sur des vues toutes différentes, accentuées par la pente de la maison. Le design a cherché en grande partie à créer des liens entre l'intérieur et le jardin sur le toit à tous les niveaux afin de conférer une sorte de « topographie » naturelle à l'ensemble. Une cabane ou resserre a été placée sur le toit telle une « petite villa ».

Sloped and angled interior spaces together with skylights enliven the volumes. Right, a stepladder leads up to the roof level.

Dachschrägen und lange Fluchten, kombiniert mit Oberlichtern, verleihen den Räumen Lebendigkeit. Rechts führt eine Leiter zum Dach.

Avec les lucarnes, les espaces intérieurs inclinés et anguleux donnent vie aux volumes. À droite, une échelle mène au toit.

PUBLIC TOILET
IN ICHIHARA

Location Itabu Station, Ichihara City, Chiba, Japan, 2012

Area: 209 m². Client: Ichihara City.
Collaboration: Nao Harikae, Naganobu Matsumura, Naoki Tamura.

Though a public toilet may not seem the most obvious place for a talented architect to challenge architectural suppositions, this is precisely what Sou Fujimoto sought to do in the case of the Public Toilet in Ichihara. Located near the Itabu Station on a local train line, this toilet consists of two units, one for women and the other which is "unisex and for people with disabilities." The area around the station is known for its scenery and in particular for the spring cherry blossoms, which posed certain design issues, as the architect explains: "A public toilet is, in a way, the smallest public facility. It is public, and, at the same time, it is a very private space. Therefore, it is the usual premise to close and to protect the location from its surroundings. However, in the midst of this beautiful environment, the question is raised of how it can be closed while remaining open. And this closed-but-openedness challenges us to reflect on a primitive form of architecture." A wooden log fence is used to enclose an area of 209 square meters that contains the toilets in their natural environment. "This multilayered divergence of internal and external boundaries blends together public and private, the sense of openness and protection, nature and architecture, internal and external, large and small, while retaining their ambiguity," says Fujimoto.

Obgleich eine öffentliche Toilette normalerweise keine Herausforderung für einen talentierten Architekten darstellt, traf das doch für Sou Fujimoto im Fall der öffentlichen Bedürfnisanstalt in Ichihara zu. Sie liegt bei der Station Itabu einer Lokalbahnlinie und besteht aus zwei Einheiten, einer für Damen und einer anderen für „Unisex und Personen mit Behinderung". Der Bereich um den Bahnhof herum ist für seine schöne landschaftliche Umgebung, vor allem während der Kirschblüte, bekannt, was die Planung natürlich beeinflusste, wie der Architekt erklärt: „Eine öffentliche Toilette ist gewissermaßen die kleinste öffentliche Einrichtung. Sie ist öffentlich und zugleich ein sehr privater Bereich. Daher ist es üblich, diesen Ort von seiner Umgebung abzuschirmen. Inmitten dieser schönen Landschaft stellt sich aber die Frage, wie man abschirmen und zugleich offen bleiben kann. Und diese Geschlossen-, aber doch Offenheit hat uns herausgefordert, über eine primitive Form der Architektur nachzudenken." Ein Zaun aus Holzbalken umschließt eine Fläche von 209 m², auf der sich die Toiletten in ihrem natürlichen Umfeld befinden. „Diese vielschichtige Abweichung von inneren und äußeren Begrenzungen vermischt Öffentliches und Privates, das Empfinden von Offenheit und Sicherheit, von Natur und Architektur, innen und außen, groß und klein, bei gleichzeitigem Erhalt ihrer Doppelsinnigkeit", sagt Fujimoto.

Les toilettes publiques ne sont pas forcément l'endroit le plus évident où un architecte de talent peut remettre en question des postulats architecturaux, c'est pourtant ce que Sou Fujimoto a fait avec les toilettes publiques d'Ichihara. Situées près de la gare d'Itabu, sur la ligne de chemin de fer locale, elles sont composées de deux unités, l'une pour les femmes et l'autre « unisexe et pour les personnes handicapées ». La zone qui entoure la gare est réputée pour la beauté de son paysage, et surtout pour les bourgeons de cerisiers au printemps, ce qui a posé question en termes de design, comme l'explique l'architecte : « Les toilettes publiques sont pour ainsi dire le plus petit des espaces publics. C'est un lieu public, et en même temps un endroit très personnel. C'est pourquoi on part généralement du principe qu'elles doivent être closes et protégées de ce qui les entoure. Mais ici, dans cet environnement magnifique, la question se pose de les laisser ouvertes tout en les fermant. Ce caractère clos-mais-ouvert nous met au défi de revenir à une forme primitive d'architecture. » Une clôture en rondins de bois entoure un espace de 209 mètres carrés où sont placées les toilettes en pleine nature. « Cette divergence complexe entre les frontières intérieures et extérieures mêle le public et le privé, le sentiment d'ouverture et celui de protection, la nature et l'architecture, l'interne et l'externe, le grand et le petit, tout en gardant son ambiguïté », selon Fujimoto.

This surprising tiny public toilet is an unexpected combination of transparency and a bucolic setting. Perhaps challenging the usual Japanese tendency to a certain natural modesty and playing too on their fixation on toilet gadgetry, the architect in a sense inverts the usual clichés.

Diese erstaunliche kleine öffentliche Toilette ist eine ungewöhnliche Kombination aus Transparenz und einer bukolischen Landschaft. Vielleicht als Protest gegen die Tendenz der Japaner zu einer natürlichen Bescheidenheit und auch als Spiel mit ihrer Fixierung auf die Toilettenausstattung kehrt der Architekt gewissermaßen das übliche Klischee um.

Ces étonnantes toilettes publiques miniature associent avec beaucoup d'originalité la transparence et un décor bucolique. Ciblant peut-être la tendance des Japonais à une certaine modestie naturelle et jouant sur leur amour des gadgets aux toilettes, l'architecte inverse en quelque sorte les clichés habituels.

GIJS VAN VAERENBERGH

PIETERJAN GIJS was born in Leuven, Belgium, in 1983. He studied Civil Engineering and Architecture at KU Leuven (2001–06) and obtained a Master's degree in Urbanism and Territorial Development from the Université Catholique de Louvain (2006–07). In 2008, he cofounded Gijs Van Vaerenbergh. **ARNOUT VAN VAERENBERGH** was also born in 1983 in Leuven, and studied Civil Engineering and Architecture at KU Leuven (2001–06). He has worked as an architect at New + Partners (2006–09) and at noA Architecten (2009–10), cofounding Gijs Van Vaerenbergh in 2008. The work of Gijs Van Vaerenbergh "consists of site-specific interventions, installations, and constructions that generate a mutual relation with their environment." Their work includes Greenhouse Intersect (Leuven, 2010); SpinOff (Brussels, 2010); The Upside Dome (Leuven, 2010); Reading between the Lines (Borgloon, 2011, published here); Skylight (Leuven, 2012); Framework (Leuven, 2012); and Ghent 1913 – A Retroactive Monument (exhibition in DeSingel, Antwerp, 2013), all in Belgium unless otherwise indicated.

PIETERJAN GIJS wurde 1983 in Leuven, Belgien, geboren. Er studierte Ingenieurwesen und Architektur an der KU Leuven (2001–06) und absolvierte einen Master in Urbanistik und Raumplanung an der Université Catholique de Louvain (2006–07). Das Büro Gijs Van Vaerenbergh gründete er 2008 mit **ARNOUT VAN VAERENBERGH**, der ebenfalls 1983 in Leuven geboren wurde und Ingenieurwesen und Architektur an der KU Leuven studierte (2001–06). Vor Gründung des Büros arbeitete Vaerenbergh für New + Partners (2006–09) sowie noA Architecten (2009–10). Gijs Van Vaerenberghs Projekte sind oft „standortspezifische Interventionen, Installationen und Konstruktionen, die den Dialog mit ihrem Umfeld suchen". Zu ihren Projekten zählen Greenhouse Intersect (Leuven, 2010), SpinOff (Brüssel, 2010), The Upside Dome (Leuven, 2010), Reading between the Lines (Borgloon, 2011, hier vorgestellt), Skylight (Leuven, 2012), Framework (Leuven, 2012) und die Ausstellung „Ghent 1913. A Retroactive Monument" am Internationalen Kunstcampus DeSingel (Antwerpen, 2013).

Né à Louvain, en Belgique, en 1983, **PIETERJAN GIJS** étudie l'ingénierie civile et l'architecture à la KU Leuven (2001–06) et obtient un master en urbanisme et développement du territoire à l'Université catholique de Louvain (2006–07). En 2008, il est cofondateur de l'agence Gijs Van Vaerenbergh. Né également en 1983 à Louvain, **ARNOUT VAN VAERENBERGH** étudie aussi l'ingénierie civile et l'architecture à la KU Leuven (2001–06). Il travaille comme architecte chez New + Partners (2006–09) et chez noA Architecten (2009–10), et participe à la fondation de Gijs Van Vaerenbergh en 2008. Le travail de Gijs Van Vaerenbergh « consiste en interventions, installations et constructions spécifiques à un site et qui génèrent une relation avec leur environnement ». Leurs réalisations comprennent *Greenhouse Intersect* (Louvain, 2010) ; *SpinOff* (Bruxelles, 2010) ; *The Upside Dome* (Louvain, 2010) ; *Reading between the Lines* (Looz, 2011, présenté ici) ; *Skylight* (Louvain, 2012) ; *Framework* (Louvain, 2012) et « Ghent 1913. A Retroactive Monument » (exposition au centre d'art DeSingel, Anvers, 2013), tous en Belgique, sauf indication contraire.

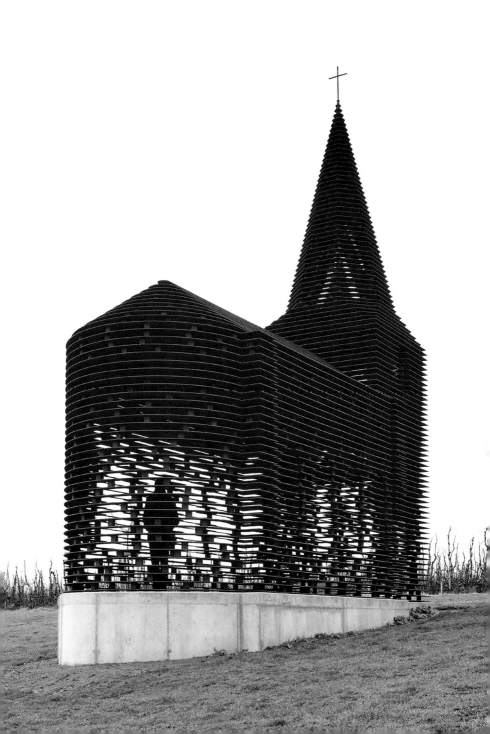

READING BETWEEN THE LINES

Borgloon, Belgium, 2011

Area: 28 m².
Client: IVA Beeldenproject.

Built in a rural setting outside of the Limburg town of Borgloon, this structure, based on the design of the local church, was inaugurated on September 24, 2011. It has a reinforced-concrete foundation and was made with 30 tons of COR-TEN steel and 2000 columns. It is not a piece of architecture in the usual sense, but rather a "transparent object of art." Gijs Van Vaerenbergh explain that their work can be seen as a reflection on architectural themes, such as scale or the plan, but also as a commentary on the fact that many churches no longer fulfill their past functions since they are quite empty, in the region of Limburg and elsewhere. The work can also be seen as a kind of line drawing in space. Despite the use of such "solid" materials as reinforced concrete and steel, Reading between the Lines retains a fundamental fragility, which is what makes it interesting.

Das Projekt, außerhalb der limburgischen Stadt Borgloon auf dem Land gelegen und der örtlichen Kirche nachempfunden, wurde am 24. September 2011 eingeweiht. Auf einem Fundament aus Stahlbeton ruht eine Konstruktion aus 30 t Corten-Stahl und 2000 Querträgern. Dies ist keine Architektur im herkömmlichen Sinn, sondern vielmehr ein „transparentes Kunstobjekt". Gijs Van Vaerenbergh verstehen ihren Entwurf sowohl als Auseinandersetzung mit architektonischen Konzepten wie Maßstab und Grundriss als auch als Kommentar zu der Entwicklung, dass viele Kirchen in Limburg und andernorts zunehmend leer sind und ihre ursprüngliche Bestimmung nicht mehr erfüllen. Das Projekt lässt sich auch als „räumliche Zeichnung" lesen. Trotz massiver Materialien wie Stahl und Beton ist „Reading between the Lines" von einer Fragilität, die dem Projekt einen besonderen Reiz verleiht.

Construit dans un environnement rural près de Looz, dans le Limbourg, ce bâtiment dont la forme s'inspire de l'église locale a été inauguré le 24 septembre 2011. Trente tonnes d'acier Corten et 2000 piliers ont été utilisés pour sa construction sur des fondations en béton armé. Il ne s'agit pas d'un objet architectural dans le sens habituel, mais plutôt d'un « objet d'art transparent ». Selon Gijs Van Vaerenbergh, leur création peut être vue comme une réflexion sur des thèmes architecturaux comme l'échelle ou le plan, mais aussi comme un commentaire sur le fait que de nombreuses églises ne remplissent plus leurs fonctions passées puisqu'elles sont quasiment vides, dans le Limbourg comme ailleurs. Le projet peut aussi être vu comme un dessin dans l'espace. En dépit de l'emploi de matériaux solides comme l'acier et le béton armé, *Reading Between the Lines* conserve une fragilité fondamentale qui en fait l'intérêt.

The schematic outline of a church stands out on its country hillside, a commentary on architecture, but also on religion.

Die stilisierte Kontur einer Kirche erhebt sich über der hügeligen Landschaft: ein Kommentar zur Architektur, aber auch zur Religion.

La silhouette schématique d'une église se détache sur la campagne vallonnée, un commentaire sur l'architecture comme sur la religion.

GIJS VAN VAERENBERGH

Although the exact size of this "church" is not readily grasped from a distance, when seen closer up, it becomes apparent that it is quite small.

Die tatsächliche Größe der „Kirche" ist aus der Ferne nicht eindeutig auszumachen. Erst aus relativer Nähe erschließt sich, dass der Bau recht klein ist.

La taille exacte de cette « église », qui n'est pas immédiatement perceptible à distance, se révèle bien petite quand on s'en approche.

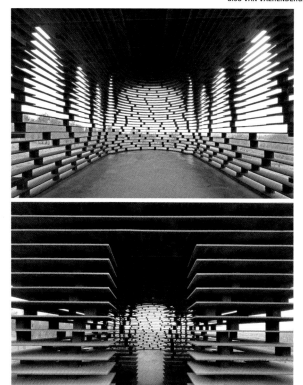

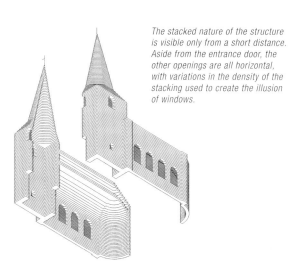

The stacked nature of the structure is visible only from a short distance. Aside from the entrance door, the other openings are all horizontal, with variations in the density of the stacking used to create the illusion of windows.

Auch das Schichtprinzip des Baus wird erst aus größerer Nähe deutlich. Abgesehen vom Eingang sind alle weiteren Öffnungen horizontal; Variation ergibt sich durch die Dichte der Schichtelemente, die auch Fenster andeutet.

L'empilement caractéristique de sa structure n'est visible que de près. Hormis la porte d'entrée, toutes les ouvertures sont horizontales, avec des variations de densité de l'empilement qui créent l'illusion de fenêtres.

Though the idea of Reading between the Lines seems quite simple, the designers have used the concept to create a poetic structure that is sculptural in its essence even if it does evoke architecture.

Bien que l'idée de Reading Between the Lines semble assez simple, les designers se sont servis du concept pour créer une structure poétique d'essence sculpturale, même si elle évoque l'architecture.

Die Idee von Reading between the Lines scheint zunächst simpel, doch den Planern gelingt es, mit ihrem Konzept eine poetische Konstruktion zu schaffen, die vor allem skulptural ist, auch wenn sie an architektonische Formen anknüpft.

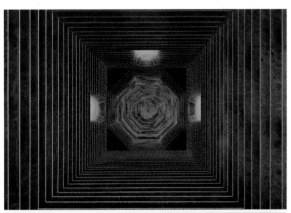

JORGE GRACIA GARCÍA

JORGE GRACIA GARCÍA was born in 1973 in Tijuana, Mexico, and graduated from the Universidad Iberoamericana Noroeste (Tijuana, 1991–97). He worked in the Sebastian Mariscal Studio (2003–04), before creating his own firm in 2004. His recent projects include the GA House (Tijuana, 2004); Todos Santos House (Todos Santos, Baja California Sur, 2006); the Becerril House (Tijuana, 2006); a Culinary School (Tijuana, 2008); a Design Center in Brickell (Miami, Florida, USA, 2006/09–); and La Caja Art Gallery (Tijuana, 2009). More recently he has worked on the Endémico Resguardo Silvestre (Valle de Guadalupe, 2010–11, published here); the Plaza Internacional (Ensenada, 2012); CAS Hotel (Tijuana, 2012); and Liverpool Department Stores in Cancun, Playa del Carmen, and La Paz, all in Mexico unless stated otherwise.

JORGE GRACIA GARCÍA wurde 1973 in Tijuana, Mexiko, geboren und studierte dort an der Universidad Iberoamericana Noroeste (1991–97). Er arbeitete im Studio Sebastian Mariscal (2003–04), bevor er sich 2004 selbstständig machte. Zu seinen jüngeren Projekten zählen die Casa GA (Tijuana, 2004), die Casa Todos Santos (Todos Santos, Baja California Sur, 2006), die Casa Becerril (Tijuana, 2006), eine Kochschule (Tijuana, 2008), ein Designcenter in Brickell (Miama, Florida, seit 2006/09) und die Kunstgalerie La Caja (Tijuana, 2009). In jüngerer Zeit hat er am Endémico Resguardo Silvestre (Valle de Guadalupe, 2010–11, hier vorgestellt), dem Projekt Plaza Internacional (Ensenada, 2012), dem Hotel CAS (Tijuana, 2012) und den Liverpool-Kaufhäusern in Cancun, Playa del Carmen und La Paz gearbeitet, alle in Mexiko, wenn nicht anders angeben.

JORGE GRACIA GARCÍA, né en 1973 à Tijuana, au Mexique, est diplômé de l'Universidad Iberoamericana Noroeste (Tijuana, 1991–97). Il a travaillé dans le studio de Sebastian Mariscal (2003–04) avant de créer son agence en 2004. Ses projets récents comprennent la Maison GA (Tijuana, 2004) ; la maison Todos Santos (Todos Santos, Basse-Californie du Sud, 2006) ; la maison Becerril (Tijuana, 2006) ; une école de cuisine (Tijuana, 2008) ; un centre du design à Brickell (Miami, Floride, 2006/09–) et la galerie d'art La Caja (Tijuana, 2009). Plus récemment, il a travaillé au projet Endémico Resguardo Silvestre (Valle de Guadalupe, 2010–11, publié ici) ; au Plaza Internacional (Ensenada, 2012) ; à l'hôtel CAS (Tijuana, 2012) et aux grands magasins Liverpool de Cancun, Playa del Carmen et La Paz, tous au Mexique sauf mention contraire.

ENDÉMICO RESGUARDO SILVESTRE

Valle de Guadalupe, Ensenada, Mexico, 2010–11

Area: 20 rooms, each 20 m².
Client: Grupo Encuentro.

This "design hotel" is located on a 99-hectare site in the wine-producing region of Baja California, about one and a half hours from San Diego, California. The Encuentro Guadalupe project also includes a winery and residences. Given the concept of the project ("endémico" means "endemic" in Spanish), the architect was asked to respect the natural setting to the greatest extent possible. A steel skeleton permitted a minimum amount of contact with the soil. COR-TEN steel was used for exterior surfaces because of its weathering properties, but also to emphasize the continuity between the architecture and the natural environment. Given the location of the hotel and its concept, the architect imagined the hotel rooms as a luxury camping site, where clients can be in close proximity to nature and still have their basic requirements taken care of by the hotel.

Das „Designhotel" befindet sich auf einem 99 ha großen Areal im Weinanbaugebiet von Baja California, rund anderthalb Stunden von San Diego, Kalifornien, entfernt. Zum Encuentro-Guadalupe-Projekt gehören außerdem eine Kelterei und Wohnhäuser. Dem Konzept des Projekts gemäß („endémico" bedeutet so viel wie „einheimisch"), war der Architekt angehalten, so wenig wie irgend möglich in die natürliche Umgebung einzugreifen. Stahlgerüste sorgen für einen minimalen Kontakt mit dem Untergrund. Für die Außenfassaden wurde Corten-Stahl verwendet, wegen seiner Witterungseigenschaften, aber auch um die Kontinuität zwischen Architektur und natürlicher Umgebung zu betonen. Angesichts der Lage und des Konzepts interpretierte der Architekt das Hotel als luxuriösen Campingplatz, wo die Gäste der Natur nah sein können, während der Hotelservice sich um ihre Grundbedürfnisse kümmert.

Cet « hôtel design » occupe un site de 99 hectares dans la région viticole de Basse-Californie, à une heure et demie environ de San Diego, en Californie. Le projet Encuentro Guadalupe comprend aussi un établissement viticole et des résidences. Étant donné le concept (« endémico » signifie « endémique » en espagnol), l'architecte a été prié de respecter le plus possible le cadre naturel. Un squelette en acier permet un contact minimal avec le sol. L'acier Corten a été choisi pour les surfaces extérieures en raison de sa résistance aux intempéries, mais aussi pour souligner la continuité entre l'architecture et le décor naturel. En raison de l'emplacement et du concept de l'hôtel, l'architecte a conçu les chambres comme un camping de luxe où les clients sont à proximité immédiate de la nature tout en voyant leurs exigences de base prises en charge.

Set up off the ground to preserve the natural setting, the cabins provide individual space and privacy to this hotel.

Die Häuser sind aufgeständert, um die natürliche Umgebung zu schützen, und bieten in diesem Hotel individuellen Raum und Privatsphäre.

Surélevées pour préserver le cadre naturel, les chambres offrent des espaces individuels et l'intimité aux clients de l'hôtel.

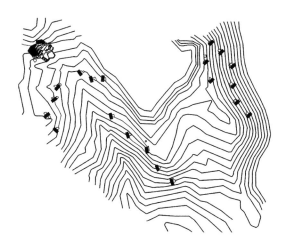

Left, a topographical site plan
shows the cabins in the hilly
environment. Above, a cabin terrace
offers a spectacular view of the
mountains.

Links zeigt ein topografischer
Lageplan die Häuser im hügeligen
Gelände. Die Terrassen bieten einen
spektakulären Blick auf die Berge
(oben).

À gauche, un plan topographique du
site montre les chambres dans leur
environnement vallonné. Ci-dessus,
vue spectaculaire sur les montagnes
depuis la terrasse d'une chambre.

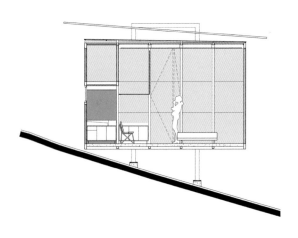

Interiors offer generous glazing and openings to the exterior deck. Left, a section drawing shows the volume set up on steel struts, creating horizontal surfaces where the terrain is steeply sloped.

Die Innenräume zeichnen sich durch großzügige Verglasung und Öffnungen zur Terrasse hin aus. Links verdeutlicht ein Querschnitt die Aufständerung des Gebäudes auf Stahlstreben, wodurch in dem steilen Gelände horizontale Flächen entstehen.

Les intérieurs offrent un vitrage généreux et des ouvertures vers la terrasse. À gauche, vue en coupe du volume posé sur des supports en acier, qui créent une surface horizontale malgré la forte pente du terrain.

*Right, a plan of the interior of a
cabin. Below, interior fittings are
simple but obviously chosen with
a good sense of the quality of
the design.*

*Rechts ein Grundriss eines der
Häuser. Die Armaturen sind schlicht,
aber offensichtlich mit einem guten
Gespür für das Gesamtbild des
Entwurfs gewählt (unten).*

*À droite, plan de l'intérieur d'une
chambre. Ci-dessous, les équipements sont simples mais manifestement choisis avec un sens élevé
de la qualité du design.*

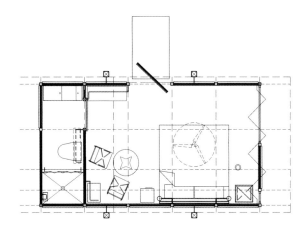

ZAHA HADID

ZAHA HADID (1950–2016) studied Architecture at the Architectural Association (AA) in London, beginning in 1972, and was awarded the Diploma Prize in 1977. She then became a partner of Rem Koolhaas in OMA and taught at the AA. She also taught at Harvard, the University of Chicago, in Hamburg, and at Columbia University in New York. In 2004, Zaha Hadid became the first woman to win the Pritzker Prize. As well as the exhibition design for *The Great Utopia* (Solomon R. Guggenheim Museum, New York, USA, 1992), her work includes the Vitra Fire Station (Weil am Rhein, Germany, 1990–94); the Lois & Richard Rosenthal Center for Contemporary Art (Cincinnati, Ohio, USA, 1999–2003); Phaeno Science Center (Wolfsburg, Germany, 2001–05); the Central Building of the new BMW Assembly Plant in Leipzig (Germany, 2005); and the MAXXI, the National Museum of 21st Century Arts (Rome, Italy, 1998–2009). More recent projects include the Sheik Zayed Bridge (Abu Dhabi, UAE, 2003–10); the Guangzhou Opera House (Guangzhou, China, 2005–10); the Aquatics Center for the London 2012 Olympic Games (London, UK, 2005–11); the CMA CGM Tower (Marseille, France, 2008–11); and the Messner Mountain Museum Corones (Enneberg/Pieve di Marebbe, Italy, 2015). Her office continues to operate under the leadership of Patrik Schumacher.

ZAHA HADID (1950–2016) studierte ab 1972 Architektur an der Architectural Association (AA) in London und erwarb 1977 den Diploma Prize. Dann wurde sie Partnerin von Rem Koolhaas beim OMA und lehrte an der AA. Sie lehrte auch in Harvard, an der University of Chicago, in Hamburg und an der Columbia University. 2004 gewann Zaha Hadid als erste Frau den Pritzker Prize. Außer der Ausstellungsgestaltung „The Great Utopia" (Solomon R. Guggenheim Museum, New York, USA, 1992) zählen zu ihren Werken das Feuerwehrhaus auf dem Vitra-Gelände (Weil am Rhein, Deutschland, 1990–94), das Lois & Richard Rosenthal Center for Contemporary Art (Cincinnaty, Ohio, USA, 1999–2003), das Phaeno Science Center (Wolfsburg, Deutschland, 2001–05), das BMW-Zentralgebäude in Leipzig (Deutschland, 2005) und das MAXXI, Museo nazionale delle arti del XXI secolo (Rom, Italien, 1998–2009). Neuere Projekte sind die Brücke Sheik Zayed (Abu Dhabi, Vereinigte Arabische Emirate, 2003–10), das Opernhaus in Guangzho (Guangzhou, China, 2005–10), das Aquatics Center für die Olympischen Spiele in London 2012 (London, UK, 2005–11), der CMA CGM Tower (Marseille, Frankreich, 2008–11) und das Messner Mountain Museum (Enneberg/Pieve di Marebbe, Italien, 2015). Zaha Hadids Büro wird unter der Leitung von Patrik Schumacher weitergeführt.

ZAHA HADID (1950–2016) a étudié l'architecture à l'Architectural Association (AA) de Londres de 1972 à 1977, date à laquelle elle a reçu le prix du diplôme. Elle est ensuite devenue partenaire de Rem Koolhaas à l'OMA et a enseigné à l'AA, ainsi qu'à Harvard, à l'université de Chicago, à Hambourg et à l'université Columbia à New York. En 2004, elle a été la première femme à remporter le très convoité prix Pritzker. Outre la conception de l'exposition The Great Utopia (Solomon R. Guggenheim Museum, New York, 1992), elle a réalisé le poste d'incendie pour Vitra (Weil am Rhein, Allemagne, 1990–94) ; le Centre Lois & Richard Rosenthal pour l'art contemporain (Cincinnati, Ohio, USA, 1999–2003) ; le Centre scientifique Phaeno (Wolfsburg, Allemagne, 2001–05) ; le bâtiment central de la nouvelle usine BMW à Leipzig (Allemagne, 2005) et le Musée national des arts du XXIᵉ siècle MAXXI (Rome, 1998–2009). Ses projets plus récents comprennent le pont Sheik Zayed (Abou Dhabi, EAU, 2003–2010) ; l'Opéra de Canton (Chine, 2005–10) ; le Centre des sports aquatiques pour les Jeux olympiques de Londres 2012 (2005–11) ; la tour CMA CGM (Marseille, 2008–11) et le Messner Mountain Museum Corones (Enneberg/Pieve di Marebbe, Italie, 2015). Son agence poursuit son œuvre sous la direction de Patrik Schumacher.

BURNHAM PAVILION
Chicago, USA, 2009

Area: 45 m². Client: Burnham Plan Centennial.
Collaboration: Fabric Images (General Contractor & Fabricator),
Dear Productions (Lighting), The Gray Circle (Media Content).

One of a number of small structures commissioned to celebrate the 100th anniversary of the Burnham Plan for Chicago, this pavilion is made of bent aluminum. Each element was shaped and welded while inner and outer fabric skins were wrapped around this skeleton. The architect suggests that the structure contains "hidden traces of Burnham's organizational structure." The fabric serves as a screen for video installations within the pavilion. Intended to be easily dismantled or recycled, the pavilion is also meant to be assembled in another location in the future. Zaha Hadid Architects states: "The presence of the new structure triggers the visitor's intellectual curiosity whilst an intensification of public life around and within the pavilion supports the idea of public discourse."

Dieser Pavillon ist einer von mehreren Bauten, die anlässlich der 100-Jahr-Feier des Burnham-Masterplans der Stadt Chicago in Auftrag gegeben wurde. Der Pavillon besteht aus gebogenen Aluminiumelementen, die einzeln geformt und geschweißt wurden. Über dieses Skelett wurde eine Innen- und Außenhaut aus Textil gespannt. Der Architektin zufolge zeigen sich in der Konstruktion „unterschwellige Spuren der von Burnham entworfenen Organisationsstruktur". Die Textilbespannung dient zugleich als Leinwand für Videoinstallationen im Pavillon. Der leicht demontierbare und recycelbare Pavillon lässt sich in Zukunft auch an anderen Standorten installieren. Die Architektin erklärt: „Die Präsenz des neuen Baus weckt die intellektuelle Neugier der Besucher und belebt zugleich das öffentliche Leben im und um den Pavillon. So wird ein öffentlicher Diskurs gefördert."

Ce pavillon, commandé dans le cadre d'un programme de petites constructions lancé à l'occasion des célébrations du centième anniversaire du Plan Burnham pour Chicago, a été réalisé en aluminium cintré. Ses éléments mis en forme et soudés constituent un squelette qui est enveloppé de « peaux » de toile à l'extérieur et à l'intérieur. L'architecte aime imaginer que cette structure contient des « traces cachées de la structure organisée de Burnham ». À l'intérieur, la toile tendue sert d'écran à des installations vidéo. Conçu pour être facilement démonté ou recyclé, le pavillon pourra être éventuellement transporté dans un autre lieu. « La présence d'une nouvelle construction suscite la curiosité intellectuelle du visiteur, tandis que l'intensification de la vie et des échanges autour du pavillon et à l'intérieur de celui-ci développe une idée de discours public », explique l'agence.

Like a glowing UFO, the pavilion does indeed challenge visitors to think again about space, and about the surrounding city.

Der wie ein leuchtendes UFO wirkende Pavillon hält seine Besucher unweigerlich dazu an, über Raumfragen und die gebaute Umwelt Chicagos nachdenken.

Comme un Ovni lumineux, le pavillon invite les spectateurs à repenser leur perception de l'espace et de la ville.

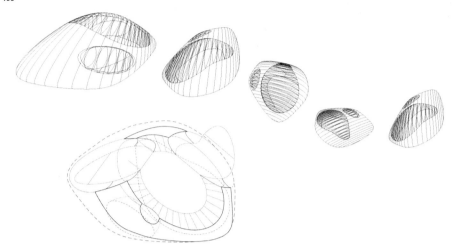

With its continuous curving forms and changing colors, the pavilion is in a sense all that the architecture around is not: non-geometric, challenging, and new.

Mit seinen geschwungenen Formen und der wechselnden Farbgebung ist der Pavillon gewissermaßen all das, was die umgebende Architektur nicht ist: winkellos, kontrovers, neuartig.

À travers ses courbes continues et ses couleurs changeantes, le pavillon est un peu tout ce que l'architecture environnante n'est pas : non orthogonal, provocateur et nouveau.

HAKUHODO

ATSUSHI MUROI was born in Hiroshima, Japan, in 1975. He received a B.Arch. degree from Tokyo University of Science. He worked on the AND Market (Kasumigaseki, Tokyo, 2011, published here) with **HATTORI KIMITARO**, who was born in Gifu, Japan (1977), and graduated from the Tokyo University of the Arts. They both work for Hakuhodo, a firm specialized in advertising, corporate communications, and marketing. Hakuhodo is the second largest advertising agency in Japan. Atsushi Muroi has also worked on the Nissan Omoiyari Balloon (Yokohama, 2009); Docomo Smartphone Lounge (Tokyo, 2010); and Zoff Park Harajuku (Tokyo, 2011), all in Japan.

ATSUSHI MUROI wurde 1975 in Hiroshima geboren. Seinen B. Arch. machte er an der Naturwissenschaftlichen Universität Tokio. Am AND Market (Kasumigaseki, Tokio, 2011, hier vorgestellt) arbeitete er gemeinsam mit **HATTORI KIMITARO**, geboren 1977 in Gifu, Japan, der sein Studium an der Universität der Künste Tokio abschloss. Beide sind für Hakuhodo tätig, eine Agentur für Werbung, Kommunikation und Marketing. Hakuhodo ist Japans zweitgrößte Werbeagentur. Atsushi Muroi arbeitete außerdem an folgenden Projekten: Nissan Omoiyari Balloon (Yokohama, 2009), Docomo Smartphone Lounge (Tokio, 2010) und Zoff Park Harajuku (Tokio, 2011), alle in Japan.

ATSUSHI MUROI est né à Hiroshima en 1975. Il est titulaire d'un B.Arch de l'Université des sciences de Tokyo. Il a travaillé au projet AND Market (Kasumigaseki, Tokyo, 2011, publié ici) avec **HATTORI KIMITARO**, né à Gifu, Japon (1977) et diplômé de l'Université des arts de Tokyo. Ils sont tous les deux employés par Hakuhodo, une agence de publicité, communication d'entreprise et marketing – la deuxième agence de publicité du Japon. Atsushi Muroi a également collaboré au Nissan Omoiyari Balloon (Yokohama, 2009) ; au Smartphone Lounge Docomo (Tokyo, 2010) et au Zoff Park d'Harajuku (Tokyo, 2011).

AND MARKET

Kasumigaseki, Tokyo, Japan, 2011

Area: 31 m².
Client: NEC Mobiling, Ltd.

The AND Market concept was developed by Atsushi Muroi and Hattori Kimitaro for Japan's first smart phone retailer that is not part of a major mobile phone company. Customers can buy phones, accessories, and applications, and benefit from various membership services, not confined to any one certain carrier both in the retail shop and on their web site. Atsushi Muroi states: "Our project includes concept development, brand portfolio strategy, brand name and CI/VI development, and overall brand design, such as the retail shop, web site, promotional tools, and characters." The designer describes the concept as "neutral" meaning "achromatic in terms of design." For Muroi: "Without any heightened color, not even black or white, our design symbolizes the brand essence by depicting the balance of brightness between black and white. You cannot associate AND Market with traditional colors, since it is quite unique both in its services and brand designs."

Atsushi Muroi und Hattori Kimitaro entwickelten das Konzept des AND Market für Japans ersten netzwerkunabhängigen Smartphone-Anbieter. Die Kunden können in der Filiale wie auch im Webshop Telefone, Accessoires und Apps wählen und verschiedene Mitgliedervorteile nutzen, ohne an einen bestimmten Netzwerkbetreiber gebunden zu sein. Atsushi Muroi erklärt: „Unser Projekt war ein Gesamtpaket aus Konzeptentwicklung, Markenportfolio-Strategie, Entwicklung von Markennamen, Corporate Identity und Erscheinungsbild sowie dem gesamten Branding, einschließlich Filialgeschäft, Website, Werbemitteln und Typografie." Ihm zufolge ist das Konzept „neutral" im Sinne eines „achromatischen Designs". Muroi fügt hinzu: „Unser Design verzichtet auf prägnante Farben, einschließlich Schwarz und Weiß, und symbolisiert den Kern der Marke durch ein Gleichgewicht der Helligkeit zwischen Schwarz und Weiß. AND Market lässt sich nicht mit üblichen Farben assoziieren, schließlich sind Service und Markendesign einzigartig."

Le concept AND Market a été créé par Atsushi Muroi et Hattori Kimitaro pour le premier distributeur japonais de smart phones, qui n'appartient à aucune grande société de téléphonie mobile : les clients membres peuvent y acheter des téléphones, des accessoires, des applications et bénéficier de divers services sans être limités à un opérateur unique, que ce soit dans la boutique ou sur le site Web. Pour Atsushi Muroi : « Notre projet associe le développement conceptuel, la stratégie de portefeuille de marque, le nom commercial et développement CI/VI et le design de marque global par le biais de la boutique, du site Web, des outils promotionnels et des personnages. » Le designer décrit le concept comme « neutre », soit « achromatique en termes de design. Sans rehausser aucune couleur, pas même le noir ou le blanc, notre design incarne l'essence même de la marque en représentant l'équilibre de clarté entre le noir et le blanc. AND Market ne peut être associé à aucune couleur traditionnelle, car le concept est quasi unique par ses services et ses designs de marques ».

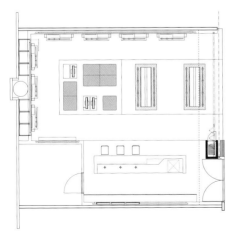

By pushing the logic of a black-and-white design, with repetitive elements such as the circular, disklike lighting fixtures, to its logical extreme, the designers create an unusual, intriguing space.

Indem sie die Logik ihres Schwarz-Weiß-Entwurfs mit wiederkehrenden Elementen wie den runden, scheibenförmigen Leuchten konzeptuell zuspitzen, gelingt es den Gestaltern, einen ungewöhnlich faszinierenden Raum zu realisieren.

En poussant à l'extrême la logique d'un design en noir et blanc aux éléments répétitifs comme les lampes circulaires en forme de disques, les designers ont créé un espace inédit et fascinant.

HAUGEN/ZOHAR

MARIT JUSTINE HAUGEN was born in 1973 in Oslo, Norway. She received her degree in Architecture from the Norwegian University of Science and Technology (Trondheim, 1995–2001) and a Master's degree from the Academy of Art (Oslo, 2003–05). **DAN ZOHAR** was born in 1972 in Tel Aviv, Israel. He also studied Architecture at the Norwegian University of Science and Technology (1996–2002). They established their firm in 2006. They have received the Norwegian Center for Design and Architecture prize for young talents in 2007, and Architectural Review Awards for Emerging Architecture in 2009 and 2011. They were invited participants for both the 2010 and the 2012 *Venice Architecture Biennale*. Their work includes the Fireplace for Children (Trondheim, 2010) and Cave for Children (Trondheim, 2012), both published here; House for Sister and Brother (Oslo, 2012); Lofts and Flats, an ongoing project to convert existing residences in Oslo (2009–); and a number of exhibition installations and art-related projects, all in Norway.

MARIT JUSTINE HAUGEN wurde 1973 in Oslo geboren. Sie absolvierte ihr Architekturstudium an der Technisch-Naturwissenschaftlichen Universität Norwegen (Trondheim, 1995–2001) und machte den Master an der Kunsthochschule Oslo (2003–05). **DAN ZOHAR** wurde 1972 in Tel Aviv geboren. Auch er studierte an der Technisch-Naturwissenschaftlichen Universität Norwegen (1996–2002). Ihr gemeinsames Büro gründeten sie 2006. Sie erhielten 2007 den Nachwuchspreis des norwegischen Zentrums für Design und Architektur und 2009 und 2011 Architectural Review Awards for Emerging Architecture. 2010 und 2012 waren sie eingeladene Teilnehmer der Architekturbiennale in Venedig. Zu ihren Arbeiten gehören die Feuerstelle für Kinder (Trondheim, 2010) und die Höhle für Kinder (Trondheim, 2012, beide hier vorgestellt), das Haus für Schwester und Bruder (Oslo, 2012), Lofts und Wohnungen, ein laufendes Umbauprojekt von Mietshäusern (seit 2009), und eine Reihe von Ausstellungsinstallationen und kunstverwandter Projekte, alle in Norwegen.

MARIT JUSTINE HAUGEN est née en 1973 à Oslo. Elle est diplômée en architecture de l'Université norvégienne des sciences et technologies (Trondheim, 1995–2001) et possède un master de l'Académie des arts (Oslo, 2003–05). **DAN ZOHAR** est né en 1972 à Tel Aviv. Il a aussi fait des études d'architecture à l'Université norvégienne des sciences et technologies (1996–2002). Ils ont créé leur société en 2006. Ils ont reçu le prix des jeunes talents du Centre norvégien de design et architecture en 2007 et les prix de l'Architectural Review pour l'architecture émergente en 2009 et 2011. Ils ont été invités à participer à la Biennale d'architecture de Venise en 2010 et 2012. Leurs réalisations comprennent le Foyer pour enfants (Trondheim, 2010) et la Caverne pour enfants (Trondheim, 2012), publiés tous les deux ici ; la Maison pour frère et sœur (Oslo, 2012) ; des lofts et appartements – un projet en cours de conversion de résidences existantes à Oslo (2009–) et de nombreuses installations dans des expositions et projets artistiques, tous en Norvège.

CAVE FOR CHILDREN

Trondheim, Norway, 2012

Area: 16 m².
Client: Municipality of Trondheim.

Built at the Breidablikk Kindergarten in Trondheim, the Cave for Children had a very low budget. The architects explain: "The inspiration for the project comes from natural caves, offering qualities such as collection of sunrays and rain, hiding and climbing." Leftover materials (1.5 tons of "pre-industrial waste") were used, hollowed out, layered, and glued together. The basic material is XP foam used for automobile dashboards, or industrial packaging, recovered in this instance from a number of European manufacturers. The lightness of the material and the nature of the design permitted the architects to put it to good use and avoid the usual burning or use as landfill of the leftover foam.

Für die Höhle, die vor dem Breidablikk-Kindergarten in Trondheim errichtet wurde, stand nur ein sehr kleines Budget zur Verfügung. Die Architekten: „Zu diesem Projekt haben uns natürliche Höhlen inspiriert, in die Sonnenstrahlen einfallen und Regen, wo man sich verstecken und herumklettern kann." Verwendet wurde Verschnittmaterial (1,5 t „vorindustrieller Abfall"), das man aushöhlte, übereinanderschichtete und zusammenklebte. Das Grundmaterial ist XP-Schaumstoff, der in Autos bei Armaturenbrettern oder als industrielles Verpackungsmaterial verwendet wird und den man sich für das Projekt von einer Reihe europäischer Hersteller sichern konnte. Die Leichtigkeit des Materials und die Art des Entwurfs ermöglichten den Architekten, es sinnvoll zu nutzen und so zu verhindern, dass der übrig gebliebene Kunststoff wie üblicherweise verbrannt wurde oder auf die Müllkippe wanderte.

Installée près du jardin d'enfants Breidablikk de Trondheim, la Caverne disposait d'un très petit budget. Les architectes expliquent que « le projet est inspiré des grottes naturelles et de certaines de leurs propriétés telles que la pénétration des rayons du soleil et de la pluie ou des possibilités de se cacher et de grimper ». Des matériaux de récupération (1,5 t de « déchets préindustriels ») ont été exploités, évidés, empilés et collés. Le matériau de base est de la mousse PIR utilisée pour les tableaux de bord automobiles, ou encore des emballages industriels récupérés chez bon nombre de constructeurs européens. La légèreté du matériau et la nature même du design ont permis aux architectes d'en faire bon usage et d'éviter la combustion ou l'enfouissement de la mousse, procédés sinon habituels.

The unexpected density of the structure and its unusual materials readily attract children to this small pavilion.

Die unerwartete Kompaktheit und die ungewöhnlichen Materialien des kleinen Pavillons faszinieren die Kinder sofort.

La surprenante densité de la structure et les matériaux inhabituels attirent irrésistiblement les enfants vers le petit pavillon.

Images and the drawings below
show that the interior of the Cave is
considerably more complex than the
cubic exterior would suggest.

Bilder und Zeichnungen unten
zeigen, dass das Innere der Höhle
um einiges komplexer ist, als das
kubische Äußere vermuten lässt.

Les photos et les plans ci-dessous
le montrent, l'intérieur de la caverne
est beaucoup plus complexe que
sa forme extérieure cubique ne le
suggère.

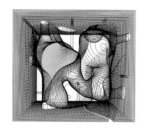
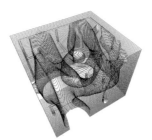

Offering a place to hide and play or perhaps to observe while not being seen, the inside of the Cave has a clearly geological source of inspiration, like layered stone.

Das Innere der Höhle ist offenkundig von der Geologie inspiriert, Gesteinsschichten etwa, und bietet Raum zum Verstecken und Spielen, vielleicht auch zum Beobachten, während man selbst unsichtbar bleibt.

Lieu où se cacher et jouer, ou peut-être observer sans être vu, l'intérieur de la caverne est clairement d'inspiration géologique, comme des roches stratifiées.

FIREPLACE FOR CHILDREN

Trondheim, Norway, 2010

Area: 30 m².
Client: Municipality of Trondheim.

This clever, simple structure made of recycled wood has a central, open fireplace like old huts or ancient shelters.

Wie eine Hütte oder ein Unterschlupf aus alten Zeiten verfügt dieses raffinierte, aber simple Bauwerk aus recyceltem Holz über eine zentrale offene Feuerstelle.

La structure simple et astucieuse en bois recyclé possède un foyer central ouvert comme les huttes d'autrefois ou les anciens refuges.

This project, which also had a "very limited budget," involved the recuperation of unused material from a neighboring construction site. Short pieces of wood were used to create a design based on traditional Norwegian huts. A light concrete base was used for the structure that is made of "80 layered circles." The radius and center point of the circles varies, but each is made of 28 pieces of pine, and they are placed to encourage a chimney effect. A double curved sliding door is used to close the outdoor fireplace, which was erected near the Skjermvegen Kindergarten. The project received an Honorable Mention in the Trondheim Municipality Building Prize, and was included in the top 25 entries for the AR Emerging Architecture Awards 2009.

Bei diesem Projekt, für das ebenfalls nur ein „sehr begrenztes Budget" zur Verfügung stand, kam ungenutztes Baumaterial einer nahe gelegenen Baustelle zum Einsatz. Aus kurzen Holzstücken wurde eine Form geschaffen, die sich an traditionellen norwegischen Hütten orientiert. Die aus „80 geschichteten Kreisen" bestehende Konstruktion ruht auf einem leichten Betonfundament. Radius und Mittelpunkt der Kreise, die aus jeweils 28 Stück Pinienholz bestehen und deren Anordnung einen Kamineffekt erzielen soll, variieren. Die Feuerstelle, gleich neben dem Skjermvegen-Kindergarten errichtet, kann mit einer doppelt gewölbten Schiebetür verschlossen werden. Das Projekt erhielt bei der Verleihung des Städtischen Baupreises von Trondheim eine lobende Erwähnung und schaffte es unter die besten 25 der AR Emerging Architecture Awards 2009.

Ce projet au budget lui aussi « très limité » comprenait la récupération de matériaux inutilisés sur un chantier voisin. Des morceaux de bois courts ont permis de créer un design inspiré des huttes traditionnelles norvégiennes. La structure de « 80 cercles empilés » a été dotée d'une base en béton légère. Le rayon et le centre de chaque cercle varient, mais chacun est fait de 28 morceaux de pin, et ils sont disposés de manière à favoriser l'effet cheminée. Une double porte coulissante arrondie ferme le foyer extérieur érigé près du jardin d'enfants Skjermvegen. Le projet a reçu une mention honorable au prix du bâtiment de la municipalité de Trondheim et faisait partie des 25 premiers pour le prix ar+d pour l'architecture naissante 2009.

Children gathered around the fire find not so much a place to play as a meeting or teaching area where the elements are kept at bay to some extent by the open hearth.

Für die um das Feuer versammelten Kinder ist der Ort, an dem die Elemente auf gewisse Weise durch die offene Feuerstelle ferngehalten werden, eher ein Treffpunkt oder Unterrichtsraum als ein Spielplatz.

Les enfants rassemblés autour du feu trouvent ici, moins un endroit où jouer qu'un lieu de réunion ou d'enseignement où les éléments sont dans une certaine mesure tenus à distance par le foyer ouvert.

Drawings show the basic circular form with its irregular upper opening. As the images demonstrate, a pattern of openings has been left in the external shell, making the structure glow more fully in the dark.

Die Zeichnungen zeigen die grundlegende Kreisform mit der abweichenden oberen Öffnung. Wie die Bilder belegen, sorgt ein Muster von Öffnungen in der Hülle dafür, dass das Gebäude im Dunklen regelrecht glüht.

Plans de la forme de base circulaire et son ouverture irrégulière en haut. Des ouvertures ont été laissées dans la coque extérieure et forment un motif qui fait briller la construction de tous ses feux dans l'obscurité.

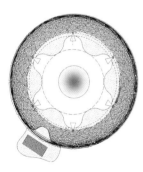

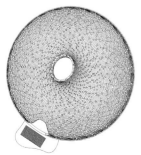

HAWORTH TOMPKINS

GRAHAM HAWORTH studied Architecture at the Universities of Nottingham and Cambridge. After graduation in 1984, he worked in the US for Skidmore, Owings & Merrill, and Holt Hinshaw Pfau Jones. On returning to the UK, he worked for Bennetts Associates, before forming Haworth Tompkins with **STEVE TOMPKINS** in 1991. Steve Tompkins studied Architecture at Bath University and traveled in Asia, before joining Arup Associates in London. He was a founding member of Bennetts Associates in 1987 prior to forming Haworth Tompkins with Graham Haworth. Projects by the practice include the Coin Street Housing and Neighborhood Center (South Bank, London, 2001–07); The Young Vic (London, 2006); Aldeburgh Music Creative Campus (Snape Maltings, Aldeburgh, 2009); Dovecote Studio (Snape Maltings, Snape, 2009, published here); the Open Air Theater, Regent's Park (London, 2000–12); and The London Library, St. James's Square (London, 2007–13). Current work includes the Royal College of Art (London, 2009–14); the Chichester Festival Theater (2014); and the National Theater South Bank (London, 2013–15), all in the UK.

GRAHAM HAWORTH studierte Architektur an den Universitäten von Nottingham und Cambridge. Nach seinem Diplom 1984 arbeitete in den USA bei Skidmore, Owings & Merrill und bei Holt Hinshaw Pfau Jones sowie nach seiner Rückkehr in das Vereinigte Königreich bei Bennetts Associates, bis er 1991 mit **STEVE TOMPKINS** das Büro Haworth Tompkins gründete. Steve Tompkins studierte Architektur an der Bath University und reiste durch Asien, danach ging er zu Arup Associates in London. Er war 1987 Mitbegründer von Bennetts Associates, bevor er mit Graham Haworth das Büro Haworth Tompkins gründete. Zu dessen Projekten zählen die Wohnbebauung und das Nachbarschaftszentrum Coin Street (South Bank, London, 2001–07); The Young Vic (London, 2006); der Aldeburgh Music Creative Campus (Snape Maltings, Aldeburgh, 2009); das Dovecote Studio (Snape Maltings, Snape, 2009, hier veröffentlicht); das Freilichttheater im Regent's Park (London, 2000–12) und die London Library, St. James's Square (London, 2007–13). Aktuelle Arbeiten sind das Royal College of Art (London, 2009–14); das Chichester Festival Theatre (2014) und das National Theatre South Bank (London, 2013–15), alle im Vereinigten Königreich.

GRAHAM HAWORTH a étudié l'architecture aux universités de Nottingham et de Cambridge. Après son diplôme (1984), il a travaillé aux USA pour Skidmore, Owings & Merrill et Holt Hinshaw Pfau Jones. De retour en Grande-Bretagne, il a travaillé pour Bennetts Associates avant de fonder Haworth Tompkins avec **STEVE TOMPKINS** en 1991. Steve Tompkins a fait des études d'architecture à l'université de Bath et a voyagé en Asie avant de rejoindre Arup Associates à Londres. Il a été l'un des fondateurs de Bennetts Associates en 1987 avant de créer Haworth Tompkins avec Graham Haworth. Parmi les projets réalisés par l'agence figurent le logement et centre de voisinage de Coin Street (South Bank, Londres, 2001–07) ; le théâtre Young Vic (Londres, 2006) ; le campus de musique créative d'Aldeburgh (Snape Maltings, Aldeburgh, 2009) ; le studio Dovecote (Snape Maltings, Snape, 2009, publié ici) ; le théâtre en plein air de Regent's Park (Londres, 2000–12) et la bibliothèque London Library de St James's Square (2007–13). Les travaux en cours sont le Royal College of Art (Londres, 2009–14) ; le théâtre du festival de Chichester (2014) et le théâtre national de South Bank (Londres, 2013–15), tous au Royaume-Uni.

DOVECOTE STUDIO

Snape Maltings, Snape, Suffolk, UK, 2009

Area: 29 m². Client: Aldeburgh Music.
Cost: £155 000. Collaboration: Marianne Løbersli Sørstrøm.

Converted from the ruins of a 19th-century dovecote (home for domesticated pigeons), this studio is intended for a single artist and forms part of the music campus at Snape Maltings, founded by Benjamin Britten in a group of former industrial buildings on the Suffolk coast of England. The studio is made with a welded COR-TEN steel monocoque shell, which was lined in spruce plywood. It was fabricated on site and then placed in its final location with a crane to avoid undue disturbance to the vegetation. The architects state: "A large north-facing roof window, ground-floor double doors, and a small mezzanine workspace enable the studio to be used for writing, music, visual arts, or performance. A corner window from the mezzanine gives long views over the reed beds to the North Sea."

Dieses in den Ruinen eines Taubenhauses aus dem 19. Jahrhundert errichtete Studio ist für einen einzelnen Künstler konzipiert und gehört zu dem von Benjamin Britten gegründeten Musikcampus Snape Maltings, der in einer Reihe von Industriebauten an der Küste von Suffolk untergebracht ist. Das Studio besteht aus einer geschweißten, einschaligen Hülle aus Corten-Stahl und ist mit Fichtensperrholz ausgekleidet. Es wurde vor Ort gefertigt und mithilfe eines Krans platziert, um die Vegetation nicht in Mitleidenschaft zu ziehen. Die Architekten: „Wegen eines großes Dachfensters auf der Nordseite, Doppeltüren im Erdgeschoss und eines kleinen Mezzanin-Arbeitsplatzes eignet sich das Studio sowohl für Autoren als auch für bildende Künstler und Performancekünstler. Ein Eckfenster im Mezzanin-Geschoss gewährt einen weiten Ausblick über das Röhricht hin zur Nordsee."

Issu de la reconversion des ruines d'un colombier du XIXᵉ siècle, le studio est destiné à accueillir un artiste célibataire, il fait partie du campus de musique de Snape Maltings fondé par Benjamin Britten dans un ensemble d'anciens bâtiments industriels sur la côte anglaise du Suffolk. Il est fait d'une monocoque en acier Corten soudé, doublée de contreplaqué d'épicéa. Fabriqué sur le site même, il a été mis en place à l'aide d'une grue afin de ne pas détruire indûment la nature. Les architectes expliquent : « Une large fenêtre dans le toit face au nord, les doubles portes du rez-de-chaussée et un petit espace de travail sur une mezzanine permettent au studio d'être utilisé pour l'écriture, la musique, les arts plastiques ou les performances. Une fenêtre dans l'angle de la mezzanine offre des vues très larges des roselières vers la mer du Nord. »

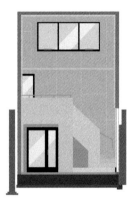
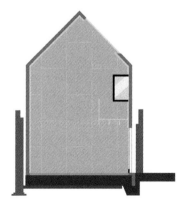

The double-slope roof has a generous skylight on one side that compensates for the relatively closed steel façades.

Auf einer Seite des Spitzdachs befindet sich ein großes Dachfenster und gleicht die relative Geschlossenheit der Stahlfassade aus.

Le toit à double pente est percé d'une généreuse lucarne sur un côté qui compense le caractère sinon assez clos des façades en acier.

*Left page, full spruce plywood
surfaces on the interior correspond
to the relatively closed and blank
exterior COR-TEN walls. The roof
opening nonetheless floods the
space with natural light.*

*Die Oberflächen aus Fichten-
sperrholz im Innenbereich (linke
Seite) korrespondieren mit der
eher geschlossenen und rohen
Außenwand aus Corten-Stahl. Dafür
taucht die Dachöffnung den Raum in
natürliches Licht.*

*Page de gauche, les surfaces inté-
rieures entièrement couvertes de
contreplaqué d'épicéa font pendant
aux murs extérieurs en acier Corten
relativement fermés et nus. L'ouverture dans le toit suffit à inonder
l'espace de lumière naturelle.*

*A corner window gives an un-
expectedly generous view of the
surroundings. The interior forms
of the building are very much in
harmony with the exterior, though
lighter colors predominate.*

*Das Eckfenster bietet eine überra-
schend großzügige Aussicht auf die
Umgebung. Die Formen im Innern
des Gebäudes stimmen mit dem
Äußeren überein, wobei hellere
Farben dominieren.*

*Une fenêtre d'angle ouvre une vue
étonnamment large des alentours.
Les formes intérieures du bâtiment
sont très largement harmonisées
avec l'extérieur, mais les couleurs
dominantes sont plus claires.*

TIMOTHY HURSLEY

TIMOTHY HURSLEY was born in 1955 in Detroit, Michigan, where he apprenticed in architectural photography with the Hungarian photographer Balthazar Korab, beginning in 1972. His apprenticeship continued until he moved to Little Rock, Arkansas, in 1980. There, he started his own architectural photography studio, The Arkansas Office. From 1982 to 1987, he made architectural photographs of Andy Warhol's last Factory on Madison Avenue and 34th Street in Manhattan. In 1990, Hursley was given an Honor Award for his architectural photography by the American Institute of Architects. In 1994, Timothy Hursley began documenting the work of the architect Samuel Mockbee's Rural Studio and continues to do so today. This has resulted in two books: *Rural Studio: Samuel Mockbee and an Architecture of Decency* (Princeton Architectural Press, 2002) and *Proceed and Be Bold* (Princeton Architectural Press, 2005). He is currently working on a third volume celebrating 20 years of Rural Studio. Other architects Hursley has worked closely with during his career include Gunnar Birkerts, Fay Jones, Antoine Predock, Moshe Safdie, I. M. Pei, and Mack Scogin. Published here is Alabama Silo (Greensboro, Alabama, USA).

TIMOTHY HURSLEY wurde 1955 in Detroit, Michigan, geboren, wo er 1972 bei dem ungarischen Fotografen Balthazar Korab eine Ausbildung zum Architekturfotografen begann, die bis zu seinem Umzug 1980 nach Little Rock, Arkansas, dauerte. Dort gründete er 1980 sein eigenes Studio für Architekturfotografie, The Arkansas Office. Zwischen 1982 und 1987 fotografierte er Andy Warhols letzte Factory in Manhattan (Madison Avenue, Ecke 34th Street). Für sein architekturfotografisches Werk erhielt Hursley einen Honor Award des American Institute for Architects. 1994 begann er, die Arbeiten des Architekten Samuel Mockbee und seines Rural Studios zu dokumentieren, was er bis heute tut. Dabei entstanden zwei Bücher: *Rural Studio: Samuel Mockbee and an Architecture of Decency* (Princeton Architectural Press, 2002) und *Proceed and Be Bold* (Princeton Architectural Press, 2005). Derzeit arbeitet er an einem dritten Band anlässlich des 20. Jubiläums von Rural Studio. Weitere Architekten, mit denen Hursley im Lauf seiner Karriere eng zusammengearbeitet hat, sind u. a. Gunnar Birkerts, Fay Jones, Antoine Predock, Moshe Safdie, I. M. Pei und Mack Scogin. Hier vorgestellt wird sein Alabama Silo (Greensboro, Alabama).

TIMOTHY HURSLEY est né en 1955 à Detroit où il a fait son apprentissage de photographe architectural avec le photographe hongrois Balthazar Korab à partir de 1972 et jusqu'à son départ pour Little Rock, dans l'Arkansas, en 1980. C'est là qu'il a ouvert son studio de photographie architecturale, The Arkansas Office. De 1982 à 1987, il a photographié la dernière factory d'Andy Warhol dans Madison Avenue et la 34ᵉ Rue à Manhattan. En 1990, Hursley a reçu un prix honorifique de l'American Institute of Architects. Timothy Hursley a commencé en 1994 à documenter le travail du Rural Studio de l'architecte Samuel Mockbee et il continue encore aujourd'hui, ce qui a donné lieu à la publication de deux livres : *Rural Studio: Samuel Mockbee and an Architecture of Decency* (Princeton Architectural Press, 2002) et *Proceed and Be Bold* (Princeton Architectural Press, 2005). Il travaille actuellement à un troisième pour les 20 ans de Rural Studio. Il a collaboré étroitement avec d'autres architectes au cours de sa carrière, notamment Gunnar Birkerts, Fay Jones, Antoine Predock, Moshe Safdie, I. M. Pei et Mack Scogin. Nous publions ici son Alabama Silo (Greensboro, Alabama).

ALABAMA SILO

Greensboro, Alabama, USA

Area: ø 4.6 m.
Client: Tim Hursley.

In 2007, Timothy Hursley discovered and photographed a silo in Greensboro, Alabama, damaged by a tornado in about 1993, while documenting the work of Rural Studio. The 14-meter-high structure had been twisted and bent by the force of the winds. In 2010, the photographer purchased the silo but not the land it stands on with the understanding that he would remove the structure within seven years. In 2011, he set up a surveillance camera at the silo shooting frames every 12 seconds. In March 2012, he released a short film from this series as a time-lapse video on *Oxford American*'s channel on YouTube. Hursley's interest in this former farm structure might well be likened to the documentary work of Hilla and Bernd Becher, though the documentation of industrial buildings carried out by the German photographers did not focus on damaged buildings.

Während seiner Dokumentation der Arbeiten von Rural Studio entdeckte und fotografierte Timothy Hursley 2007 ein Silo in Greensboro, Alabama, das um 1993 herum von einem Tornado beschädigt worden war. Die Wucht des Sturms hatte das 14 m hohe Gebäude verdreht und abgeknickt. Der Fotograf erwarb das Silo 2010, jedoch nicht den Grund, auf dem es stand, mit dem Vorhaben, das Gebäude innerhalb von sieben Jahren abzutransportieren. 2011 installierte er eine Überwachungskamera, die alle 12 sec ein Bild machte. Zusammen mit dem *Oxford American* veröffentlichte er im März 2012 auf YouTube einen Kurzfilm mit Bildern der Serie im Zeitraffer. Zwischen Hursleys Interessen an diesem ehemaligen landwirtschaftlichen Gebäude und dem dokumentarischen Werk Bernd und Hilla Bechers lassen sich durchaus Parallelen feststellen, auch wenn sich die beiden deutschen Fotografen bei ihrer Beschäftigung mit Industriekultur nicht auf beschädigte Gebäude konzentrierten.

En 2007, alors qu'il documente le travail de Rural Studio, Timothy Hursley découvre et photographie un silo endommagé par une tornade en 1993 à Greensboro, dans l'Alabama. La structure haute de 14 m avait été tordue et pliée par la force des vents. En 2010, le photographe achète le silo, mais pas le terrain où il est situé, à la condition qu'il se débarrasse du silo dans les sept ans. En 2011, il place une caméra de surveillance à proximité qui prend une photo toutes les 12 secondes. En mars 2012, il réalise avec le magazine *Oxford American* un court-métrage à partir de ces images en accéléré, hébergé sur youtube. L'intérêt de Hursley pour cet ancien bâtiment agricole pourrait être comparé au travail documentaire de Hilla et Bernd Becher, mais les Allemands ne se sont pas intéressés aux constructions abîmées dans leur inventaire de bâtiments industriels.

As much a piece of architectural art generated by a storm as a real building, the Silo assumes a sculptural presence in its site.

Als Werk architektonischer Kunst, geschaffen von einem Sturm, ebenso wie als reales Gebäude, besitzt das Silo an seinem Standort eine starke skulpturale Präsenz.

Autant œuvre d'art architecturale créée par une tornade que bâtiment réel, le silo dégage une présence sculpturale.

CRISTINA IGLESIAS

CRISTINA IGLESIAS was born in San Sebastián, Spain, in 1956. She lives and works in Madrid. She studied chemical sciences in her hometown (1976–78) and then, after a brief period in Barcelona working on ceramics and drawing, she studied sculpture at the Chelsea School of Art in London, UK (1980–82). She was granted a Fulbright scholarship to study at the Pratt Institute (New York, 1988). In 1995 she was appointed Professor of Sculpture at the Akademie der bildenden Künste in Munich (Germany) and in 1999 she won Spain's National Visual Arts Prize. In 2012 she won the Grosse Kunstpreis Berlin. She has represented Spain twice at the *Venice Biennale*, in 1986 and 1993. She also represented Spain at *Expo '92* in Seville, and at the Hanover World Fair, *Expo 2000*. Her public commissions include Laurel Leaves—Moskenes (Lofoten Island, Norway); Deep Fountain (Leopold de Waelplaats, Antwerp, Belgium, 2006); the threshold-entrance for the Prado Museum extension (Madrid, Spain, 2007); the Estancias Sumergidas, an underwater sculpture in the Cortes Sea near Espiritu Santo Island, in Baja California (Mexico, 2010); and Vegetation Room Inhotim (Inhotim, Belo Horizonte, Brazil, 2010–12, published here). Recent solo exhibitions have been held at the Marian Goodman Gallery (New York, USA, 2011) and at the Reina Sofia National Museum (Madrid, Spain, 2013).

CRISTINA IGLESIAS wurde 1956 in San Sebastián, Spanien, geboren. Sie lebt und arbeitet in Madrid. Sie studierte in ihrer Heimatstadt Chemie (1976–78) und, nach einer Zeit in Barcelona, während der sie sich mit Keramik und Zeichnen beschäftigte, Skulptur an der Chelsea School of Art in London (1980–82). Mit einem Fulbright-Stipendium studierte sie zudem am Pratt Institute (New York, 1988). An der Akademie der bildenden Künste in München wurde sie 1995 Professorin für Skulptur. 1999 bekam sie den Spanischen Staatspreis der bildenden Künste verliehen, 2012 den Großen Kunstpreis Berlin. Sie hat Spanien zweimal bei der Biennale in Venedig vertreten, 1986 und 1993, ebenso bei der Expo 1992 in Sevilla und 2000 in Hannover. Zu ihren öffentlichen Aufträgen zählen Laurel Leaves – Moskenes (Lofoten, Norwegen), Deep Fountain (Leopold de Waelplaats, Antwerpen, 2006), das Eingangstor für den Anbau des Prado (Madrid, 2007), die Estancias Sumergidas, eine Unterwasserskulptur im Golf von Kalifornien bei der Isla Espiritu Santo (Baja California, Mexiko, 2010) und der Vegetation Room Inhotim (Inhotim, Belo Horizonte, Brasilien, 2010–12, hier vorgestellt). Einzelausstellungen waren zuletzt in der Marian Goodman Gallery (New York, 2011) und im Museum Reina Sofia (Madrid, 2013) zu sehen.

CRISTINA IGLESIAS est née à Saint-Sébastien, en Espagne, en 1956. Elle vit et travaille à Madrid. Elle a fait des études de chimie dans sa ville natale (1976–78) puis, après une courte période à Barcelone où elle a travaillé sur la céramique et le dessin, elle a étudié la sculpture à la Chelsea School of Art de Londres (1980–82). Elle a bénéficié d'une bourse Fulbright pour étudier à l'Institut Pratt (New York, 1988). Elle a été nommée professeur de sculpture à l'Académie d'art plastiques de Munich en 1995 et a remporté le prix national d'Espagne en arts plastiques en 1999. Elle a également gagné le prix Grosse Kunstpreis de Berlin en 2012. Elle a représenté deux fois l'Espagne à la Biennale de Venise, en 1986 et 1993, ainsi qu'aux expositions universelles Expo '92 de Séville et Expo 2000 de Hanovre. Ses commandes publiques comprennent *Les Feuilles de laurier* – Moskenes (îles Lofoten, Norvège); *Fontaine profonde* (place Leopold de Wael, Anvers, Belgique, 2006); l'entrée de l'extension du musée du Prado (Madrid, 2007); les *Estancias Sumergidas*, une sculpture immergée dans la mer de Cortes, près de l'île du Saint-Esprit, en Basse-Californie (Mexique, 2010) et la *Vegetation Room Inhotim* (Inhotim, Belo Horizonte, Brésil, 2010–12, publiée ici). Des expositions personnelles ont eu lieu récemment à la galerie Marian Goodman (New York, 2011) et au musée Reina Sofia (Madrid, 2013).

VEGETATION ROOM INHOTIM

Inhotim, Belo Horizonte, Brazil, 2010–12

Area: 81 m² (9 x 9 x 3 meters).
Client: Inhotim Contemporary Art Institute.

Inhotim was founded in 2006 by the collector Bernardo Paz to house his art collection. A botanical garden designed by Roberto Burle Marx in 1984 is part of the property. In the 300 hectares of native forest there are 110 other botanical collections with more than 5000 species, and 450 sculptures and installations by international artists, most of them commissioned expressly for their current location, are part of the scheme. The Vegetation Room Inhotim is located in an area of scrubland between the garden and the forest. The exterior structure is a nine-meter square covered in polished stainless steel that reflects the surrounding vegetation. Designed like a maze, its curved walls are covered with vegetal carvings and bronze powder resin. Of the four entrances of the square, only one leads to a central space where a stream runs. Cristina Iglesias first visited Inhotim in 2009. "By then," she says, "I had been doing plant rooms, but this is the first on such a large scale." The materials employed are bronze, resin, fiberglass, stainless steel, and water.

Inhotim wurde 2006 von dem Sammler Bernardo Paz gegründet, der dort seine Kunstsammlung unterbringen wollte. Ein botanischer Garten, 1984 von Roberto Burle Marx gestaltet, gehört zum Gelände. Auf den 300 ha urwüchsigen Waldes finden sich 110 botanische Sammlungen mit mehr als 5000 Pflanzenarten, das Gesamtbild ergänzen zudem 450 Skulpturen und Installationen internationaler Künstler, die meisten davon speziell für diesen Standort in Auftrag gegeben. Der Vegetation Room Inhotim liegt in buschigem Gelände zwischen Garten und Wald. Von außen ist ein quadratisches Gebäude von 9 m Seitenlänge zu sehen, mit polierten rostfreien Stahlplatten verkleidet, in denen sich die umgebende Vegetation spiegelt. Der Innenraum ist labyrinthisch gestaltet, die geschwungenen Wände sind mit pflanzenartigen Reliefs und Kunstharz mit Bronzepuder bedeckt. Von den vier Eingängen des Quaders führt nur ein einziger zu einem Raum in der Mitte, wo ein Bach fließt. Cristina Iglesias war 2009 zum ersten Mal in Inhotim. „Bis dahin", sagt sie, „hatte ich schon Pflanzräume gestaltet, aber das hier ist der erste in dieser Größe." Zu den verwendeten Materialien gehören Bronze, Kunstharz, Fiberglas, rostfreier Stahl und Wasser.

Inhotim a été créé en 2006 par le collectionneur Bernardo Paz pour accueillir sa collection d'art. La propriété comprend un jardin botanique, conçu par Roberto Burle Marx en 1984. Les 300 hectares de forêt naturelle abritent 110 autres collections botaniques de plus de 5000 espèces et 450 sculptures et installations d'artistes internationaux, la plupart spécialement commandées pour l'emplacement. La *Vegetation Room Inhotim* est placée dans une zone de brousse, entre le jardin et la forêt. La structure extérieure est un carré de neuf mètres de côté, recouvert d'acier inoxydable poli qui reflète la végétation environnante. Conçu comme un labyrinthe, les courbes de ses murs sont couvertes de sculptures végétales et de résine de poudre de bronze. Le carré à quatre entrées, dont une seule mène à l'espace central traversé par un ruisseau. Cristina Iglesias a visité Inhotim pour la première fois en 2009. « Jusqu'alors, explique-t-elle, j'avais fait des "plant rooms", mais jamais à aussi grande échelle. » Les matériaux employés sont le bronze, la résine, la fibre de verre, l'acier inoxydable et l'eau.

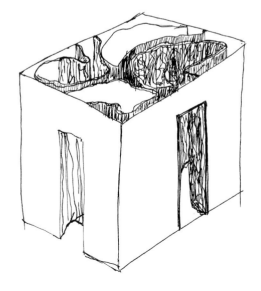

Left, a model of the work and, to the
right, a sketch showing the design.
Above, a photo of the mirrored
exterior of the Vegetation Room.

Links ein Modell der Arbeit, rechts
eine Skizze, die den Entwurf zeigt.
Oben ein Foto der gespiegelten
Umgebung des Vegetation Room.

À gauche, maquette de l'œuvre et à
droite, un croquis du design.
Ci-dessus, photo de l'environnement
extérieur de la Vegetation Room.

The contrast between the mirrored exterior and the open doorway leading to the interior of the work is one of surfaces, either a smooth reflection of the forest, or a three-dimensional representation of dense vegetation.

Der Kontrast zwischen dem spiegelnden Äußeren und dem offenen Eingang, der ins Innere der Arbeit führt, zeigt sich in den Oberflächen, der glatten Reflexion des Waldes bzw. der dreidimensionalen Repräsentation dichter Vegetation.

Le contraste entre l'extérieur qui se reflète et la porte ouverte qui mène à l'intérieur de l'œuvre est un contraste de surfaces, reflet lissé de la forêt ou représentation tridimensionnelle d'une végétation luxuriante.

A sketch by the artist (below) and an image of the interior where the work of art seems to be in symbiosis with the forest itself.

Eine Zeichnung der Künstlerin (unten) und ein Bild des Innenraums, wo das Kunstwerk eine Symbiose mit dem Wald einzugehen scheint.

Croquis de l'artiste (ci-dessous) et une vue de l'intérieur où l'œuvre semble fusionner avec la forêt.

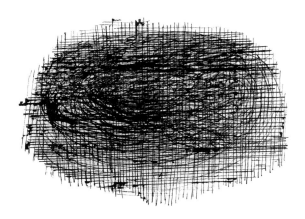

JUNYA ISHIGAMI

JUNYA ISHIGAMI was born in Kanagawa, Japan, in 1974. He studied at the Tokyo National University of Fine Arts and Music in the Architecture Department, graduating in 2000. He worked in the office of Kazuyo Sejima & Associates (now SANAA) from 2000 to 2004, establishing Junya Ishigami + Associates in 2004. Given his age, his list of projects is not long, but he has designed a number of tables, including one 9.5 meters long and three millimeters thick made of prestressed steel, and a project for the Hotel Kaiyo and housing (2007). Aside from the Kanagawa Institute of Technology KAIT workshop (Japan, 2007–08), he has designed a New York store for Yohji Yamamoto (USA, 2008) in the so-called Meatpacking District, and participated in the 2008 *Venice Architecture Biennale* (Greenhouses for the Japanese Pavilion, Venice, Italy, published here). Despite his limited number of completed works Junya Ishigami has emerged as one of the more significant young Japanese architects.

JUNYA ISHIGAMI wurde 1974 in Kanagawa, Japan, geboren. Er studierte an der Fakultät für Architektur der Staatlichen Kunst- und Musikhochschule Tokio, wo er 2000 seinen Abschluss machte. Zwischen 2000 und 2004 arbeitete er für Kazuyo Sejima & Associates (inzwischen SANAA) und gründete 2004 sein Büro Junya Ishigami + Associates. Angesichts seines Alters ist seine Projektliste nicht lang, doch hat Ishigami bereits mehrere Tische entworfen, darunter den 9,5 m langen Table aus 3 mm starkem Spannstahl sowie ein Projekt für die Kaiyo Hotel- und Wohnanlage (2007). Neben dem Werkstattgebäude für das Kanagawa Institute of Technology (KAIT; Japan, 2007–08) gestaltete er einen Yohji Yamamoto Store im New Yorker Meatpacking District (2008) und war 2008 auf der Architektur-Biennale in Venedig vertreten (Gewächshäuser für den japanischen Pavillon, Venedig, hier vorgestellt). Trotz der geringen Anzahl gebauter Projekte hat sich Junya Ishigami als einer der maßgeblichen jungen japanischen Architekten etabliert.

JUNYA ISHIGAMI, né en 1974 à Kanagawa au Japon, a étudié au département d'architecture de l'Université nationale des beaux-arts et de musique de Tokyo, dont il est sorti diplômé en 2000. Il a travaillé chez Kazuyo Sejima & Associates (aujourd'hui SANAA) de 2000 à 2004 et a créé l'agence Junya Ishigami + Associates en 2004. Son jeune âge explique que sa liste de réalisations ne soit pas très longue, mais il a dessiné un certain nombre de tables, dont une de 9,5 mètres de long et de 3 millimètres d'épaisseur en acier précontraint (Table), et un projet pour l'hôtel Kaiyo et des logements (2007). En dehors d'installations pour l'Institut de technologie Kanagawa (2007–08), il a conçu le magasin new-yorkais du couturier japonais Yohji Yamamoto (2008) dans le quartier du Meatpacking. Il a participé à la Biennale d'architecture de Venise en 2008 (serres pour le pavillon japonais, publiées ici). Malgré ce nombre limité de projets achevés, Ishigami apparaît comme l'un des jeunes architectes japonais les plus prometteurs.

GREENHOUSES, JAPANESE PAVILION

Venice Architecture Biennale, Venice, Italy, 2008

Area: 20 m², 6 m², 11 m², 6 m². Client: The Japan Foundation.
Collaboration: Taro Igarashi (Commissioner), Hideaki Ohba (Botanist),
Jun Sato (Structural Engineer).

For the 2008 *Venice Architecture Biennale*, Junya Ishigami designed a series of small glass greenhouses that he set around the building in the *giardini*. Each of the greenhouses was conceived as an actual building, pushing the limits of structural soundness thanks to sophisticated calculations. His intention was to suggest "the future possibilities of architecture." Ishigami also refers to Joseph Paxton's Crystal Palace at the *Great Exhibition* in London (1851), which took the form of a greenhouse. Ishigami worked with the botanist Hideaki Ohba, who carefully selected varieties of plants that at first seemed to be native to the environment, but in fact represent a "slight disturbance in the landscape of the park." Wooden furniture was placed in the garden, suggesting the ambiguity or more precisely "simultaneity" of interior and exterior space, while the inside of the Pavilion itself was essentially empty except for delicate drawings on the white walls.

Für die Architektur-Biennale 2008 entwarf Junya Ishigami eine Reihe kleinerer Gewächshäuser, die er rund um den Pavillon in die Giardini platzierte. Jedes Gewächshaus war als eigenständiger Bau konzipiert und dank ausgeklügelter Berechnungen eben gerade in der Lage stabil aufrecht zu stehen. Seine Absicht war es, „künftige Möglichkeiten der Architektur" aufzuzeigen. Zugleich nimmt Ishigami auf Joseph Paxtons Kristallpalast Bezug, der 1851 zur Londoner Weltausstellung erbaut worden und ebenfalls wie ein Gewächshaus angelegt war. Ishigami arbeitete mit dem Botaniker Hideaki Ohba, der sorgsam Pflanzen auswählte, die zunächst einheimisch wirkten, tatsächlich aber „eine subtile Störung der Parklandschaft" darstellten. Außerdem wurden im Garten Holzmöbel aufgestellt, eine Anspielung auf die Mehrdeutigkeit oder vielmehr „Simultaneität" von Innen- und Außenraum. Die Innenräume des Pavillons selbst waren bis auf wenige zarte Zeichnungen an den weißen Wänden so gut wie leer.

Junya Ishigami a conçu pour la Biennale de Venise 2008 une série de petites serres en verre disposées autour du pavillon japonais dans les Giardini. Chacune a été conçue comme une vraie construction, dont la stabilité a fait l'objet de calculs sophistiqués. Son intention était de suggérer «les possibilités futures de l'architecture». Ishigami se réfère également au Crystal Palace construit par Joseph Paxton pour la grande exposition de Londres (1851), qui était aussi en forme de serre. Il a travaillé avec le botaniste Hideaki Ohba qui a sélectionné méticuleusement différentes plantes apparemment natives du lieu, mais qui, en fait, représentent un «léger dérangement dans le paysage du parc». Le mobilier de bois a été disposé dans les jardins pour suggérer une ambiguïté, ou plus précisément une «simultanéité», entre l'intérieur et l'extérieur, tandis que l'intérieur du pavillon lui-même reste essentiellement vide, à part quelques délicats dessins sur ses murs blancs.

At first glance, the vegetation contained in Ishigami's greenhouses appears to be indigenous, but on closer examination reveals itself to be more exotic.

Die auf den ersten Blick einheimisch wirkenden Pflanzen in Ishigamis Gewächshäusern erweisen sich bei näherem Hinsehen als exotischere Gattungen.

À première vue, la végétation contenue dans les serres d'Ishigami semble indigène, mais elle est en fait plutôt exotique.

The inside space almost looks white in these images, but the walls are covered with delicate drawings. Below, a drawing of the outdoor structures in their natural setting.

Auch im Innern des Pavillons, der auf den Fotos fast weiß wirkt, erkennt man erst auf den zweiten Blick die ungemein feinen Wandzeichnungen. Unten eine Zeichnung der von Bäumen umstandenen Gewächshäuser.

Bien que l'espace intérieur semble presque blanc sur ces reproductions, les murs sont recouverts de délicats dessins. Ci-dessous, une représentation des serres dans leur cadre naturel.

ARATA ISOZAKI

Born in Oita City on the island of Kyushu, Japan, in 1931, **ARATA ISOZAKI** graduated from the Architectural Faculty of the University of Tokyo in 1954 and established Arata Isozaki & Associates in 1963, having worked in the office of Kenzo Tange. Winner of the 1986 RIBA Gold Medal, his notable buildings include the Museum of Modern Art, Gunma (Gunma, Japan, 1971–74); the Tsukuba Center Building (Tsukuba, Japan, 1978–83); the Museum of Contemporary Art (Los Angeles, California, USA, 1981–86); Art Tower Mito (Mito, Japan, 1986–90); Higashi Shizuoka Convention and Arts Center (Shizuoka, Japan, 1993–98); and Ohio's Center of Science and Industry (COSI, Columbus, Ohio, USA, 1994–99). Recent work includes the Shenzhen Cultural Center (Shenzhen, China, 1997–2008); Central Academy of Fine Art, Museum of Art (Beijing, China, 2003–08); Obscured Horizon (Pioneertown, California, USA, 2008–10, published here); Qatar National Convention Center (Doha, Qatar, 2004–11); the ongoing Milano Fiera (Milan, Italy, 2003–); and Himalayas Center (Shanghai, China, 2007–12).

ARATA ISOZAKI, 1931 in Oita auf der Insel Kyushu geboren, schloss sein Studium 1954 an der Fakultät für Architektur der Universität Tokio ab. Anschließend arbeitete er im Büro von Kenzo Tange und gründete 1963 Arata Isozaki & Associates. 1986 wurde er mit der RIBA-Goldmedaille ausgezeichnet. Zu seinen wichtigsten Bauten zählen das Museum für moderne Kunst in Gunma (Gunma, Japan, 1971–74), das Tsukuba Center (Tsukuba, Japan, 1978–83), das Museum of Contemporary Art (Los Angeles, Kalifornien, 1981–86), der Art Tower Mito (Mito, Japan, 1986–90), das Messe- und Kunstzentrum Higashi Shizuoka (Shizuoka, Japan, 1993–98) und das Zentrum für Wissenschaft und Industrie von Ohio (COSI, Columbus, Ohio, 1994–99). Neuere Arbeiten sind u. a. das Kulturzentrum Shenzhen (China, 1997–2008), das Kunstmuseum der Zentralen Akademie der schönen Künste in Peking (2003–08), Obscured Horizon (Pioneertown, Kalifornien, 2008–10, hier vorgestellt), das Nationale Kongresszentrum von Katar (Doha, Katar, 2004–11), das laufende Projekt Fiera Milano (Mailand, seit 2003) und das Himalayas Center (Schanghai, China, 2007–12).

Né à Oita, sur l'île de Kyushu, au Japon, en 1931, **ARATA ISOZAKI** obtient son diplôme d'architecte à l'université de Tokyo en 1954. Il fonde Arata Isozaki & Associates en 1963 après avoir travaillé dans l'agence de Kenzo Tange. Il obtient la médaille d'or du RIBA en 1986. Parmi ses réalisations les plus remarquées, on trouve le Musée d'art moderne de Gunma (Japon, 1971–74) ; le Centre civique de Tsukuba (Japon, 1978–83) ; le Musée d'art contemporain de Los Angeles (1981–86) ; la tour de l'art Mito (Mito, Japon, 1986–90) ; le Centre des congrès et des arts Higashi Shizuoka (Shizuoka, Japon, 1993–98) et le Centre des sciences et de l'industrie COSI (Columbus, Ohio, 1994–99). Ses récents travaux comprennent le Centre culturel de Shenzhen (Chine, 1997–2008) ; le musée de l'École nationale des beaux-arts (Pékin, 2003–08) ; Obscured Horizon (Pioneertown, Californie, 2008–10, publié ici) ; le Centre national des congrès du Qatar (Doha, 2004–11) ; le Milano Fiera, en cours (Milan, 2003–) et le complexe Himalayas (Shanghai, 2007–12).

OBSCURED HORIZON

Pioneertown, California, USA, 2008–10

Area: 9 m².
Client: Eba and Jerry Sohn.

Located in the Mojave Desert where rain is very rare, this project consists of a series of freestanding pavilions that have neither electricity nor water. The project was carried out in collaboration with the artist Lawrence Weiner. The owner and the architect agreed to make three beds reflecting the different seasons in different areas of the property. "The Summer bed is a concrete platform set 1.8 meters off the ground to avoid the danger of snakes. The Spring and Fall bed has a ceiling to avoid morning dew, and Winter is surrounded by walls." All the same size, these "bed rooms" have "the desert as a floor, the sky as a ceiling, and no walls but unframed landscape" in the words of Arata Isozaki. The architect, like some of his younger Japanese colleagues such as Sou Fujimoto, has sought, with such a "fundamental" series of small structures, to address issues that concern the very nature of architecture. "Here," he says, "we should be referring to the property size as 'as far as you can see' or the height of the building as 'the height of the sky.'"

Das mitten in der regenarmen Mojave-Wüste gelegene Projekt besteht aus einer Reihe freistehender Pavillons, die weder über Strom noch Wasser verfügen. Realisiert wurde das Projekt in Zusammenarbeit mit dem Künstler Lawrence Weiner. Auftraggeber und Architekt kamen überein, drei „Betten" zu entwerfen, die an verschiedenen Standorten auf dem Grundstück symbolisch für die Jahreszeiten stehen. „Das Sommerbett ist eine Plattform aus Beton, die 1,8 m über dem Boden aufge-ständert ist, um Schutz vor Schlangen zu bieten. Das Frühlings- und Herbstbett hat ein Dach, um vor Morgentau zu schützen, der Winter ist von Wänden umschlossen." Diese „Betträume" sind jeweils gleich groß und „haben die Wüste zum Boden, den Himmel als Decke und keine Wände, sondern ungerahmte Landschaft", so Arata Isozaki. Wie andere japanische Kollegen, darunter auch der jüngere Sou Fujimoto, beschäftigt sich Isozaki, besonders bei einer Reihe „fundamentaler" Kleinbauten, mit Definitionen von Architektur schlechthin. „Hier", erklärt Isozaki, „lässt sich die Größe des Grundstücks mit den Worten ‚so weit das Auge reicht' beschreiben, die Höhe der Bauten als ‚himmelhoch'."

Mis en œuvre en plein désert de Mojave où les pluies sont rares, ce projet conçu en collaboration avec l'artiste concep-tuel Lawrence Weiner se compose d'une série de pavillons indépendants qui ne possèdent ni eau ni électricité. Le pro-priétaire et l'architecte se sont accordé sur la construction de trois « lits » rappelant les différentes saisons et implantés à différents endroits de la propriété. « Le lit d'été est une plate-forme de béton suspendue à 1,8 mètre du sol pour se protéger des serpents. Le lit du printemps et de l'automne possède un plafond qui abrite de la rosée matinale, et celui d'hiver est entouré de murs. » Toutes de mêmes dimensions, ces « chambres à coucher » ont « le désert pour sol, le ciel pour plafond, et, dépourvues de murs, s'ouvrent sur un paysage sans limite », selon Arata Isozaki. Comme certains de ses plus jeunes confrères dont Sou Fujimoto, l'architecte cherche par une série « fondatrice » de petites structures à aborder des problèmes qui concernent la nature même de l'architecture. « Ici, dit-il, les expressions "aussi loin que l'on peut voir" et "aussi haut que le ciel" définissent les dimensions de la propriété. »

Isozaki's work in this instance is closer to sculpture or installation art than it is to architecture in the traditional sense—or rather, it is an effort to define what represents the minimalist limit of any building.

Isozakis Entwurf ist hier eher Skulptur oder Installationskunst als Architektur im klassischen Sinn – bzw. vielmehr der Versuch zu entdecken, was die Minimalgrenzen eines Gebäudes sein könnten.

Ici, l'intervention d'Isozaki est plus proche de la sculpture ou de l'installation que de l'architecture au sens traditionnel. Plus précisé-ment, elle représente un effort de définition des limites minimales de toute construction.

Placed in a voluntary way in the vast western landscape, Isozaki's interventions can also be likened to the garden follies of another era, albeit on a willfully reduced scale.

Man könnte die willkürlich in der weiten Landschaft des Westens platzierten Interventionen mit Follies vergleichen, Fantasiebauten der Gartenkunst früherer Zeiten. Allerdings fallen Isozakis Arbeiten bewusst kleiner aus.

Positionnées de manière très précise dans cet immense paysage, les interventions d'Isozaki peuvent aussi se comparer aux « folies » de jardins d'autres époques, mais à une échelle volontairement réduite.

TOYO ITO

Born in 1941 in Seoul, South Korea, **TOYO ITO** graduated from the University of Tokyo in 1965 and worked in the office of Kiyonori Kikutake until 1969. He created his own office, Urban Robot (URBOT), in Tokyo in 1971, assuming the name of Toyo Ito & Associates, Architects in 1979. He was awarded the Golden Lion for Lifetime Achievement from the 8th *International Venice Architecture Biennale* in 2002, the RIBA Gold Medal in 2006, and the Pritzker Prize in 2013. One of his most successful and widely published projects, the Sendai Mediatheque, was completed in 2001, while in 2002 he designed a temporary Pavilion for the Serpentine Gallery in London (UK). More recently, he has completed TOD'S Omotesando Building (Shibuya-ku, Tokyo, Japan, 2002–04); the Island City Central Park Grin Grin (Fukuoka, Japan, 2002–05); the Tama Art University Library (Hachioji City, Tokyo, Japan, 2004–07); the Za-Koenji Public Theater (Tokyo, Japan, 2005–08); and the Toyo Ito Museum of Architecture (Imabari, Ehime, Japan, 2011). The Home-for-All in Rikuzentakata (Iwate, Japan, 2012, published here) was the result of close collaboration between people who were affected by the March 2011 earthquake-tsunami and the architects Toyo Ito, Kumiko Inui, Sou Fujimoto, and Akihisa Hirata.

TOYO ITO, geboren 1941 in Seoul, Südkorea, machte 1965 seinen Abschluss an der Universität Tokio und arbeitete dann bis 1969 im Büro von Kiyonori Kikutake. Mit Urban Robot (URBOT) gründete er 1971 sein eigenes Büro in Tokio und änderte den Namen 1979 in Toyo Ito & Associates. Auf der VIII. Internationalen Architekturbiennale 2002 in Venedig erhielt er einen Goldenen Löwen für sein Lebenswerk, 2006 die RIBA-Goldmedaille und 2013 den Pritzker-Preis. Eines seiner erfolgreichsten und bekanntesten Projekte, die Mediathek von Sendai, wurde 2001 fertiggestellt, 2002 entwarf er einen temporären Pavillon für die Serpentine Gallery in London. In jüngerer Zeit hat er das Omotesando-Gebäude von TOD'S (Shibuya-ku, Tokio, 2002–04), das Island City Central Park Grin Grin (Fukuoka, Fukuoka, Japan, 2002–05), die Bibliothek der Kunsthochschule Tama (Hachioji, Tokio, 2004–07), das Theater Za-Koenji (Tokio, 2005–08) und das Toyo-Ito-Architekturmuseum (Imabari, Ehime, Japan, 2011) realisiert. Das Home-for-All in Rikuzentakata (Iwate, Japan, 2012, hier vorgestellt) ist das Ergebnis einer engen Zusammenarbeit mit Menschen, die im März 2011 von Erdbeben und Tsunami in Mitleidenschaft gezogen wurden, und den Architekten Toyo Ito, Kumiko Inui, Sou Fujimoto und Akihisa Hirata.

Né en 1941 à Séoul, **TOYO ITO** est diplômé de l'université de Tokyo (1965) et a travaillé dans l'agence de Kiyonori Kikutake jusqu'en 1969. Il a fondé son agence, Urban Robot (URBOT) à Tokyo en 1971 et a repris le nom Toyo Ito & Associates, Architects en 1979. Il a gagné le Lion d'or pour l'ensemble de son œuvre à la VIIIᵉ Biennale internationale d'architecture de Venise en 2002, la médaille d'or du RIBA en 2006 et le prix Pritzker en 2013. L'un de ses projets les plus célèbres et largement publiés, la médiathèque de Sendai, a été achevé en 2001, et il a créé un pavillon temporaire pour la Serpentine Gallery de Londres en 2002. Plus récemment, il a réalisé l'immeuble TOD'S d'Omotesando (Shibuya-ku, Tokyo, 2002–04); le parc Grin Grin de l'île de Fukuoka (Fukuoka, Japon, 2002–05); la bibliothèque universitaire d'art de Tama (Hachioji City, Tokyo, 2004–07); le théâtre public Za-Koenji (Tokyo, 2005–08); et le musée d'architecture Toyo Ito (Imabari, Ehime, Japon, 2011). La Maison pour tous de Rikuzentakata (Iwate, Japon, 2012, publiée ici) est le résultat d'une collaboration étroite entre les populations victimes du tremblement de terre et tsunami de mars 2011 et les architectes Toyo Ito, Kumiko Inui, Sou Fujimoto et Akihisa Hirata.

HOME-FOR-ALL
IN RIKUZENTAKATA

Rikuzentakata, Iwate, Japan, 2012

Area: 30 m². Collaboration: Kumiko Inui, Sou Fujimoto,
Akihisa Hirata, Naoya Hatakeyama.

Intended as a place for local residents to regain their peace of mind after the tsunami disaster that hit Japan, the Home-for-All is made in good part of Japanese cedar.

Das Home-for-All, gedacht als ein Ort für die Anwohner, um dort nach der Tsunami-Katastrophe in Japan zur Ruhe zu kommen, besteht zum Großteil aus japanischer Zeder.

Conçue comme un lieu destiné à aider les habitants de la région à retrouver la paix de l'esprit après le tsunami qui a frappé le Japon, la Maison pour tous est majoritairement construite en cèdre du Japon.

The structure spirals upward and offers terrace space that seems to be a continuation of the tree-like pillars.

Das Gebäude schraubt sich empor und verfügt über Terrassen, die wie eine Fortsetzung der baumartigen Stützpfeiler wirken.

La construction monte en spirale vers une terrasse qui semble une continuation des piliers arborescents.

This ten-meter-high Japanese cedar structure has two stories above ground. It was built on the Sanriku Coast in Rikuzen-takata, which was over 70% destroyed by the earthquake of March 11, 2011. Toyo Ito called on three younger architects— Kumiko Inui, Sou Fujimoto (also featured in this book), and Akihisa Hirata—to plan a "Home for All" in this town. The concept was to create a place for residents to "gain peace of mind and nurture their energy for the city's reconstruction." The architects developed their plan after consultations with residents who had suffered from the results of the earthquake and subsequent tsunami. They wish to point out that major contributions were made to the project by the photographer Naoya Hatakeyama, the Japan Foundation, and a large number of other supporting corporations, organizations, and individuals. Their work was displayed in the 13th *Venice Architecture Biennale* in 2012 in the Japan Pavilion in the Giardini, where it was awarded the Golden Lion for Best National Participant.

Dieses 10 m hohe Bauwerk aus japanischer Zeder besteht aus zwei Stockwerken. Errichtet wurde es an der Sanriku-Küste in Rikuzentakata, die das Erdbeben vom 11. März 2011 zu über 70 % zerstört hatte. Toyo Ito bat drei jüngere Architekten – Kumiko Inui, Sou Fujimoto (ebenfalls in diesem Buch vorgestellt) und Akihisa Hirata – ein „Heim für alle" für diese Stadt zu planen. Die Idee war, einen Ort zu schaffen, wo die Bewohner „zur Ruhe kommen und Kraft sammeln können für den Wiederaufbau ihrer Stadt". Die Architekten erarbeiteten ihren Entwurf nach Gesprächen mit Ortsansässigen, die von den Folgen des Erdbebens und des darauffolgenden Tsunamis betroffen waren. Es ist ihnen wichtig darauf hinzuweisen, dass zum Gelingen des Projekts außerdem der Fotograf Naoya Hatakeyama, die Japan Foundation und eine große Anzahl weiterer Unternehmen, Organisationen und Einzelpersonen maßgeblich beigetragen haben. Ihre Arbeit war während der XIII. Biennale in Venedig 2012 im Japanischen Pavillon in den Giardini zu sehen, wo sie mit dem Goldenen Löwen für den besten nationalen Beitrag ausgezeichnet wurde.

La structure de 10 m de haut en cèdre du Japon a deux étages. Elle a été bâtie sur la côte de Sanriku, à Rikuzentakata, ville détruite à plus de 70 % par le tremblement de terre du 11 mars 2011. Toyo Ito a fait appel à trois architectes plus jeunes – Kumiko Inui, Sou Fujimoto (également présent dans ce livre) et Akihisa Hirata – pour créer une « Maison pour tous » dans cette ville. L'idée était de créer un lieu de séjour où « retrouver la paix de l'esprit et s'alimenter en énergie pour reconstruire la ville ». Les architectes ont dessiné leur plan après avoir consulté les habitants qui avaient souffert des conséquences du tremblement de terre et du tsunami qui a suivi. Ils souhaitent souligner que les contributions majeures au projet ont été celles du photographe Naoya Hatakeyama, de la Fondation du Japon et d'un grand nombre d'autres entreprises, organisations et individus. L'œuvre a été présentée à la XIIIe Biennale d'architecture de Venise (2012) dans le pavillon du Japon des Giardini et a reçu le Lion d'or de la meilleure participation nationale.

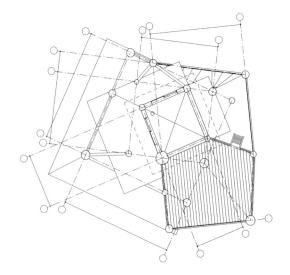

The plan left shows the spiraling pattern of the design. Right, an interior view with the exposed cedar pillars penetrating the space and offering generous ceiling heights.

Der Grundriss links verdeutlicht das spiralartige Moment des Entwurfs. Die Innenansicht rechts zeigt die freiliegenden Zedernpfeiler, die den Raum durchbohren und für großzügige Deckenhöhen sorgen.

Le plan à gauche montre la forme en spirale de la construction. À droite, une vue intérieure avec les piliers en cèdre visibles à l'extérieur qui pénètrent l'espace et permettent de généreuses hauteurs sous plafonds.

INSIDE IN
Tokyo, Japan, 2010

Area: 61 m². Client: The National Museum of Modern Art, Tokyo.
Collaboration: Inoue Industries (Construction), NUNO (Fabrics), Izumi,
Okayasu Lighting Design (Lighting).

This museum installation Inside in constructed in April 2010, was made with fabric, steel pipes, acrylic opal panels, aluminum mesh, and sheet polypropylene and is related in its polyhedron structure to the Imabari Toyo Ito Architecture Museum currently being designed by the architect in Omishima, Ehime, Japan. Seeking to create a "soft and topologically distorted space," Toyo Ito employed polyhedrons half the size of the ones to be used in Imabari. He states: "We were eager to create new spatial experiences that are beyond our imagination with the polyhedrons, and through this exhibition we have the opportunity to experiment with the modules to create exciting internal spaces." Ito's polyhedrons were set in the midst of a larger (196 m²) gallery in the museum for this temporary exhibition.

Die im April 2010 errichtete Museumsinstallation inside in bestand aus Textil, Stahlrohren, Milchglassegmenten aus Acrylglas, Aluminiummaschendraht und Polypropylenfolie und ähnelt der Polyeder-Konstruktion, die der Architekt derzeit für das Toyo Ito Architekturmuseum in Imabari auf Omishima, Präfektur Ehime, Japan, entwickelt. Toyo Ito, dem es darum ging, einen „weichen und topologisch verzerrten Raum" zu schaffen, arbeitete mit Polyedern, die halb so groß sind wie die Polyeder in Imabari. Er führt aus: „Wir wollten mit den Polyedern unbedingt neue räumliche Erfahrungen schaffen. Mit dieser Ausstellung haben wir die Gelegenheit, mit den Modulen zu experimentieren und faszinierende Innenräume zu gestalten." Itos Polyeder befanden sich im Zentrum eines großen (196 m²) Ausstellungsraums im Museum, der dieser Sonderschau gewidmet war.

L'installation inside in, montée dans une galerie de 196 m² d'un musée en avril 2010, a été réalisée en tissu, tubes d'acier, panneaux d'acrylique opalin, maillage d'aluminium et feuilles de polypropylène. Sa structure polyédrique rappelle le projet du Musée d'architecture Toyo Ito Imabari que conçoit actuellement l'architecte pour Omishima, dans la préfecture d'Ehime au Japon. Cherchant à créer un « espace doux et topologiquement déformé », Toyo Ito a utilisé des polyèdres de la moitié de la taille de ceux retenus pour Imabari. « À travers ces polyèdres, nous avons voulu créer de nouvelles expériences spatiales qui aillent au-delà de notre imagination, et cette exposition nous a donné l'opportunité d'expérimenter ces modules pour créer des espaces étonnants et stimulants. »

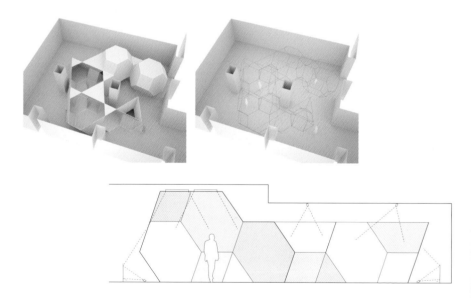

Using basic geometric forms and such materials as acrylic opal panels, Toyo Ito succeeds in altering the visitor's perception of space.

Mit einfachen geometrischen Formen und Materialien wie Milchglassegmenten aus Acrylglas gelingt es Toyo Ito, die Raumwahrnehmung der Besucher zu beeinflussen.

À partir de formes géométriques basiques et de matériaux comme les panneaux d'acrylique opalin, Toyo Ito réussit à modifier la perception de l'espace.

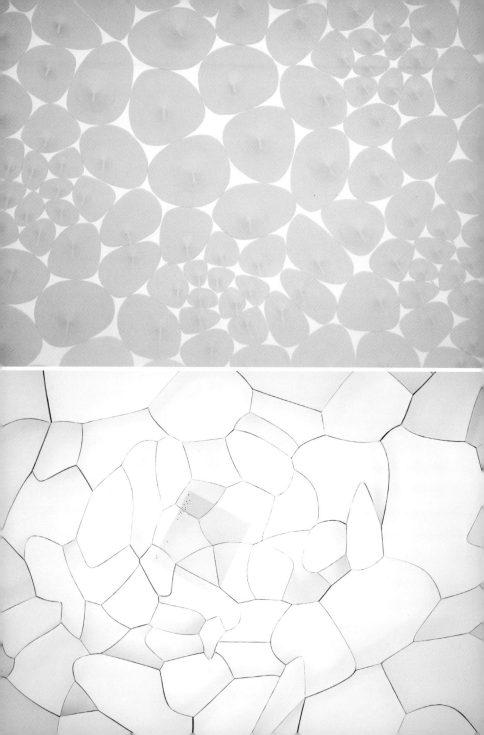

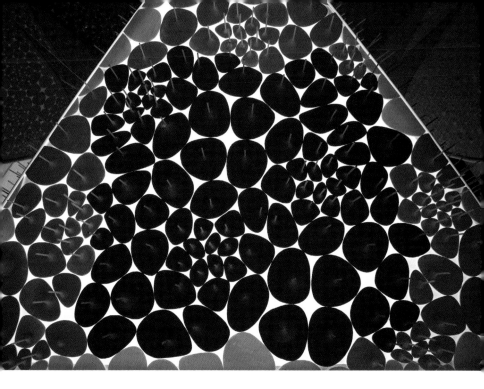

Toyo Ito has always shown an interest in forms that create a series of sensory dislocations—much in the same way that his younger colleagues of SANAA have done in recent years.

Toyo Ito interessiert sich schon immer für Formen, mit denen sich räumliche Desorientierung erzeugen lässt – ähnlich wie seine jüngeren Kollegen von SANAA in den letzten Jahren.

Toyo Ito a toujours fait preuve d'un grand intérêt pour les formes qui provoquent une dislocation sensorielle, attitude assez proche de ce que ses jeunes confrères de SANAA ont tenté ces dernières années.

JAKOB+MACFARLANE

DOMINIQUE JAKOB was born in 1966 and holds a degree in Art History from the Université de Paris I (1990) and a degree in Architecture from the École d'Architecture Paris-Villemin (1991). Born in New Zealand in 1961, **BRENDAN MACFARLANE** received his B.Arch. at SCI-Arc, Los Angeles (1984), and his M.Arch. degree at the Harvard Graduate School of Design (1990). From 1995 to 1997, MacFarlane was an architecture critic at the Architectural Association (AA) in London. They founded their own agency in 1992 in Paris, and were also cofounders with E. Marin-Trottin and D. Trottin of the exhibition and conference organizer Periphériques (1996–98). Their main projects include the T House (La-Garenne-Colombes, 1994, 1998); the Georges Restaurant (Pompidou Center, Paris, 1999–2000); the restructuring of the Maxim Gorky Theater (Petit-Quevilly, 1999–2000); and the Renault International Communication Center (Boulogne, 2004). Recent work includes the City of Fashion and Design (Paris, 2007–08); the Orange Cube (Lyon, 2010); and the FRAC Contemporary Art Center in Orléans (2006–11), all in France.

DOMINIQUE JAKOB wurde 1966 geboren und schloss ihr Studium der Kunstgeschichte an der Université de Paris I (1990) sowie der Architektur an der École d'Architecture Paris-Villemin (1991) ab. **BRENDAN MACFARLANE**, geboren 1961 in Neuseeland, absolvierte seinen B. Arch. am SCI-Arc, Los Angeles (1984), und seinen M. Arch. an der Harvard Graduate School of Design (1990). Von 1995 bis 1997 war MacFarlane Architekturkritiker an der Architectural Association (AA) in London. 1992 gründeten die beiden ihre eigene Agentur in Paris. Gemeinsam mit E. Marin-Trottin und D. Trottin waren sie Mitbegründer der Ausstellungs- und Messeagentur Periphériques (1996–98). Ihre wichtigsten Projekte sind u. a. das Maison T (La-Garenne-Colombes, 1994, 1998), das Restaurant Georges (Centre Pompidou, Paris, 1999–2000), der Umbau des Maxim-Gorki-Theaters (Petit-Quevilly, 1999–2000) sowie das Internationale Kommunikationszentrum von Renault (Boulogne, 2004). Zu ihren jüngeren Arbeiten zählen die Cité de la Mode et du Design (Paris, 2007–08), der Orange Cube (Lyon, 2010) sowie das Zentrum für zeitgenössische Kunst FRAC in Orléans (2006–11), alle in Frankreich.

DOMINIQUE JAKOB, née en 1966, est diplômée en histoire de l'art de l'université de Paris I (1990) et en architecture de l'École d'architecture Paris-Villemin (1991). Né en Nouvelle-Zélande en 1961, **BRENDAN MACFARLANE** a obtenu son B. Arch. au SCI-Arc (Los Angeles, 1984), et son M. Arch. à Harvard GSD (1990). De 1995 à 1997, il a été critique de projets à l'Architectural Association de Londres. Ils ont fondé leur agence à Paris en 1992 à Paris et ont aussi été cofondateurs, avec E. Marin-Trottin et D. Trottin, de l'agence Périphériques (1996–98). Parmi leurs principaux projets, tous en France : la maison T (La-Garenne-Colombes, 1994, 1998) ; le restaurant Georges (Centre Pompidou, Paris, 1999–2000) ; la restructuration du Théâtre Maxime Gorki (Petit-Quevilly, 1999–2000) et le Centre international de communication Renault (Boulogne-Billancourt, 2004). Plus récemment, ils ont réalisé la Cité de la mode et du design (Paris, 2007–08) ; un projet immobilier sur un quai de la Saône, le Cube Orange (Lyon, 2010) et le FRAC d'Orléans (2006–11).

PINK BAR

Centre Pompidou, Paris, France, 2006

Area: 22 m². Client: Georges Restaurant.
Cost: €100 000.

Returning to the Georges Restaurant run by the Costes family that they designed on the top floor of the Piano and Rogers Centre Pompidou in 2000, Jakob+MacFarlane made new use of a volume previously used for the cloakroom and restrooms. As they explain: "This new 'Pink' space, as second generation project, is conceived as a resultant element based on the same grid of the original restaurant project. Instead of deforming the grid to create the surfaced volumes, we carved out a resultant volume from a 3D matrix of 40 cubic centimeters, a micro division of the original building grid at the Centre Pompidou. This matrix is built from 10-millimeter aluminum sheets using laser cutting technology." Furniture for the Pink Bar was designed by Jakob+MacFarlane and produced by Cappellini, while lighting was done by iGuzzini.

In dem von der Familie Costes geführten Restaurant Georges, das sie 2000 im obersten Geschoss des Centre Pompidou von Piano und Rogers entworfen hatten, gestalteten Jakob+MacFarlane einen früher für Garderoben und Toiletten genutzten Bereich um. Sie erläutern den Entwurf wie folgt: „Dieser neue rosafarbene Bereich, ein Projekt der zweiten Generation, wurde als Element auf dem gleichen Raster der ursprünglichen Restaurantplanung konzipiert. Anstatt das Raster zu verformen, um die erforderlichen Flächen zu gewinnen, schnitten wir ein weiteres Volumen aus einer 3-D-Matrix von 40 cm³ – ein kleiner Teil des ursprünglichen Rasters des Centre Pompidou. Diese Matrix besteht aus 10 mm starken Aluminiumplatten, die mit Lasertechnologie geschnitten wurden." Die Möbel für die Pink Bar wurden von Jakob+MacFarlane entworfen und von Cappellini produziert, die Beleuchtung stammt von iGuzzini.

De retour au Georges, le restaurant géré par la famille Costes qu'ils avaient conçu au dernier étage du Centre Pompidou par Piano et Rogers en 2000, Jakob et MacFarlane ont réutilisé un volume affecté au vestiaire et aux toilettes. « Ce nouvel espace Rose, projet de seconde génération, est un élément résultant de la trame du projet d'origine du restaurant. Au lieu de déformer cette trame pour créer des volumes, nous avons creusé le volume résultant dans une matrice en 3D de 40 cm³, en une microdivision de la trame originale du Centre Pompidou. Cette matrice est en tôle d'aluminium de 10 mm d'épaisseur découpée au laser ». Le mobilier du bar a également été conçu par les deux architectes et produit par Cappellini, tandis que l'éclairage a été réalisé par iGuzzini.

The bar structure and furniture were all custom-designed by the architects for this location on the top floor of the Centre Pompidou in Paris.

Die Barkonstruktion und die Möbel wurden von den Architekten speziell für dieses Lokal auf dem obersten Geschoss des Centre Pompidou in Paris entworfen.

La structure et le mobilier du bar ont été spécialement dessinés par les architectes pour ce lieu situé au dernier niveau du Centre Pompidou à Paris.

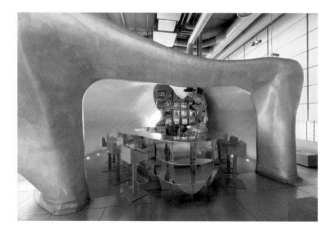

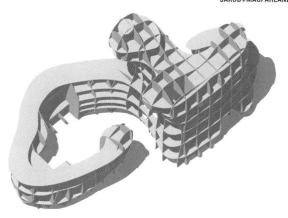

The drawing above shows the structure that is covered with a smooth, visible metallic skin. Bar stools, poufs, and tables were manufactured by Cappellini.

Diese Zeichnung zeigt die Konstruktion, die mit einer glatten Metallhaut verkleidet ist. Barstühle, Hocker und Tische wurden von Cappellini gefertigt.

Le dessin montre la structure qui a été recouverte d'une peau métallique lisse. Les tabourets, les poufs et les tables ont été fabriqués par Cappellini.

ADAM KALKIN

ADAM KALKIN was born in 1965 and attended Vassar College (class of 1984), the Washington University School of Architecture (1990), and the Architectural Association in London (1992). He was a winner of the Progressive Architecture Young Architects Award (1990). He has written a number of books about temporary architecture, such as *Quik Build, Adam Kalkin's ABC of Container Architecture* (Bibliotheque McLean, London, 2008). He is one of the more active architects in the area of container-based structures, having used them to design luxury homes, refugee housing, and a museum extension. In fact, Kalkin has frequently said that he does not consider himself an architect. He devised the Quik House, a prefabricated residence (2004–ongoing) made from five shipping containers that can be completed in three months. Kalkin has also worked in such unusual circumstances as collaboration with the fashion model Natalia Vodianova and the Naked Heart Foundation to build 200 playhouses for poor children across Russia, or with the US Army in Kabul. Although he most frequently reuses shipping containers, he has found a broad variety of potential uses for these, such as the illy Push Button House (2007, published here).

ADAM KALKIN wurde 1965 geboren und besuchte das Vassar College (Abschlussklasse 1984), die Fakultät für Architektur der Washington University (1990) und die Architectural Association in London (1992). 1990 wurde er mit dem Progressive Architecture Young Architects Award ausgezeichnet. Er schrieb mehrere Bücher über zeitgenössische Architektur, darunter *Quik Build, Adam Kalkin's ABC of Container Architecture* (Bibliotheque McLean, London, 2008). Er zählt zu den aktiveren Architekten im Bereich Bauen mit Containern und nutzte sie bereits für Entwürfe von Luxushäusern, Flüchtlingsunterkünften und die Erweiterung eines Museums. Tatsächlich äußerte Kalkin des Öfteren, er verstehe sich nicht als Architekt. Er konzipierte das Quik House, ein Fertighaus aus fünf Containern (2004–andauernd), das in nur drei Monaten fertiggestellt werden kann. Kalkin hat darüber hinaus unter ungewöhnlichen Umständen gearbeitet, etwa bei der Realisierung von 200 Spielhäusern für Kinder in Armut in Russland, eine Kollaboration mit dem Model Natalia Vodianova und der Naked Heart Foundation oder mit der US Army in Kabul. Obwohl er zumeist mit gebrauchten Frachtcontainern arbeitet, hat er eine große Bandbreite potenzieller Nutzungsformen gefunden, etwa mit seinem illy Push Button House (2007, hier vorgestellt).

ADAM KALKIN, né en 1965, a étudié à Vassar College à partir de 1984, à l'École d'architecture de Washington University (1990) et à l'Architectural Association de Londres (1992). Il a remporté le prix des jeunes architectes de Progressive Architecture (1990) et a écrit un certain nombre d'ouvrages sur l'architecture temporaire comme *Quik Build, Adam Kalkin's ABC of Container Architecture* (Bibliothèque McLean, Londres, 2008). C'est un des architectes les plus actifs dans le secteur de la construction à base de conteneurs qu'il utilise pour réaliser des logements de luxe, des logements pour réfugiés ou l'extension d'un musée. En fait, Kalkin a fréquemment affirmé qu'il ne se considérait pas comme un architecte. Il a conçu la Quik House, résidence préfabriquée (à partir de 2004, projet en cours) composée de cinq conteneurs et réalisable en trois mois. Il a également travaillé dans des circonstances inhabituelles comme, par exemple, lors de sa collaboration avec le top-modèle Natalia Vodianova et la Naked Heart Foundation pour construire 200 maisons de récréation destinées aux enfants pauvres de Russie, ou avec l'armée américaine à Kaboul. Il a imaginé une multiplicité d'utilisations potentielles des conteneurs, comme dans l'illy Push Button House (2007, publiée ici).

ILLY PUSH BUTTON HOUSE

Venice, Italy, and other locations, 2007

Area: 44.6 m². Client: illy. Collaboration: Quik Build.

The Italian coffee firm illy collaborated with Adam Kalkin to create "a dramatic work of living art—the illy Push Button House, a 'five-room home' with a kitchen, dining room, bedroom, living room, and library constructed within a standard industrial shipping container." The structure transforms using a hydraulic system at the push of a button from what appears to be a perfectly normal container into a very open and schematic representation of a home, which could coincidentally be used to serve coffee. The Push Button House was first shown at the *Venice Biennale* in June 2007. In December 2007, it was exhibited in New York City at the Time Warner Center. As part of the New York Wine & Food Festival, in October 2008, the Push Button House was again seen in Manhattan's Meatpacking District.

Im Zuge einer Kollaboration des italienischen Kaffeeherstellers illy mit Adam Kalkin entstand „ein dramatisches, lebendes Kunstwerk – das illy Push Button House, eine ‚5-Zimmer-Wohnung' mit Küche, Esszimmer, Schlafzimmer, Wohnzimmer und Bibliothek, gebaut aus einem Standard-Frachtcontainer". Die Konstruktion verwandelt sich dank eines Hydrauliksystems per Knopfdruck: Aus einem normalen Container wird ein offenes, schematisiertes Haus, das sich zufälligerweise auch für den Ausschank von Kaffee eignet. Erstmals präsentiert wurde das Push Button House auf der Biennale von Venedig im Juni 2007. Im Dezember 2007 wurde es im Time Warner Center in New York ausgestellt. Im Oktober 2008 war das Push Button House ein weiteres Mal im Rahmen des New York Wine & Food Festival im Meatpacking District zu sehen.

La marque de café italienne illy a collaboré avec Adam Kalkin pour créer « une œuvre d'art vivant spectaculaire, l'illy Push Button House, une résidence de cinq pièces avec cuisine, salle à manger, chambre, séjour et bibliothèque construite à partir de conteneurs d'expédition industriels standard ». Grâce à un système hydraulique commandé par un bouton, la structure passe de l'état de conteneur normal à celui d'une maison schématique ouverte, qui peut également servir de cafétéria. Elle a été présentée pour la première fois à la Biennale de Venise en juin 2007. En décembre 2007, elle a été exposée au Time Warner Center à New York, puis dans le quartier du Meatpacking dans le cadre du festival « Wine & Food » de New York en octobre 2008.

With careful study of space within the framework of the industrial container, Adam Kalkin creates an entire "home" that pops out of this foldable structure.

In Adam Kalkins durchdachter Raumstudie entfaltet sich aus dem Gerüst eines Frachtcontainers ein komplettes „Eigenheim", das mithilfe eines Klappmechanismus ausgefahren wird.

Grâce à une étude approfondie du volume intérieur d'un conteneur industriel, Adam Kalkin a créé une « maison » qui naît du déploiement de sa structure.

TETSUO KONDO

TETSUO KONDO was born in Ehime Prefecture, Japan, in 1975. He graduated from the Nagoya Institute of Technology in 1999, and worked in the office of Kazuyo Sejima (SANAA) until 2006. He established his own firm the same year. His recent completed work includes House with Gardens (Kanagawa, 2008); A Path in the Forest in the context of the European Capital of Culture, Urban Installations Festival LIFT11 (Tallinn, Estonia, 2011); and the House in Chayagasaka (Aichi, 2012, published here). He is currently working on the Tiny House (Ehime, 2012–), and the N House (Ishikawa, 2012–), all in Japan unless stated otherwise.

TETSUO KONDO wurde 1975 in der Präfektur Ehime, Japan, geboren. Seinen Abschluss machte er 1999 an der Technischen Hochschule Nagoya und arbeitete dann bis 2006 im Büro von Kazuyo Sejima (SANAA). Im selben Jahr machte er sich selbstständig. Zu seinen unlängst realisierten Arbeiten zählen das Haus mit Gärten (Kanagawa, 2008), A Path in the Forest im Rahmen der Kulturhauptstadt Europas/Urban Installations Festival LIFT11 (Tallinn, Estland, 2011) und das Haus in Chayagasaka (Aichi, 2012, hier vorgestellt). Derzeit arbeitet er am Winzigen Haus (Ehime, seit 2012) und dem Haus N (Ishikawa, seit 2012), alle in Japan, wenn nicht anders angegeben.

TETSUO KONDO est né dans la préfecture d'Ehime, au Japon, en 1975. Il est diplômé de l'Institut de technologie de Nagoya (1999) et a travaillé dans l'agence de Kazuyo Sejima (SANAA) jusqu'en 2006, année où il a créé son agence. Ses travaux achevés les plus récents comprennent une maison avec jardins (Kanagawa, 2008) ; *A Path in the Forest* pour la capitale européenne de la culture, dans le cadre du festival d'installations urbaines LIFT11 (Tallin, Estonie, 2011) et la maison à Chayagasaka (Aichi, 2012, publiée ici). Il travaille actuellement à la Maison minuscule (Ehime, 2012–) et à la Maison N (Ishikawa, 2012–), tous au Japon sauf mention contraire.

HOUSE IN CHAYAGASAKA

Nagoya, Aichi, Japan, 2011–12

Area: 90 m². Collaboration: Yasutaka Konishi/
Konishi Structural Engineers.

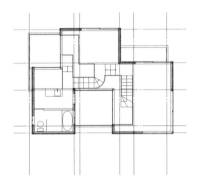
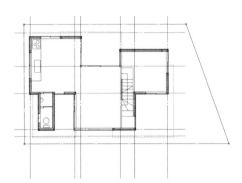

This house was built near a Nagoya metro station for a couple and their two small children. Since the couple wanted as many "common" spaces as possible, the architect states: "I decided to build a one-room house, with a subtle balance between connected and separated areas." Tetsuo Kondo sought to make the house able to "welcome a large variety of things" and the changing situation of the family as the children grow, in particular. "This architecture," he says, "is not one dominated by a strong system or built in a well-ordered manner, but rather one that incorporates various meanings, and it seems difficult to understand why it was made that way." The architect has an interesting, and perhaps relatively new approach to "order" in his design. "The order should not constrain the system," he states, "but it should rather loosely define its relationships. I aimed to create an architecture based on soft order."

Dieses Haus wurde für ein Paar und seine beiden kleinen Kinder gebaut und liegt in der Nähe einer U-Bahn-Station in Nagoya. Das Paar wollte so viel „gemeinschaftlichen" Raum wie möglich. Der Architekt dazu: „Ich entschied mich also, ein Ein-Raum-Haus zu entwerfen mit einer subtilen Balance zwischen verbundenen und abgetrennten Bereichen." Tetsuo Kondo versuchte, das Haus „offen für eine Vielzahl von Möglichkeiten" zu gestalten, besonders für die Veränderungen innerhalb der Familie mit ihren heranwachsenden Kindern. „Diese Architektur", sagt er, „ist nicht von einem strengen Ordnungssystem dominiert oder sonderlich penibel in der Bauweise, sondern versucht eher, verschiedene Bedeutungen einfließen zu lassen, wobei es auf den ersten Blick schwerfallen mag, den Grund dafür zu erkennen." Der Architekt verfolgt bei seinen Entwürfen in Bezug auf „Ordnung" einen interessanten und womöglich recht neuen Ansatz. „Die Ordnung sollte nicht das System behindern", so Kondo, „sondern die Bezüge lose definieren. Ich habe versucht, eine Architektur der weichen Ordnung zu entwerfen."

La maison a été construite près d'une station du métro de Nagoya pour un couple et ses deux jeunes enfants. Pour répondre à leur demande du plus possible d'espaces « communs », l'architecte explique : « J'ai décidé de construire une maison à pièce unique et à l'équilibre très subtil entre parties raccordées les unes aux autres et parties séparées. » Tetsuo Kondo a cherché à rendre la maison capable d'« accueillir une grande diversité de choses » et les changements dans la situation familiale, notamment lorsque les enfants grandiront. « Cette architecture, déclare-t-il, n'est pas dominée par un système fort ni construite de manière ordonnée, mais plutôt de manière à intégrer des significations diverses, et il semble difficile de comprendre pourquoi cela a été fait de cette manière. » L'architecte a adopté une approche intéressante, et sans doute relativement nouvelle, de l'« ordre » pour sa création. « L'ordre ne doit pas forcer le système, affirme-t-il, mais plutôt définir vaguement ses relations. J'ai voulu créer une architecture basée sur un ordre souple. »

The house is composed of a series of rectangles that overlap each other and provide overhangs. Left, plans of the two main levels.

Das Haus besteht aus einer Reihe von Quadern, deren versetzte Anordnung Überhänge entstehen lässt. Links Grundrisse der beiden zentralen Ebenen.

La maison consiste en une série de rectangles qui se chevauchent de manière à créer des surplombs. À gauche, plans des deux niveaux principaux.

274

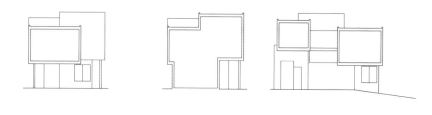

Interior volumes all seem to penetrate each other, with landings and interior glazing offering an unusual degree of openness.

Die Innenräume scheinen sich zu durchdringen, Podeste und Innenverglasung sorgen für ein ungewohntes Maß an Offenheit.

Les volumes intérieurs donnent l'impression de s'interpénétrer, tant les paliers et le vitrage intérieur permettent un degré d'ouverture inédit.

Section drawings show how the orthogonal volumes are layered and inserted into each other, creating unusual open interior spaces.

Querschnitte zeigen, wie die recht-eckigen Raumelemente geschichtet und ineinander verschachtelt sind und so ungewöhnlich offene Innen-räume entstehen lassen.

Les plans en coupe montrent comment les volumes orthogonaux sont empilés et insérés les uns dans les autres afin de créer des espaces intérieurs inhabituellement ouverts.

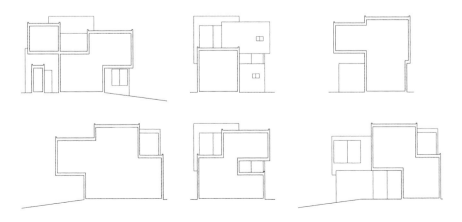

KENGO KUMA

Born in 1954 in Kanagawa, Japan, **KENGO KUMA** graduated in 1979 from the University of Tokyo with an M.Arch. degree. In 1987 he established the Spatial Design Studio, and in 1991 he created Kengo Kuma & Associates. His recent work includes the Great (Bamboo) Wall Guesthouse (Beijing, China, 2002); One Omotesando (Tokyo, 2003); LVMH Osaka (Osaka, 2004); the Nagasaki Prefectural Art Museum (Nagasaki, 2005); Zhongtai Box, Z58 building (Shanghai, China, 2003–06); Steel House (Bunkyo-ku, Tokyo, 2005–07); Tiffany Ginza (Tokyo, 2008); Nezu Museum (Tokyo, 2007–09); Museum of Kanayama (Ota City, Gunma, 2009); Glass Wood House (New Canaan, Connecticut, USA, 2007–10); Yusuhara Marche (Yusuhara, Kochi, 2009–10); the Yusuhara Wooden Bridge Museum (Yusuhara-cho, Takaoka-gun, Kochi, 2010) all in Japan unless stated otherwise. The small projects published here (Même Experimental House, Hokkaido, 2011–12; and Hojo-an, Kyoto, 2012) demonstrate the architect's attachment to innovative structures, often based on historic precedents.

KENGO KUMA wurde 1954 in Kanagawa, Japan, geboren und schloss ein Studium an der Universität Tokio mit einem M. Arch. ab. 1987 gründete er das Büro Spatial Design, 1991 folgte die Gründung von Kengo Kuma & Associates. Zu seinen jüngeren Arbeiten zählen das Great (Bamboo) Wall Guesthouse (Peking, 2002), One Omotesando (Tokio, 2003), LVMH Osaka (Osaka, 2004), das Kunstmuseum der Präfektur Nagasaki (2005), die Zhongtai Box, Z 58 (Schanghai, 2003–06), das Steel House (Bunkyo-ku, Tokio, 2005–07), Tiffany Ginza (Tokio, 2008), das Nezu-Museum (Tokio, 2007–09), das Museum von Kanayama (Ota City, Gunma, Japan, 2009), das Glass Wood House (New Canaan, Connecticut, USA, 2007–10), Yusuhara Marché (Yusuhara, Kochi, Japan, 2009–10) und das Yusuhara Wooden Bridge Museum (Yusuhara-cho, Takaoka-gun, Kochi, Japan, 2010). Die hier vorgestellten kleineren Projekte (Même Experimental House, Hokkaido, 2011–12 und Hojo-an, Kioto, 2012) belegen den Hang des Architekten zu innovativen Bauweisen, die oft auf historische Beispiele zurückgehen.

Né en 1954 à Kanagawa (Japon), **KENGO KUMA** a reçu son M.Arch de l'université de Tokyo (1979). En 1987, il crée le Spatial Design Studio et, en 1991, Kengo Kuma & Associates. Ses réalisations récentes comprennent la maison d'hôtes de la Grande muraille (de bambou) (Pékin, 2002) ; l'immeuble One Omotesando (Tokyo, 2003) ; l'immeuble LVMH Osaka (2004) ; le Musée d'art de la préfecture de Nagasaki (Nagasaki, 2005) ; l'immeuble Zhongtai Box, Z58 (Shanghai, 2003–06) ; la Steel House (Bunkyo-ku, Tokyo, 2005–07) ; l'immeuble Tiffany Ginza (Tokyo, 2008) ; le musée Nezu (Tokyo, 2007–09) ; le musée de Kanayama (Ota City, Gunma, 2009) ; la Glass Wood House (New Canaan, Connecticut, 2007–10) ; le marché de Yusuhara (Yusuhara, Kochi, 2009–10) ; le musée du Pont de bois de Yusuhara (Yusuhara-cho, Takaoka-gun, Kochi, 2010), toutes au Japon sauf mention contraire. Les petits projets présentés ici (maison expérimentale Même, Hokkaido, 2011–12 et Hojo-an, Kyoto, 2012) montrent l'attachement de l'architecte aux structures innovantes, souvent basées sur des précédents historiques.

HOJO-AN
Kyoto, Japan, 2012

Area: 9 m².
Collaboration: Ejiri Structural Engineering.

Kamono Chomei (1155–1216), the author of *Hojo-ki* (An Account of My Hut), lived in a movable house that is often described as the prototype of Japan's compact housing. This project aimed to reconstruct his house with modern ideas and methods, on the same site in the precinct of the Shimogamo Jinja Shrine. The word *hojo* implies a small cottage approximately 3 x 3 meters in size. Kengo Kuma employed ETFE sheets that can be rolled up, making the structure portable. Cedar strips combined with powerful magnets were used to create a "kind of tensegrity structure" which, when combined into a single unit, form a "hard box."

Kamono Chomei (1155–1216), Autor von *Hojo-ki* (Aufzeichnungen aus meiner Hütte), lebte in einem bewegbaren Haus, das oft als Prototyp der japanischen Kompaktbauweise beschrieben wird. Ziel dieses Projekt war es, mithilfe moderner Ideen und Methoden sein Haus am ursprünglichen Standort auf dem Gelände des Shimogama-Jinja-Schreins zu rekonstruieren. „*Hojo*" bezeichnet eine kleine Hütte von ungefähr 3 x 3 m Größe. Kengo Kuma verwendet aufrollbare ETFE-Folien, um die Transportfähigkeit des Hauses zu gewährleisten. Aus mit starken Magneten versehenen Zedernlatten entstand „eine Art Tensegrity-System", aus dem sich, zu einer Einheit zusammengesetzt, eine „stabile Kiste" bauen lässt.

Kamono Chomei (1155–1216), l'auteur de *Hojo-ki* (*Notes de ma cabane de moine*), habitait une maison mobile souvent décrite comme le prototype du logement japonais compact. Le projet visait à reconstruire cette maison avec des idées et des méthodes modernes sur le même site, dans l'enceinte du sanctuaire Shimogamo Jinja. Le mot *hojo* désigne une petite maison rurale d'environ 3 x 3 m. Kengo Kuma a utilisé des feuilles d'EFTE qui peuvent être roulées pour porter la structure. Des bandes de cèdre associées à de puissants aimants créent une « sorte de système de tenségrité » qui, assemblé en une entité unique, forme une « boîte rigide ».

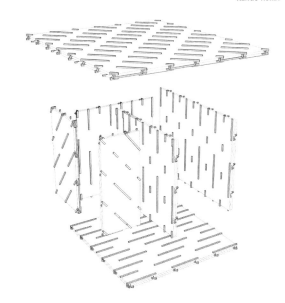

The unusual concept of the recon-
stitution of an ancient building with
modern materials was taken up by
Kengo Kuma. Right, drawings show
the layering of ETFE sheeting.

Kengo Kuma nahm das nicht
alltägliche Vorhaben in Angriff, ein
historisches Gebäude mit modernen
Materialien zu rekonstruieren.
Rechts zeigen Zeichnungen die
Schichtung der ETFE-Folie.

Le concept inédit qui consiste à
reconstituer un bâtiment ancien
avec des matériaux modernes a été
repris par Kengo Kuma. À droite, les
schémas montrent les empilements
des feuilles d'ETFE.

 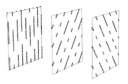

Magnets and strips of wood are
used to hold the structure together,
as seen in the detail image
to the left.

Magneten und Holzlatten halten das
Bauwerk zusammen, wie auf der
Detailaufnahme links zu sehen ist.

Des aimants et des bandes de bois
servent à maintenir la structure
assemblée, comme on le voit sur
le détail à gauche.

MÊME EXPERIMENTAL HOUSE

Hokkaido, Japan, 2011–12

Area: 79 m². Client: LIXIL JS Foundation.
Collaboration: Yasushi Moribe (Structural Engineer).

In this instance, the architect explored the traditional housing of the Ainu people of Hokkaido, called *Chise*—a "house of grass and earth." The roof and walls of these houses are entirely covered with sedge or bamboo grass because of their insulating properties. *Chise* have a fireplace in the center that burns throughout the year. The architect explains: "We wrapped a wooden frame made of Japanese larch with a polyester fluorocarbon coating, and an inner part with a removable glass-fiber-cloth membrane. Between the two membranes, the designers inserted a polyester insulator recycled using PET bottles. This composition is based on the idea that by creating air convection, the internal environment could be kept comfortable." The ample presence of natural light in the house was also assured with the membrane materials.

In diesem Fall ließ sich der Architekt von den traditionellen Häusern der Ainu in Hokkaido inspirieren, die „Chise" heißen – „Haus aus Gras und Erde". Dach und Wände der Häuser wurden wegen der isolierenden Eigenschaften vollständig mit Riet- oder Bambusgras verkleidet. Chise haben in der Mitte eine Feuerstelle, die ganzjährig genutzt wird. „Wir bezogen ein Tragwerk aus japanischer Lärche von außen mit einer Polyester-Fluorocarbon-Hülle und einen Teil des Innenbereiches mit einer entfernbaren Membran aus Glasfasergewebe. Zwischen die beiden Schichten füllten die Architekten aus recycelten PET-Flaschen gewonnenes Dämmmaterial. Diese Anordnung resultierte aus der Überlegung, dass das Raumklima im Innenbereich durch das Entstehen von Konvektion angenehm würde." Die Membranmaterialien sorgen außerdem für reichlich natürliches Licht.

L'architecte a ici exploré l'habitat traditionnel des Ainus d'Hokkaido, aussi appelés *Chise* – une « maison d'herbe et de terre ». Le toit et les murs sont entièrement recouverts de laîche ou de bambou, choisis pour leurs propriétés isolantes. Un foyer au centre de la maison brûle toute l'année. L'architecte explique : « Nous avons emballé la charpente en mélèze du Japon dans un revêtement de polyester et fluorocarbone, ainsi qu'une partie de l'intérieur dans une membrane amovible de fibre de verre et de tissu. Entre les deux, les designers ont inséré un isolant polyester recyclé utilisant des bouteilles en PET. Cette combinaison est basée sur l'idée que créer une convection de l'air maintiendra l'atmosphère intérieure agréable. » Les matériaux des membranes permettent également à la lumière naturelle de pénétrer largement dans la maison.

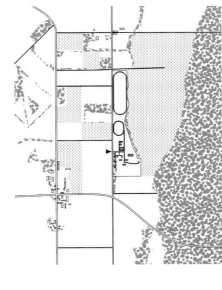

The structure fits in with neighboring farm buildings (left page) in its bucolic setting. Below, the structure glows from within at night.

Das Haus passt sich an die benachbarten Farmgebäude in der ländlichen Umgebung an (linke Seite). Unten: Nachts leuchtet das Innere des Gebäudes.

La structure s'accorde avec les bâtiments agricoles voisins (page de gauche) dans son cadre bucolique. Ci-dessous, la construction éclairée de l'intérieur la nuit.

The interior volume is generous, as seen in the images to the left and above. While the larch frame of the house was coated with polyester fluorocarbon, the inner volume is coated with a glass-fiber cloth membrane.

Wie auf den Abbildungen links und oben zu sehen ist, ist das Innere des Hauses großzügig gestaltet. Sein Tragwerk aus Lärche wurde mit einer Polyester-Fluorocarbon-Hülle versehen, der Innenbereich mit einer Membran aus Glasfasergewebe verkleidet.

Le volume intérieur est généreux, on le voit sur les photos à gauche et ci-dessus. La charpente en mélèze a été recouverte d'un revêtement de polyester fluorocarbure, tandis que le volume intérieur est habillé d'une membrane en tissu de fibre de verre.

LAAC

KATHRIN ASTE was born in 1969 in Innsbruck and received her diploma from the Faculty of Architecture of Innsbruck University in 2000. She cofounded LAAC with **FRANK LUDIN**, who was born in Weil am Rhein, Germany, in 1972. He also received his degree in Innsbruck in 2004. LAAC was founded in 2009 as the successor of astearchitecture, a firm founded in Innsbruck in 2004 "to provide an intersection point between teaching, research and realization." The research work is done in the design studios of the Technical Faculty of Innsbruck University. Under the name "Built by Velocity," the firm designs ski jumps, bob runs, and sprint toboggan runs, as well as panoramic platforms, such as the Mountain Platform published here (Top of Tyrol Mountain Platform, Stubai Glacier, Tyrol, 2007–08). Works include the Roof Landscape SOHO II (Innsbruck, 2010); a Multifunction Hall and Rehearsal Room (Weissenbach am Lech, 2010); and a Ski Jump Center (Astana, Kazakhstan, 2008–11), all in Austria unless stated otherwise.

KATHRIN ASTE wurde 1969 in Innsbruck geboren und absolvierte ihr Diplom 2000 an der Fakultät für Architektur der Universität Innsbruck. Ihr Büro LAAC gründete sie gemeinsam mit **FRANK LUDIN**, 1972 geboren in Weil am Rhein. Ludin schloss sein Studium 2004 ebenfalls an der Universität Innsbruck ab. 2009 wurde LAAC Nachfolger des Vorgänger-büros astearchitecture, das 2004 als „Schnittstelle für Lehre, Forschung und Praxis" in Innsbruck gegründet worden war. Forschungsprojekte werden in den Studios für Entwerfen an der Fakultät für Bauingenieurwissenschaften verfolgt. Unter dem Namen „Built by Velocity" entwirft das Büro Skischanzen, Bobbahnen, Sprintrodelbahnen sowie Aussichtsplattformen, darunter auch die hier vorgestellte Gipfelplattform (Top of Tyrol, Aussichtsplattform am Stubaier Gletscher, Tirol, 2007–08). Realisierte Projekte umfassen eine Dachlandschaft SOHO II (Innsbruck, 2010), einen Mehrzwecksaal und Probenraum (Weißenbach am Lech, 2010) sowie ein Skischanzen-Zentrum in Astana (Kasachstan, 2008–11), alle in Österreich, sofern nicht anders angegeben.

KATHRIN ASTE, née en 1969 à Innsbruck, est diplômée de la Faculté d'architecture de l'Université d'Innsbruck (2000). Elle a fondé LAAC avec **FRANK LUDIN**, né à Weil-am-Rhein (Allemagne) en 1972, également diplômé d'Innsbruck (2004). LAAC a été fondée en 2009 pour succéder à astearchitecture, agence créée à Innsbruck en 2004, « point d'intersection entre l'enseignement, la recherche et la réalisation ». Le travail de recherche est effectué dans les ateliers de conception de la Faculté polytechnique de l'Université d'Innsbruck. Sous le label d'ensemble de « Built by Velocity », l'agence conçoit des tremplins de saut à ski, des pistes de bobsleigh et des toboggans de saut, ainsi que des plates-formes panoramiques comme la Gipfel Platform publiée ici (plate-forme du sommet du Tyrol, glacier du Stubai, Tyrol, 2007–08). Ses réalisations récentes comprennent un projet d'aménagement paysager de toiture SOHO II (Innsbruck, 2010) ; un hall multifonctions, une salle de répétitions (Weissenbach-am-Lech, 2010) et un centre de saut à ski (Astana, Kazakhstan, 2008–11).

TOP OF TYROL
MOUNTAIN PLATFORM

Mount Isidor, Stubai Glacier, Tyrol, Austria, 2007–08

Area: 80 m². Client: Wintersport Tirol AG &
CO Stubaier Bergbahnen KG. Cost: € 300 000.

The platform is visible to the left at the bottom of this panoramic mountain view.

Unten links auf diesem Berg- panorama ist die Plattform zu sehen.

À gauche, la plate-forme semble minuscule dans cette vue panoramique.

Located an hour's drive from Innsbruck, the Stubai Glacier is in the heart of a tourist area, and this platform aims to revive interest in summer hiking or mountain climbing. The platform is only open in winter when weather conditions permit. The architects were directly commissioned by the client. The structure is located near the Schaufeljoch station of the Stubai Gletscher Bahn (3180 meters above sea level). In clear weather, no less than 109 3000-meter peaks are visible from the platform. The architects say that their goal was to create a "situation in space more than a building." Weather-resistant COR-TEN steel was chosen as a "contrast to the zinc-covered steel structures of the surrounding ski region." Handrails and a bench are made of larch, filled with stainless-steel netting. Nineteen tons of COR-TEN steel were used for the structure, carried in appropriately sized pieces to the site by helicopter.

Nur eine Autostunde von Innsbruck liegt der Stubaier Gletscher mitten im Herzen eines Urlaubsgebiets. Die Plattform soll Lust auf sommerliche Wanderungen oder Klettertouren wecken. Geöffnet ist sie nur im Winter bei geeigneten Witterungsverhältnissen. Die Architekten wurden direkt vom Bauherrn beauftragt. Das Bauwerk liegt unweit der Station Schaufeljoch der Stubaier Gletscherbahn (3180 m ü.N.N.). Bei klarem Wetter sind von der Plattform aus nicht weniger als 109 Dreitausendergipfel zu sehen. Den Architekten ging es nach eigener Aussage eher darum, „eine Situation im Raum" als „ein Bauwerk" zu schaffen. Als „Kontrast zu den zinkverblendeten Stahlbauten des umliegenden Skigebiets" entschied man sich für wetterbeständigen Cortenstahl. Handläufe und eine Bank wurden aus Lärchenholz gefertigt und mit einem Kern aus Edelstahldraht versehen. Um die Konstruktion zu realisieren, wurden 19 Tonnen Cortenstahl verbaut, die in entsprechend kleinen Segmenten per Hubschrauber zum Bauplatz transportiert wurden.

À une heure de voiture d'Innsbruck, le glacier du Stubai s'étend au cœur d'une vaste région touristique. Cette plateforme a pour objectif de réveiller l'intérêt des touristes pour l'alpinisme ou la marche en montagne. Elle n'est ouverte en hiver que lorsque les conditions climatiques le permettent. Il s'agit d'une commande directe. Cet objet architectural se trouve près de la gare de Schaufeljoch du télécabine du glacier du Stubai, à 3180 mètres d'altitude. Par temps clair, on aperçoit pas moins de 109 sommets de plus de 3000 mètres d'altitude. Le propos des architectes a été plus de créer « une situation dans l'espace qu'une construction ». Un acier Corten résistant au climat a été choisi « qui contraste avec les constructions en acier recouvertes de zinc de la région touristique environnante ». Les garde-corps et la banquette sont en mélèze renforcé d'une structure en acier inoxydable. Dix-neuf tonnes d'acier Corten ont été nécessaires, réparties en éléments de dimensions et de poids adaptés à la capacité des hélicoptères de transport.

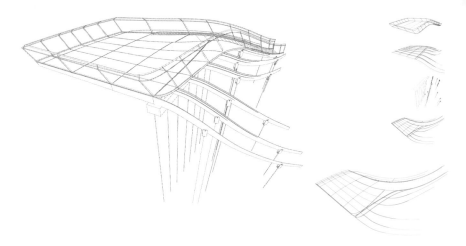

Drawings show the basic simplicity of the platform, like a wing extending over the void.

Die Zeichnungen belegen die einfache Grundform der Plattform, die wie ein Flügel über dem Abgrund schwebt.

Ces dessins illustrent la simplicité de conception de la plate-forme qui se déploie comme une aile au-dessus du vide.

The platform juts out over the
mountain edge, allowing visitors
to participate in the vertiginous
landscape more than if they were
comfortably placed on the rock of
the mountain itself.

Die Plattform ragt über die Fels-
kante hinaus und macht die
schwindelerregende Bergwelt für
die Besucher viel eindrücklicher
erfahrbar, als würden sie sicher auf
dem felsigen Berggrund stehen.

La plate-forme se projette par-
dessus l'arête de la montagne. Les
visiteurs ont davantage le sentiment
de ne faire qu'un avec le paysage
vertigineux que s'ils étaient confortablement assis sur un rocher.

LOT-EK

ADA TOLLA was born in 1964 in Potenza, Italy. She received her M.Arch. from the Architecture Faculty of the "Federico II" University (Naples, 1982–89) and did postgraduate studies at Columbia University (New York, 1990–91). She is one of the two founding partners of LOT-EK, created in Naples, Italy, in 1993 and in New York in 1995. She is currently an Associate Professor at Columbia University in the Graduate School of Architecture, Planning, and Preservation. **GIUSEPPE LIGNANO** was born in Naples, Italy, in 1963. He also received his M.Arch. degree from the "Federico II" University (1982–89) and did postgraduate studies at Columbia at the same time as Ada Tolla. He is the other founding partner of LOT-EK and is currently an Associate Professor at Columbia University in the Graduate School of Architecture, Planning, and Preservation. Their work includes X-Static Process (Deitch Projects, New York, 2003); Uniqlo Container Stores (New York, 2006); Theater for One (Princeton University, Princeton, New Jersey, 2007); PUMA DDSU (South Street Seaport, New York, 2010); APAP OpenSchool (Anyang, South Korea, 2010); and Van Alen Books (New York, , 2011, published here). Current projects include the Whitney Studio (New York, 2012, also published here); Pier 57 (New York, 2011–13); and Band of Outsiders (Tokyo, Japan, 2012–13) all in the USA unless stated otherwise.

ADA TOLLA wurde 1964 in Potenza, Italien, geboren. Sie erlangte ihren M. Arch. an der Fakultät für Architektur der Universität Frederico II (Neapel, 1982–89) und absolvierte ein Postgraduiertenstudium an der Columbia University (New York, 1990–91). Sie ist eine der zwei Gründungspartner von LOT-EK, gegründet 1993 in Neapel und 1995 in New York. Aktuell lehrt sie als Privatdozentin am Graduiertenprogramm für Architektur, Stadtplanung und Denkmalschutz der Columbia University. **GUISEPPE LIGNANO** wurde 1963 in Neapel geboren. Auch er machte seinen M. Arch. an der Universität Frederico II (1982–89) und ein Postgraduiertenstudium an der Columbia University. Er ist der zweite Gründungspartner von LOT-EK und derzeit außerordentlicher Professor am Graduiertenprogramm für Architektur, Stadtplanung und Denkmalschutz der Columbia University. Zu den Arbeiten der beiden gehören „X-Static Process" (Deitch Projects, New York, 2003), die Uniqlo Container Stores (New York, 2006), das Theater for One (Princeton University, New Jersey, 2007), PUMA DDSU (South Street Seaport, New York, 2010), die APAP OpenSchool (Anyang, Südkorea, 2010) und Van Alen Books (New York, 2011, hier vorgestellt). Aktuelle Projekte sind u. a. das Whitney Studio (New York, 2012, ebenfalls hier vorgestellt), Pier 57 (New York, 2011–13) und der Band-of-Outsiders-Shop im japanischen Tokio (2012–13), alle in den USA, sofern nicht anders angegeben.

ADA TOLLA, née en 1964 à Potenza (Italie), a obtenu son M.Arch à la faculté d'architecture de l'université Federico II de Naples (1982–89) et a effectué des études de troisième cycle à l'université Columbia (New York, 1990–91). Elle est l'une des deux associés fondateurs de l'agence LOT-EK, créée à Naples en 1993 et à New York en 1995. Elle est actuellement professeur associé à l'université Columbia (Graduate School of Architecture, Planning, and Preservation). **GIUSEPPE LIGNANO**, né à Naples en 1963, a également obtenu son M.Arch à l'université Federico II (1982–89) et étudié à l'université Columbia en même temps qu'Ada Tolla avec laquelle il a fondé LOT-EK. Il est lui aussi professeur associé à l'université Columbia (Graduate School of Architecture, Planning, and Preservation). Parmi leurs projets : l'installation *X-Static Process* (Deitch Projects, New York, 2003) ; les magasins Uniqlo Container (New York, 2006) ; le Theater for One (université de Princeton, New Jersey, 2007) ; PUMA DDSU (South Street Seaport, New York, 2010) ; l'OpenSchool APAP (Anyang, Corée-du-Sud, 2010) et Van Alen Books (New York, 2011, publié ici). Les projets actuels comprennent : le Whitney Studio (New York, 2012, également publié ici) ; Pier 57 (New York, 2011–13) et la boutique Band of Outsiders (Tokyo, 2012–13), tous aux États-Unis sauf mention contraire.

WHITNEY STUDIO

New York, USA, 2012

Area: 60 m². Client: Whitney Museum, Education Department.
Collaboration: Virginie Stolz (Project Architect).

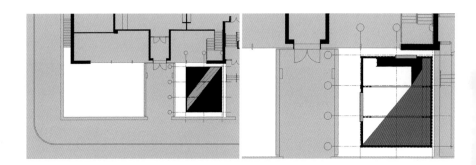

LOT-EK was commissioned to design an art studio space for the Whitney Museum of American Art, a Marcel Breuer building on Madison Avenue. The Studio houses activities for the Whitney Museum's education program, including art classes for adults, teens, and families, as well as informal lectures and special exhibits. The structure was made of six steel shipping containers stacked on two levels to form a "monolithic cube," and was specifically designed to fit within the Whitney's open moat on the south side of the entry bridge. The stack is cut diagonally along two sides and the roof of the structure, providing natural light inside at the same time as it allows those on the exterior to view the Studio's activities. A white double-height space for production and display of artworks marks the interior, together with a triangular mezzanine for art supplies and computer desks.

LOT-EK erhielt den Auftrag, Atelierräume für das Whitney Museum of American Art zu entwerfen, ein Gebäude von Marcel Breuer an der Madison Avenue. Im Studio finden im Rahmen des Bildungsangebots des Museums Veranstaltungen statt, z. B. Kunstunterricht für Erwachsene, Jugendliche und Kinder, aber auch informelle Vorträge und Sonderausstellungen. Das Gebäude besteht aus sechs stählernen Containern, die auf zwei Ebenen zu einem „monolithischen Würfel" gestapelt wurden, und wurde extra so entworfen, dass es genau in den Graben an der Südseite der Eingangsrampe passt. Der Block ist an zwei Seiten diagonal und oben aufgeschnitten, so wird Tageslicht hineingelassen, gleichzeitig kann man von außen die Aktivitäten im Studio beobachten. Das Innere besteht aus einem einzelnen, weiß getünchten Raum, der mit seiner doppelten Deckenhöhe Platz für die Herstellung und Ausstellung von Kunstwerken bietet, sowie aus einem dreieckigen Halbgeschoss mit Materiallager und Computerplätzen.

Le Whitney Museum of American Art, un bâtiment de Marcel Breuer sur Madison Avenue, a passé commande à LOT-EK d'un espace studio d'art. Le studio accueille des activités du programme pédagogique du musée, notamment des cours d'art pour les adultes, les jeunes et les familles, ainsi que des conférences informelles et des expositions spéciales. La structure est faite de six conteneurs maritimes en acier empilés sur deux niveaux pour former un « cube monolithique » et a été spéciale-ment conçue pour remplir le creux autour du Whitney, du côté sud de la passerelle d'entrée. L'ensemble est découpé en dia-gonale sur deux côtés et le toit pour y faire entrer la lumière du jour, tout en permettant aux activités du studio d'être observées depuis l'extérieur. L'intérieur se caractérise par un espace double hauteur en blanc destiné à la production et la présentation d'œuvres d'art, ainsi que par une mezzanine triangulaire accueillant les réserves de matériel et les postes informatiques.

The architects dared to insert their bright yellow container into the Madison Avenue terrace near the entrance to Marcel Breuer's Whitney Museum of American Art.

Die Architekten wagten es, ihren leuchtend gelben Container in den Terrassenbereich an der Madison Avenue gleich neben dem Eingang zu Marcel Breuers Whitney Museum of American Art einzupassen.

Les architectes n'ont pas hésité à introduire leur conteneur jaune vif Madison Avenue, près de l'entrée du Whitney Museum of American Art de Marcel Breuer.

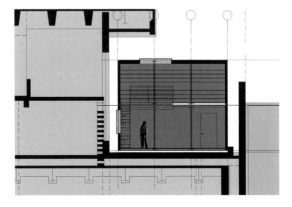

With its diagonally sliced openings, the two-story box actually sits one level below grade, poking up above the wall that separates the Museum from the Madison Avenue sidewalk.

Der zweistöckige Kasten mit seinen diagonal geschnittenen Öffnungen steht de facto im Untergeschoss und ragt hinter der Mauer hervor, die das Museum vom Gehsteig der Madison Avenue trennt.

Avec ses ouvertures découpées en diagonale, le cube a un premier étage en dessous du niveau du sol, tandis que le deuxième dépasse du mur qui sépare le musée du trottoir de Madison Avenue.

The structure is striking not only
because of its color and forms but
also because it contrasts metal
with the stony solidity of the
Whitney itself.

Der Bau besticht nicht nur durch
seine Farbe und Formensprache,
sondern auch durch den Kontrast
zwischen dem Metall und der
steinernen Festigkeit des Whitney
selbst.

La structure frappe par sa couleur
et ses formes, mais aussi par le
contraste du métal avec la solidité
de la pierre du Whitney.

Interior spaces are essentially white and angular with black detailing. Below, a section drawing shows the rectangular volume in its setting.

Die Innenräume sind, bis auf einige Details in Schwarz, vorwiegend weiß gehalten und von schrägen Winkeln geprägt. Unten zeigt ein Querschnitt das rechtwinklige Volumen an seinem Standort.

Les espaces intérieurs sont presque tous blancs et anguleux avec des détails en noir. Ci-dessous, la vue en coupe montre l'emplacement du volume rectangulaire.

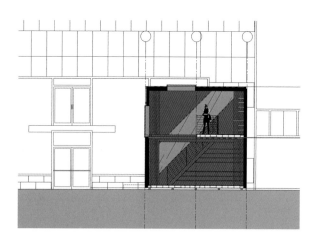

VAN ALEN BOOKS

New York, USA, 2011

Area: 47 m².
Client: Van Alen Institute.

Located at the Van Alen Institute at 30 West 22nd Street in Manhattan, this is a new architecture and design bookstore and public reading room and is the only facility of its kind in New York. Named after the American architect William Van Alen (1883–1954) who designed Manhattan's Chrysler Building, the Institute is a non-profit organization that seeks to improve design in the public domain through publications, exhibitions, and competitions. The installation includes a 4.3-meter seating platform forming large steps, or an amphitheater, that was made with 70 recycled doors. The architects explain: "The solid wood doors form a triangular installation evoking the steps of Times Square's TKTS booth, an iconic project originated through Van Alen Institute's 1999 design competition." As is often the case in the work of LOT-EK, a bright yellow color and strong graphics characterize the space.

Die in Manhattan neben dem Van Alen Institute an der 30 West 22nd Street gelegene neue Buchhandlung ist auf Architektur und Design spezialisiert und die einzige ihrer Art in New York. Das nach dem amerikanischen Architekten William Van Alen (1883–1954) – dem Baumeister des Chrysler Building in Manhattan – benannte Institut ist eine gemeinnützige Einrichtung zur Förderung von gutem Design im öffentlichen Raum. Dies geschieht durch Publikationen, Ausstellungen und Wettbewerbe. Die Rauminstallation umfasst eine 4,30 m hohe Sitzplattform bzw. ein Amphitheater mit breiten Stufen, das aus 70 recycelten Türen gebaut wurde. Die Architekten führen aus: „Die massiven Holztüren bilden eine Dreiecksform, die an die Treppenkonstruktion der TKTS-Theaterkasse am Times Square erinnert – ein echtes Wahrzeichen, das 1999 aus einem Entwurfswettbewerb hervorging, den das Van Alen Institute initiiert hatte." Wie oft bei Entwürfen von LOT-EK, wird der Raum von leuchtendem Gelb und auffälligen Schriftzügen dominiert.

Située dans l'Institut Van Alen, 30 Ouest 22ᵉ Rue à Manhattan, cette nouvelle librairie d'architecture et de design avec salle de lecture publique est la seule de ce type à New York. L'institut, qui porte le nom de l'architecte américain auteur du Chrysler Building de Manhattan William Van Alen (1883–1954), est une organisation à but non lucratif qui vise à faire progresser le design dans le domaine public par des publications, des expositions et des concours. L'ensemble comporte une plate-forme de 4,3 m formant de larges marches, ou un amphithéâtre, et est faite de 70 portes recyclées. Les architectes expliquent que « les solides portes de bois forment une installation triangulaire qui rappelle les marches du kiosque TKTS de Times Square, un projet emblématique qui doit son origine au concours de design de l'Institut Van Alen en 1999 ». Comme souvent dans les projets de LOT-EK, l'espace est marqué par le jaune vif et un graphisme très dynamique.

LOT-EK has realized a number of temporary installations with elements such as shipping containers—here their typical bright colors and an unexpected suspended stair give the small space a dynamic feeling.

LOT-EK realisierte eine Reihe temporärer Installationen mit Modulen wie Schiffscontainern – hier gewinnt der kleine Raum durch die für LOT-EK typischen leuchtenden Farben und eine ungewöhnliche abgehängte Treppenkonstruktion an Dynamik.

LOT-EK a réalisé beaucoup d'installations temporaires avec des conteneurs maritimes – leurs couleurs vives caractéristiques et un étonnant escalier suspendu donnent ici un grand dynamisme au petit espace.

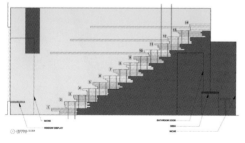

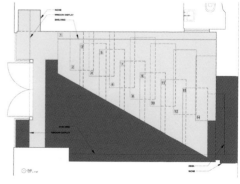

The architects made skilful use of the small space (47m²), for example making a stairway to the upper level a convenient place to sit and read or look at a book. The bright yellow shelves, walls and steps together with bright blue graphics give a fresh modern feeling to the bookstore.

Die Architekten nutzten den kleinen Raum (47 m²) sehr geschickt aus, zum Beispiel indem sie eine Treppe zum Obergeschoss in einen praktischen Platz zum Sitzen und zum Blick in ein Buch gestalteten. Die leuchtend gelben Regale, Wände und Stufen im Verein mit der leuchtend blauen Beschriftung lassen die Buchhandlung frisch und modern wirken.

Les architectes ont su exploiter intelligemment le petit espace (47 m²) en transformant par exemple un escalier en un endroit commode pour s'asseoir et lire ou regarder un livre. Avec le graphisme bleu vif, les rayonnages, murs et marches d'un jaune éclatant donnent une impression de fraîcheur et de modernité à la librairie.

KEISUKE MAEDA/
UID ARCHITECTS

KEISUKE MAEDA was born in 1974 in Hiroshima, Japan, and graduated from the Department of Architecture of Kokushikan University (1999). UID architects was established by Maeda in Hiroshima in 2003. Aside from architecture, the firm specializes in interior design, furniture, exhibition and product design, urban design, planning, consulting, and research. Keisuke Maeda presently lectures at the Hiroshima Institute of Technology. His work includes the Holocaust Education Center (Hiroshima, 2007); House in Tomonoura (Hiroshima, 2008); Art Flow House (Hiroshima, 2008); Rustic House (Fukuyama, 2009); MORI x hako (Hiroshima, 2009); Atelier Bisque Doll (Osaka, 2009); Tumuji + Hako House (Fukuyama, 2010); Nest (Hiroshima, 2010); Machi House (Fukuyama, Hiroshima, 2011); and Peanuts (Hiroshima, 2011–12, published here). Current work includes Dental Clinic O in Matsuyama (2013); and a street renovation in Fukuyama (Hiroshima, 2016), all in Japan.

KEISUKE MAEDA, geboren 1974 in Hiroshima in Japan, machte 1999 seinen Abschluss im Fachbereich Architektur der Universität Kokushikan. 2003 gründete er UID architects in Hiroshima. Außer auf Architektur ist das Büro auf Innenarchitektur, Möbelgestaltung, Ausstellungs- und Produktdesign, Städteplanung, Beratung und Forschung spezialisiert. Derzeit lehrt Keisuke Maeda am Hiroshima Institute of Technology. Zu seinen Arbeiten zählen das Holocaust-Bildungszentrum (Hiroshima, 2007), das Haus in Tomonoura (Hiroshima, 2008), das Air Flow House (Hiroshima, 2008), Rustic House (Fukuyama, 2009), MORI x hako (Hiroshima, 2009), das Atelier Bisque Doll (Osaka, 2009), das Tumuji + Hako House (Fukuyama, 2010), Nest (Hiroshima, 2010), das Machi-House (Fukuyama, 2011) und der Kindergarten Peanuts (Hiroshima, 2011–12, hier vorgestellt). Aktuelle Projekte umfassen die Zahnklinik O in Matsuyama (2013) und eine Straßeninstandsetzung in Fukuyama (2016), alle in Japan.

KEISUKE MAEDA est né en 1974 à Hiroshima, il est diplômé en architecture de l'université Kokushikan (1999). Il a créé UID architects à Hiroshima en 2003. En plus de l'architecture, l'agence est spécialisée en architecture intérieure, mobilier, design d'expositions et de produits, urbanisme, planification, conseil et recherche. Keisuke Maeda enseigne à l'Institut de technologie d'Hiroshima. Ses projets comprennent le Centre d'éducation sur l'Holocauste (Hiroshima, 2007) ; une maison à Tomonoura (Hiroshima, 2008) ; l'Art Flow House (Hiroshima, 2008) ; la Rustic House (Fukuyama, 2009) ; MORI x hako (Hiroshima, 2009) ; l'atelier Bisque Doll (Osaka, 2009) ; la maison Tumuji + Hako (Fukuyama, 2010) ; Nest (Hiroshima, 2010) ; la Machi House (Fukuyama, Hiroshima, 2011) et l'école maternelle Peanuts (Hiroshima, 2011–12, publiée ici). Ses travaux en cours comprennent la clinique dentaire O de Matsuyama (2013) et la rénovation d'une rue à Fukuyama (Hiroshima, 2016), tous au Japon.

PEANUTS

Hiroshima, Japan, 2011–12

Area: 119 m².

The curvilinear structure takes its place in a garden setting, with wide bands of glazing rising through most of its height.

Das kurvige Gebäude, dessen großzügige Glasfassade sich beinahe über die Gesamthöhe erstreckt, ist von einem Garten umgeben.

La structure curviligne occupe un jardin, de larges bandes vitrées se dressent sur presque toute sa hauteur.

This is a timber structure located on a 1500-square-meter site, and intended for use as a nursery school. The plan might be compared to two circles, one slightly larger than the other, that are joined together at the center. Vertical wooden bands are placed at regular intervals up the glazed sides of the building. Curves are present everywhere inside the building as well, where wooden surfaces are the rule. The building is surrounded by greenery designed by Toshiya Ogino. The architect writes: "One circle is a completed form because it has strong centripetal characteristics. However, overlapping two circles change the form that has various vectors and is not centripetal... I expect that children will be brought up with sensitivity in this architecture because Peanuts is not a completed form... like a plant bearing fruit in soil."

Das Gebäude aus Holz steht auf einem 1500 m² großen Grundstück und beherbergt einen Kindergarten. Der Grundriss gleicht zwei Kreisen, der eine etwas größer als der andere, die sich überschneiden. Vertikale Holzbänder ziehen sich in gleichmäßigen Abständen um die verglaste Außenfassade herum. Geschwungene Formen sind auch überall im Inneren des Gebäudes zu finden, wo Holzoberflächen das Bild dominieren. Die das Gebäude umgebende Begrünung wurde von Toshiya Ogino gestaltet. Der Architekt schreibt: „Ein Kreis ist aufgrund seiner eindeutig zentripetalen Charakteristik eine in sich ge-schlossene Form. Bei zwei sich überschneidenden Kreisen allerdings entsteht eine nicht zentripetale Form mit verschiedenen Vektoren … Ich denke, dass Kinder in dieser Architektur mit Achtsamkeit erzogen werden, weil Peanuts keine fertige Form hat … (es ist) wie eine Pflanze, deren Früchte in der Erde verborgen liegen."

La structure en bois d'œuvre est située sur un terrain de 1500 m² et destinée à accueillir une école maternelle. Le plan peut être comparé à deux cercles, l'un légèrement plus grand que l'autre, qui sont reliés au centre. Des bandes de bois verticales ponctuent à intervalles réguliers les côtés vitrés du bâtiment. Les courbes sont omniprésentes à l'intérieur aussi où les surfaces en bois sont de rigueur. Le bâtiment est entouré d'un espace vert créé par Toshiya Ogino. L'architecte décrit son œuvre par ces mots : « Le cercle est une forme achevée du fait de ses fortes caractéristiques centripètes. Mais faire se chevaucher deux cercles modifie cette forme qui présente plusieurs vecteurs et n'est plus centripète… Je compte que les enfants seront élevés avec une sensibilité pour cette architecture, car Peanuts est une forme inachevée… telle une plante portant un fruit encore dans le sol. »

Above, a curved wooden play area is surrounded by the white structure of the building, with its nearly unobstructed views of the garden.

Oben: Ein geschwungener Spielbereich in Holz wird vom weißen Tragwerk des Gebäudes umgeben, das einen nahezu unverstellten Blick in den Garten bietet.

Ci-dessus, un espace de jeu rond en bois est entouré par la structure blanche du bâtiment et sa vue presque entièrement dégagée sur le jardin.

The roof view (above) and the plan of the building reveal its amoeboid shape, compared by the architect to the intersection of two unequal circles.

Die Dachansicht (oben) und der Grundriss des Gebäudes offenbaren die amöbenartige Form, die die Architekten mit der Überschneidung zweier ungleicher Kreise vergleichen.

La vue du toit (ci-dessus) et le plan mettent en évidence la forme amibienne, comparée par l'architecte à l'intersection de deux cercles inégaux.

The curvilinear wooden play and storage area meant for small children is in keeping with the overall plan of the building, but contrasts with the harder walls or angled columns that lie at the outer periphery of the building.

Der geschwungene, in Holz gestaltete Spielbereich und der Stauraum sind für kleine Kinder geplant und fügen sich nahtlos in den Gesamtentwurf ein, kontrastieren aber mit den robusteren Wänden und abgeschrägten Stützpfeilern an der Peripherie des Gebäudes.

L'espace curviligne de jeu et de rangement en bois destiné aux jeunes enfants est assorti au plan global, mais contraste avec les murs plus durs ou les colonnes anguleuses à la périphérie extérieure du bâtiment.

FUMIHIKO MAKI

Born in Tokyo, Japan, in 1928, **FUMIHIKO MAKI** received his B.Arch. degree from the University of Tokyo in 1952, and M.Arch. degrees from the Cranbrook Academy of Art (1953) and the Harvard GSD (1954). He worked for Skidmore, Owings & Merrill in New York (1954–55) and Sert Jackson and Associates in Cambridge, Massachusetts (1955–56), before creating his own firm, Maki and Associates, in Tokyo in 1965. Notable buildings include the Fujisawa Municipal Gymnasium (Fujisawa-shi, Kanagawa, 1984); Spiral (Minato-ku, Tokyo, 1985); National Museum of Modern Art (Sakyo-ku, Kyoto, 1986); Tepia (Minato-ku, Tokyo, 1989); Nippon Convention Center Makuhari Messe (Chiba, Chiba, 1989); the Tokyo Metropolitan Gymnasium (Shibuya-ku, Tokyo, 1990); and the Center for the Arts Yerba Buena Gardens (San Francisco, California, USA, 1993), all in Japan unless stated otherwise. More recent work includes the Sam Fox School of Design and Visual Arts, Washington University (Saint Louis, Missouri, USA, 2006); the MIT Media Laboratory Expansion (Cambridge, Massachusetts, USA, 2007–09); the Novartis Oncology Consolidation Building (East Hanover, New Jersey, USA, 2012); World Trade Center Tower 4 (New York, USA, 2013); and the Aga Khan Museum in Toronto (Ontario, Canada, 2013). Published here is Haus der Hoffnung, Natori Performing Arts Center Multipurpose Hall in Natori (Miyagi, Japan, 2012).

FUMIHIKO MAKI wurde 1928 in Tokio geboren und erlangte 1952 einen B. Arch. der University of Tokyo und jeweils einen M. Arch. an der Cranbook Academy of Art (1953) und der Harvard GSD (1954). Er war für Skidmore, Owings & Merill in New York (1954–55) und Sert Jackson and Associates in Cambridge, Massachusetts (1955–56) tätig, bevor er 1965 in Tokio sein eigenes Büro, Maki and Associates, gründete. Zu seinen wichtigen Bauten zählen die Städtische Sporthalle Fujisawa (Fujisawa-shi, Kanagawa, 1984), Spiral (Minato-ku, Tokio, 1985), das Nationalmuseum für moderne Kunst Kioto (Saky-ku, 1986), Tepia (Minato-ku, Tokio, 1989), das Nippon Convention Center Makuhari Messe (Chiba, Chiba, 1989), die städtische Sporthalle Tokio (Shibuya-ku, Tokio, 1990) und das Center for the Arts Yerba Buena Gardens (San Francisco, USA, 1993), alle in Japan, soweit nicht anders angegeben. Zu seinen jüngeren Arbeiten gehören die Sam Fox School of Design and Visual Arts, Washington University (Saint Louis, Missouri, USA, 2006), die Erweiterung des MIT Media Laboratory (Cambridge, Massachusetts, USA, 2007–09), das Novartis Oncology Consolidation Building (East Hanover, New Jersey, USA, 2012), das World Trade Center Tower 4 (New York, 2013) und das Aga-Khan-Museum in Toronto (Ontario, Kanada, 2013). Hier vorgestellt wird das Haus der Hoffnung, die Mehrzweckhalle des Natori Performing Arts Center in Natori (Miyagi, Japan, 2012).

Né à Tokyo en 1928, **FUMIHIKO MAKI** est titulaire d'un B.Arch de l'université de Tokyo (1952) et de deux M.Arch de la Cranbrook Academy of Art (1953) et de la Harvard GSD (1954). Il a travaillé pour Skidmore, Owings & Merrill à New York (1954–55) et Sert Jackson and Associates à Cambridge, Massachusetts (1955–56) avant de fonder son agence, Maki and Associates, à Tokyo en 1965. Les bâtiments les plus remarquables qu'il a construits sont notamment le gymnase municipal de Fujisawa (Fujisawa-shi, Kanagawa, 1984) ; Spiral (Minato-ku, Tokyo, 1985) ; le Musée national d'art moderne (Sakyo-ku, Kyoto, 1986) ; Tepia (Minato-ku, 1989) ; le palais des congrès Makuhari Messe (Chiba, Chiba, 1989) ; le centre sportif de Tokyo (Shibuya-ku, 1990) et le Yerba Buena Center for the Arts (San Francisco, 1993), tous au Japon sauf mention contraire. Parmi ses réalisations plus récentes : la Sam Fox School of Design and Visual Arts de l'université Washington (Saint Louis, Missouri, 2006) ; l'extension du Media Laboratory du MIT (Cambridge, Massachusetts, 2007–09) ; le Novartis Oncology Consolidation Building (East Hanover, New Jersey, 2012) ; la tour 4 du World Trade Center (New York, 2013) et le musée Aga Khan de Toronto (Ontario, Canada, 2013). Nous publions la Haus der Hoffnung, salle polyvalente du Centre des arts du spectacle de Natori (Miyagi, Japon, 2012).

HAUS DER HOFFNUNG

Natori Performing Arts Center Multipurpose Hall, Natori, Miyagi, Japan, 2012

Area: 234 m².
Client: Reinhard & Sonja Ernst Foundation.

The Haus der Hoffnung (House of Hope) is a multipurpose facility intended to support communal interaction and activities of children and elderly residents of Natori City. Natori was severely damaged by the earthquake and tsunami of March 2011, and this facility serves both as practical support space for displaced residents and as a symbol of the region's recovery. Located near temporary housing shelters and adjacent to the Natori Performing Arts Center (also designed by Maki and Associates), the project was realized through the generosity of the Reinhard & Sonja Ernst Foundation—a German organization dedicated to education and the elderly. The program includes a multipurpose room and kitchen, a room for cultural events/ classes, a meeting area, and a playroom. The architecture is characterized by unusual V-shaped columns supporting a paired roof structure. Wood is the main structural material for this one-story building.

Das Haus der Hoffnung ist ein Mehrzweckgebäude, das das bürgerschaftliche Miteinander fördern und ein Ort für Kinder und alte Menschen in Natori City sein soll. Natori wurde durch das Erdbeben und den Tsunami im März 2011 schwer beschädigt, und die Einrichtung dient sowohl als praktische Anlaufstelle für Menschen, die ihre Häuser verloren haben, als auch als Symbol für das Wiedererstarken der Region. Das Projekt, in der Nähe von Notunterkünften und gleich neben dem Natori Performing Arts Center (ebenfalls von Maki and Associates entworfen) gelegen, konnte dank der Großzügigkeit der deutschen Reinhard & Sonja Ernst-Stiftung realisiert werden, die sich für Bildung und alte Menschen engagiert. Zur Einrichtung gehören ein Mehrzweckraum mit Küche, ein Raum für kulturelle Anlässe und Kurse, ein Versammlungsraum und ein Spielzimmer. Die Architektur zeichnen ungewöhnliche v-förmige Säulen aus, die eine zweiteilige Dachkonstruktion stützen. Holz ist das dominierende Baumaterial des eingeschossigen Gebäudes.

La Haus der Hoffnung (Maison de l'espoir) est un centre polyvalent destiné à favoriser l'interaction au niveau communal et les activités des enfants et habitants âgés de Natori. La ville a beaucoup souffert du tremblement de terre et du tsunami de mars 2011, et cet établissement tient lieu à la fois d'espace concret où trouver un soutien pour les habitants déplacés et de symbole du redressement de la région. Situé à proximité de logements temporaires et adjacent au Centre des arts du spectacle de Natori (également créé par Maki and Associates), le projet a pu être réalisé grâce à la générosité de la fondation Reinhard et Sonja Ernst – une organisation allemande qui se consacre à l'éducation et aux personnes âgées. L'ensemble comprend une salle polyvalente avec cuisine, une salle pour les manifestations culturelles ou les cours, une salle de réunion et une salle de jeu. L'architecture est surtout caractérisée par ses colonnes en V originales qui soutiennent un toit jumelé. Le bois est le principal matériau de construction de ce bâtiment d'un niveau.

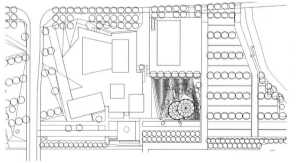

Overall site plan.

Lageplan der gesamten Anlage.

Plan global du site.

The rounded roofs of the multi-purpose facility overlie a more rectilinear plan, as the drawing to the right shows. Images give the impression of buildings that are at once modern and yet somehow related to tradition.

Les toits ronds du centre polyvalent surmontent un plan plus rectiligne, comme le montre le schéma à droite. Les images donnent l'impression de bâtiments modernes mais rattachés malgré tout à la tradition.

Die abgerundeten Dächer der Mehrzweckeinrichtung überlagern einen eher rechtwinkligen Grundriss, wie die Zeichnung rechts zeigt. Die Bilder vermitteln den Eindruck moderner Gebäude, die aber auch der Tradition verpflichtet sind.

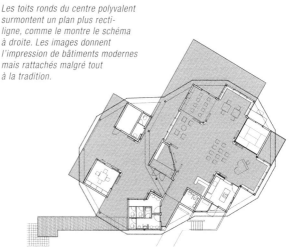

Angled wooden columns and a curving roof give a strong impression of movement. Some sliding screens reinforce the impression of a will to refer to Japanese tradition without being too specific.

Angeschrägtes Ständerwerk aus Holz und ein geschwungenes Dach vermitteln einen starken Eindruck von Bewegung. Einige verschiebbare Wände lassen den Wunsch erkennen, die japanische Tradition anklingen zu lassen, ohne aber zu spezifisch zu werden.

Les colonnes de bois à angles et la courbe du toit donnent une forte impression de mouvement. Des panneaux coulissants renforcent l'impression d'une référence voulue à la tradition japonaise, mais sans être trop spécifique.

Opposite: The generous covered wooden decks create space that is neither entirely exterior nor actually within the walls of the building.

Gegenüber: Die großzügige Überdachung der Holzterrassen lässt Räume entstehen, die weder ganz im Freien noch wirklich im Gebäudeinneren liegen.

Ci-contre : Les larges galeries couvertes en bois créent un espace, ni entièrement extérieur, ni dans les murs du bâtiment.

MARK+VIVI

MARK+VIVI is a design studio based in Montreal, Canada. It was cofounded in 2010 by **MARK FEKETE**, born in Montreal in 1971, and **VIVIANA DE LOERA**, born in Zacatecas, Mexico, in 1978, who began their collaboration after graduating with B.Arch. degrees from the College of Architecture and Environmental Design at Cal Poly (San Luis Obispo, California, 2004). Mark Fekete worked for the Jerde Partnership (Los Angeles, 2004) and Rossetti Architects (Newport Beach, California 2007–08), before creating MARK + VIVI. Like Fekete, Viviana de Loera worked for the KTGY Group (Irvine, California, 2004–08). Their first projects include the Tire Shop (Verdun, Montreal, 2010–11, published here) and the Grand Trunk House (Pointe-Saint-Charles, Quebec, 2013), both in Canada.

MARK+VIVI ist ein Architekturbüro mit Sitz in Montreal. Gegründet wurde es 2010 von **MARK FEKETE**, geboren 1971 in Montreal, und **VIVIANA DE LOERA**, geboren 1978 in Zacatecas, Mexiko, die seit ihrem Studium am College of Architecture and Environmental Design at Cal Pony (San Louis Obispo, Kalifornien, 2004) zusammenarbeiten, das beide mit einem B. Arch. abschlossen. Mark Fekete arbeitete für Jerde Partnership (Los Angeles, 2004) und Rossetti Architects (Newport Beach, Kalifornien, 2007–08), bevor MARK + VIVA entstand. Wie Fekete arbeitete auch Viviana de Loera für die KTGY Group (Irvine, Kalifornien, 2004–08). Ihre ersten Projekte als Team waren der Tire Shop (Verdun, Montreal, 2010–11, hier vorgestellt) und das Grand Trunk House (Pointe-Saint-Charles, Quebec, 2013), beide in Kanada.

MARK+VIVI est une agence de design basée à Montréal. Elle a été cofondée en 2010 par **MARK FEKETE**, né à Montréal en 1971, et **VIVIANA DE LOERA**, née à Zacatecas, au Mexique, en 1978, qui ont commencé à travailler ensemble après avoir obtenu leurs B. Arch du College of Architecture and Environmental Design de Cal Poly (San Luis Obispo, Californie, 2004). Mark Fekete a travaillé pour Jerde Partnership (Los Angeles, 2004) et Rossetti Architects (Newport Beach, Californie, 2007–08) avant de créer MARK + VIVI. Comme lui, Viviana de Loera a travaillé pour le groupe KTGY (Irvine, Californie, 2004–08). Leurs premiers projets en équipe sont The Tire Shop (Verdun, Montréal, 2010–11, publié ici) et le Grand Trunk House (Pointe-Saint-Charles, Québec, 2013).

THE TIRE SHOP PROJECT

Verdun, Montreal, Canada, 2010–11

Area: 79 m².
Client: Mark Fekete and Viviana de Loera.

The architects live and work in this small former tire shop. A spiraling black stairway saves space, and a contrast between wood beams and surfaces with bright yellow or white volumes enlivens the house.

Die Architekten leben und arbeiten in dieser kleinen ehemaligen Reifenhandlung. Eine schwarze Wendeltreppe spart Platz, und der Kontrast zwischen den Holzbalken und den hellgelb oder weiß gehaltenen Raumkomponenten macht das Haus lebendig.

Les architectes vivent et travaillent dans cet ancien magasin de pneus. Un escalier noir en colimaçon permet de gagner de la place et contraste avec les poutres en bois et les surfaces jaune vif ou blanches qui donnent vie à la maison.

The Tire Shop is MARK+VIVI's inaugural project, located in a renovated former tire shop built in 1920. They live and work in the space. The space also houses La Façade Art+Architecture, a public storefront gallery dedicated to the exhibition of local contemporary art and experimental architecture. The newly exposed structure integrates simple, raw, modern, industrial materials and efficient design. "We have had an overwhelmingly positive response from our neighborhood," states Mark Fekete. "Our goal was to create a home that served as a catalyst for the design community while providing opportunities for local artists who would otherwise not have a chance to exhibit their work. We'd like to help revitalize our city one building at a time."

Der Tire Shop ist MARK+VIVIs Erstlingsprojekt, der renovierte ehemalige Laden eines Reifenhändlers aus dem Jahr 1920. Die beiden leben und arbeiten in den Räumen. Ebenfalls dort untergebracht ist La Façade Art+Architecture, eine öffentliche Galerie, die sich lokaler zeitgenössischer Kunst und experimenteller Architektur widmet. Die freigelegte Bausubstanz kombiniert einfache, rohe, moderne und industrielle Materialien mit effizientem Design. „Aus der Nachbarschaft kamen überwältigend positive Reaktionen", so Mark Fekete. „Unser Ziel war es, ein Zuhause zu schaffen, das als Katalysator für die Designer und Architekten hier funktioniert und gleichzeitig lokalen Künstlern, die ihre Arbeiten sonst nicht würden zeigen können, die Möglichkeit bietet auszustellen. Wir würden gern mithelfen, unsere Stadt Gebäude für Gebäude wiederzubeleben."

The Tire Shop est le projet inaugural de l'agence MARK+VIVI, dans un ancien magasin de pneus construit en 1920 et rénové. Ils y vivent et y travaillent. L'endroit accueille également La Façade Art+Architecture, une galerie publique qui se consacre à l'art contemporain local et l'architecture expérimentale. La structure récente associe des matériaux simples, bruts, modernes et de fabrication industrielle à un design fonctionnel. « Les réactions du voisinage ont été extraordinairement positives », raconte Mark Fekete. « Notre but était de créer une maison qui serve de catalyseur pour la communauté design, tout en donnant une chance aux artistes locaux qui ne pourraient sinon pas exposer leur travail. Nous voudrions contribuer à redonner vie à notre ville, bâtiment après bâtiment. »

The only real exterior sign of the function of the strict brick building is the large display window near the main entrance.

Den einzigen äußeren Hinweis auf die Funktion des strengen Backsteinbaus liefert das große Schaufenster neben dem Eingang.

Le seul signe extérieur de l'ancienne fonction de cette austère maison en briques est la grande vitrine près de l'entrée principale.

Left, storage and display shelves are casual, but in keeping with the willful contrasts of colors and materials that are employed.

Links: Die Küchen- wie auch die Bücherregale wirken beinahe provisorisch, harmonieren aber mit den Kontrasten von Farben und Materialien.

À gauche, les étagères de rangement et de présentation n'ont rien de spécial, mais elles s'accordent avec les contrastes délibérés de couleurs et de matériaux employés.

Private spaces are less hetero-
geneous in appearance than the
kitchen or work space. Here, white
and black are the main colors, with
some touches of color or the presence of a wood floor (right page).

*Die Privaträume sind von der
Anmutung her weniger heterogen
als der Küchen- und Arbeitsbereich.
Hier dominieren Weiß und Schwarz,
ergänzt durch einige Farbakzente
und den Holzfußboden (rechte Seite).*

*Les espaces privés sont plus
homogènes que la cuisine ou
l'espace de travail. Le blanc et le
noir y dominent, avec quelques
touches de couleur ou un sol en
bois (page de droite).*

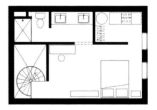

Right, plans of the two levels
of the building, with the spiral
stairway visible at the lower
left of the drawings. Above,
the bedroom.

Rechts: Grundrisse der beiden Eta-
gen, die Wendeltreppe ist auf den
Zeichnungen links unten zu sehen.
Oben: das Schlafzimmer.

À droite, plan des deux étages
avec l'escalier en colimaçon
visible à l'extrême gauche.
Ci-dessus, la chambre à coucher.

MARTE.MARTE

BERNHARD MARTE was born in 1966 in Dornbirn, Vorarlberg, Austria, and his brother, **STEFAN MARTE**, was born in the same locality in 1967. They obtained their M.Arch. degrees from the Technical University of Innsbruck. Stefan Marte worked in the office of Gohm + Hiessberger in Feldkirch until Marte.Marte was created in Weiler in 1993. Their work includes the Schanerloch Bridge (Dornbirn, 2005–06); State Pathology Hospital (Feldkirch, 2003–08); Alfenz Bridge (Lorüns, 2009–10); Grieskirchen School Center (Grieskirchen, 2003–11); Special Pedagogical Center (Dornbirn, 2008–11); Diocesan Museum (Fresach, 2010–11); Mountain Cabin (Laterns, 2010–11, published here); Maiden Tower (Dafins, 2011–12); and a Tourism School (Villach, 2011–13), all in Austria. They are currently working on the SFVV Museum (Berlin, Germany, 2013–16).

BERNHARD MARTE wurde 1966 in Dornbirn im österreichischen Vorarlberg geboren, sein Bruder Stefan Marte 1967 im selben Ort. Sie machten ihren M. Arch. an der Technischen Universität Innsbruck. **STEFAN MARTE** arbeitete im Büro Gohm + Hiessberger in Feldkirch, bis sie beide 1993 Marte.Marte in Weiler gründeten. Zu ihren ausgeführten Bauten zählen die Schanerloch-Brücke (Dornbirn, 2005, hier vorgestellt), das Pathologiegebäude des Landeskrankenhauses in Feldkirch (2003 bis 2008), die Alfenz-Brücke (Lorüns, 2009–10), das Schulzentrum Grieskirchen (Grieskirchen, 2003–11), ein Sonderschulzentrum (Dornbirn, 2008–11), das Kärntner Diözesanmuseum (Fresach, 2010–11), eine Berghütte im Laternser Tal (Laterns, 2010–11), der Mädchenturm (Dafins, 2011–12) und eine Tourismusschule (Villach, 2011–13), alle in Österreich. Gegenwärtig arbeiten sie am Museum der Stiftung Flucht, Vertreibung, Versöhnung (SFVV) in Berlin (2013–16).

BERNHARD MARTE est né en 1966 à Dornbirn, dans le Vorarlberg (Autriche), ainsi que son frère **STEFAN MARTE** en 1967. Ils sont tous les deux titulaires d'un M.Arch. de l'Université technique d'Innsbruck. Stefan Marte a travaillé dans l'agence Gohm + Hiessberger à Feldkirch avant la création de Marte.Marte à Weiler en 1993. Leurs réalisations comprennent le pont de Schanerloch (Dornbirn, 2005, publié ici) ; l'hôpital régional à pathologie (Feldkirch, 2003–08) ; le pont d'Alfenz (Lorüns, 2009–10) ; le Centre scolaire de Grieskirchen (2003–11) ; le Centre pédagogique spécial (Dornbirn, 2008–11) ; le Musée diocésain de Carinthie (Fresach, 2010–11) ; un refuge de montagne dans la vallée de Laterns (Laterns, 2010–11) ; la Maiden Tower (Dafins, 2011–12) et une école de tourisme (Villach, 2011–13), toutes en Autriche. Ils travaillent actuellement au musée SFVV (Berlin, 2013–16).

MOUNTAIN CABIN

Laterns, Austria, 2010–11

Area: 87 m².

The square plan and concrete volumes of the house are enlivened by cutouts that leave spaces for outside terraces and views of the mountain setting.

Der quadratische Grundriss und der Betonkörper des Hauses werden durch Aussparungen aufgelockert, die Raum für eine Terrasse und den Blick in die Berglandschaft schaffen.

Le plan carré et les volumes en béton sont égayés par des découpures qui ouvrent des terrasses et des vues sur les montagnes environnantes.

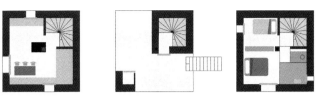

In their design, the architects used "carefully hewn rough concrete," oak front doors with anthracite-colored handrails, and untreated oak floors, as well as square windows of different sizes with solid oak frames. Inside the structure, a spiral staircase connects the living area on the upper level with the two private areas on the lower level, where the bedrooms and relaxation areas "are interlocked like a puzzle." The entire design gives an impression of solidity that is in many ways a reflection of the rather harsh beauty of the natural setting.

Die Architekten verwendeten für dieses Projekt „sorgsam bearbeiteten rauen Beton", Eingangstüren aus Eichenholz, anthrazitfarbene Handläufe und unbehandeltes Eichenholz für die Fußböden. Zudem kamen verschieden große quadratische Fenster mit massiven Eichenholzrahmen zum Einsatz. Innerhalb des Gebäudes verbindet eine Wendeltreppe den Wohnraum im Obergeschoss mit den beiden Privatbereichen im Untergeschoss, wo die Schlaf- und Entspannungsräume „wie bei einem Puzzle ineinandergreifen". Der gesamte Entwurf vermittelt einen Eindruck von Robustheit, der in vielerlei Hinsicht die durchaus raue Schönheit der Natur reflektiert.

Les architectes ont ici utilisé le « béton brut soigneusement taillé », avec des portes de devant en chêne aux rampes anthracite, des planchers de chêne brut et des fenêtres carrées de différentes tailles aux solides cadres de chêne. À l'intérieur, un escalier en colimaçon relie le séjour de l'étage aux deux espaces privés du niveau inférieur où les chambres et salles de relaxation « s'emboîtent comme un puzzle ». L'ensemble donne une impression de solidité qui reflète à bien des égards la beauté plutôt rude du cadre naturel.

Wood finishing and some added wooden furniture make the interior of the house warmer than might be expected when it is seen from the outside.

Holzflächen und Holzmobiliar lassen das Innere des Hauses wärmer erscheinen als von außen zunächst vermutet.

Les finitions en bois et le mobilier en bois ajouté rendent l'intérieur de la maison plus chaleureux qu'on ne le penserait en la voyant de l'extérieur.

MIRALLES TAGLIABUE EMBT

Born in Barcelona, Spain, in 1955 (d. 2000), **ENRIC MIRALLES** received his degree from the ETSA in that city in 1978, and went on to form a partnership with Carme Pinós in 1983. Benedetta Tagliabue was born in Milan, Italy, and graduated from the IUAV in Venice in 1989. She studied and worked in New York (with Agrest and Gandelsonas) from 1987 to 1989. She worked for Enric Miralles, beginning in 1992, first becoming a partner, then leading the studio after his death. The work of Miralles includes the Olympic Archery Ranges (Barcelona, 1989–91); Igualada Cemetery Park (Barcelona, 1985–92); La Mina Civic Center (Barcelona, 1987–92); Morella Boarding School (Castelló, 1986–94); and the Huesca Sports Hall (1988–94). The most visible recent project of the firm was the Scottish Parliament (Edinburgh, UK, 1998–2004); while other recent work includes the Rehabilitation of the Santa Caterina Market (Barcelona, 1997–2005); the Principal Building for the University Campus (Vigo, 2006); the Public Library (Palafolls, 1997–2007); headquarters for Gas Natural (Barcelona, 2007); the Camper Store (Barcelona, 2010, published here); and the Spanish Pavilion for the *Shanghai 2010 Expo* (China), all in Spain unless stated otherwise.

ENRIC MIRALLES, geboren 1955 in Barcelona (gestorben 2000), beendete sein Studium 1978 an der ETSA Barcelona und schloss sich 1983 mit Carme Pinós als Partnerin zusammen. Benedetta Tagliabue, geboren in Mailand, schloss ihr Studium 1989 an der IUAV Venedig ab. Von 1987 bis 1989 studierte und arbeitete sie in New York (bei Agrest & Gandelsonas). Ab 1992 war sie für Enric Miralles tätig, wurde Partnerin und übernahm nach seinem Tod die Leitung des Studios. Zu Miralles' Projekten zählen die Olympische Bogenschießanlage (Barcelona, 1989–91), die Gartenanlagen des Friedhofs Igualada (Barcelona, 1985–92), das Stadtteilzentrum in La Mina (Barcelona, 1987–92), ein Internat in Morella (Castelló, 1986–94) sowie das Sportzentrum in Huesca (1988–94). Bekanntestes Projekt des Büros in jüngerer Zeit ist das Schottische Parlament (Edinburgh, 1998–2004). Weitere neuere Projekte sind der Umbau der Markthalle Santa Caterina (Barcelona, 1997–2005), das Hauptgebäude auf dem Universitätscampus von Vigo (2006), die Bibliothek von Palafolls (1997–2007), die Zentrale für Gas Natural (Barcelona, 2007), der Camper Store (Barcelona, 2010, hier vorgestellt) und der Spanische Pavillon für die Expo 2010 in Schanghai (China), alle in Spanien, soweit nicht anders angegeben.

Né à Barcelone en 1955 (mort en 2000), **ENRIC MIRALLES** y a obtenu son diplôme de l'ETSA en 1978 et s'est associé à Carme Pinós en 1983. Benedetta Tagliabue est née à Milan et a obtenu son diplôme de l'IUAV à Venise en 1989. Elle a fait des études et a travaillé à New York (avec Agrest and Gandelsonas) de 1987 à 1989. Elle a travaillé pour Enric Miralles dès 1992, d'abord en tant que partenaire, et dirige l'agence depuis sa mort. Leurs réalisations comprennent : le terrain de tir à l'arc olympique (Barcelone, 1989–91); le cimetière d'Igualada (Barcelone, 1985–92); le centre administratif de La Mina (Barcelone, 1987–92); le pensionnat de Morella (Castelló, Espagne, 1986–94) et la salle de sports de Huesca (Espagne, 1988–94). Le projet récent le plus représentatif est le Parlement écossais (Édimbourg, 1998–2004); parmi les autres réalisations récentes figurent la rénovation du marché Santa Caterina (Barcelone, 1997–2005); le bâtiment directeur du campus universitaire (Vigo, 2006); la bibliothèque publique (Palafolls, 1997–2007); le siège de Gas Natural (Barcelone, 2007); la boutique Camper (Barcelone, 2010, publiée ici) et le pavillon de l'Espagne à l'Exposition universelle de Shanghai en 2010 (Chine), toutes en Espagne sauf mention contraire.

CAMPER STORE

Barcelona, Spain, 2010

Area: 52 m². Client: Camper.
Collaboration: Karl Unglaub (Project Director).

This interior design project was created with the idea of seeing fashion through children's eyes, or "shoes in front of the twisted mirrors of an amusement park." The architects also visited a Camper shoe factory where "flat leather sheets are cut and, like magic, with a couple of stitches and a mold, they become beautiful three-dimensional wrappings!" The result of this observation was that EMBT used MDF sheets "cut like shoes," creating benches, tables, and other surfaces, together with the mirrors that they also refer to. Finally, Benedetta Tagliabue states: "Camper has much to do with *el campo*, that is the countryside, the fields… to walk in the fields… and so we imagined shoes stepping on irregular surfaces, like when we walk on earth."

Hinter dieser Innenarchitektur steckt der Gedanke, Mode durch die Augen eines Kindes zu sehen, wie „Schuhe in einem Zerrspiegel auf dem Jahrmarkt". Die Architekten besuchten ein Camper-Werk, wo „Lederstücke zugeschnitten und wie durch Zauberhand mit ein paar Stichen und einem Leisten zu wunderschönen dreidimensionalen Hüllen werden!" Diese Beobachtungen veranlassten EMBT, mit MDF-Platten zu arbeiten, die „wie Schuhe zugeschnitten" wurden, um Bänke, Tische und weitere Präsentationsflächen zu schaffen, die mit den eingangs erwähnten Spiegelelementen kombiniert wurden. Benedetta Tagliabue resümiert: „Camper hat viel mit *el campo* zu tun, dem Land, den Feldern… Spaziergängen in den Feldern… weshalb wir ein bestimmtes Bild vor Augen hatten: Schuhe, die auf unebenen Grund treten, so als würden wir über erdigen Grund laufen."

Ce projet d'architecture intérieure a été créé avec l'idée de voir la mode à travers les yeux d'enfant ou « des chaussures dans les miroirs déformants d'un parc de loisirs ». Les architectes ont visité une usine de chaussures Camper et vu « les feuilles de cuir découpées à plat devenir, comme par magie, avec un ou deux points de couture et une forme, de superbes emballages en trois dimensions ». À la suite de cette observation, EMBT a choisi d'utiliser des feuilles MDF « coupées à la manière de chaussures », créant bancs, tables et autres surfaces avec les miroirs qu'ils évoquent. Benedetta Tagliabue conclut : « Camper est très proche d'*el campo*, la campagne, les champs… marcher à travers champs… nous avons donc imaginé des chaussures qui arpentent des surfaces irrégulières, comme lorsque nous marchons sur la terre. »

Above, three-dimensional drawings show the design of the display stands, visible in situ in the images to the right. An ordinary shop interior is transformed by the addition of this irregular, seemingly mobile installation.

Dreidimensionale Zeichnungen (oben) veranschaulichen das Design der Präsentationsinseln, rechts auf einer Aufnahme vor Ort. Die asymmetrische, scheinbar mobile Installation verwandelt den gewöhnlichen Verkaufsraum.

Ci-dessus, plans 3D du design du présentoir visible in situ sur les photos de droite. L'installation aux formes irrégulières et en apparence mobiles transforme l'intérieur d'une boutique ordinaire.

KOTA MIZUISHI

KOTA MIZUISHI was born in 1973 in Osaka, Japan. He received his B.Arch. degree from the Yokohama National University (1997) and an M.Arch. degree from the Tokyo National University of Fine Arts and Music (2000). He worked with Atelier Y Associates (Tokyo, 2000), before establishing TKO-M (2003). He created his present office, Mizuishi Architect Atelier, in 2009. His work includes the House in Kodaira (Tokyo, 2009); Riverside House (Suginami, Tokyo, 2010–11, published here); House in Nukuikitamachi (Tokyo, 2011); House in Shirogane (Tokyo, 2011); and the Ootakanomori Animal Hospital (Nagareyama, Chiba, 2012), all in Japan.

KOTA MIZUISHI wurde 1973 in Osaka in Japan geboren. Er erlangte seinen B. Arch. an der Yokohama National University (1997) und einen M. Arch. an der Tokyo National University of Fine Art and Music (2000). Er arbeitete bei Atelier Y Associates (Tokio, 2000), bevor er TKO-M gründete (2003). Sein derzeitiges Büro, Mizuishi Architect Atelier, gründete er 2009. Einige seiner Arbeiten sind das Haus in Kodera (Tokio, 2009), das Riverside House (Suginami, Tokio, 2010–11, hier vorgestellt), das Haus in Nukuikitamachi (Tokio, 2011), das Haus in Shirogana (Tokio, 2011) und die Tierklinik Ootakanomori (Nagareyama, Chiba, 2012), alle in Japan.

KOTA MIZUISHI est né en 1973 à Osaka. Il est titulaire d'un B.Arch de l'Université nationale de Yokohama (1997) et d'un M.Arch de l'Université nationale des beaux-arts et de musique de Tokyo (2000). Il a travaillé avec Atelier Y Associates (Tokyo, 2000) avant de fonder TKO-M (2003). Il a créé son agence actuelle, Mizuishi Architect Atelier, en 2009. Ses réalisations comprennent la maison à Kodaira (Tokyo, 2009); la Riverside House (Suginami, Tokyo, 2010–11, publiée ici); une maison à Nukuikitamachi (Tokyo, 2011); une maison à Shirogane (Tokyo, 2011) et l'hôpital vétérinaire d'Ootakanomori (Nagareyama, Chiba, 2012), toutes au Japon.

RIVERSIDE HOUSE

Suginami, Tokyo, Japan, 2010–11

Area: 55 m².

Built on a 52-square-meter triangular site between a river and a road, the very small house was designed for a couple and their young daughter. The architect wished to emphasize the relation of the residence to the river. The dining area and kitchen on the west side occupy the largest proportion of the floor area. The central living area has a low ceiling and windows on both sides. A "spare room" on the east side "is a space watching the light." A loft area with two skylights looks down on the river and up at the sky. The two-story building is made of wood with a galvanized steel sheet roof. Interior floors are in solid birch. Furnishings are in linden plywood.

Das sehr kleine Haus, errichtet auf einem 52 m² großen, dreieckigen Grundstück zwischen einem Fluss und einer Straße, wurde für ein Paar und deren kleine Tochter entworfen. Dem Architekten war es wichtig, die Beziehung des Hauses zum Fluss hervorzuheben. Essbereich und Küche auf der Westseite nehmen den Großteil des Erdgeschosses ein. Der zentrale Lebensbereich hat eine niedrige Decke und Fenster zu beiden Seiten. Ein „Extrazimmer" auf der Ostseite „ist ein Ort, der das Licht beobachtet". Von einem Loftbereich mit zwei Oberlichtern aus schaut man auf den Fluss und nach oben in den Himmel. Das zweistöckige Gebäude besteht aus Holz und hat ein Dach aus feuerverzinktem Stahlblech. Die Böden im Innern sind aus massiver Birke, die Möbel aus Lindensperrholz.

Construite sur une parcelle triangulaire de 52 m² entre une rivière et une route, cette toute petite maison a été conçue pour un couple et leur fillette. L'architecte a voulu mettre en valeur le lien entre l'habitation et la rivière. L'espace salle à manger et la cuisine, du côté ouest, occupent la majeure partie de la surface au sol. L'espace séjour central est bas de plafond et a des fenêtres de chaque côté. Une « chambre d'amis » à l'est « forme un espace regardant la lumière ». L'espace sous les combles, percé de deux lucarnes, donne sur la rivière vers le bas et sur le ciel vers le haut. Le bâtiment de deux niveaux est en bois couvert d'un toit en feuille d'acier galvanisé. À l'intérieur, les sols sont en bouleau massif. Le mobilier est en tilleul contreplaqué.

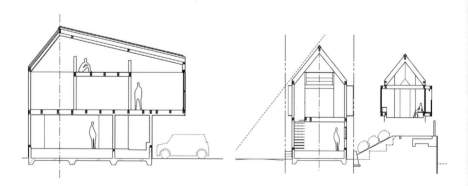

Within this tiny house, the architect creates a spatial interest with angles and a sloping roof. A suspended loft area hangs over the living and dining space.

In diesem winzigen Haus schafft der Architekt mittels Winkeln und einem abfallenden Dach räumliche Spannung. Ein Loftbereich schwebt über dem Wohn- und Essraum.

Dans une maison minuscule, l'architecte a créé un intérêt spatial avec des angles et un toit en pente. Un espace loft est suspendu au-dessus du salon-salle à manger.

Making use of a tiny lot, the architect created an intriguing narrow volume with a long overhang on one side.

Auf einem winzigen Grundstück schuf der Architekt ein verblüffend schmales Gebäude mit einem weiten Überstand auf der einen Seite.

Sur une parcelle minuscule, l'architecte a imaginé un curieux volume étroit avec un long surplomb d'un côté.

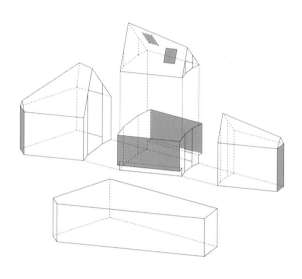

Below, a view of the ground-level bedroom that appears to be quite ample in size, though appearances can be deceiving. Left, an exploded axonometric drawing.

Unten eine Ansicht des Schlafzimmers im Erdgeschoss, das zwar recht geräumig wirkt, doch der Schein trügt. Links eine axonometrische Explosionszeichnung.

Une vue de la chambre à coucher au niveau du sol qui paraît assez spacieuse, mais les apparences sont parfois trompeuses. À gauche, croquis axonométrique éclaté.

On this page a bright bathroom and the upper-level loft space. Below, the projecting volume, called a "spare space" in the plans, is glazed and offers a comfortable working area.

Das helle Bad und der höher gelegene Loftbereich (diese Seite). Unten das auskragende Gebäude- element, in den Plänen „Extra- zimmer" genannt, das beidseitig verglast ist und einen angenehmen Arbeitsplatz bietet.

Une salle de bains claire et l'espace sous les combles. Ci-dessous, le volume en saillie, appelé « chambre d'amis » sur les plans, est vitré et offre un lieu de travail agréable.

TATZU NISHI

TATZU NISHI is an artist who also goes by the names Tazu Rous, Tatzu Oozu, Tatsurou Bashi, and Tazro Niscino. He was born in Nagoya, Japan, in 1960. He studied at the Musashino Art University (Tokyo, 1981–84) and the Kunstakademie Münster (Germany, 1989–97). He currently lives and works in Berlin and Tokyo. His work includes the installations Hotel Continental (Aachen, Germany, 2002); Villa Victoria (Liverpool, UK, 2002); Engel (Basel, Switzerland, 2004); Café in the Sky—Moon Rider (Dublin, Ireland, 2005); Kariforunia, the Museum of Contemporary Art (Los Angeles, USA, 2006); Chéri in the Sky, Maison Hermès (Tokyo, Japan, 2006); Sometimes Extraordinary, Sometimes Less Than Common, Aichi Prefectural Museum of Art (Nagoya, Japan, 2009); Villa Cheminée (Cordemais, France, 2011); the Merlion Hotel (Singapore, 2012); Hotel Gent (Ghent, Belgium, 2012); and Discovering Columbus (New York, USA, 2012, published here).

TAZU NISHI ist Künstler und arbeitet auch unter den Namen Tazu Rous, Tatzu Oozu, Tatsurou Bashi und Tazro Niscino. Er wurde 1960 in Nagoya, Japan, geboren. Nishi studierte an der Musashino Kunsthochschule (Tokio, 1981–84) und der Kunstakademie in Münster (1989–97). Zurzeit lebt und arbeitet er in Berlin und Tokio. Zu seinen Arbeiten zählen die Installationen Hotel Continental (Aachen, 2002), Villa Victoria (Liverpool, 2002), Engel (Basel, 2004), Café in the Sky – Moon Rider (Dublin, 2005), Kariforunia am Museum of Contemporary Art (Los Angeles, 2006), Chéri in the Sky im Maison Hermès (Tokio, 2006), Sometimes Extraordinary, Sometimes Less Than Common im Museum für Kunst der Präfektur Aichi (Nagoya, 2009), Villa Cheminée (Cordemais, Frankreich, 2011) sowie das Merlion Hotel (Singapur, 2012), das Hotel Gent (Gent, Belgien, 2012) und Discovering Columbus (New York, 2012, hier vorgestellt).

L'artiste **TATZU NISHI** se fait également appeler Tazu Rous, Tatzu Oozu, Tatsurou Bashi ou Tazro Niscino. Né à Nagoya, au Japon, en 1960, il fait ses études à l'Université d'art de Musashino (Tokyo, 1981–84) et à l'Académie des beaux-arts de Münster (Allemagne, 1989–97). Il vit et travaille entre Berlin et Tokyo. Parmi ses réalisations, on trouve *Hotel Continental* (Aix-la-Chapelle, Allemagne, 2002) ; *Villa Victoria* (Liverpool, 2002) ; *Engel* (Bâle, 2004) ; *Café in the Sky – Moon Rider* (Dublin, 2005) ; *Kariforunia* au Musée d'art contemporain (Los Angeles, 2006) ; *Chéri in the Sky* à la Maison Hermès (Tokyo, 2006) ; *Sometimes Extraordinary, Sometimes Less Than Common* au Musée préfectoral d'art d'Aichi (Nagoya, Japon, 2009) ; *Villa Cheminée* (Cordemais, France, 2011) ; l'hôtel Merlion (Singapour, 2012) ; l'hôtel Gent (Gand, Belgique, 2012) et *Discovering Columbus* (New York, 2012, présenté ici).

DISCOVERING COLUMBUS

New York, USA, 2012

Area: 12 m² (hallway); 75 m² (living room).
Client: Public Art Fund. Collaboration: Amiko Takimoto,
Gerner Kronick + Valcarcel PC.

Those familiar with Manhattan have surely noticed the statue of Christopher Columbus that stands on a 23-meter-high column at Columbus Circle. Tatzu Nishi, faithful to other installations that have involved a similar approach to spaces that normally cannot be acceded to, has actually built a domestic environment around the sculpture. "I am constructing a living room around it—as if to envelop this statue that has for years watched over New York as its immigrants came in—and it will be open to the public. The object, which passersby could previously only see from the sidewalk, will now occupy this room like a familiar sculpture, bringing viewers face to face with it at eye level for the first time in the plaza's over 100-year-long history." Visitors were invited to climb stairs attached to scaffolding, to pass through a long narrow hallway and to enter the "living room." The artist explains: "The interior design is similar to apartments commonly seen in the neighborhood with the exceptions of the presence of an unnaturally large sculpture and the original wallpaper, which is based on my drawings that take American culture and history as their inspiration. The building design and interior only need to serve the minimal function of enabling the contradictory concept of a public sculpture that occupies an indoor 'private' space."

Wer New York kennt, kennt sicher die Statue von Christoph Kolumbus, die auf einer 23 m hohen Säule über dem Columbus Circle steht. Tazu Nishi, der bereits mehrere Installationen schuf, die Räume und Orte thematisieren, die üblicherweise unzugänglich sind, hat einen fiktiven Wohnraum um diese Skulptur herum errichtet. „Ich baue ein Wohnzimmer um die Skulptur herum, um sie gewissermaßen zu verhüllen, nachdem sie jahrelang, während immer neue Einwanderer den Weg in die Stadt finden, über New York gewacht hat, und öffne dieses Wohnzimmer der Öffentlichkeit. Bisher konnten Passanten die Skulptur nur vom Gehweg aus sehen. Jetzt dominiert sie als etwas sehr Vertrautes den Raum, und zum ersten Mal in der über 100-jährigen Geschichte des Columbus Circle können Besucher ihr geradewegs in die Augen sehen." Besucher konnten eine Treppe das Gerüst hinaufsteigen und über einen schmalen Gang das Zimmer betreten. Der Künstler hierzu: „Abgesehen von der überdimensionalen Skulptur und der originellen Tapete mit von mir gezeichneten Motiven aus der US-amerikanischen Kultur und Geschichte, ist die Inneneinrichtung konventionell. Architektur und Inneneinrichtung erfüllen lediglich die Funktion, den Widerspruch zu illustrieren, der darin liegt, einer Skulptur des öffentlichen Raums in einem ‚privaten' Wohnraum zu begegnen."

Ceux qui connaissent Manhattan auront sûrement remarqué la statue de Christophe Colomb qui s'élève sur une colonne de 23 m de haut à Columbus Circle. Tatzu Nishi, fidèle à d'autres installations impliquant une approche similaire aux espaces habituellement inaccessibles, a construit un environnement domestique autour de la sculpture. « Je construis un salon tout autour, comme pour envelopper cette statue qui a surveillé New York à l'arrivée des immigrants pendant des années, et il sera ouvert au public. Cet objet, que les passants ne pouvaient voir que du trottoir, occupera maintenant cette pièce comme une sculpture familière, mettant les spectateurs au même niveau qu'elle pour la première fois depuis plus de cent ans que la place existe. » Les visiteurs étaient conviés à grimper les escaliers attachés à l'échafaudage, puis à traverser un long couloir étroit pour entrer dans le « salon ». Selon l'artiste, « le design intérieur est semblable aux appartements du voisinage à l'exception de la présence d'une énorme sculpture et du papier peint créé d'après mes dessins, qui s'inspirent de l'histoire et de la culture de l'Amérique. Le design du bâtiment et de l'intérieur ont pour fonction minimale d'exposer au grand jour le concept antinomique d'une sculpture publique occupant un espace intérieur "privé" ».

The artist has perched an intention-
ally very ordinary domestic space
on the top of the column where this
sculpture of Columbus is placed.
Scale, function, and location are all
questioned in an original way.

Der Künstler versetzt ganz bewusst
einen konventionellen Wohnraum an
die Spitze einer Säule, auf der die
Kolumbusstatue steht. So hinterfragt
er ironisch Maßstab, Funktion und
Standort zugleich.

L'artiste a perché un espace domes-
tique délibérément très banal au
sommet de la colonne où est placée
cette statue de Christophe Colomb.
Il questionne ainsi échelle, fonction
et emplacement de façon originale.

RYUE NISHIZAWA

RYUE NISHIZAWA was born in Tokyo in 1966. He graduated from Yokohama National University with an M.Arch. in 1990, and joined the office of Kazuyo Sejima & Associates in Tokyo the same year. In 1995, he established SANAA with Kazuyo Sejima, and two years later his own practice, the Office of Ryue Nishizawa. He has worked on all the significant projects of SANAA and has been a Visiting Professor at Yokohama National University (2001–), the University of Singapore (2003), Princeton (2006), and the Harvard GSD (2007). His work outside SANAA includes a Weekend House (Gunma, 1998); the N Museum (Kagawa, 2005); Moriyama House (Tokyo, 2006); House A (East Japan, 2006); Towada Art Center (Aomori, 2006–08); the Teshima Museum (Teshima, Kagawa, 2009–10); a garden and house (Tokyo, 2010–11); the Hiroshi Senju Museum (Karuizawa, Nagano, 2011); and Fukita Pavilion in Shodoshima (Shodoshima, Kagawa, 2013, published here), all in Japan.

RYUE NISHIZAWA wurde 1966 in Tokio geboren und schloss sein Studium 1990 mit einem M. Arch. an der Nationaluniversität in Yokohama ab. Noch im selben Jahr schloss er sich dem Büro von Kazuyo Sejima & Associates in Tokio an. Gemeinsam mit Kazuyo Sejima gründete er 1995 SANAA, zwei Jahre später sein eigenes Büro Ryue Nishizawa. Er war an sämtlichen Schlüsselprojekten von SANAA beteiligt und hatte Gastprofessuren an der Nationaluniversität Yokohama (seit 2001), der Universität von Singapur (2003), in Princeton (2006) sowie an der Harvard GSD (2007). Zu seinen Projekten unabhängig von SANAA zählen ein Wochenendhaus (Gunma, 1998), das N Museum (Kagawa, 2005), das Haus Moriyama (Tokio, 2006), das Haus A (Ostjapan, 2006), das Towada Art Center (Aomori, 2006–08), das Kunstmuseum auf Teshima (Teshima, Kagawa, 2009–10), Garten und Haus (Tokio, 2010–11), das Hiroshi Senju Museum (Karuizawa, Nagano, 2011) und den Fukita Pavilion in Shodoshima (Shodoshima, Kagawa, 2013, hier vorgestellt), alle in Japan.

RYUE NISHIZAWA, né à Tokyo en 1966, a obtenu son M.Arch. à l'Université nationale de Yokohama (1990). Il a commencé à travailler dans l'agence de Kazuyo Sejima & Associates à Tokyo la même année, avant qu'ils ne fondent ensemble SANAA en 1995 et sa propre agence Office of Ryue Nishizawa deux ans plus tard. Il a été professeur invité à l'Université nationale de Yokohama (2001–), aux universités de Singapour (2003), Princeton (2006) et la Harvard GSD (2007). Il est intervenu sur tous les grands projets de SANAA. Son œuvre personnel comprend une maison de week-end (Gunma, 1998) ; le musée N (Kagawa, 2005) ; la maison Moriyama (Tokyo, 2006) ; la maison A (Japon oriental, 2006) ; le Centre d'art Towada (Aomori, 2006–08) ; le Musée d'art de Teshima (île de Teshima, Kagawa, 2009–10) ; un jardin et maison (Tokyo, 2010–11) ; le musée Hiroshi Senju (Karuizawa, Nagano, 2011) et le Fukita Pavilion de Shodoshima (Shodoshima, Kagawa, 2013, publié ici), le tout au Japon.

FUKITA PAVILION

Shodoshima, Kagawa, Japan, 2013

Area: 185 m². Client: Shodoshima Town Office.
Collaboration: Mitsuhiro Kanada (Structural Engineer, Arup Japan).

This unusual structure is a pavilion for a restaurant located on the premises of a shrine, next to the gymnasium of the Fukuda Elementary School in Shodoshima, an island in the Seto Inland Sea of Japan. It is comprised of two overlapping, curved sheets of steel, the corners of which are welded together, while the steel plate that forms the floor is prevented from flattening by the plate that serves as the roof. In turn, the roof plate is supported by the steel floor as it slightly "slouches" in the center. The space thus created between the two sheets of metal provides seating for visitors, and also serves as a playground for children in the area leading to the temple. Despite its rather ephemeral appearance, this is a permanent structure, although without any foundations. "It is a simple arrangement, as if the pavilion had just been brought along and placed there," the architects say.

Dieses ungewöhnliche Bauwerk ist ein Restaurant-Pavillon auf dem Gelände eines Schreins neben der Sporthalle der Fukuda Elementary School auf Shodoshima, einer Insel in der japanischen Seto-Inlandsee. Es besteht aus zwei sich über-schneidenden, gekrümmten Stahlplatten, die an den Ecken zusammengeschweißt sind, während die den Boden bildende Stahlplatte durch die das Dach darstellende Platte am Ausbeulen gehindert wird. Diese Dachplatte wiederum wird vom Stahlboden getragen, der in der Mitte leicht „durchhängt". Der so durch die beiden Metallplatten entstandene Raum bietet Sitzplätze für Besucher und dient auch zum Spielen für Kinder im Vorbereich zum Tempel. Trotz seines eher vergänglichen Erscheinungbilds ist dies ein dauerhaftes Bauwerk, wenn auch ohne Fundament. „Es ist eine schlichte Anordnung, als wäre der Pavillon gerade erst angeliefert und dort hingestellt", sagen die Architekten.

Cette structure originale est un pavillon construit pour un restaurant à côté d'un sanctuaire, près du gymnase de l'école élémentaire Fukuda de Shodoshima, une île de la Mer intérieure du Japon. Il se compose de deux feuilles d'acier recourbées qui se chevauchent, soudées aux angles, celle qui sert de toit empêche celle du bas de s'aplatir, tandis que cette dernière la soutient au centre là où elle « s'affale » légèrement. L'espace créé entre les deux plaques de métal permet aux visiteurs de s'asseoir et tient lieu de terrain de jeux pour les enfants sur le chemin vers le temple. Malgré son apparence éphémère, il s'agit d'une structure destinée à durer, sans la moindre fondation. Pour les architectes, « c'est une composition simple, comme si le pavillon avait simplement été apporté et disposé ici ».

Though it looks like it might be made of cloth, the pavilion is formed with steel sheets that seem to hang from the trees, almost without other visible means of support. The usual elements of architecture have been replaced by two curving plates of metal.

Obgleich der Pavillon wie aus Stoff gemacht aussieht, ist er aus Stahlplatten geformt, die scheinbar von den Bäumen hängen, fast ohne irgendwelche sichtbaren tragenden Teile. Die üblichen Architektur-elemente wurden durch zwei gekrümmte Metallplatten ersetzt.

Bien qu'il ait l'air l'air en toile, le pavillon est fait de feuilles d'acier qui semblent pendre des arbres, sans presque aucun autre soutien visible. Les éléments architecturaux habituels ont été remplacés par deux plaques de métal courbes.

OBRA ARCHITECTS

PABLO CASTRO was born in San Juan, Argentina, attended the Universidad Nacional de San Juan, Argentina (1987), and received his M.S. in Advanced Architectural Design from the Columbia University Graduate School of Architecture in 1989. He worked in the office of Richard Meier in New York (1989–92) and with Steven Holl (1995–2000), before cofounding OBRA Architects with Jennifer Lee in 2000. **JENNIFER LEE** attended Harvard College (1990) and received her B.Arch. degree from the Cooper Union School of Architecture (New York, 1997). Their work includes Red+Housing, National Art Museum of China (Beijing, China, 2009, published here); and the Internationale Bauausstellung Smart Price Houses Competition (Hamburg, Germany, 2010). More recent work includes the Inside Out Museum (Beijing, China, 2012) and the Casa Osa (Cerro Osa, Osa Peninsula, Costa Rica, 2013).

PABLO CASTRO wurde in San Juan, Argentinien, geboren, besuchte die Universidad Nacional de San Juan, Argentinien (1987) und absolvierte seinen M.S. in Advanced Architectural Design (Aufbaustudiengang Entwerfen) an der Architektur-fakultät der Columbia University (1989). Er arbeitete im Büro von Richard Meier in New York (1989–92) und für Steven Holl (1995–2000), ehe er 2000 gemeinsam mit **JENNIFER LEE** das Büro OBRA Architects gründete. Jennifer Lee studierte am Harvard College (1990) und absolvierte ihren B. Arch. an der Architekturfakultät der Cooper Union (New York, 1997). Zu ihren Projekten zählen Red+Housing, Chinesisches Nationalmuseum für Kunst (Peking, China, 2009, hier vorgestellt) und der Wett-bewerbsbeitrag Internationale Bauausstellung Hamburg/Smart Price Houses (2010). Neuere Projekte sind u. a. das Inside Out Museum (Peking, China, 2012) und die Casa Osa (Cerro Osa, Halbinsel Osa, Costa Rica, 2013).

PABLO CASTRO, né à San Juan, Argentine, a étudié à l'Universidad Nacional de San Juan (Argentine, 1987). Il a obtenu son M.S. en conception architecturale avancée à l'École d'architecture de l'université Columbia (1989). Il a travaillé dans les agences de Richard Meier à New York (1989–92) et de Steven Holl (1995–2000), avant de fonder OBRA Architects avec Jennifer Lee en 2000. **JENNIFER LEE** a étudié au Harvard College (1990) et passé son diplôme de B. Arch à l'École d'architecture de la Cooper Union (New York, 1997). À leur actif figurent un projet de logement d'urgence Red+Housing pour le Musée national d'art de Chine (Pékin, Chine, 2009, publié ici) et leur participation au concours des maisons à prix réduit de l'Internationale Bauausstellung (Hambourg, Allemagne, 2010). Parmi les autres réalisations récentes figurent l'Inside Out Museum (Pékin, Chine, 2012) et la Casa Osa (Cerro Osa, péninsule d'Osa, Costa Rica, 2013).

RED+HOUSING: ARCHITECTURE ON THE EDGE OF SURVIVAL

Beijing, China, 2009

Area: 45 m². Client: National Art Museum of China. Cost: estimated future production cost $5000.
Collaboration: Shin Kook Kang (Project Architect).

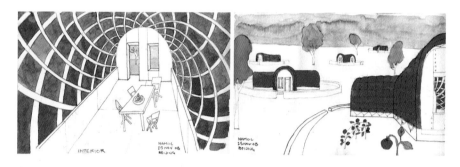

This project involved an emergency housing prototype commissioned as part of the exhibit *Crossing* which occurred one year after the Sichuan earthquake. "Emergency housing from the point of view of design," declare the architects, "is only an extreme form of architecture." The structure is intended to be economical, transportable, easy to assemble, made with renewable materials, and digitally prefabricated. The prototype shown in China was made of red parachute cloth and plywood. The architects further said: "We feel architecture can contribute not only to the physical but also emotional and psychological well-being of disaster victims." OBRA also created plywood furniture for the project.

Bei diesem Projekt ging es um den Entwurf eines Prototyps für Notunterkünfte im Rahmen der Ausstellung „Crossing", die ein Jahr nach dem Erdbeben von Sichuan stattfand. „Notunterkünfte sind aus gestalterischer Sicht nichts weiter als eine extreme Form von Architektur", so die Architekten. Vorgesehen ist, die Konstruktion ökonomisch, transportabel und leicht montierbar zu halten und mit digitalen Methoden aus erneuerbaren Materialien vorzufertigen. Der in China vorgestellte Prototyp bestand aus roter Fallschirmseide und Sperrholz. Die Architekten führen weiter aus: „Wir glauben, dass Architektur nicht nur physisch, sondern auch emotional und psychologisch zum Wohlbefinden von Katastrophenopfern beitragen kann." OBRA entwarf darüber hinaus Möbel aus Sperrholz für das Projekt.

Ce projet portait sur un prototype de logement d'urgence proposé dans le cadre de l'exposition « Crossing », organisée un an après le tremblement de terre du Sichuan. « Du point de vue de la conception, expliquent les architectes, le logement d'urgence n'est qu'une forme extrême d'architecture. » La structure est économique, transportable, facile à assembler, faite de matériaux renouvelables, et est préfabriquée à l'aide de machines à commandes numériques. Le prototype exposé en Chine a été réalisé en toile de parachute rouge et en contreplaqué. « Nous pensons que l'architecture peut contribuer au bien-être non seulement physique, mais également émotionnel et psychologique des victimes d'une catastrophe », ont déclaré les architectes. OBRA a également créé des meubles en contreplaqué pour ce projet.

Drawings and photos with the red parachute cloth giving a warm impression of the interiors of this emergency relief housing.

Zeichnungen und Fotos der mit roter Ballonseide bespannten Notunterkünfte vermitteln etwas von der Wärme des Innenraums.

Dessins et photos sur la mise en place de la toile de parachute rouge qui crée une atmosphère chaleureuse dans ces logements d'urgence.

A series of photos showing the assembly of the Red+Housing installation at the National Art Museum.

Eine Bildsequenz illustriert den Montageprozess der Red+Housing Notunterkünfte am National Art Museum.

Photos de l'installation de Red+Housing au Musée national d'art.

A view of the installation in Beijing, and a series of drawings showing the assembly of the structures.

Ansicht der Installation in Peking und verschiedene Montage-zeichnungen.

Vue de l'installation à Pékin, et dessins détaillant le principe de construction des logements.

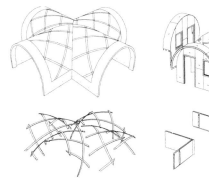

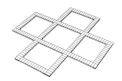

OFFICE OF MOBILE DESIGN

Born in 1965 in New York, **JENNIFER SIEGAL** obtained her M.Arch. degree from the SCI-Arc in 1994. She was an apprentice and resident at Arcosanti (Codes Junction, Arizona, 1987) and then worked in the offices of Skidmore, Owings & Merrill in San Francisco (1988), Mark Mack (1992), and Hodgetts + Fung (1994–95). She has been the Principal of the Office of Mobile Design in Venice, California, since 1998. The work of OMD includes Swellhouse, a mass-customized/prefabricated eco-friendly house (Los Angeles, California, 2003); Portable House, a prefabricated eco-friendly mobile house (San Diego, California, 2003); and Seatrain Residence, a custom residence composed of two pairs of stacked ISO shipping containers sheltered under a 15-meter steel-and-glass roof membrane (Los Angeles, California, 2003). More recent work includes the Country School: Middle School (North Hollywood, California, 2008); Taliesin Mod.Fab (Scottsdale, Arizona, 2009, published here); the OMD Prefab Show House (Joshua Tree, California, 2006/2010, also published here); and the Big Sur Prefab Residence (Big Sur, California, 2010), all in the USA.

JENNIFER SIEGAL wurde 1965 in New York geboren und absolvierte ihren M. Arch. 1994 am SCI-Arc. Sie war Auszubildende und Stipendiatin in Arcosanti (Codes Junction, Arizona, 1987). Davor hatte sie für Skidmore, Owings & Merrill in San Francisco (1988), Mark Mack (1992) und Hodgetts + Fung (1994–95) gearbeitet. Seit 1998 leitet sie das Office of Mobile Design in Venice, Kalifornien. Zu den Projekten von OMD zählen Swellhouse, ein umweltfreundliches, massengefertigtes, nach Kundenwunsch modifiziertes Fertighaus (Los Angeles, Kalifornien, 2003), Portable House, ein umweltfreundliches mobiles Fertighaus (San Diego, Kalifornien, 2003) sowie die Seatrain Residence, ein nach Kundenwunsch gefertigtes Haus aus zwei übereinandergestapelten ISO-Containern unter einem 15 m großen Schutzdach aus Glas und Stahl (Los Angeles, Kalifornien, 2003). Jüngere Projekte sind die Country School: Middle School (North Hollywood, Kalifornien, 2008), Taliesin Mod.Fab (Scottsdale, Arizona, 2009, hier vorgestellt), OMD Fertigbau-Musterhaus (Joshua Tree, Kalifornien, 2006/2010, ebenfalls hier vorgestellt) sowie das Big Sur Fertighaus (Big Sur, Kalifornien, 2010), alle in den USA.

Née en 1965 à New York, **JENNIFER SIEGAL** a obtenu son M. Arch au SCI-Arc (1994). Elle a été apprentie et résidente à Arcosanti (Codes Junction, Arizona, 1987) et a travaillé dans les agences Skidmore, Owings & Merrill à San Francisco (1988), Mark Mack (1992) et Hodgetts + Fung (1994–95). Elle dirige l'Office of Mobile Design à Venice, en Californie, depuis 1998. Les références d'OMD comprennent : la Swellhouse, une maison écologique personnalisée/préfabriquée (Los Angeles, 2003) ; la Portable House, maison écologique mobile préfabriquée (San Diego, 2003), et la Seatrain Residence, une résidence composée de deux paires de conteneurs ISO empilés abrités sous une toiture d'acier et de verre de 15 m de haut (Los Angeles, 2003). Plus récemment, elle a réalisé une école (Hollywood Nord, Californie, 2008) ; la maison modèle préfabriquée Taliesin Mod.Fab House (Scottsdale, Arizona, 2009, publiée ici) ; la maison d'exposition préfabriquée OMD Prefab Show House (Joshua Tree, Californie, 2006/2010, publiée ici) et la Big Sur Prefab Residence (Big Sur, Californie, 2010).

OMD PREFAB SHOW HOUSE

Joshua Tree, California, USA, 2006/2010

Area: 70 m². Client: Chris Hanley.
Cost: $150 000.

This prototype house was originally located on Abbot Kinney Boulevard and was used to display the work of OMD. It is now placed in 32 hectares of wilderness land. The steel-frame structure measures 3.5 x 18 meters and has a 3.8-meter ceiling height inside. The design makes use of radiant heat ceiling panels and tankless water heaters, but also includes a central, luxurious Boffi kitchen. The architect states: "Whether briefly situated in an urban lot, momentarily located in the open landscape, or positioned for a more lengthy stay, the Joshua Tree Prefab accommodates a wide range of needs and functions."

Dieser Hausprototyp stand ursprünglich am Abbot Kinney Boulevard und wurde von OMD zur Präsentation ihrer Projekte genutzt. Inzwischen steht es auf einem 32 ha großen Wüstengrundstück. Die Stahlrahmenkonstruktion misst 3,5 x 18 m und hat innen eine Deckenhöhe von 3,8 m. Ausgestattet ist der Bau mit einer Deckenheizung und Durchlauferhitzern, jedoch auch mit einer luxuriösen Boffi-Küche. Die Architektin erklärt: „Ob kurzfristig auf einem Stadtgrundstück, vorübergehend in der offenen Landschaft oder auch an einem langfristigeren Standort, das Joshua Tree Prefab wird einer großen Bandbreite von Anforderungen und Funktionen gerecht."

Cette maison prototype a été dressée au départ sur Abbot Kinney Boulevard où elle servait à présenter le travail de l'agence. Elle est aujourd'hui installée dans un petit domaine naturel de 32 ha. La construction en acier de 3,5 m de large par 18 m de long bénéficie d'un plafond de 3,8 m de haut. Elle fait appel à des panneaux de chauffage radiant pour son plafond et des radiateurs à eau, mais comprend également une luxueuse cuisine Boffi. « Qu'elle soit brièvement installée sur une parcelle urbaine, momentanément installée dans un paysage dégagé en attendant une implantation plus durable, la Maison préfabriquée de Joshua Tree répond à un grand nombre de besoins et de fonctions », a précisé l'architecte.

With a form that recalls that of ship-ping containers, the OMD Prefab Show House sits, above, in its loca-tion in Joshua Tree, California.

Von außen erinnert das OMD Prefab Show House an Seefrachtcontainer. Oben eine Ansicht des Baus vor Ort in Joshua Tree, Kalifornien.

La maison d'exposition préfabriquée OMD sur site, à Joshua Tree en Californie. Sa forme rappelle celle de conteneurs de transport.

Above, the house being transported on a flatbed truck. Below, it is seen installed in its wilderness site.

Oben der Transport des Hauses auf einem Tieflader. Unten nach dem Aufbau auf dem Wüstengrundstück.

Ci-dessus la maison transportée par camion. Ci-dessous son installation dans le désert.

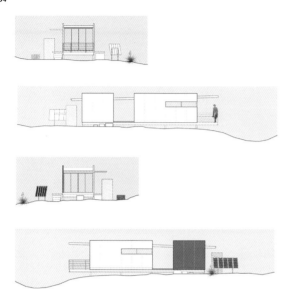

Elevation drawings and an image of
the house in a more urban setting,
where its long, thin design makes
it fit readily into a small lot.

Aufrisse und eine Ansicht des
Hauses in wesentlich urbanerem
Kontext. Hier fügt sich die lange,
schmale Gebäudeform problemlos
in ein kleines Baugrundstück.

Ces élévations et la photo
ci-dessous situent la maison dans
son cadre urbain. Le plan en longueur est adapté à la petite taille
de la parcelle.

A floor plan and interior views show the modern, generous spaces, with minimal walls reserved only for the enclosed toilet and kitchen areas.

Grundriss und Innenansichten der modernen großzügigen Räume. Die wenigen Innenwände umschließen lediglich Bad und Küchenbereich.

Le plan au sol et les vues de l'intérieur illustrent l'ampleur des volumes intérieurs, les seuls murs sont réservés à la séparation des sanitaires et de la cuisine.

TALIESIN MOD.FAB

Frank Lloyd Wright School of Architecture,
Taliesin West, Scottsdale, Arizona, USA, 2009

Area: 56 m². Client: Frank Lloyd Wright School of Architecture.
Collaboration: Michael P. Johnson, Design/Build students at Taliesin.

Jennifer Siegal points out that Frank Lloyd Wright created a scheme to build prefabricated houses early in the 20th century (American System of Housing). The Taliesin Mod.Fab is a prototype for "simple, elegant, and sustainable living in the desert." The one-bedroom steel-frame residence can be transported on normal roads and makes use of passive and active (solar panels) energy saving measures. The project is a result of a design/build studio class on prefabricated construction co-taught by Jennifer Siegal and Michael Johnson. The prototype was built almost entirely by students with low-tech hand and power tools. The building sits cantilevered over a desert wash and is used as a guesthouse for visiting scholars.

Jennifer Siegal weist darauf hin, dass Frank Lloyd Wright bereits Anfang des 20. Jahrhunderts ein Fertighaussystem entwickelt hat (American System of Housing). Das Taliesin Mod.Fab ist der Prototyp für „einfaches, elegantes und nachhaltiges Wohnen in der Wüste". Die 2-Zimmer-Stahlrahmenkonstruktion kann auf regulären Straßen transportiert werden und nutzt sowohl passive als auch durch Solarzellen aktive Energiesparstrategien. Das Projekt entstand im Rahmen einer Studioklasse für Entwerfen und Bauen zum Thema Fertigbau unter Leitung von Jennifer Siegal und Michael Johnson. Der Prototyp wurde fast ausschließlich von Studierenden mit einfachen Hand- und Elektrowerkzeugen gebaut. Das Haus kragt über einen erosionsbedingten Wüstenabhang aus und wird als Gästehaus für Wissenschaftler genutzt.

Jennifer Siegal fait remarquer que Frank Lloyd Wright avait eu un projet de construction de maisons préfabriquées dès le début du XXᵉ siècle («American System of Housing»). Le Taliesin Mod.Fab est le prototype d'une « maison simple, élégante et durable pour vivre dans le désert». Cette petite résidence de deux pièces à ossature en acier, transportable sur routes normales, fait appel à des dispositifs actifs et passifs d'économie d'énergie. Le projet est aussi l'aboutissement d'un programme d'enseignement en atelier sur la construction préfabriquée, donné par Jennifer Siegal et Michael Johnson. Ce prototype a été presque entièrement construit par des étudiants à l'aide d'un outillage classique. En porte-à-faux au-dessus d'un ravin dans le désert, il sert de maison d'hôtes pour des chercheurs invités.

Intended for desert living, the Taliesin Mod.Fab house harkens back in its references to schemes by Frank Lloyd Wright, but does not retain the older architect's organic approach to design.

Das Taliesin-Mod.Fab-Haus wurde für das Wüstenklima konzipiert und nimmt Bezug auf Wohnbauprojekte Frank Lloyd Wrights. Allerdings setzt es die organische Architekturauffassung des älteren Architekten nicht fort.

Conçue pour le désert, cette maison modèle préfabriquée Taliesin va chercher des références du côté de Frank Lloyd Wright, mais sans retenir l'approche organique du grand architecte.

OLSON KUNDIG

TOM KUNDIG received his B.A. in Environmental Design (1977) and his M.Arch. (1981) degrees from the University of Washington. He was a Principal of Jochman/Kundig (1983–84), before becoming a Principal of Olson Kundig Architects (since 1986). Tom Kundig is the recipient of the 2008 National Design Award in Architecture Design, awarded by the Smithsonian's Cooper-Hewitt National Design Museum. As Olson Sundberg Kundig Allen Architects the firm received the 2009 National AIA Architecture Firm Award. **JIM OLSON** is the founding partner and owner of Olson Kundig. The firm's work includes the Olson Cabin (Longbranch, Washington, 1959/2003, published here); Outpost Residence (Bellevue, Idaho, 2008); Montecito Residence (Montecito, California, 2008); Gulf Islands Cabin (Gulf Islands, British Columbia, Canada, 2008, also published here); and Hong Kong Villa (lead architect Jim Olson, Shek-O, China, 2008); The Pierre (San Juan Islands, Washington, 2008–10); Art Stable (Seattle, Washington, 2010); Studio Sitges (Sitges, Spain, 2010); Sol Duc Cabin (Olympic Peninsula, Washington, 2010–11, also published here); Charles Smith Wines Tasting Room and Headquarters (Walla Walla, Washington, 2011); and the Bill and Melinda Gates Foundation Visitor Center (Seattle, Washington, 2012), all in the USA unless stated otherwise.

TOM KUNDIG machte seinen B. A. in Umweltgestaltung (1977) und seinen M. Arch. (1981) an der Universität Washington. Er war Mitinhaber von Jochman/Kundig (1983–84), bevor er Mitinhaber von Olson Kundig Architects wurde (seit 1986). Tom Kundig erhielt 2008 den National Design Award in Architecture Design, verliehen vom Smithsonian's Cooper-Hewitt National Design Museum. Als Olson Sundberg Kundig Allen Architects bekam das Büro 2009 den National AIA Architecture Firm Award. **JIM OLSON** ist Gründungspartner und Mitinhaber von Olson Kundig. Zu den Arbeiten des Büros gehören die Olson Cabin (Longbranch, Washington, 1959/2003, hier vorgestellt), die Outpost Residence (Bellevue, Idaho, 2008), die Montecito Residence (Montecito, Kalifornien, 2008), die Gulf Island Cabin (Gulf Islands, British Columbia, Kanada, 2008, ebenfalls hier vorgestellt), die Hong Kong Villa (leitender Architekt: Jim Olson, Shek-O, China, 2008), The Pierre (San Juan Islands, Washington, 2008–10), der Art Stable (Seattle, 2010), das Studio Sitges (Sitges, Spanien, 2010), die Sol Duc Cabin (Olympic Peninsula, Washington, 2010–11, ebenfalls hier vorgestellt), Weinproberaum und Firmensitz von Charles Smith (Walla Walla, Washington, 2011) und das Besucherzentrum der Bill und Melinda Gates Foundation (Seattle, 2012), alle in den USA, wenn nicht anders angegeben.

TOM KUNDIG a obtenu son B.A. en conception environnementale (1977) et son M.Arch. (1981) à l'université de Washington. Il a été dirigeant de Jochman/Kundig (1983–84) avant de diriger Olson Kundig Architects depuis 1986. Il a reçu le prix national de conception architecturale 2008 du Smithsonian's Cooper-Hewitt National Design Museum. Sous la dénomination d'Olson Sundberg Kundig Allen Architects, l'agence a reçu en 2009 le prix national de l'agence d'architecture de l'année de l'AIA. **JIM OLSON** est associé et dirigeant d'Olson Kundig. Les réalisations de l'agence comprennent la cabane Olson (Longbranch, Washington, 1959/2003, publiée ici) ; la résidence Outpost (Bellevue, Idaho, 2008) ; la résidence Montecito (Montecito, Californie, 2008) ; la cabane des îles Gulf (îles Gulf, Colombie-Britannique, Canada, 2008, également publiée ici) ; la villa Hong-Kong (architecte principal Jim Olson, Shek-O, Chine, 2008) ; la maison The Pierre (îles San Juan, Washington, 2008–10) ; l'Art Stable (Seattle, 2010) ; le studio Sitges (Sitges, Espagne, 2010) ; la cabane Sol Duc (péninsule Olympique, Washington, 2010–11, également publiée ici) ; la salle de dégustation et le siège de Charles Smith Wines (Walla Walla, Washington, 2011) et le centre d'accueil de la fondation Bill and Melinda Gates (Seattle, 2012), toutes aux États-Unis sauf mention contraire.

SOL DUC CABIN

Olympic Peninsula, Washington, USA, 2010–11

Area: 36 m².
Collaboration: Edward Lalonde (Project Manager).

This steel-clad cabin is lifted up on four steel columns because of occasional flooding in the area, and can be entirely closed with sliding steel shutters. It was built with unfinished mild steel and structural insulated panels. The client wanted "a compact, low-maintenance, virtually indestructible building to house himself and his wife during fishing expeditions." Entry, dining, and kitchen areas are located on the lower floor, while a sleeping loft with minimal shelving is set above. The floor of the loft space was made with leftover lumber provided by the client. A cantilevered steel deck extends from the lower level, providing views of the river. The cabin also has a cantilevered roof designed to provide shading and protection from storms.

Diese stahlverkleidete Hütte steht wegen der gelegentlichen Überschwemmungen in der Gegend auf vier stählernen Pfeilern und kann mit verschiebbaren stählernen Platten vollständig verschlossen werden. Sie wurde aus unveredeltem Baustahl und Isolierbauplatten konstruiert. Der Kunde wollte „ein kompaktes, pflegeleichtes, geradezu unzerstörbares Gebäude für sich und seine Frau für ihre gemeinsamen Angelausflüge". Eingangsbereich, Ess- und Küchenbereich befinden sich im unteren Geschoss, darüber ein Schlafboden mit ein paar Regalen. Der Zwischenboden wurde aus Bauholzresten gefertigt, das der Bauherr selbst beisteuerte. Von einer auskragenden, stählernen Terrasse im unteren Geschoss aus kann man den Fluss sehen. Die Hütte hat zudem ein weit vorstehendes Dach, das Schatten und Schutz vor Unwettern bietet.

La cabane revêtue d'acier est perchée sur quatre colonnes d'acier pour échapper aux crues occasionnelles dans la région et peut être entièrement fermée par des volets coulissants en acier. Elle a été construite avec de l'acier doux sans finitions et des panneaux structurels isolants. Le client voulait « un bâtiment compact, nécessitant peu d'entretien et quasiment indestructible pour l'abriter lui et sa femme pendant leurs expéditions de pêche ». L'entrée, les espaces salle à manger et cuisine occupent l'étage inférieur, tandis que le haut sert de chambre à coucher, garni de rayonnages minimalistes. Le sol en a été réalisé avec du bois de charpente récupéré fourni par le client. Un ponton en acier fait saillie à partir du niveau inférieur et a vue sur la rivière. Le toit en encorbellement est conçu pour ombrager la cabane et la protéger des tempêtes.

Elevated to avoid flooding, this cabin seems like a nearly solid block of steel hanging above the site. A drawing (right) shows the shutter opening.

Diese Hütte, aufgeständert, um vor Hochwasser geschützt zu sein, wirkt wie ein nahezu massiver, über seinem Standort schwebender Stahlklotz. Die Zeichnung rechts zeigt, wie der Fensterladen geöffnet wird.

Surélevée pour éviter les inondations, cette cabane ressemble à un solide bloc d'acier suspendu au-dessus du site. Le schéma de droite montre le système d'ouverture du volet.

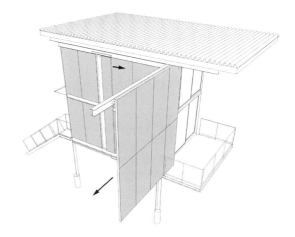

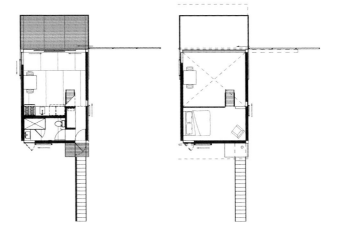

Double-height space gives way to a mezzanine above the kitchen (left page). Above, the main sliding shutter of the house seen in open and closed positions. Plans show the very basic simplicity of the design, made spectacular by its height and by the fact that it is fully lifted off the ground.

Der Raum mit doppelter Deckenhöhe bietet Platz für die Empore oberhalb der Küche (linke Seite). Oben der zentrale verschiebbare Fensterladen in offenem und geschlossenem Zustand. Die Pläne zeigen die Schlichtheit des Entwurfs, der durch seine Höhe und den Umstand, dass er vollständig aufgeständert ist, dennoch spektakulär wirkt.

Un espace double hauteur cède la place à une mezzanine au-dessus de la cuisine (page de gauche). Ci-dessus, le principal volet coulissant en position ouverte et fermée. Les schémas montrent la simplicité élémentaire du plan, que la hauteur et la position surélevée par rapport au sol rend remarquable.

GULF ISLANDS CABIN

Gulf Islands, British Columbia, Canada, 2008

Area: 18 m² + 14 m² (porches).

Located on a small island off the coast of Vancouver Island, this single-room cabin "is a no-maintenance retreat where the emphasis is on the experience of nature." According to the architect: "It's so small you have to go outside. That's the point!" The design consists in a retaining wall made of rammed earth built against an untreated mild steel-clad box with highly insulated glazing. The weathered steel is meant to blend in with the landscape. A wood stove is used to heat the interior that includes a bed, toilet, and kitchenette. The interiors are clad mainly in cedar from fallen trees that were on the property, and a demolished local bridge. A sliding steel panel slides in place to cover the glass façade and doubles as a shield for an open-air shower.

Diese Ein-Raum-Hütte, gelegen auf einer kleinen Insel vor der Küste von Vancouver Island, „ist eine pflegeleichte Zuflucht, bei der das Naturerlebnis ganz im Vordergrund steht". „Sie ist so klein, man muss einfach raus. Darum geht es!", so der Architekt. Der Entwurf besteht aus einer Rückwand aus gestampfter Erde vor einem mit unbehandeltem Baustahl verkleideten Kasten mit hocheffektiven Thermofenstern. Der verwitterte Stahl soll sich in die Landschaft einfügen. Ein Holzofen heizt den Innenbereich mit Bett, Toilette und Kochnische. Die Einbauten bestehen zum Großteil aus Zedernholz von auf dem Gelände umgefallenen Bäumen und einer abgerissenen Brücke in der Nähe. Die Glasfassade kann mit einer verschiebbaren Stahlplatte verschlossen werden, die der Außendusche gleichzeitig als Sichtschutz dient.

Située sur une petite île au large de celle de Vancouver, cette cabane à pièce unique « est une retraite ne nécessitant aucun entretien, centrée sur la vie dans la nature ». Selon l'architecte : « C'est tellement petit qu'il faut sortir. C'est tout l'intérêt ! » L'ensemble se compose d'un mur de soutènement en terre battue, érigé contre un cube revêtu d'acier doux non traité au vitrage extrêmement isolant. L'acier patinable est conçu pour se fondre dans le paysage. L'intérieur composé d'un lit, de toilettes et d'une kitchenette est chauffé par un poêle à bois. Les murs en sont majoritairement revêtus de cèdre récupéré sur des arbres tombés sur la propriété et un pont du voisinage démoli. Un panneau coulissant en acier peut être remis en place pour couvrir la façade vitrée et protéger des regards une douche extérieure.

Left, page a general view of the cabin in its site. Seen with its side door open, the cabin has a wood-burning stove. Below, an overall site plan shows the forested location of the structure.

Links eine Gesamtansicht der Hütte an ihrem Standort. Die Hütte verfügt über einen Holzofen, wie ein Blick durch die Seitentür zeigt. Unten zeigt ein Lageplan den Standort des Gebäudes im Wald.

Page de gauche, vue d'ensemble de la cabane dans son décor naturel. La porte latérale ouverte montre le poêle à bois de la cabane. Ci-dessous, plan d'ensemble du site présentant l'emplacement boisé de la construction.

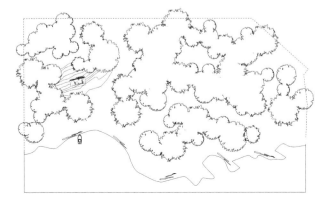

Solid in appearance, the cabin
provides for little or no frills. Even a
shower (above right) is located outside under the projecting roof. Left,
a section drawing of the cabin.

Die Hütte, schon vom Erscheinungsbild solide, verzichtet auf alles Überflüssige. Sogar die Dusche (oben
rechts) befindet sich draußen unter
dem schützenden Vordach. Links ein
Querschnitt der Hütte.

D'apparence robuste, la cabane
est extrêmement simple. Même la
douche (en haut à droite) est placée
à l'extérieur, sous l'avancée du toit.
À gauche, schéma en coupe
de la cabane.

A skillful mixture of stone, wood, and steel gives the house a rough but still warm feeling, evidenced in particular by the wooden interiors. Right, a floor plan of the structure.

Eine raffinierte Mischung aus Stein, Holz und Stahl verleiht dem Hause eine raue, aber trotzdem warme Anmutung, wofür vor allem die in Holz gehaltenen Innenräume verant- wortlich sind. Rechts ein Grundriss des Gebäudes.

Un mélange habile de pierre, bois et acier confère à la maison une impression rustique mais néanmoins chaleureuse, due essentiellement au bois de l'intérieur. À droite, plan de niveau de la structure.

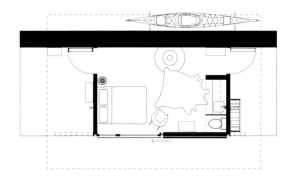

Wood is present as the main cladding material inside, with glazing that is nearly full height offering an open view of the natural setting.

Holz ist im Inneren als wichtigster Baustoff allgegenwärtig, während die beinahe deckenhohe Verglasung den Blick in die Natur freigibt.

Le bois est le principal matériau de revêtement à l'intérieur, tandis que le vitrage sur presque toute la hauteur offre une vue dégagée sur le décor naturel.

OLSON CABIN

Longbranch, Washington, USA, 1959/2003

Area: 111 m². Client: Jim Olson.
Collaboration: Ellen Cecil, Derek Santo.

The property on which the Olson Cabin was built has belonged to the architect's family for nearly a century. An earlier wood-frame cabin was designed while Olson was still working on his degree. As is the case with some other cabins by the firm, a manifest desire to "melt into the woods" is expressed in this design. In 2003, while doubling the area of the cabin, Olson sought to unify the original cabin and its later additions using galvanized steel columns and laminated wood beams. The living room has a full-height glazed opening that is intended to give the impression that there is no barrier between interior and exterior. Elements of the original cabin are visible as inner walls in the new structure, which employed only certified lumber.

Das Grundstück, auf dem die Olson Cabin errichtet wurde, gehört seit beinahe einem Jahrhundert der Familie des Architekten. Eine frühere Hütte in Holzrahmenbauweise entstand, als Olson noch an seinem Universitätsabschluss arbeitete. Wie bei einigen anderen Bauten der Firma kommt auch in diesem Entwurf der offenkundige Wunsch zum Ausdruck, das Bauwerk solle „mit dem Wald verschmelzen". 2003 verdoppelte Olson die Grundfläche der Hütte, indem er unter Verwendung verzinkter Stahlträger und Schichtholzbalken den Originalbau mit neueren Anbauten verband. Das Wohnzimmer verfügt über ein deckenhohes Panoramafenster, das den Eindruck vermitteln soll, es gebe keine Trennung zwischen innen und außen. Elemente der ursprünglichen Hütte sind als Wände im neuen Gebäude sichtbar, bei dem ausschließlich Holz aus nachhaltiger Forstwirtschaft verwendet wurde.

La propriété sur laquelle la cabane Olson a été construite appartient à la famille de l'architecte depuis près d'un siècle. Olson y avait déjà construit une cabane à charpente en bois alors qu'il préparait son diplôme de fin d'études. À l'instar d'autres cabanes de l'agence, la conception exprime un désir manifeste de « se fondre dans les bois ». En 2003, Olson a doublé la surface de la première cabane et cherché à unifier la construction d'origine et les ajouts ultérieurs au moyen de colonnes en acier galvanisé et de poutres en bois lamellé. Le salon ouvre par une baie vitrée sur toute sa hauteur pour donner l'impression que toute barrière a disparu entre intérieur et extérieur. Des éléments de la cabane d'origine restent visibles sous forme de parois intérieures dans le nouveau bâtiment, dont tout le bois de construction est certifié.

Set on a sloped site, as seen in the drawing to the left, the cabin is isolated in the forest. Images show the more modern (left page) and weathered (this page) aspects of the structure.

Die Hütte steht tief im Wald auf einem abschüssigen Gelände, wie auf der Zeichnung links zu erkennen ist. Die Bilder zeigen sowohl die moderne Anmutung des Gebäudes (linke Seite) als auch Spuren der Verwitterung (diese Seite).

Placée sur un terrain en pente, comme on le voit sur le schéma de gauche, la cabane est aussi isolée dans la forêt. Les photos montrent ses aspects plus modernes (page de gauche) et patinables (ci-dessous).

The drawing on this page suggests the incremental aspect of the construction and design. Though comfortable, the interior confirms the somewhat rustic aspect of the architecture.

Die Zeichnung auf dieser Seite verdeutlicht den Charakter von Bau und Entwurf. Trotz aller Behaglichkeit unterstreichen die Innenräume das Rustikale der Architektur nochmals.

Le schéma de cette page laisse apparaître le caractère progressif de la construction et du projet. Bien que confortable, l'intérieur confirme l'apparence quelque peu rustique de l'architecture.

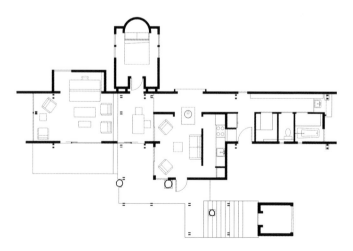

The alcove seen above is also
present on the plan on the left page.
Views of the forest and water are
generously provided for.

*Der Alkoven oben ist auf dem
Grundriss ebenfalls gut zu erkennen.
Er bietet großzügige Ausblicke auf
Wald und Wasser.*

*L'alcôve ci-dessus figure aussi
sur le plan page de gauche.
La cabane est généreusement
pourvue de vues sur la forêt et
l'eau.*

JOHN PAWSON

Born in Halifax in central England in 1949, **JOHN PAWSON** worked in his family's textile mill before going to Japan for four years. On his return, he studied at the Architectural Association (AA) in London and set up his own firm in 1981. He has worked on numerous types of buildings, including the flagship store for Calvin Klein in New York, airport lounges for Cathay Pacific airlines at the Chek Lap Kok Airport in Hong Kong, and a small apartment for the author Bruce Chatwin. Some of his recent work includes Lansdowne Lodge Apartments (London, UK, 2003); Hotel Puerta America in Madrid (Spain, 2005); the Tetsuka House (Tokyo, Japan, 2003–06); Calvin Klein Apartment (New York, USA, 2006); the Sackler Crossing in the Royal Botanic Gardens (Kew, London, UK, 2006); work and renovation of a wing of the Monastery of Our Lady of Nový Dvůr (Czech Republic, 2004; second phase 2009); the Martyrs Pavilion Saint Edward's School (Oxford, UK, 2009); and a number of apartments in New York (Schrager Penthouse, 50 Gramercy Park North, Hoppe Apartment, etc., 2009). In 2010 he realized the House of Stone (Milan, Italy, published here); and his work was the object of a solo exhibition, *John Pawson Plain Space* in the Design Museum (London, UK). Current work includes several houses in France, Greece, Portugal, Spain, the UK, and the USA.

JOHN PAWSON, 1949 in Halifax in England geboren, arbeitete in der Textilfabrik seiner Familie, ehe er für vier Jahre nach Japan ging. Nach seiner Rückkehr studierte er an der AA in London und eröffnete 1981 sein eigenes Büro. Er war mit zahlreichen Projekten befasst, darunter der Flagshipstore von Calvin Klein in New York, Flughafenlounges für Cathay Pacific am Flughafen Chek Lap Kok in Hongkong sowie ein kleines Apartment für den Schriftsteller Bruce Chatwin. Eine Auswahl jüngerer Projekte umfasst u. a. die Lansdowne Lodge Apartments (London, 2003), das Hotel Puerta America in Madrid (2005), das Haus Tetsuka (Tokio, 2003–06), ein Apartment für Calvin Klein (New York, 2006), die Sackler-Crossing-Brücke in Kew Gardens (Kew, London, 2006), Neubauten und Sanierung eines Gebäudeflügels am Kloster Nový Dvůr (Tschechische Republik, 2004, zweite Bauphase 2009), den Martyrs Pavilion für die Saint Edward's School (Oxford, 2009) sowie mehrere Apartments in New York (Schrager Penthouse, 50 Gramercy Park North, Hoppe Apartment u. a., 2009). 2010 realisierte er das Steinhaus (Mailand, 2010, hier vorgestellt). Im gleichen Jahr widmete ihm das Design Museum London die Einzelausstellung „John Pawson Plain Space". Zu seinen aktuellen Projekten zählen mehrere Privathäuser in Frankreich, Griechenland, Portugal, Spanien, Großbritannien und den USA.

Né à Halifax en Angleterre en 1949, **JOHN PAWSON**, travaille dans l'usine de textile familiale, avant de séjourner quatre ans au Japon. À son retour, il étudie à l'Architectural Association de Londres et crée son agence en 1981. Il est intervenu sur de nombreux types de projets, dont le magasin-phare de Calvin Klein à New York, les salons de la compagnie Cathay Pacific à l'aéroport de Chek Lap Kok à Hong Kong ou un petit appartement pour l'écrivain Bruce Chatwin. Parmi ses réalisations récentes : les Lansdowne Lodge Apartments (Londres, 2003) ; l'hôtel Puerta America à Madrid (2005) ; la maison Tetsuka (Tokyo, 2003–06) ; l'appartement de Calvin Klein (New York, 2006) ; le pont du Sackler Crossing dans les Jardins botaniques royaux (Kew, Londres, 2006) ; la rénovation d'une aile du monastère de Notre-Dame de Nový Dvůr (République tchèque, 2004, seconde phase en 2009) ; le pavillon des Martyrs de l'École Saint Edward (Oxford, 2009) et un certain nombre d'appartements à New York (penthouse Schrager ; 50 Gramercy Park North ; appartement Hoppe, etc., 2009). En 2010, il a réalisé la maison de pierre (Milan, publiée ici), et son œuvre a fait l'objet d'une exposition personnelle, « John Pawson Plain Space » au Design Museum de Londres. Il travaille actuellement sur plusieurs projets de maisons en France, en Grèce, au Portugal, en Espagne, au Royaume-Uni et aux États-Unis.

HOUSE OF STONE
Milan, Italy, 2010

Area: 43 m². Client: Interni Think Tank.
Collaboration: Alfredo Salvatori S.r.l. (Sponsoring Partner).

In the course of the 2010 Milan Furniture Fair, the Interni Think Tank sponsored an event where architects and designers were assigned a manufacturing partner and asked to create installations for sites within the Università degli Studi. John Pawson was paired with Alfredo Salvatori S.r.l., maker of Lithoverde, a 100% recycled stone material. It is made with 99% scrap and 1% natural resin. The House of Stone makes use of this material and takes into account the double-arcaded courtyard where it was set. The architect states: "In a defining gesture, the structure was sliced along its ridge and through its midsection, opening the interior to the changing play of sunlight and the vagaries of the weather. At night, internal sources of illumination transformed the cuts into blades of light." The House of Stone is to be permanently installed in the park of the *Milan Triennale.*

Im Zuge der Mailänder Möbelmesse 2010 initiierte der Interni Think Tank als Sponsor ein Event, bei dem Architekten und Designer je einem Hersteller zugeteilt wurden und den Auftrag erhielten, Installationen auf dem Gelände der Università degli Studi zu realisieren. John Pawson wurde Alfredo Salvatori S.r.l. zugeteilt, dem Hersteller von Lithoverde, einem zu 100 % recycelten Material. Es besteht zu 99 % aus Steinabfällen und zu 1 % aus natürlichem Harz. Das Steinhaus nutzt dieses Material und stellt zugleich einen Bezug zu dem Hof mit seinen Doppelarkaden her, in dem es steht. Der Architekt erklärt: „In einer bezeichnenden Geste wurde der Bau entlang des Firsts sowie quer aufgeschnitten, wodurch der Innenraum für das Spiel des Sonnenlichts und die Launen des Wetters geöffnet wird. Nachts werden die Einschnitte durch eine Lichtquelle im Inneren zu Klingen aus Licht." Das Steinhaus soll dauerhaft im Park der Mailänder Triennale stehen.

À l'occasion du Salon du meuble de Milan 2010, le Think Tank du magazine Interni a sponsorisé un événement où architectes et designers se sont vu attribuer un fabricant pour créer des installations temporaires à l'intérieur de l'Université degli Studi. John Pawson a été associé avec Alfredo Alvadori S.r.l., fabricant de Lithoverde, un matériau à base de pierre 100 % recyclable, composé de 99 % de déchets de pierre et de 1 % de résine naturelle. La Maison de pierre réalisée dans ce matériau a pris en compte son environnement, une cour à double arcade. «Dans un geste puissant, la structure a été tranchée selon l'axe de son faîte et en deux parties égales, permettant ainsi à l'intérieur de s'ouvrir au jeu de la lumière et des changements du temps. La nuit, des éclairages internes transforment ces découpes en lames de lumière», explique Pawson. La maison de pierre sera installée en permanence dans le parc de la Triennale de Milan.

Known precisely for his strict, minimalist vocabulary, John Pawson uses a traditional house shape, but renders it original with its long slit openings in the ceiling and walls.

John Pawson, bekannt für seine strenge, minimalistische Formensprache, greift auf eine traditionelle Hausform zurück, die er jedoch mit langen Schlitzen in Decke und Wänden ungewöhnlich interpretiert.

Connu pour son vocabulaire architectural d'un minimalisme strict, John Pawson utilise ici la forme traditionnelle d'une maison qu'il singularise en pratiquant de longues ouvertures dans les plafonds et les murs.

JIM POTEET

JIM POTEET was born in 1959 in Richmond, Virginia. He received his M.Arch. at the University of Texas at Austin (1987). From 1990 to 1992, he worked with Kieran Timberlake & Harris (Philadelphia), before creating his own firm in San Antonio in 1998. Recent work includes Capps Residence (2008); Linda Pace Foundation Offices (2008); the Container GuestHouse (2009–10, published here); Ricos Products Headquarters (2010); Hill Residence (2012); Causeway Advisory Group Offices (2012), Elmendorf Residence (2013) and the Condon Residence (2013), all in San Antonio, Texas.

JIM POTEET wurde 1959 in Richmond, Virginia, geboren. Er erwarb seinen M. Arch. an der University of Texas in Austin (1987). Von 1990 bis 1992 arbeitete er bei Kieran Timberlake & Harris (Philadelphia) und gründete 1998 sein eigenes Büro in San Antonio. Zu seinen neueren Werken zählen das Wohnhaus Capps (2008), das Bürohaus der Linda Pace Foundation (2008), das Container Guest House (2009–10, hier veröffentlicht), die Hauptverwaltung der Firma Ricos Products (2010), das Wohnhaus Hill (2012), das Bürohaus der Causeway Advisory Group (2012), das Wohnhaus Elmendorf (2013) und das Wohnhaus Condon (2013), alle in San Antonio, Texas.

JIM POTEET est né en 1959 à Richmond (Virginie). Il possède un M. Arch. de l'université du Texas à Austin (1987). De 1990 à 1992, il a travaillé avec Kieran Timberlake & Harris (Philadelphie), puis a créé son agence à San Antonio en 1998. Ses réalisations récentes comprennent : Capps Residence (2008) ; les bureaux de la Fondation Linda Pace (2008) ; la Container Guesthouse (2009–10, publiée ici) ; le siège de Ricos Products (2010) ; Hill Residence (2012) ; les bureaux du groupe de consulting Causeway (2012) ; Elmendorf Residence (2013) et Condon Residence (2013), toutes à San Antonio, Texas.

CONTAINER GUESTHOUSE

San Antonio, USA, 2009–10

Area: 30 m². Client: Stacey Hill.
Collaboration: Brett Freeman, Isadora Sintes, Shane Valentine.

The architect has made considerable efforts to investigate the "repurposing of existing structures for new uses." Comparing the Container GuestHouse to an "art project," Jim Poteet sought to "create the maximum effect with the minimum of architectural gesture." The client was interested in experimenting with shipping containers because she lives in a warehouse located in a former industrial site. The guesthouse has a shower and composting toilet, and a large glazed sliding door and end window. A garden on the roof is elevated to allow free airflow. The insulated interior is lined with bamboo plywood, while the rear of the container has mesh panels that are covered with evergreen vines for shading. Recycled telephone poles were used for the foundation, and exterior light fixtures were made with blades from a tractor disk plow.

Der Architekt hat sich eingehend mit der „Umnutzung bestehender Konstruktionen" auseinandergesetzt und vergleicht sein Container GuestHouse mit einem „Kunstprojekt". Jim Poteet war daran gelegen, „einen größtmöglichen Effekt durch eine minimale architektonische Geste" zu erzielen. Die Kundin wollte gern mit Schiffscontainern experimentieren, da sie ein Lagergebäude auf einem ehemaligen Industriegelände bewohnt. Das Gästehaus ist mit einer Dusche, einer Komposttoilette, einer großen Glasschiebetür und einem Fenster an der Endseite des Containers ausgestattet. Der Dachgarten wurde etwas angehoben, damit die Luft zirkulieren kann. Die isolierten Innenräume sind mit Bambussperrholz verschalt, an der Container-rückseite befinden sich Maschengitter, die mit schattenspendendem, immergrünem Wein bedeckt sind. Für das Fundament wurden Telefonmasten wiederverwendet. Die Außenleuchten sind aus den Scheiben eines Häufelpflugs gefertigt.

L'architecte s'est ici efforcé d'explorer « la nouvelle conception de structures existantes pour de nouveaux usages ». Comparant sa maison d'hôtes à un « projet artistique », Jim Poteet a cherché à « produire l'effet maximal avec une intervention architecturale minimale ». La cliente était intéressée par une expérimentation avec des conteneurs maritimes, car elle habite un hangar dans un ancien site industriel. La chambre d'hôtes possède une douche et des toilettes à compost, ainsi qu'une large porte vitrée coulissante et une fenêtre à son extrémité. Un jardin sur le toit est surélevé pour permettre à l'air de circuler librement. L'intérieur isolé est revêtu de contreplaqué de bambou, tandis que l'arrière du conteneur est garni de panneaux de treillis couverts de vigne à feuilles persistantes qui l'ombragent. Des poteaux de téléphone recyclés ont été utilisés pour les fondations, et les luminaires extérieurs sont faits avec les lames d'une charrue à disques de tracteur.

Though made with a shipping container, the dark blue house, with a garden on the roof, has all the attributes of a modern cabin: it's easy to transport, requires very little construction work, and is ready to go.

Das dunkelblaue Haus mit Dachgarten besteht aus einem Frachtcontainer, verfügt aber über alle Eigenschaften einer modernen Hütte. Es ist leicht zu transportieren, kann mit wenig Aufwand aufgebaut werden und ist schnell zur Nutzung bereit.

Bien que constituée d'un conteneur maritime, la maison peinte en bleu foncé avec un jardin sur le toit présente toutes les caractéristiques d'une cabane moderne, facile à transporter, ne nécessitant que très peu de travaux de construction et prête à l'emploi.

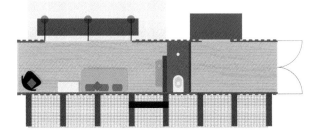

RAAAF/ATELIER DE LYON

RONALD RIETVELD was born in 1972, in Gorinchem, The Netherlands. He graduated from the Academy of Architecture in Amsterdam (2003) and won a Prix de Rome in 2006. After that he founded RAAAF (Rietveld Architecture-Art-Affordances) together with his brother **ERIK RIETVELD**, born in 1969, also in Gorinchem. The studio operates "at the crossroads of architecture, art, and science." RAAAF was elected Dutch Architect of the Year 2013 and has shown installations at international exhibitions at the Museum Boijmans Van Beuningen (Rotterdam), Centraal Museum (Utrecht), and was curator of the Dutch Pavilion at the *12th Architecture Biennale of Venice* in 2010 (Vacant NL). The project published here, Bunker 599 (Diefdijklinie, Zijderveld, The Netherlands, 2010), was carried out in collaboration with the Atelier de Lyon. The Atelier de Lyon was created by the artist **ERICK DE LYON**, whose work is based on his observations of the Dutch landscape.

RONALD RIETVELD wurde 1972 in Gorinchem, Niederlande, geboren. Er erwarb sein Diplom an der Academy of Architecture in Amsterdam (2003) und gewann 2006 einen Prix de Rome. Danach gründete er das Büro RAAAF (Rietveld Architecture-Art-Affordances), gemeinsam mit seinem Bruder **ERIC RIETVELD**, geboren 1969 ebenfalls in Gorinchem. Das Atelier arbeitet „am Schnittpunkt von Architektur, Kunst und Wissenschaft". RAAAF wurden 2013 zu den holländischen „Architekten des Jahres" ernannt; sie haben Installationen auf internationalen Ausstellungen im Museum Boijmans Van Beuningen (Rotterdam) und im Centraal Museum (Utrecht) gezeigt und waren 2010 die Kuratoren des Holländischen Pavillons auf der 12. Architekturbiennale in Venedig (Vacant NL). Das hier veröffentlichte Projekt, Bunker 599 (Diefdijklinie, Niederlande, 2010), wurde in Zusammenarbeit mit dem Atelier de Lyon ausgeführt. Dieses wurde vom Künstler **ERICK DE LYON** gegründet, dessen Arbeiten auf seinen Betrachtungen der holländischen Landschaft beruhen.

RONALD RIETVELD est né en 1972 à Gorinchem, aux Pays-Bas. Il est diplômé de l'Académie d'architecture d'Amsterdam (2003) et a gagné un prix de Rome en 2006. Il a ensuite fondé RAAAF (Rietveld Architecture-Art-Affordances) avec son frère **ERIK RIETVELD**, né en 1969 à Gorinchem. L'agence travaille « au croisement de l'architecture, de l'art et de la science ». RAAAF a été élu architecte néerlandais de l'année en 2013 et a présenté des installations dans des expositions internationales au musée Boijmans Van Beuningen (Rotterdam) et au Centraal Museum (Utrecht), il était conservateur du pavillon néerlandais à la XIIe Biennale d'architecture de Venise en 2010 (Vacant NL). Le projet publié ici, Bunker 599 (Diefdijklinie, Pays-Bas, 2010) a été réalisé en collaboration avec l'Atelier de Lyon. L'Atelier de Lyon a été créé par l'artiste **ERICK DE LYON** dont l'œuvre repose sur ses observations du paysage des Pays-Bas.

BUNKER 599

Zijderveld, The Netherlands

Area 30 m².
Client: DLG (Dutch Service for Land and Water Management).

Bunker 599 forms part of the New Dutch Waterline (NDW), a military line of defense in use from 1815 until 1940, which protected the cities of Muiden, Utrecht, Vreeswijk, and Gorinchem by means of intentional flooding. The designers explain: "A seemingly indestructible bunker with monumental status is sliced open. The design thereby opens up the minuscule interior of one of NDW's 700 bunkers, the insides of which are normally cut off from view completely. In addition, a long wooden boardwalk cuts through the extremely heavy construction leading visitors to a flooded area and to the footpaths of the adjacent natural reserve." Also visible from the main A2 highway, Bunker 599 aims to make an unexpected part of Dutch history accessible and tangible for visitors.

Bunker 599 bildet einen Teil der New Dutch Waterline (NDW), einer militärischen Verteidigungslinie, die von 1815 bis 1940 betrieben wurde und die Städte Muiden, Utrecht, Vreeswijk und Gorinchem durch beabsichtigte Flutung schützen sollte. Die Planer erklären: „Ein scheinbar unzerstörbarer Bunker mit monumentaler Wirkung ist aufgeschlitzt. Dadurch wird das klitzekleine Innere eines der 700 NDW-Bunker sichtbar, deren Innenräume normalerweise total unsichtbar bleiben. Außerdem durchschneidet ein langer Bohlenweg das äußerst schwere Bauwerk und führt die Besucher zu einem überfluteten Bereich und zu den Fußwegen im anschließenden Naturschutzgebiet." Der Bunker 599 ist auch von der Autobahn A2 aus sichtbar und soll den Besuchern ein unvermutetes Stück holländischer Geschichte zugänglich und erlebbar machen.

Bunker 599 fait partie de la Nouvelle ligne d'eau de Hollande (NDW), une ligne de défense militaire qui a servi de 1815 à 1940 et protégeait les villes de Muiden, Utrecht, Vreeswijk et Gorinchem en menaçant de les inonder intentionnellement. Les designers décrivent leur projet comme suit : « Un bunker en apparence indestructible, véritable monument, est ouvert par une tranchée. La conception dévoile l'intérieur exigu de l'un des 700 bunkers de la NDW, normalement fermé aux regards. Une longue promenade en bois traverse aussi la construction d'une lourdeur extrême et mène les visiteurs à une zone inondée et aux sentiers de la réserve naturelle voisine. » Visible de l'autoroute A2, Bunker 599 vise à rendre accessible et tangible une partie inattendue de l'histoire des Pays-Bas.

By slicing a seemingly impenetrable bunker in half, the designers make it into a work of art, something surely not on the mind of the original architects. Light and free passage cut through the middle of the concrete, reversing the buried presence of the structure, opening it to the sky.

Durch Aufschlitzen eines scheinbar undurchdringlichen Bunkers machen ihn die Gestalter zu einem Kunstwerk. Licht und freier Zugang mitten durch den Beton kehren die Wirkung des in der Erde verhafteten Bauwerks um und öffnen es zum Himmel.

En coupant en deux un bunker en apparence impénétrable, les designers en ont fait une œuvre d'art. La lumière et le passage tranchent le béton en son milieu, retournant la présence enterrée du bâtiment et l'ouvrant sur le ciel.

RAUMLABORBERLIN

Raumlaborberlin is a group of architects and urban designers based in Berlin, Germany, created in 1999. Working in "various interdisciplinary teams they investigate strategies for urban renewal." They have experimented in urban design and planning, architecture, interactive environments, research, and the design of public space and art installations. The group is made up of eight architects: **FRANCESCO APPUZZO** (born in Naples, 1972), **MARKUS BADER** (born in Karlsruhe, 1968), **BENJAMIN FOERSTER-BALDENIUS** (born in Stuttgart, 1968), **ANDREA HOFMANN** (born in Osnabrück, 1969), **JAN LIESEGANG** (born in Cologne, 1968), **CHRISTOF MAYER** (born in Wangen im Allgäu, 1969), **MATTHIAS RICK** (born in Versmold, 1965), and **AXEL TIMM** (born in Hanover, 1973). Recent work includes Moderato Cantabile (Graz, Austria, 2008); temporary Houses of Literature for Children (unbuilt, 2009); the Promising Land, an installation along the Liverpool-Leeds Canal (UK, 2009); Spacebuster (New York, USA, 2009, published here); *Soap Opera*, an installation for the opening ceremony of "Ruhr.2010 European Capital of Culture" (Essen, Germany, 2010); and Open House, a vertical village and social sculpture in Anyang for APAP 2010 (South Korea, 2010).

Raumlaborberlin ist eine Gruppe von Architekten und Stadtplanern in Berlin und wurde 1999 gegründet. Die Mitglieder arbeiten in „verschiedenen interdisziplinären Teams, die Strategien für urbane Erneuerung entwickeln". Ihre Versuchsfelder sind Stadtentwurf und -planung, Architektur, interaktive Räume, Forschung sowie die Gestaltung von öffentlichem Raum und Kunstinstallationen. Die Gruppe besteht aus acht Architekten: **FRANCESCO APPUZZO** (geboren 1972 in Neapel), **MARKUS BADER** (geboren 1968 in Karlsruhe), **BENJAMIN FOERSTER-BALDENIUS** (geboren 1968 in Stuttgart), **ANDREA HOFMANN** (geboren 1969 in Osnabrück), **JAN LIESEGANG** (geboren 1968 in Köln), **CHRISTOF MAYER** (geboren 1969 in Wangen im Allgäu), **MATTHIAS RICK** (geboren 1965 in Versmold) und **AXEL TIMM** (geboren 1973 in Hannover). Zu ihren jüngeren Projekten zählen Moderato Cantabile (Graz, Österreich, 2008), temporäre Kinderliteraturhäuser (nicht realisiert, 2009), The Promising Land, eine Installation am Liverpool-Leeds-Kanal (Großbritannien, 2009), Spacebuster (New York, 2009, hier vorgestellt), Soap Opera, eine Installation für das Eröffnungsfest von „Ruhr.2010 Kulturhauptstadt Europas" (Essen, 2010) sowie Open House, vertikales Dorf und soziale Skulptur in Anyang für APAP 2010 (Südkorea, 2010).

Raumlaborberlin est un groupe d'architectes et d'urbanistes basé à Berlin, créé en 1999. Travaillant en « équipes interdisciplinaires de configurations variées, ils étudient des stratégies de renouveau urbain ». Ils interviennent dans les champs de la conception et de la programmation urbanistiques, l'architecture, les environnements interactifs, la recherche et la conception d'espaces publics et d'installations artistiques. Le groupe se compose de huit architectes: **FRANCESCO APPUZZO** (né à Naples, 1972), **MARKUS BADER** (né à Karlsruhe, 1968), **BENJAMIN FOERSTER-BALDENIUS** (né à Stuttgart, 1968), **ANDREA HOFMANN** (né à Osnabrück, 1969), **JAN LIESEGANG** (né à Cologne, 1968), **CHRISTOF MAYER** (né à Wangen im Allgäu,1969), **MATTHIAS RICK** (né à Versmold, 1965) et **AXEL TIMM** (né à Hanovre, 1973). Parmi leurs travaux récents : Moderato Cantabile (Graz, Autriche, 2008) ; des maisons de la littérature pour enfants temporaires (non construites, 2009) ; *Terre promise*, une installation le long du canal Liverpool-Leeds (GB, 2009) ; Spacebuster (New York, 2009, publié ici) ; *Soap Opera*, une installation pour la cérémonie d'ouverture de « Ruhr.2010 capitale européenne de la culture » (Essen, Allemagne, 2010), et Open House (« Maison ouverte »), un village vertical et une sculpture sociale à Anyang pour l'APAP 2010 (Corée du Sud, 2010).

SPACEBUSTER

New York, USA, 2009

Area: 100 m².
Client: Storefront for Art and Architecture.

Spacebuster is intended to "transform architectural and social space." It is made up of a van and an inflatable space for up to 80 people that comes out of the back of the van. Visitors enter through the passenger door of the vehicle and enter the translucent bubble. The architects describe the membrane as a semi-permeable border between public and more private space and liken its use to public theater. Desks, chairs, or dining tables are added to the bubble space as required. Another advantage of the scheme is that the bubble can be squeezed into available space where the van parks. In 2009, the architects hosted nine consecutive evenings in Manhattan and Brooklyn. The inventors of the project explain: "As a research tool the Spacebuster disclosed peoples' relation to urban space and to quite a number of invisible borders within the city that shape the built and social space."

Ziel des Spacebusters ist es, den „architektonischen und sozialen Raum" zu verändern. Der Spacebuster besteht aus einem Kleinlaster mit einem aufblasbaren Raum für bis zu 80 Personen, der sich aus der Rückseite des Busses entfaltet. Besucher betreten den Raum durch die Beifahrertür des Wagens und treten hinaus in die transparente Blase. Die Architekten beschreiben die Membran als semipermeable Grenze zwischen öffentlichem und tendenziell privatem Raum und vergleichen deren Einsatz mit einer öffentlichen Theateraufführung. Je nach Bedarf wird die Blase mit Schreibtischen, Stühlen oder Esstischen ausgestattet. Ein weiterer Vorteil des Entwurfs ist, dass die Blase im verfügbaren Laderaum verstaut werden kann, wenn der Bus parkt. 2009 realisierten die Architekten eine Reihe von neun Abendveranstaltungen in Manhattan und Brooklyn. Die Erfinder des Projekts führen aus: „Als Forschungsinstrument entlarvt der Spacebuster die Beziehung von Menschen zum urbanen Raum und zu zahlreichen unsichtbaren Grenzen in der Stadt, die den gebauten und sozialen Raum definieren."

Le Spacebuster se propose de «transformer l'espace architectural et social». L'installation se compose d'une camionnette et d'une structure gonflable pouvant contenir jusqu'à 80 personnes qui se déploie de l'arrière du camion. Les visiteurs entrent par la portière passager du véhicule, puis pénètrent dans la bulle translucide. Les architectes présentent cette membrane comme une frontière semi-perméable entre l'espace public et un espace plus privatif qu'ils comparent à un théâtre. Des bureaux, des sièges ou des tables pour les repas sont installés dans la bulle selon les besoins. Celle-ci peut aussi se loger dans l'espace disponible lorsque la camionnette est stationnée. En 2009, les architectes ont organisé neuf manifestations consécutives en soirée à Manhattan et Brooklyn : «En tant qu'espace de recherche, le Spacebuster met en lumière les relations des gens avec l'espace urbain et un certain nombre de limites urbaines invisibles qui contribuent à la mise en forme de l'espace social et construit.»

A bulbous additional space expands from within the confines of the Spacebuster van, implying questions about the very nature of architectural space.

Aus der Enge des Hecks des Spacebuster-Busses wölbt sich eine Raumblase: Hier werden herkömmliche Vorstellungen von Architektur und Raum infrage gestellt.

Le volume additionnel se déploie en forme de bulle à partir de la camionnette, posant au passage des questions sur la nature même de l'espace architectural.

In its expanded state, the Space-buster can accommodate up to 80 people in a completely ephemeral space that requires no structural adaptation other than a flat, empty area to expand into.

In aufgeblasenem Zustand bietet der Spacebuster Platz für bis zu 80 Personen. Der ephemere Raum erfordert keinerlei Stützkonstruktion, sondern lediglich eine ebene, freie Fläche, um sich zu entfalten.

Déployé, le Spacebuster peut rece-voir jusqu'à 80 personnes dans un espace totalement éphémère qui ne demande rien d'autre qu'un lieu plat et dégagé pour être mis en place.

RECETAS URBANAS

SANTIAGO CIRUGEDA was born in Seville, Spain, in 1971, and studied Architecture at the ETSA in his native city. He founded Recetas Urbanas in Seville in 2004. He calls himself an "artist with the title of architect." His work has consisted of the production of a number of temporary, usually parasitic, structures that call into question the very nature of architecture and its materials. He has participated extensively in debates, workshops, and exhibitions. He has frequently flirted with illegality in the realization of these projects, again questioning the rules that govern construction and urban development. He refers to a number of his projects as "strategies for subversive occupation." He participated in the 2003 *Venice Biennale*. His projects include the Recycling of a High-Voltage Equipment Building (Olmeda de la Cuesta, Cuenca, 2009); Trucks, Containers, Collectives (various locations, 2007–10); Extension 2010 + Chill-Out for Zanfoña Aldana (Coca Piñera, Seville, 2010); Rooftop Housing (Madrid, 2010); and Cement Recycling (Maimona Saints, Badajoz, 2010). More recent projects are Proyectalab, the Reuse of a Train Station (Benicassim, 2011); Varuma Circus School (Seville, 2011); Aula Abierta / La Araña (Seville, 2011/12, published here); and the Open Classroom (Seville, 2012), all in Spain.

SANTIAGO CIRUGEDA wurde 1971 in Sevilla geboren und studierte in seiner Heimatstadt an der ETSA Architektur. 2004 gründete er dort Recetas Urbanas. Er selbst bezeichnet sich als „Künstler mit Architektentitel". Sein Werk besteht aus einer Reihe temporärer, meist parasitärer Bauwerke, die das Wesen der Architektur selbst und ihrer Materialien infrage stellen. Er war an zahlreichen Debatten, Workshops und Ausstellungen beteiligt und hat bei der Realisierung seiner Projekte die Grenzen der Legalität zuweilen übertreten und damit wiederum die Regeln, die Bauwesen und Stadtentwicklung bestimmen, hinterfragt. Einige seiner Projekte bezeichnet er daher als „Strategien subversiver Besetzung". 2003 hat er an der Biennale in Venedig teilgenommen. Zu seinen Projekten gehören das Recycling eines Umspannwerks (Olmeda de la Cuesta, Cuenca, 2009), Trucks, Containers, Collectives (verschiedene Standorte, 2007–10), Erweiterung 2010 + Chill-out für La Zanfoña (Coca Pieñera, Sevilla, 2010), Dachwohnung (Madrid, 2010) sowie Zement-Recycling (Maimona Saints, Badajoz, 2010). Zu den jüngeren Projekten zählen das Proyectalab, die Umnutzung eines Bahnhofs (Benicassim, 2011), die Zirkusschule Varuma (Sevilla, 2011), Aula Abierta/La Araña (Sevilla, 2011/2012, hier vorgestellt) und der Offene Klassenraum (Sevilla, 2012), alle in Spanien.

SANTIAGO CIRUGEDA est né à Séville en 1971 et y a étudié l'architecture à l'ETSA. Il a fondé Recetas Urbanas à Séville en 2004. Il se définit lui-même comme un « artiste avec le titre d'architecte ». Son œuvre consiste en de multiples structures temporaires, souvent parasites, qui remettent en question la nature même de l'architecture et de ses matériaux. Il a déjà participé à de très nombreux débats, ateliers et expositions. La réalisation de ses projets a souvent été à la limite de l'illégalité, remettant là aussi en question les règlements et décrets en matière de construction et d'urbanisme. Il en parle comme de « stratégies d'occupation subversive ». Il a participé à la Biennale de Venise 2003. Ses projets comprennent le recyclage du bâtiment d'un condensateur haute tension (Olmeda de la Cuesta, Cuenca, 2009) ; *Camions, conteneurs, collectifs* (lieux divers, 2007–10) ; Extension 2010 + Chill-Out for Zanfoña Aldana (Coca Piñera, Séville, 2010) ; logement sur le toit (Madrid, 2010) et Cement Recycling (Maimona Saints, Badajoz, 2010). Ses réalisations plus récentes sont Proyectalab, la reconversion d'une gare (Benicassim, 2011) ; l'école du cirque Varuma (Séville, 2011) ; l'Aula Abierta/La Araña (Séville, 2011–2012, publié ici) et la salle de classe ouverte (Séville, 2012), toutes en Espagne.

AULA ABIERTA/LA ARAÑA

Seville, Spain, 2011/12

Area: 80 m² (Aula Abierta), 30 m² (La Araña). Client: Bifa and Cia.
Collaboration: Rehasa Estructuras and friends.

Santiago Cirugeda explains: "Since 1996, I have developed a critical practice through subversive projects in diverse urban environments, all of which ultimately demand the revision of city planning regulations and ordinances." Aula Abierta is meant to activate an abandoned lot in a residential area in the periphery of Seville, at a time when public administration in the city is not supporting projects related to culture and the arts. The project started in 2004 when a group of students from the University of Granada assembled a classroom from materials gathered by dismantling a building that was set to be demolished. In January 2012, students helped dismantle this project and the materials were transported to Seville, where it was received by Recetas Urbanas and the technical team of the Varuma Theater. Aula Abierta Sevilla is part of an expanded project called "Espacio Artístico—La Carpa" (Artistic Space—The Tent), which is the headquarters of the Varuma Theater and the future Circus School of Andalucía. La Araña (The Spider) was also made for the same site with recuperated materials including shipping containers.

„Seit 1996", erklärt Santiago Cirugeda, „habe ich anhand subversiver Projekte in verschiedenen städtischen Zusammenhängen eine kritische Praxis entwickelt, all diese Projekte verlangen letztendlich die Revision stadtplanerischer Regularien und Bestimmungen." Mit Aula Abierta soll eine Brache in einer Wohngegend am Rande Sevillas belebt werden, gerade zu einer Zeit, in der die Stadtverwaltung keinerlei Projektförderungen im Bereich Kunst und Kultur gewährt. Mit dem Projekt ging es 2004 los, als Studenten der Universität Granada einen Seminarraum aus Materialien zusammenbauten, die sie aus einem zum Abriss freigegebenen Gebäude geholt hatten. Im Januar 2012 wurde das Gebäude wieder demontiert, das Material nach Sevilla transportiert und von Recetas Urbanas und den Technikern des Varuma-Theaters in Empfang genommen. Aula Abierta Sevilla gehört zu einem größeren Projekt namens „Espacio Artístico – La Carpa" (Kunstraum – Das Zelt), in dem das Varuma-Theater und die zukünftige Zirkusschule von Andalusien untergebracht sind. La Araña (die Spinne) wurde auf demselben Grundstück aus recycelten Materialien, u. a. Containern, errichtet.

Santiago Cirugeda explique : « Depuis 1996, j'ai développé une pratique critique à travers des projets subversifs dans divers environnements urbains qui exigent tous en fin de compte la révision des règlements et décrets en matière d'urbanisme. » L'Aula Abierta vise à redonner vie à un terrain abandonné d'une zone résidentielle en périphérie de Séville, à une époque où les pouvoirs publics municipaux ne financent plus les projets dans les domaines de la culture et de l'art. Le projet a commencé en 2004, lorsqu'un groupe d'étudiants de l'université de Grenade a monté une salle de classe à partir de matériaux provenant d'un édifice destiné à être démoli. En janvier 2012, les étudiants ont aidé à démonter la construction, et les matériaux ont été transportés jusqu'à Séville, où Recetas Urbanas les a réceptionnés avec les techniciens du théâtre Varuma. L'ensemble fait aujourd'hui partie d'un projet plus vaste appelé « Espacio Artístico – La Carpa » (Espace artistique – Le Chapiteau), siège de la troupe de théâtre Varuma et de la future école du cirque d'Andalousie. La Araña (l'araignée) sur le même site a également été construite avec des matériaux de récupération, dont des conteneurs maritimes.

The metal legs of La Araña are seen to the right. Working with recuperated materials the architect has willfully invested abandoned urban or quasi-urban sites, seeking to make the best use of existing unoccupied land.

Rechts sind die metallenen Beine von La Araña zu sehen. Der Architekt, der mit wiederverwertetem Material arbeitet, hat gezielt städtische oder stadtnahe Brachen besetzt, um unbebaute Flächen optimal zu nutzen.

On voit à droite les pattes métalliques de La Araña. Travaillant avec des matériaux de récupération, l'architecte a délibérément investi des sites urbains ou quasi urbains abandonnés pour tirer le meilleur parti du terrain inoccupé.

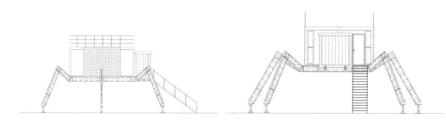

La Araña seen in different variations, set up off the ground in order
to make better use of available
space, and having a decidedly me-
chanical appearance often favored
by Santiago Cirugeda.

La Araña, aus verschiedenen Pers-
pektiven gesehen und zur besseren
Flächennutzung aufgebockt, bietet
einen entschieden technischen
Anblick, wie er häufig bei Santiago
Cirugeda anzutreffen ist.

La Araña en différentes variations,
surélevée pour mieux exploiter
l'espace disponible, elle présente
un aspect résolument mécanique
comme les aime Santiago Cirugeda.

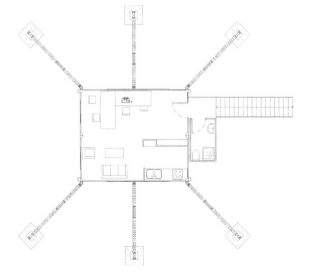

REX

JOSHUA PRINCE-RAMUS received a B.A. in Philosophy from Yale in 1991 and an M.Arch. from Harvard University in 1996. He was the founding partner of OMA New York, the American affiliate of the Office for Metropolitan Architecture (OMA) / Rem Koolhaas in The Netherlands, and served as its Principal until he renamed the firm REX in 2006. He was Partner in charge of the Guggenheim-Hermitage Museum in Las Vegas and the Seattle Central Library by OMA. He is now the Principal of REX. Recently completed projects include the Madison Avenue (Doll)House (New York, USA, 2008, published here); the AT&T Performing Arts Center Dee and Charles Wyly Theater (Dallas, Texas, USA, 2006–09); the Vakko Fashion Center and Power Media Center in Istanbul (Turkey, 2008–10); and Museum Plaza (Lexington, Kentucky, USA, 2005–11). Current work includes McDonald's Prototypes (worldwide, 2011–); Yongsan International Business District "Project R6" (Seoul, South Korea, 2012–); and 2050 M Street (Washington, D.C., USA, 2015–).

JOSHUA PRINCE-RAMUS schloss sein Studium mit einem B. A. in Philosophie an der Universität Yale sowie mit einem M. Arch. an der Universität Harvard ab. Er war einer der Gründungspartner von OMA New York, der amerikanischen Niederlassung des Office for Metropolitan Architecture (OMA)/Rem Koolhaas in den Niederlanden, und war dort leitender Architekt, bis er das Büro 2006 unter dem Namen REX fortführte. Bei OMA war er verantwortlich für Projekte wie das Guggenheim-Hermitage-Museum in Las Vegas und die Seattle Central Library. Inzwischen ist er Direktor von REX. In letzter Zeit fertiggestellt wurden u. a. das Madison Avenue (Doll)House (New York, 2008, hier vorgestellt), das Dee & Charles Wyly Theater des AT&T Performing Arts Center in Dallas (Texas, 2006–09), das Vakko Fashion Center und das Power Media Center in Istanbul (2008–10) und die Museum Plaza (Lexington, Kentucky, 2005–11). Zu den laufenden Projekten gehören Prototypen für McDonald's (weltweit, seit 2011), der Yongsan International Business District „Project R6" (Seoul, Südkorea, seit 2012) und die 2050 M Street (Washington, D.C., 2015–).

JOSHUA PRINCE-RAMUS a obtenu son B.A. en philosophie à l'université Yale (1991) et son M.Arch. à l'université Harvard (1996). Il a été l'un des fondateurs de l'agence OMA New York, branche américaine de l'Office for Metropolitan Architecture (OMA/ Rem Koolhaas) aux Pays-Bas, et l'a dirigée avant de la renommer REX en 2006. Il a été partenaire en charge du musée Guggenheim-Hermitage à Las Vegas et de la bibliothèque centrale de Seattle signée OMA. Il dirige actuellement REX. Parmi ses projets récemment achevés figurent : *Madison Avenue (Doll)House* (New York, 2008, publié ici) ; le théâtre Dee and Charles Wyly du Centre des arts du spectacle AT&T (Dallas, Texas, 2006–09) ; le Centre de la mode de Vakko et siège de Power Media à Istanbul (2008–10) et le Museum Plaza (Lexington, Kentucky, 2005–11). Il travaille actuellement aux prototypes de McDonald's (à l'international, 2011–) ; au quartier international d'affaires « Projet R6 » de Yongsan (Séoul, 2012–) ; et au 2050 M Street (Washington, D.C., 2015–).

MADISON AVENUE (DOLL)HOUSE

New York, USA, 2008

Area: 4 m² (Dollhouse), 190 m² (Concept House).
Client: Calvin Klein, Inc.

REX was approached by an official of Calvin Klein's company to design a concept house showcasing pieces from the company's apparel, accessory, and home lines. The house would be realized in miniature and displayed in the main window of Calvin Klein's Madison Avenue store during the 2008–09 holiday season. A response to two different scales and purposes, the smaller structure, dubbed the "(Doll)House" by the architects, had to reconcile the contradictory constraints of a concept house and a dollhouse in a single project. The concept house was to be designed for the "Calvin Klein woman," a professed city-dweller. Suspended in air, the concept house remained a freestanding residence while capitalizing on underutilized urban space. Undeniably frivolous, the Madison Avenue (Doll)House could be seen closely in the round and from a distance, and could be opened from all sides for play. REX made use of the precedent of the minimalist design originally created by the designer of the store, John Pawson. The interiors and roof terrace were furnished with miniature replicas of pieces from the company's apparel, accessory, and home lines.

REX war von der Geschäftsführung Calvin Kleins gebeten worden, ein Konzepthaus zu entwerfen, in dem ausgewählte Stücke der Produktlinien Kleidung, Accessoires und Einrichtung präsentiert werden sollten. Das Haus sollte als Modell realisiert und während des Weihnachtsgeschäfts 2008–09 im großen Schaufenster der Calvin-Klein-Filiale an der Madison Avenue ausgestellt werden. Vor dem Hintergrund zweier unterschiedlicher Maßstäbe und Nutzungskonzepte musste das kleine Bauwerk, von den Architekten (Doll)House genannt, die widersprüchlichen Anforderungen eines Konzept- und eines Puppenhauses in einem einzigen Projekt miteinander in Einklang bringen. Konzipiert wurde das Haus für die „Calvin-Klein-Frau", eine bekennende Städterin. Durch die Deckenhängung verkörperte das Konzepthaus eine autarke Wohneinheit, die aus ungenutztem urbanen Raum Nutzen schlägt. Das zweifellos provokante Madison Avenue (Doll)House war weithin gut sichtbar, konnte aber auch von allen Seiten aus der Nähe inspiziert und zum Spielen geöffnet werden. REX adaptierte die minimalistische Formensprache seines Vorgängers John Pawson, dem ursprünglichen Designer des Ladens. Innenräume und Dachterrasse wurden mit Miniaturrepliken aus den Calvin-Klein-Linien Kleidung, Accessoires und Einrichtung ausgestattet.

REX a été contacté par un responsable de Calvin Klein pour une concept house présentant des articles de la gamme de produits habillement et accessoires. Elle devait être construite en miniature et exposée dans la principale vitrine du magasin Calvin Klein de Madison Avenue pendant les vacances 2008–09. Destinée à répondre à deux échelles et objectifs différents, la petite structure appelée « (Doll)House » par les architectes devait concilier les exigences contradictoires de la concept house et de la maison de poupées dans un seul projet. La concept house devait être créée pour la ligne « Calvin Klein Woman », résolument citadine. Suspendue dans les airs, elle devait rester indépendante, tout en tirant parti de l'espace urbain sous-exploité. Incontestablement moins sérieuse, la Madison Avenue (Doll)House pouvait être vue entièrement de près ou de loin et être ouverte de tous les côtés pour jouer. REX a tiré parti du décor minimaliste du magasin, création originale du designer John Pawson. L'intérieur et la terrasse du toit ont été meublés de répliques miniatures d'articles de la gamme de produits habillement et accessoires.

Seen in the context of its presentation in a Madison Avenue store of Calvin Klein, the (Doll)House is made to hang in space, quite visible and also rather incongruous or perturbing.

Das (Doll)House, hier zu sehen im Rahmen seiner Präsentation in der Calvin-Klein-Filiale an der Madison Avenue, hängt frei im Raum, gut sichtbar und gleichzeitig seltsam unpassend, sogar verstörend.

Présentée dans le contexte de son installation dans un magasin Calvin Klein de Madison Avenue, la (Doll) House est conçue pour être suspendue, très visible et aussi quelque peu incongrue ou dérangeante.

The scale model of the concept
house designed by REX, the (Doll)
House has all the fittings of a real
residence that just happens to
hover in space.

Das maßstäbliche Modell des von
REX entworfenen Konzepthauses
(Doll)House ist ausgestattet wie
ein echtes Haus, das eben in der
Luft schwebt.

Modèle réduit de la concept house
créée par REX, la (Doll)House présente tous les équipements d'une
véritable habitation qui flotterait
simplement dans les airs.

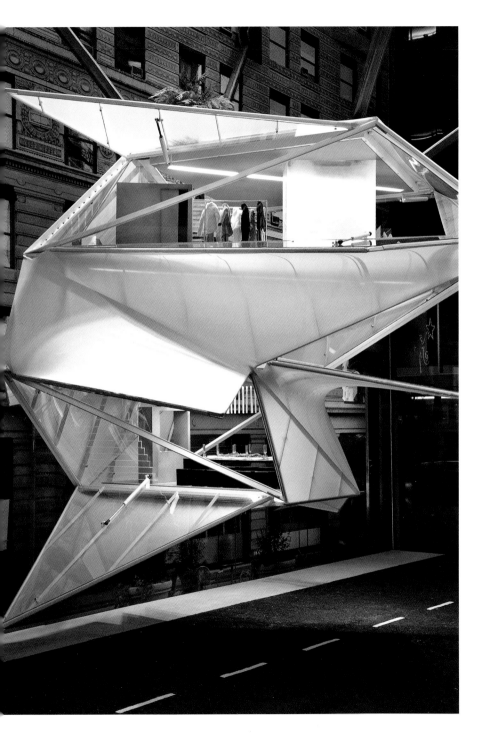

RINTALA EGGERTSSON

Rintala Eggertsson Architects was established in 2007 by the Finnish architect **SAMI RINTALA** and the Icelandic architect **DAGUR EGGERTSSON**. Today the office also includes the architects Vibeke Jenssen, Kaori Watanabe, and Masae Asada. Seeking to "occupy the space between architecture and public art," their work has been seen in the Victoria and Albert Museum in London, the MAXXI Museum in Rome, and in the *Venice Biennale*. Sami Rintala was born in 1969 in Helsinki, Finland. He obtained his degree in Architecture from the Helsinki University of Technology (1990–99). Dagur Eggertsson was born in 1965 in Reykjavik, Iceland. He obtained his M.Arch. degree from the Helsinki University of Technology (1995–97), having previously studied at the Oslo School of Architecture and Design (1986–92). Their work includes the Ark Booktower (Victoria and Albert Museum, London, UK, 2010, published here); an Arboretum (Gjövik, Norway, 2011); Seljord Watchtower (Seljord, Telemark, Norway, 2011, also published here); Hut to Hut (Kagala, Karnataka, India, 2012, also published here); and Suidal Bridge (Suidal, Norway, 2013).

Rintala Eggertsson Architects wurde 2007 von dem finnischen Architekten **SAMI RINTALA** und dem isländischen Architekten **DAGUR EGGERTSSON** gegründet. In dem Büro arbeiten heute zudem Vibeke Jenssen, Kaori Watanabe und Masae Asada. Ihre Arbeiten, mit denen sie „den Raum zwischen Architektur und Kunst im öffentlichen Raum besetzen" wollen, waren im Victoria and Albert Museum in London, dem MAXXI-Museum in Rom und bei der Biennale in Venedig zu sehen. Sami Rintala wurde 1969 in Helsinki geboren. Seinen Architekturabschluss machte er an der Technischen Hochschule Helsinki (1990–99). Dagur Eggertsson wurde 1965 in Reykjavík geboren. Er erlangte seinen M. Arch. an der Technischen Hochschule Helsinki (1995–97), nachdem er bereits an der Hochschule für Architektur und Design in Oslo studiert hatte (1986–92). Zu ihren Arbeiten gehören der Ark Booktower (Victoria and Albert Museum, London, 2010, hier vorgestellt), ein Arboretum (Gjövik, Norwegen, 2011), der Seljord Watchtower (Seljord, Telemark, Norwegen, 2011, ebenfalls hier vorgestellt), Hut to Hut (Kagala, Karnataka, Indien, 2012, ebenfalls hier vorgestellt) und die Brücke in Suidal (Norwegen, 2013).

Rintala Eggertsson Architects a été fondé en 2007 par les architectes finlandais **SAMI RINTALA** et islandais **DAGUR EGGERTSSON**. L'agence emploie aujourd'hui les architectes Vibeke Jenssen, Kaori Watanabe et Masae Asada. Cherchant à « occuper l'espace entre architecture et art public », leur travail a été exposé au Victoria and Albert Museum de Londres, au musée MAXXI de Rome et à la Biennale de Venise. Sami Rintala est né en 1969 à Helsinki. Il a obtenu son diplôme d'architecte à l'Université de technologie d'Helsinki (1990–99). Dagur Eggertsson est né en 1965 à Reykjavik. Il a obtenu son M.Arch à l'Université de technologie d'Helsinki (1995–97), après des études à l'École d'architecture et de design d'Oslo (1986–92). Leurs réalisations comprennent l'*Ark Booktower* (Victoria and Albert Museum, 2010, publiée ici) ; un arboretum (Gjövik, Norvège, 2011) ; la tour d'observation de Seljord (Seljord, Telemark, Norvège, 2011, également publiée ici) ; Hut to Hut (Kagala, Karnataka, Inde, 2012, également publiée ici) et le pont de Suidal (Suidal, Norvège, 2013).

HUT TO HUT
Kagala, Karnataka, India, 2012

Area: 27 m². Client: Panchabhuta Foundation.
Cost: $75 000.

The hut was developed in a design and building workshop with students from the University of Science and Technology in Trondheim, following an international seminar about the future of ecotourism in the Western Ghats region in India. The aim was to use locally produced materials and renewable energy sources. A group of houses can form a shaded courtyard coherent with local traditions. The resulting building is completely off-grid, with solar panels on the roof, and a composting latrine that produces biogas. The architects explain: "The hut represents a possibility for the local population to invest in the growing environmentally conscious segment of the tourist market while maintaining their traditional culture and lifestyle."

Die Hütte wurde im Rahmen eines Entwurfs- und Bauworkshops gemeinsam mit Studenten der Universität der Wissenschaft und Technik Trondheim entwickelt – im Anschluss an ein internationales Seminar zur Zukunft des Ökotourismus in den Westghats in Indien. Das Ziel war es, lokal produzierte Materialien und erneuerbare Energien zu verwenden. Eine Häusergruppe kann einen schattigen Innenhof bilden, der im Einklang mit Traditionen der Region steht. Das dabei entworfene Gebäude ist völlig unabhängig dank Solarmodulen auf dem Dach und einer Komposttoilette, die Biogas produziert. Die Architekten erklären: „Das Gebäude symbolisiert die Option der lokalen Bevölkerung, in das wachsende Segment umweltbewussten Tourismus zu investieren, gleichzeitig aber ihre traditionelle Kultur und Lebensweise zu bewahren."

La cabane a été développée dans le cadre d'un atelier de design et construction avec des étudiants de l'Université de sciences et technologie de Trondheim qui faisait suite à un séminaire international sur le futur de l'écotourisme dans la région indienne des Ghâts occidentaux. Il s'agissait d'utiliser des matériaux produits sur place et des sources d'énergies renouvelables. Un groupe de maisons peut former une cour ombragée en cohérence avec les traditions locales. Le bâtiment obtenu est totalement indépendant du réseau électrique avec des panneaux solaires sur le toit et des toilettes à compostage qui produisent du biogaz. Les architectes expliquent que « cela incarne une possibilité pour la population locale d'investir dans le secteur en expansion du tourisme sensibilisé aux questions d'environnement tout en conservant sa culture et son style de vie traditionnels ».

Elegant and light, the hut corresponds fully to local traditions insofar as materials and buildings techniques are concerned, but it does possess a sense of modernity that has been brought to the project by the architects.

Was Materialien und Bauweise betrifft, entspricht die Hütte, elegant und leicht wie sie ist, vollkommen den lokalen Traditionen, gleichzeitig verliehen die Architekten ihr etwas dezidiert Modernes.

Élégante et légère, la cabane correspond parfaitement aux traditions locales en ce qui concerne les matériaux et techniques de construction, mais elle y insuffle une touche de modernité ajoutée par les architectes.

The structures are connected by a wooden walkway, with different forms evolving from the same general vocabulary imposed by Rintala Eggertsson.

Die Gebäude sind durch einen hölzernen Steg miteinander verbunden, sie unterscheiden sich in der Formgebung, entstehen aber beide aus demselben von Rintala Eggertsson entwickelten Grundvokabular.

Les deux constructions sont reliées par des passerelles en bois, les différences de formes parlent le même langage général imposé par Rintala Eggertsson.

The climate allows for generous openings and spaces that are neither clearly defined as being interiors nor exteriors. The structures are simple but have an unusual, original appearance.

Das Klima gestattet großzügige Öffnungen und Bereiche, die weder eindeutig Innen- noch Außenraum sind. Die Bauten sind schlicht, verfügen aber dennoch über ein ungewöhnliches, originelles Erscheinungsbild.

Le climat permet des ouvertures généreuses et des espaces dont l'appartenance intérieure ou extérieure n'est pas clairement définie. Les constructions sont simples mais présentent un aspect original et inhabituel.

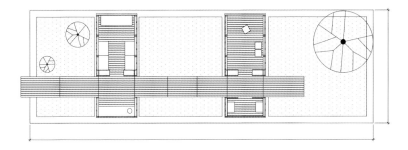

A site plan shows the two structures and their linking walkway. The visual and physical link is seen in the photos on this page.

Ein Lageplan zeigt die beiden Gebäude und den sie verbindenden Steg. Die visuelle und physische Verbindung ist auf den Fotos auf dieser Seite zu sehen.

Le plan du site montre les deux structures et la passerelle qui les relie. Les photos montrent ce lien visuel et physique.

SELJORD WATCHTOWER

Seljord, Telemark, Norway, 2011

Area: 70 m². Client: Seljord Municipality.
Cost: €300 000.

The Seljord Watchtower, located in the Telemark region of southern Norway, makes reference to a local myth concerning sightings of a serpent in the lake.

Der Seljord-Wachturm in der Region Telemark in Südnorwegen nimmt Bezug auf den lokalen Mythos einer Schlange, die im See gesichtet worden sein soll.

La tour d'observation de Seljord, dans la région du Telemark, au sud de la Norvège, fait référence à un mythe local concernant un serpent qui aurait été vu dans le lac.

Over a long period, a myth has been created about a sea serpent sighted in the lake of Seljord. In 2008, the municipality decided to use this feature as a point of departure for a development program for the area. Part of the scheme was conceived as a design-build workshop with art and architecture students and teachers from the Nuova Accademia di Belle Arte and Politecnico in Milan and stage design students from the Norwegian Theater Academy under Rintala Eggertsson's leadership. The workshop was thematically focused on the issue of anchoring man-made installations to characteristic features in the landscape without dominating them. The three installations were grouped under the title "Into the Landscape." Rintala Eggertsson was also commissioned to design the central feature that is essentially a viewing platform and a small shelter for exhibitions. The architects decided to divide the program in two and place the two functions on each side of the trees, with a connecting deck in between. The viewing platform was given the form of a tower with a space at the top overlooking the lake and two smaller spaces on the way to the top. The platform was given a connection to a nearby parking area with a narrow walkway designed by the associate landscape architects Feste Grenland.

Der Mythos, es sei eine Seeschlange im Seljord-See gesichtet worden, existiert schon sehr lange. 2008 entschied die Stadtverwaltung, das zum Ausgangspunkt eines Entwicklungsprogramms für die Gegend zu machen. Teil des Vorhabens war ein Gestaltungs- und Bauworkshop unter der Leitung von Rintala Eggertsson mit Kunst- und Architekturstudenten und Lehrkräften der Nuova Accademia di Belle Arte and Politecnico in Mailand und Bühnenbild-Studenten der Theaterakademie Norwegen. Thema war die Verankerung von Bauten aus Menschenhand in Charakteristika einer Landschaft, ohne diese zu dominieren. Die drei Installationen wurden unter dem Titel „Into the Landscape" zusammengefasst. Rintala Eggertsson erhielt zudem den Auftrag, den zentralen Bau zu entwerfen, eine Aussichtsplattform und ein kleines Ausstellungsgebäude. Die Architekten entschieden sich für eine Zweiteilung und verlegten die beiden Funktionen auf je eine Seite der Bäume und verbanden sie mit einem Steg. Die Aussichtsplattform wurde als Turm gestaltet, dessen oberster Raum den See überblickt und der noch über zwei kleinere Räume verfügt. Der Aussichtsturm ist durch einen schmalen Pfad, gestaltet von den Landschaftsarchitekten Feste Grenland, mit einem nahe gelegenen Parkplatz verbunden.

Pendant longtemps, le mythe a persisté d'un serpent de mer aperçu dans le lac de Seljord. En 2008, la municipalité a décidé d'en faire le point de départ d'un programme de développement de la zone. Le projet a été conçu en partie comme un atelier de design-construction avec des étudiants et enseignants d'art et architecture de la Nuova Accademia di Belle Arte et Politecnico de Milan et des étudiants en décoration de théâtre de l'Académie norvégienne de théâtre, sous la direction de Rintala Eggertsson. L'atelier avait pour thème central la question de l'ancrage d'installations faites par l'homme dans des endroits caractéristiques du paysage sans le dominer. Les trois installations ont été regroupées sous le nom *Into the Landscape*. Rintala Eggertsson a également été chargé de concevoir l'élément central, composé pour l'essentiel d'une plate-forme d'observation et d'un petit abri pour des expositions. Les architectes ont décidé de couper le projet en deux et ont placé les deux fonctions de chaque côté des arbres, reliées par un pont. La plate-forme d'observation a reçu la forme d'une tour avec un espace tout en haut qui domine le lac et deux espaces plus petits à des niveaux intermédiaires. Elle a été reliée à un parking voisin par un passage étroit créé par l'architecte paysagiste associé Feste Grenland.

Left, visitors seem to have spotted the famous serpent. Above, the inner wooden structure of the tower essentially houses a stairway with two extra spaces located on the way up to the main platform.

Links haben die Besucher offenbar die berühmte Schlange entdeckt. Oben: Die Holzkonstruktion des Turms beherbergt im Wesentlichen die Treppe, auf dem Weg nach oben finden sich zudem zwei kleine Räume.

À gauche, des visiteurs semblent avoir localisé le monstre. Ci-dessus, la structure intérieure en bois de la tour abrite essentiellement un escalier et deux espaces sur la montée vers la plate-forme.

ARK BOOKTOWER

Victoria and Albert Museum, London, UK, 2010

Area: 9 m². Client: Victoria and Albert Museum.
Cost: £38 000.

Part of an exhibition at the Victoria and Albert that allowed architects to erect small temporary structures within the museum, the Ark Booktower was located at the base of a stairway in the National Art Library.

Der Ark Booktower, Teil einer Ausstellung im Victoria and Albert Museum, bei der Architekten kleine, temporäre Gebäude innerhalb des Museums errichten konnten, wurde am Fuß eines Treppenaufgangs in der National Art Library positioniert.

Construite pour une exposition au Victoria and Albert où des architectes ont pu ériger de petites structures temporaires dans le musée, l'Ark Booktower fut placée au pied d'un escalier à la National Art Library.

Using books and wood for their structure the architects sought to elicit a feeling of "organic familiarity" with their design.

Durch die Nutzung von Büchern und Holz wollten die Architekten mit ihrem Entwurf ein Gefühl „organischer Vertrautheit" erzeugen.

En construisant avec des livres et du bois, les architectes ont cherché à susciter un sentiment de « familiarité organique » avec leur création.

Part of the exhibition *1:1 Architects Build Small Spaces* at London's Victoria and Albert Museum (June 15 to August 30, 2010), this temporary freestanding wooden tower was intended to offer visitors information on biodiversity. It was placed in the National Art Library stairwell. The architects refer to an "escape from the physical space of the museum into the mental space of literature." Secondhand books were collected for use in the tower during 2009 and 2010 from publishers, libraries, and universities. The architects explain: "Outside, only the white paper of the books is shown, creating a unified minimal wall surface together with the bright wooden surface of the tower. This uniform representation of spatial elements in the tower is meant to emphasize the organic familiarity of materials in the books and the construction. The interior is, on the other hand, a contrasting collage of colors, titles, and themes. To learn of the contents of the books, one has to enter the tower."

Die Idee hinter diesem temporären, frei stehenden Turm aus Holz, der bei der Ausstellung „1:1 Architects Build Small Spaces" im Londoner Victoria and Albert Museum (15. Juni – 30. August 2010) gezeigt wurde, war es, die Besucher mit dem Thema Biodiversität zu konfrontieren. Platziert wurde er im Treppenhaus der National Art Library. Die Architekten verstehen ihn als „Fluchtmöglichkeit aus dem physikalischen Raum des Museums hinein in den mentalen Raum der Literatur". Von Verlagen, Bibliotheken und Universitäten wurden 2009 und 2010 benutzte Bücher für den Turm gesammelt. Die Architekten dazu: „Von außen ist nur das weiße Papier der Bücher zu sehen, die gemeinsam mit dem hellen Holz des Turms eine minimalistische Wandfläche bilden. Diese uniforme Darstellungsweise räumlicher Elemente im Turm soll die organische Vertrautheit der Materialien der Bücher und der Konstruktion betonen. Im Gegensatz dazu ist das Innere eine kontrastierende Collage aus Farben, Titeln und Themen. Um an die Inhalte der Bücher heranzukommen, muss man den Turm betreten."

Dans le cadre de l'exposition « 1:1 Architects Build Small Spaces » au Victoria and Albert Museum de Londres (du 15 juin au 30 août 2010), cette tour de bois temporaire avait pour but de fournir aux visiteurs des informations sur la biodiversité, placée dans la cage d'escalier de la National Art Library. Les architectes évoquent un moyen d'« échapper à l'espace physique du musée vers l'espace mental de la littérature ». Des livres d'occasion ont été réunis pour la tour en 2009 et 2010 auprès des éditeurs, bibliothèques et universités. Les architectes expliquent : « De l'extérieur, on ne voit que le papier blanc des livres qui crée une surface murale minimale unifiée avec le bois clair de la tour. Cette représentation uniforme d'éléments spatiaux à l'intérieur de la tour est destinée à souligner la familiarité organique des matériaux dont sont faits les livres et la construction. L'intérieur en revanche est un patchwork contrasté de couleurs, titres et sujets. Pour voir le contenu des livres, il faut entrer dans la tour. »

The used books collected by the architects were all turned so that only their white pages are visible from the exterior, with the more colorful bindings being seen from the interior of the tower.

Die gesammelten, gebrauchten Bücher wurden umgedreht, sodass das Weiß ihrer Seiten nur von außen, die farbigen Einbände nur im Innern des Turms zu sehen sind.

Les livres usagés rassemblés par les architectes étaient tous tournés de manière à ce que seules leurs pages blanches soient visibles de l'extérieur, tandis que les reliures plus colorées ne pouvaient être vues que depuis l'intérieur de la tour.

ROJKIND ARQUITECTOS

MICHEL ROJKIND was born in 1969 in Mexico City, where he studied Architecture and Urban Planning at the Universidad Iberoamericana. In 2002, he established his own firm, Rojkind Arquitectos, in Mexico City. **GERARDO SALINAS** joined the firm as a partner in 2010. He received his B.Arch. from the Universidad Nacional Autonoma de Mexico (Mexico City, 1993) and his M.Arch. from the University of Maryland (Baltimore, 1995). Their work includes the Nestlé Chocolate Museum (Toluca, 2007); Nestlé Application Group (Querétaro, 2009); the Tori Tori Restaurant (Polanco, Mexico City, 2011); the Liverpool Department Store (Mexico City, 2011); Cineteca Nacional del Siglo XXI (Mexico City, 2011–12); Portal of Awareness (Mexico City, 2012, published here); and High Park (Monterrey, 2010–13).

MICHEL ROJKIND wurde 1969 in Mexiko-Stadt geboren, wo er an der Universidad Iberoambericana Architektur und Stadtplanung studierte. 2002 gründete er dort sein eigenes Büro, Rojkind Arquitectos. **GERARDO SALINAS** stieß 2010 als Partner dazu. Er erlangte seinen B. Arch. an der Universidad Nacional Autonoma de Mexico (Mexiko-Stadt, 1993) und seinen M. Arch. an der University of Maryland (Baltimore, 1995). Zu ihren Arbeiten zählen das Nestlé-Schokoladenmuseum (Toluca, 2007), die Nestlé Application Group (Querétaro, 2009), das Restaurant Tori Tori (Polcano, Mexiko-Stadt, 2011), der Liverpool Department Store (Mexiko-Stadt, 2011), die Cineteca Nacional des Siglo XXI (Mexiko-Stadt, 2011–12), das „Portal des Bewusstseins" (Mexiko-Stadt, 2012, hier vorgestellt) und High Park (Monterrey, 2010–13).

MICHEL ROJKIND est né en 1969 à Mexico où il a étudié l'architecture et l'urbanisme à l'Université ibéro-américaine. En 2002, il ouvre son agence, Rojkind Arquitectos, à Mexico. **GERARDO SALINAS** l'a rejoint en 2010. Il a obtenu son B. Arch à l'Université nationale autonome de Mexico (1993) et son M.Arch à l'université du Maryland (Baltimore, 1995). Parmi leurs projets figurent le musée Nestlé du chocolat (Toluca, 2007) ; le Nestlé Application Group (Querétaro, 2009) ; le restaurant Tori Tori (Polanco, Mexico, 2011) ; le grand magasin Liverpool (Mexico, 2011) ; la Cineteca Nacional del Siglo XXI (Mexico, 2011–12) ; le *Portal of Awareness* (Mexico, 2012, publié ici) et High Park (Monterrey, 2010–13).

PORTAL OF AWARENESS
Mexico City, Mexico, 2012

Area: 49 m². Client: Nescafé. Cost: $11 000.
Collaboration: Alfredo Hernandez, Arie Willem, Hendrik de Jongh.

Located on one of Mexico City's most important avenues, the Paseo de la Reforma, the Portal of Awareness is an installation commissioned by Nescafé. The overall project involved seven artists working with Michel Rojkind. The program required the use of about 1500 metal coffee mugs. Rojkind used a primary structure made up of rebar woven in a pattern that generated 1497 nodes for the cups to be hung from. The architect explains: "The final shape of the portal, along with the different colors of the mugs selected, reinforces the sense of movement of the piece… Steel planters anchor the structure and allow for the vines to grow in between the rebar, with the idea that in time they will cover the entire structure in green foliage on the outside, while the inside displays the mugs' chromatics."

Das „Portal des Bewusstseins", am Paseo de la Reforma gelegen, einer der Hauptverkehrsadern von Mexiko-Stadt, ist eine Installation, die von Nescafé in Auftrag gegeben wurde. Bei dem Projekt arbeiteten insgesamt sieben Künstler mit Michel Rojkind zusammen. Laut Konzept galt es, rund 1500 metallene Kaffeebecher zu verwenden. Rojkind verwob Bewehrungsstäbe zu einem Gitter mit 1497 Knoten, an die die Becher gehängt wurden. Der Architekt erklärt: „Die schlussendliche Formgebung des Portals, gemeinsam mit den verschiedenfarbigen Bechern, verstärkt den Eindruck, als bewege sich die Arbeit … aus stählernen Blumenkästen, in denen das Gerüst verankert ist, wachsen Ranken an den Metallstreben hoch und sollen im Lauf der Zeit das ganze Gebilde von außen mit einer grünen Laubschicht bedecken, während im Innern die Chromatik der Becher zu bewundern ist."

Situé dans le Paseo de la Reforma, l'une des principales avenues de Mexico, le Portail de la conscience est une installation commandée par Nescafé. Le projet global a fait intervenir sept artistes coordonnés par Michel Rojkind. L'ensemble a nécessité environ 1500 tasses de café en métal. Rojkind a opté pour une structure primaire, faite d'un treillis de barres d'armature formant un motif avec 1497 nœuds auxquels les tasses sont accrochées. L'architecte explique : « La forme définitive du portail, avec les différentes couleurs des tasses choisies, renforce l'impression de mouvement… La structure est ancrée dans des jardinières en acier plantées de vigne qui grimpe entre les barres d'armature, l'idée étant qu'avec le temps elle recouvrira l'ensemble de feuillage à l'extérieur, tandis que l'intérieur affichera toujours la chromatique des tasses. »

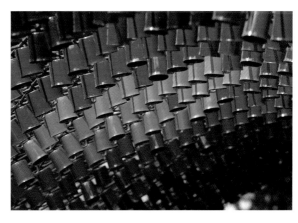

The architects took up the unexpected challenge of creating an architectural object essentially based on suspended coffee cups. A red portal located on Mexico City's main avenue surely evokes the subject of coffee, but also the interest of small structures.

Die Architekten nahmen die unerwartete Herausforderung an, ein architektonisches Objekt zu erschaffen, das im Wesentlichen aus aufgehängten Kaffeebechern besteht. Das rote Portal an der Hauptverkehrsader von Mexiko-Stadt lässt zweifellos an Kaffee denken, weckt aber ebenso das Interesse an kleinen Gebäuden.

Les architectes ont relevé le défi inattendu de créer un objet architectural à partir de tasses à café suspendues. Le portail rouge sur la principale avenue de Mexico évoque sans aucun doute le café, mais aussi l'intérêt des petites structures.

FERNANDO ROMERO

FERNANDO ROMERO was born in 1971 in Mexico City. He received his degree in Architecture from the Universidad Iberomaericana (Mexico City). Prior to creating his own firm, FR-EE, in Mexico City in 2000, Romero worked in the office of OMA in Rotterdam. His rising influence was noted in 2002 when he was among the recipients of the Global Leader of Tomorrow Award at the World Economic Forum (Davos). As well as the Children's Room (Mexico City, 2001, published here), his work includes the Bicentennial Moebius Ring (Mexico City, 2009); Chapel in Central de Abastos (Mexico City, 2009); Casa Toluca (Toluca, 2009–10); The Pyramid (Merida, 2009–10); Mercedes-Benz Business Center (Yerevan, Armenia, 2010); Soumaya Museum (Mexico City, 2005–11); Reforma Tower (Mexico City, 2011); New York Tower (New York, USA, 2011); a Museum in Panama (Panama, 2011); a Museum in Tulum (Quintana Roo, 2011); La Villa, a mixed-use project in front of the Basilica of Guadalupe (Mexico City, 2011); and the Miami Chapel (Miami, Florida, USA, 2012–13); all in Mexico unless stated otherwise.

FERNANDO ROMERO wurde 1971 in Mexiko-Stadt geboren. Sein Architekturstudium schloss er dort an der Universidad Iberoamericana ab. Bevor er in Mexiko-Stadt sein eigenes Büro FR-EE gründete, hatte Romero bei OMA in Rotterdam gearbeitet. 2002 war er unter den Preisträgern des Global Leader of Tomorrow Award auf dem Weltwirtschaftsforum in Davos, ein deutliches Zeichen für seinen wachsenden Einfluss. Zu seinen Entwürfen zählen neben dem Kinderzimmer (Mexiko-Stadt, 2001, hier vorgestellt) der Moebius-Ring zur 200-Jahr-Feier (Mexiko-Stadt, 2009), eine Kapelle in Central de Abastos (Mexiko-Stadt, 2009), die Casa Toluca (Toluca, 2009–10), Die Pyramide (Merida, 2009–10), das Mercedes-Benz Business Center (Jerewan, Armenien, 2010), das Soumaya-Museum (Mexiko-Stadt, 2005–11), der Reforma Tower (Mexiko-Stadt, 2011), der New York Tower (New York, 2011), ein Museum in Panama (2011), ein Museum in Tulum (Quintana Roo, 2011), La Villa, ein Komplex mit Mischnutzung unweit der Basilika der Jungfrau von Guadalupe (Mexiko-Stadt, 2011), und die Miami Chapel (Miami, Florida, 2012–13), alle in Mexiko, soweit nicht anders angegeben.

FERNANDO ROMERO, né en 1971 à Mexico, est diplômé en architecture de l'Université ibéro-américaine (Mexico). Avant de fonder son agence FR-EE à Mexico en 2000, il a travaillé chez OMA à Rotterdam. Son influence grandissante a été saluée en 2002 par le prix du «Global Leader of Tomorrow» au Forum économique mondial de Davos. En plus de la Chambre d'enfants (Mexico, 2001, publiée ici), ses réalisations comprennent l'anneau de Moebius du Bicentenaire (Mexico, 2009); la chapelle de Central de Abastos (Mexico, 2009); la maison Toluca (Toluca, 2009–10); la Pyramide (Merida, 2009–10); le Centre Mercedes-Benz (Erevan, Arménie, 2010); le musée Soumaya (Mexico, 2005–11); la tour Reforma (Mexico, 2011); la tour New York (New York, 2011); un musée à Panama (2011) ; un musée à Tulum (Quintana Roo, 2011); La Villa, un projet à usage mixte face à la basilique de Guadalupe (Mexico, 2011) et la chapelle Miami (Miami, 2012–13), toutes au Mexique sauf mention contraire.

CHILDREN'S ROOM

Mexico City, Mexico, 2001

Area: 135 m².

With its curving forms and white coloring, the structure appears to have indefinite boundaries, without any obstructions or right angles.

Die geschwungenen Formen, das Weiß und das Fehlen jeglicher Hindernisse oder rechter Winkel lassen die Grenzen des Gebäudes verschwimmen.

Avec ses formes courbes et sa couleur blanche, sans le moindre obstacle ni angle droit, la construction semble avoir des limites indéfinies.

The figure in the image above shows that the volume is ample, somehow evoking a space for meditation as much as a children's room.

Die Gestalt auf dem Bild oben zeigt, wie geräumig der Bau ist, der sowohl an einen Meditationsraum als auch an ein Kinderzimmer denken lässt.

Le personnage ci-dessus met en évidence l'ampleur du volume créé – qui pourrait évoquer aussi bien un espace de méditation qu'une chambre d'enfants.

The structure was designed as an annex for a residence in the southern part of Mexico City. In intentional contrast to the main house, the space was meant—as its name implies—as a play area for children, with a connection to the parent's bedroom. The architects state: "The children's room is a surface folded onto itself. Where unfolded, it creates a ramp that connects to the garden and also serves as a structural counterweight. This extension is a fantastic bubble where the limits of right angles disappear completely, giving way to a continuous soft skin that allows the children to experiment with the gravity of objects and of their own bodies." The steel skeleton of the structure was lined with poured concrete, creating a seamless skin that rests on a single point in the garden.

Das Gebäude wurde als Anbau eines Wohnhauses im Süden von Mexiko-Stadt entworfen. Der Ort sollte, in ganz bewusstem Kontrast zum Haupthaus, als – der Name deutet es bereits an – Spielbereich für Kinder fungieren und eine Verbindung zum Elternschlafzimmer haben. Der Architekt dazu: „Das Kinderzimmer ist eine in sich gefaltete Fläche. An einer Stelle entfaltet, entsteht eine Rampe zum Garten hin, die gleichzeitig als bauliches Gegengewicht dient. Der Anbau ist eine fantasievolle Blase, in der die Einengung durch rechte Winkel vollständig verschwindet und von einer durchgehenden weichen Oberfläche abgelöst wird, auf der die Kinder mit der Schwerkraft von Gegenständen und der ihrer eigenen Körper experimentieren können." Das Stahlskelett des Baus wurde mit Gussbeton verschalt, wobei eine nahtlose Hülle entstand, die nur an einem Punkt im Garten aufliegt.

La structure a été conçue comme annexe à une maison dans le sud de Mexico. Contrastant délibérément avec le bâtiment principal, l'espace créé était destiné – comme son nom l'indique – à servir de salle de jeu pour les enfants, tout en étant relié à la chambre des parents. Les architectes expliquent : « La chambre d'enfants forme une surface pliée sur elle-même. Lorsqu'elle est dépliée, elle ouvre une rampe vers le jardin et sert de contrepoids structurel. C'est une bulle imaginaire qui prolonge la maison et où les limites fixées par les angles droits disparaissent entièrement pour céder la place à une enveloppe souple continue qui permet aux enfants de tester la gravité des objets et de leur propre corps. » Le squelette en acier de la structure a été doublé de béton coulé afin de créer une « peau » ininterrompue qui repose sur un point unique dans le jardin.

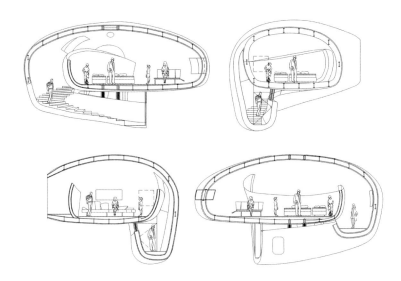

The womb-like form of the Children's Room is visible both in the photographs and in the section drawings

Die an eine Gebärmutter erinnernde Form des Kinderzimmers wird sowohl auf den Bildern als auch im Querschnitt deutlich.

La forme utérine de la chambre d'enfants est visible sur les photos et sur les plans en coupe.

438

ROTOR

The principals of the non-profit organization Rotor call it "a platform for the endorsement of industrial waste reuse. Rotor wants, among other things, to encourage contacts between producers of 'interesting' waste and potential reusers from the field of industry, design or architecture." **MAARTEN GIELEN** was born in Aalst, Belgium, in 1984. He is a founding member of Rotor, created in 2005. **TRISTAN BONIVER** was born in Brussels in 1976 and his currently finishing his M.Arch. at La Cambre Architecture Institute, Brussels. He is another founding member of the team. **LIONEL DEVLIEGER** was born in Rwamagana, Rwanda, in 1972. He obtained his Master's in Architecture and Urbanism degree from Ghent University (1996) and a Ph.D. in Engineering Sciences—Architecture from the same university in 2005. He has been an active member of Rotor since 2006. **MIA SCHMALLENBACH** was born in Canberra, Australia, in 1982. She received her Master's in Industrial Design from La Cambre Art Institute, Brussels (2008), and was an active member of Rotor from 2006 to 2008. Their recent projects include RDF181, temporary offices (Brussels, Belgium, 2007, published here); *Deutschland im Herbst* exhibition at the Ursula Blickle Stiftung (Kraichtal, Germany, 2008); and the Kunstenfestivaldesarts 2009 (Festival Center, Brussels, Belgium, 2009).

Die Partner der gemeinnützigen Organisation Rotor definieren sich als „Plattform für die Wiederverwertung von Industriemüll. Rotor will, unter anderem, Kontakte zwischen den Produzenten ‚interessanter' Abfälle und potenzieller Wiederverwender in Industrie, Design und Architektur fördern." **MAARTEN GIELEN** wurde 1984 in Aalst, Belgien, geboren. Er war eines der Gründungsmitglieder von Rotor. **TRISTAN BONIVER** wurde 1976 in Brüssel geboren und absolviert derzeit seinen M. Arch. am Architekturinstitut der Kunsthochschule La Cambre in Brüssel. Auch er zählt zu den Gründungsmitgliedern des Teams. **LIONEL DEVLIEGER** wurde 1972 in Rwamagana, Ruanda, geboren. Er absolvierte seinen Master in Architektur und Stadtplanung an der Universität Gent (1996) und promovierte 2005 in Ingenieurwissenschaften/Architektur an derselben Universität. Er ist seit 2006 aktives Mitglied bei Rotor. **MIA SCHMALLENBACH** wurde 1982 in Canberra, Australien, geboren. Sie absolvierte ihren Master in Industriedesign an der Kunsthochschule La Cambre, Brüssel (2008), und war zwischen 2006 und 2008 aktives Mitglied bei Rotor. Ihre jüngsten Projekte sind u. a. RDF181, temporäre Büros (Brüssel, 2007, hier vorgestellt), „Deutschland im Herbst", Ausstellung der Ursula Blickle Stiftung (Kraichtal, Deutschland, 2008), sowie das KunstenfestivaldesArts 2009 (Festival Center, Brüssel, 2009).

Les responsables de Rotor, association à but non lucratif créée en 2005, la présentent comme une « plate-forme pour la défense de la réutilisation des déchets industriels ». Rotor souhaite, entre autres, encourager les contacts entre les producteurs de déchets "intéressants" et leurs réutilisateurs potentiels dans le domaine de l'industrie, du design et de l'architecture ». **MAARTEN GIELEN**, né à Aalst (Belgique) en 1984, est membre fondateur de Rotor. **TRISTAN BONIVER**, né à Bruxelles en 1976, termine actuellement son M.Arch à l'Institut d'architecture de La Cambre à Bruxelles et a également participé à la fondation de Rotor. **LIONEL DEVLIEGER**, né à Rwamagana (Rwanda) en 1972, a obtenu son mastère en architecture et urbanisme de l'Université de Gand (1996), et son Ph. D en sciences de l'ingénierie-architecture de la même université, en 2005. Il est membre actif de Rotor depuis 2006. **MIA SCHMALLENBACH**, née à Canberra (Australie) en 1982, a passé son mastère en design industriel à l'Institut d'art de La Cambre Art (2008) et a été membre actif de Rotor de 2006 à 2008. Leurs projets récents comprennent RDF181, les bureaux temporaires du groupe (Bruxelles, 2007, publié ici) ; « Deutschland im Herbst », exposition à la Fondation Ursula Blickle (Kraichtal, Allemagne, 2008) et le KunstenfestivaldesArts 2009 (Centre des festivals, Bruxelles, 2009).

RDF181

Brussels, Belgium, 2007

Area: 60 m² (plus 60 m² terrace). Client: Rotor Vzw.
Cost: €3000 + 500 hours of voluntary work.

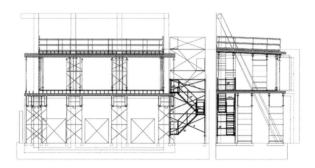

This "parasite" structure was designed as an office for Rotor. It was entirely made of waste materials: "A rejected lot of plastic film, old exhibition material and transparent sailcloth for the windows, EVA1 foam to insulate the roof, plastic van cladding as terrace paving, and materials they have borrowed from building firms for the structure: props, struts, and formwork beams." Located on a site where a developer intended to build a new structure, RDF181 was built without any application for planning permission, but with the permission of the owner, a situation Rotor calls "legal squatting." The owner required the use of the ground level for parking, thus the structure is lifted off the ground. RDF181 was in place for one year and served as a demonstration of the group's thesis that other methods of construction and occupation of cities are possible. Similar efforts exist in other countries, such as Recetas Urbanas in Spain (Santiago Cirugeda).

Die „parasitäre" Konstruktion wurde als Büroraum für Rotor geplant. Sie besteht vollständig aus Abfallmaterialien: „Ein ausgemusterter Posten Plastikfolie, alte Ausstellungsmaterialien und transparentes Segeltuch für die Fenster, EVA-1-Schaumstoff zur Dämmung des Dachs, Kunststoff-LKW-Plane als Terrassenbelag und Materialien, die von Baufirmen leihweise zur Verfügung gestellt wurden: Stützen, Druckstreben und Schalungsgerüstelemente." RDF181 wurde auf einem Grundstück errichtet, auf dem ein Neubau in Planung war. Ohne Baugenehmigung, jedoch mit Genehmigung des Eigentümers war das Vorgehen Rotor zufolge eine „legale Hausbesetzung". Der Eigentümer nutzte die Straßenebene als Parkplatz, weshalb der Bau aufgeständert wurde. RDF181 bestand ein Jahr und ist ein Beleg für die These der Gruppe, dass alternative Bau- und Nutzungsmodelle in der Stadt möglich sind. Ähnliche Initiativen gibt es auch in anderen Ländern, etwa Recetas Urbanas (Santiago Cirugeda) in Spanien.

Cette structure « parasite » a été conçue pour servir de bureaux à Rotor. Elle a été entièrement réalisée en matériaux de récupération : « Un lot de film plastique rejeté, une vieille toile transparente, du vieux matériel d'exposition et de la toile de voile pour les fenêtres, de la mousse EVA1 pour isoler le toit, de l'habillage plastique de caravanes pour servir de pavement en terrasse et des matériaux obtenus auprès d'entreprises de construction pour la structure : poteaux, étrésillons et poutres de coffrage. » Implanté sur un terrain sur lequel un promoteur projetait un nouvel immeuble, RDF181 a été construit sans demande de permis de construire, mais avec l'autorisation du propriétaire – situation qualifiée de « squat légal » par Rotor. Le propriétaire souhaitait conserver l'utilisation du sol pour garer des voitures, ce qui explique que la structure soit suspendue. RDF181 est resté en place pendant un an et a servi à démontrer la thèse du groupe qui veut que d'autres méthodes de construction et d'occupation sont possibles dans les villes. Des expériences similaires ont été tentées dans d'autres pays, comme celle de Recetas Urbanas en Espagne (Santiago Cirugeda).

An intentionally temporary extrusion above an empty lot, RDF181 is a commentary on the voids that populate modern cities.

RDF181 ist ein bewusst temporärer Anbau über einem ungenutzten Baugrundstück und zugleich ein Kommentar zu den Brachflächen, die sich durch die modernen Städte ziehen.

Bâtiment temporaire qui se projette au-dessus d'une parcelle vide, le RDF181 est aussi un commentaire sur les vides urbains dans les villes modernes.

Materials and spaces are in keeping
with the ephemeral nature of the
structure. Rough materials echo the
external appearance of the office.

Materialien und Räume spiegeln die
kurzlebige Natur des Baus wider. Die
groben Materialien korrespondieren
mit dem äußeren Erscheinungsbild
des Büros.

Les matériaux et les volumes sont
en accord avec la nature éphémère
de cette construction. Les matériaux
bruts s'harmonisent avec l'aspect
extérieur de ces bureaux.

The office grafts itself onto the
existing elements of the site—a
building wall or a leaning support
column.

*Das Büro schreibt sich in die beste-
henden architektonischen Elemente
des Grundstücks ein – sei es eine
Brandmauer oder eine Druckstrebe.*

*Les bureaux se greffent sur des
éléments existants : le mur d'un
immeuble ou des étais de soutien.*

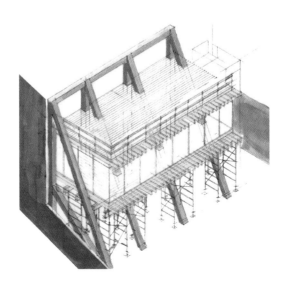

444

DAVID SALMELA

Born in 1945 in Minnesota, USA, **DAVID SALMELA** has worked in architecture since 1969, but is self-trained. He founded his firm, Salmela Architecture, in 1994, and has received an Honorary Doctorate of Humane Letters (University of Minnesota, 2007) and an AIA Minnesota Gold Medal (2008). His Bagley Outdoor Classroom Building (University of Minnesota Duluth, 2010) received a 2012 National AIA COTE Top Ten Green Project Award. Other work includes the Streeter House (Deephaven, Minnesota, 2005), which won the Home of the Year Award from *Architect Magazine* (2006); the Clure Project (Duluth, Minnesota, 2007); Hawks Boots (Duluth, Minnesota, 2008); and the Yingst Pavilion and Sauna (Traverse City, Michigan, 2010, published here), all in the USA.

DAVID SALMELA, geboren 1945 in Minnesota, USA, ist seit 1969 im Architekturbereich tätig, ist aber Autodidakt. 1994 gründete er sein Büro, Salmela Architecture, ist seit 2007 Ehrendoktor der University of Minnesota und erhielt 2008 eine Goldmedaille der AIA Minnesota. Sein Bagley Outdoor Classroom Building (University of Minnesota Duluth, 2010) wurde 2012 mit einem National AIA COTE Top Ten Green Project Award ausgezeichnet. Zu seinen weiteren Arbeiten gehören u. a. das Streeter House (Deephaven, Minnesota, 2005), das 2006 mit dem Preis Home of the Year des *Architect Magazine* ausgezeichnet wurde, das Clure Project (Duluth, Minnesota, 2007), Hawks Boots (Duluth, Minnesota, 2008) und der Pavillon und die Sauna des Ferienhauses Yingst (Traverse City, Michigan, 2010, hier vorgestellt), alle in den USA.

Né en 1945 dans le Minnesota, **DAVID SALMELA** travaille dans l'architecture depuis 1969, mais est autodidacte. Il a fondé son agence, Salmela Architecture, en 1994. Il a été nommé docteur honoris causa de lettres (université du Minnesota, 2007) et a reçu une médaille d'or de l'AIA Minnesota (2008). Sa salle de classe extérieure Bagley (université du Minnesota Duluth, 2010) a été récompensée par le prix national AIA COTE 2012 Top Ten Green Project. Ses autres réalisations comprennent la Streeter House (Deephaven, Minnesota, 2005) qui a remporté le prix de la maison de l'année de l'*Architect Magazine* (2006) ; le projet Clure (Duluth, Minnesota, 2007) ; Hawks Boots (Duluth, 2008) et le pavillon et sauna Yingst (Traverse City, Michigan ; 2010, publié ici), toutes aux États-Unis.

YINGST PAVILION AND SAUNA

Traverse City, Michigan, USA, 2010

Area: 39 m². Client: Bonnie and Doug Yingst.
Cost: $23 000.

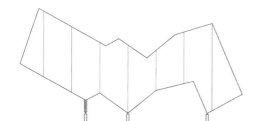

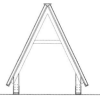

This metal pavilion assumes an unusual shape, as seen in the photo
and particularly in the elevation
drawing on the left page.

*Der metallene Pavillon hat eine
ausgefallene Form, wie das Foto,
vor allem aber die Ansichtszeich-
nung auf der linken Seite belegen.*

*Ce pavillon métallique présente
une forme inhabituelle, comme le
montrent la photo et surtout le plan
en élévation sur la page de gauche.*

An exploded axonometric drawing
(left) shows the structure, also
revealed by the image (above) of the
space in use in the summer.

*Eine axonometrische Explosions-
zeichnung (links) verdeutlicht den
Aufbau, den auch das Bild des Gebäudes (oben) während der Nutzung
im Sommer zeigt.*

*Le schéma axonométrique éclaté
(à gauche) montre la structure telle
qu'elle est aussi révélée par la
photo (ci-dessus) de l'espace utilisé
en été.*

Located on a wooded 6.5-hectare site five kilometers from Lake Michigan, the Yingst Pavilion and Sauna are part of a larger retreat that includes a house and annex structures also designed by David Salmela. For the pavilion, three structural timber frames were used to create an armature for two 9.7-meter flat trusses that were laid at angles and then fastened. Black Richlite panels were used for exterior cladding. The pavilion is situated near a bocce ball court. The architect states: "From simple techniques, the exposed framing beneath inherits complexity and intrigue disguised by the relatively flat façade. Seen from the house, the pavilion rests beyond the courtyard against the backdrop of a forest. It is a unique, black object that stimulates the imagination in both intellectual and emotional ways." The white sauna has a sod roof that makes it blend into the forest background. The Yingst Pavilion was awarded a 2011 National AIA Small Projects Award.

Der Pavillon und die Sauna des Ferienhauses Yingst liegen auf einem 6,5 ha großen Waldgrundstück 5 km vom Lake Michigan entfernt und gehören zu einem größeren Komplex mit Haupthaus und verschiedenen Anbauten, die ebenfalls David Salmela entworfen hat. Für den Pavillon wurde mittels dreier Holzrahmen eine Trägerkonstruktion für zwei flache Traversen von je 9,7 m Länge geschaffen, die im Winkel zueinander fixiert wurden. Für die äußere Verblendung wurden schwarze Richlite-Platten verwendet. Gleich neben dem Pavillon befindet sich eine Bocciabahn. Der Architekt erklärt: „Komplexität und Faszination der freiliegenden Unterkonstruktion, verborgen von der relativ unscheinbaren Fassade, fußen auf eher simplen Techniken. Vom Haupthaus aus gesehen, steht der Pavillon jenseits des Hofes vor dem Hintergrund des Waldes. Es ist ein schwarzes, einmaliges Objekt, das die Fantasie sowohl intellektuell als auch emotional anregt." Das weiße Saunahaus hat ein Rasendach, das mit dem Wald im Hintergrund optisch eins wird. Der Yingst-Pavillon erhielt 2011 den National AIA Small Projects Award.

Construits sur un terrain boisé de 6,5 ha à 5 km du lac Michigan, le pavillon et le sauna Yingst font partie d'un complexe plus important qui comprend une maison de repos et d'autres structures annexes, également conçues par David Salmela. La charpente en bois d'œuvre du pavillon forme trois armatures pour deux fermes de 9,7 m qui ont été posées en biais et fixées. Des panneaux de Richlite noir ont été utilisés pour le revêtement extérieur. Le pavillon est situé à proximité d'un terrain de boules. L'architecte constate : « À partir de techniques simples, la charpente apparente sous la toiture hérite de la complexité et du mystère dissimulés par la façade relativement plane. Vu de la maison, le pavillon repose au fond de la cour avec la forêt en toile de fond. C'est un objet noir original qui stimule l'imagination sur le plan émotionnel autant qu'intellectuel. » Le sauna blanc a un toit recouvert de mottes de gazon qui le fait se fondre dans le décor forestier. Le pavillon Yingst a reçu un prix national de l'AIA du petit projet en 2011.

The sauna has extremely simple lines and is hidden in a forest grove. A green roof participates in the bucolic image of this realization.

Die Linienführung der in einem Waldstück versteckten Sauna ist extrem schlicht. Das grüne Dach trägt zur bukolischen Anmutung des Baus bei.

Le sauna a des lignes extrêmement simples et est caché dans un bosquet. Le toit végétalisé contribue à son image bucolique.

TODD SAUNDERS

TODD SAUNDERS was born in 1969 in Gander, Newfoundland, Canada. He obtained his M.Arch. from McGill University (Montreal, Canada, 1993–95) and a Bachelor of Environmental Planning from the Nova Scotia College of Art and Design (1988–92). He has worked in Austria, Germany, Russia, Latvia, and Norway (since 1996). He teaches part-time at the Bergen School of Architecture. His work includes the Aurland Lookout (with Tommie Wilhelmsen, Aurland, 2006); Villa Storingavika (Bergen, 2004–07); Villa G (Hjellestad, Bergen, 2007–09); Sogn og Fjordane Summer Cabin (Rysjedalsvika, 2007–10, published here); and Solberg Tower and Park (Sarpsborg, Østfold, 2010), all in Norway. He is currently realizing the Fogo Island Studios (Fogo Island, Newfoundland, Canada, 2010–11), four of which out of a program of six have been completed as well as the Fogo Island Inn (2013) in the same location.

TODD SAUNDERS wurde 1969 in Gander, Neufundland, Kanada, geboren. Er machte seinen M. Arch. an der McGill University (Montreal, 1993–95) sowie einen Bachelor in Umweltplanung am Nova Scotia College of Art and Design (1988–92). Er war in Österreich, Deutschland, Russland, Lettland und Norwegen (seit 1996) tätig, wo er in Teilzeit an der Architekturfakultät von Bergen lehrt. Zu seinen Projekten zählen der Aurland-Aussichtspunkt (mit Tommie Wilhelmsen, Aurland, 2006), die Villa Storingavika (Bergen, 2004–07), die Villa G (Hjellestad, Bergen, 2007–09), das Ferienhaus Sogn og Fjordane (Rysjedalsvika, 2007–10, hier vorgestellt) und der Solberg-Turm und -Park (Sarpsborg, Østfold, 2010), alle in Norwegen. Aktuell arbeitet er an den Fogo Island Studios, vier der insgesamt sechs Ateliers für Künstler (Fogo Island, Neufundland, 2010–11) sowie das Fogo Island Inn (2013) am selben Standort sind bereits fertiggestellt.

Né en 1969 à Gander (Terre-Neuve, Canada), **TODD SAUNDERS** a obtenu son M.Arch à l'université McGill (Montréal, 1993–95) et un bachelor en planification environnementale au Collège d'art et de design de la Nouvelle-Écosse (1988–92). Il a travaillé en Autriche, Allemagne, Russie, Lituanie et Norvège (depuis 1996). Il enseigne à temps partiel à l'École d'architecture de Bergen. Parmi ses réalisations, toutes en Norvège : le belvédère d'Aurland (avec Tommie Wilhelmsen, Aurland, 2006) ; la villa Storingavika (Bergen, 2004–07) ; la villa G (Hjellestad, Bergen, 2007–09) ; la maison de vacances Sogn og Fjordane (Rysjedalsvika, 2007-10, publiée ici) et la tour et le parc Solberg (Sarpsborg, Østfold, 2010). Il travaille en ce moment aux ateliers sur l'île de Fogo (Terre-Neuve, Canada, 2010–11), où quatre sur six ateliers et l'hôtel Fogo Island Inn (2013) sont déjà achevés.

SOGN OG FJORDANE
SUMMER CABIN
Rysjedalsvika, Norway, 2007–10

Area: 80 m². Client: Inger Løland and Svein Halvorsen.
Cost: $344 600. Collaboration: Tommie Wilhelmsen.

"This little vacation cabin is essentially two separate freestanding parts linked together by a common floating roof," explains Todd Saunders. Located in the western county of Sogn og Fjordane, the sloped site offers views of the fjord. One rectangular volume contains the parents' bedroom and bathroom, kitchen, and sitting area, while the smaller part contains two bedrooms for children. Interior cladding is in birch plywood. The roof, supported by metal columns, offers covering for outdoor terraces and, as the architect explains: "The whole structure floats above the ground, creating as minimal an interference with the existing natural landscape as possible."

„Dieses kleine Ferienhaus besteht im Grunde aus zwei separaten, frei stehenden Teilen, die durch ein gewöhnliches flaches Dach verbunden sind", erläutert Todd Saunders. Der abschüssige Standort in der westlichen Provinz Sogn og Fjordane bietet einen Blick auf den Fjord. Das eine rechteckige Gebäude enthält das Elternschlafzimmer sowie Bad, Küche und Wohnbereich, im kleineren Teil befinden sich zwei Kinderzimmer. Die Innenausbauten bestehen aus Birkensperrholz. Das Dach, gestützt von Metallstützen, schützt den Terrassenbereich im Freien. „Die ganze Konstruktion scheint zu schweben", so der Architekt. „Sie soll so wenig wie möglich in die natürliche Umgebung eingreifen."

«Cette petite maison de vacances est essentiellement composée de deux parties indépendantes reliées par un toit flottant commun», explique Todd Saunders. Situé dans le comté occidental de Sogn og Fjordane, le terrain en pente a vue sur le fjord. Un volume rectangulaire abrite la chambre des parents et la salle de bains, la cuisine et un espace salon, tandis que la partie plus petite contient deux chambres d'enfants. L'intérieur est revêtu de bouleau contreplaqué. Le toit, porté par des colonnes métalliques, couvre aussi les terrasses et, comme l'explique l'architecte : «La structure dans son ensemble flotte au-dessus du sol pour limiter le plus possible les interférences avec le paysage naturel.»

The rather thick connecting roof, an essential part of the project, is seen here connecting the two elements of the design but also covering the outdoor passage and terrace.

Hier ist das recht wuchtige Dach zu sehen, ein zentraler Bestandteil des Projekts, der nicht nur die beiden Elemente des Entwurfs verbindet, sondern auch Zwischengang und Terrasse Schutz bietet.

On voit ici l'épais toit commun, un élément essentiel du projet, qui relie les deux parties de la maison et couvre le passage extérieur et la terrasse.

KAZUYO SEJIMA

Born in Ibaraki Prefecture, Japan, in 1956, **KAZUYO SEJIMA** received her M.Arch. degree from the Japan Women's University in 1981 and went on to work in the office of Toyo Ito the same year. She established Kazuyo Sejima & Associates in Tokyo in 1987. Ryue Nishizawa was born in Tokyo in 1966, and graduated from the National University (Yokohama, 1990). He began working with Sejima the same year, and the pair created the new firm Kazuyo Sejima + Ryue Nishizawa / SANAA in 1995. SANAA was awarded the 2010 Pritzker Prize. The work of SANAA includes the 21st Century Museum of Contemporary Art (Kanazawa, Ishikawa, Japan, 2002–04); and abroad, for the first time, the Glass Pavilion of the Toledo Museum of Art (Ohio, USA, 2003–06); and a theater and cultural center in Almere (De Kunstlinie, The Netherlands, 2004–07). In terms of media exposure, they reached still higher with the New Museum of Contemporary Art, located on the Bowery in New York (New York, USA, 2005–07); and the vast open spaces of the Rolex Learning Center at the EPFL in Lausanne (Switzerland, 2007–09). Recent work of SANAA includes the Louvre-Lens (Lens, France, 2009–12). The Tsuchihashi House (Tokyo, Japan, 2011, published here) and the Inujima Art House Project (Okayama, Japan, 2009–10, also published here) were the work of Sejima's original firm, Kazuyo Sejima & Associates.

Die in der Präfektur Ibaraki geborene **KAZUYO SEJIMA** erlangte ihren M. Arch. 1981 an der Japanischen Frauenuniversität und begann noch im selben Jahr, für Toyo Ito zu arbeiten. 1987 gründete sie in Tokio ihr Büro Kazuyo Sejima & Associates. Ryue Nishizawa wurde 1966 in Tokio geboren und schloss sein Studium 1990 an der Nationaluniversität in Yokohama ab. Noch im selben Jahr begann er, mit Sejima zu arbeiten. Gemeinsam gründeten sie 1995 das neue Büro Kazuyo Sejima + Ryue Nishizawa/SANAA. 2010 wurde SANAA mit dem Pritzker-Preis ausgezeichnet. Zum Werk von SANAA zählen das Museum für Kunst des 21. Jahrhunderts (Kanazawa, Ishikawa, Japan, 2002–04) und, als erstes Projekt im Ausland, der Glaspavillon am Toledo Museum of Art (Ohio, 2003–06) sowie ein Theater und Kulturzentrum in Almere (De Kunstlinie, Niederlande, 2004–07). Noch größere Aufmerksamkeit der Medien wurde dem Team durch das New Museum of Contemporary Art an der Bowery in New York (2007) und die weitläufigen, offenen Räume des Rolex Learning Center an der EPFL in Lausanne (Schweiz, 2009) zuteil. Zu den jüngeren Projekten von SANAA gehört der Louvre-Lens (Lens, Frankreich, 2009–12). Das Tsuchihashi House (Tokio, 2011, hier vorgestellt) und das Inujima Art House Projekt (Okayama, Japan, 2009–10, ebenfalls hier vorgestellt) sind Entwürfe von Sejimas ursprünglichem Büro, Kazuyo Sejima & Associates.

Née dans la préfecture d'Ibaraki en 1956, **KAZUYO SEJIMA** obtient son M.Arch de l'Université féminine du Japon en 1981 et est engagée par Toyo Ito la même année. Elle crée l'agence Kazuyo Sejima & Associates à Tokyo en 1987. Ryue Nishizawa, né à Tokyo en 1966, est diplômé de l'Université nationale de Yokohama (1990). Il a commencé à travailler avec Sejima la même année avant qu'ils ne fondent ensemble Kazuyo Sejima + Ryue Nishizawa / SANAA en 1995. SANAA a reçu le prix Pritzker en 2010. Parmi les réalisations de l'agence figurent : le Musée d'art contemporain du XXIᵉ siècle (Kanazawa, Ishikawa, 2002–04) ; le pavillon de verre du Musée d'art de Toledo (Ohio, 2003–06), première de leurs réalisations à l'étranger, et un théâtre et centre culturel à Almere (De Kunstlinie, Pays-Bas, 2004–07). Leur notoriété internationale s'est encore élargie avec des œuvres comme le New Museum of Contemporary Art sur le Bowery à New York (2005–07) et les vastes espaces ouverts du Rolex Learning Center à l'EPFL de Lausanne (Suisse, 2007–09). Leurs projets récents comprennent le Louvre-Lens (France, 2009–12). La maison Tsuchihashi (Tokyo, 2011, publiée ici) et le projet de la maison d'art Inujima (Okayama, Japon, 2009–10, également publiée ici) sont l'œuvre de l'agence d'origine de Sejima, Kazuyo Sejima & Associates.

TSUCHIHASHI HOUSE

Tokyo, Japan, 2011

Area: 30 m².

Verticality is stressed in this house that has a full-height atrium that connects interior levels while allowing natural light to be very present. Stairways link the levels, on alternating sides of the interior. The basement level is occupied by the main living space, kitchen and dining area are at ground level, and bathroom and bedrooms above. The floors are formed by 25-millimeter corrugated steel decking on steel plate. A rooftop terrace provides even more direct contact with "nature" than the interior light, although the Japanese consider light or breeze to be a manifestation of nature in a more direct way than might be assumed in the West.

Die Betonung liegt auf Vertikalität bei diesem Haus, dessen Atrium sich über die Gesamthöhe erstreckt, die verschiedenen Ebenen miteinander verbindet und für viel natürliches Licht im Haus sorgt. An wechselnden Seiten führen Treppen auf die verschiedenen Ebenen. Der zentrale Lebensbereich befindet sich im Untergeschoss, Küche und Essbereich liegen ebenerdig und Bad und Schlafzimmer oben. Die Böden bestehen aus stählernen Profilplatten von 25 mm Stärke, die auf Stahlschwellen aufliegen. Eine Dachterrasse ermöglicht einen noch direkteren Kontakt zur „Natur" als nur durch das einfallende Licht, auch wenn sich für Japaner in Licht oder Wind die Natur bereits wesentlich unmittelbarer manifestiert, als im Westen angenommen wird.

Cette maison met l'accent sur la verticalité avec l'atrium sur toute la hauteur, qui fait communiquer les différents niveaux à l'intérieur tout en laissant entrer beaucoup de lumière naturelle. L'escalier relie les différents niveaux disposés de manière alternée. Le sous-sol est occupé par le principal espace séjour, la cuisine et le coin repas sont au niveau du sol, la salle de bains et les chambres au-dessus. Les sols sont faits d'acier ondulé de 25 mm sur des plaques d'acier. Une terrasse sur le toit offre un contact encore plus direct que la seule luminosité intérieure avec la « nature », même si les Japonais considèrent la lumière ou le vent comme des manifestations de la nature plus directes qu'on ne le penserait en Occident.

Like a number of her architect colleagues, Sejima has wholeheartedly taken up the idea of houses that are very open inside, with mezzanine levels and stairways connecting them, as seen in the images on this double page.

Wie viele ihrer Kollegen hat auch Sejima sich vorbehaltlos dem Ideal eines im Innern sehr offenen Hauses verschrieben, mit Zwischengeschossen und verbindenden Treppen, wie auf den Bildern dieser Doppelseite zu sehen ist.

Comme bon nombre de ses collègues architectes, Sejima a repris sans réserves l'idée de maisons très ouvertes à l'intérieur, avec des mezzanines et des escaliers pour les relier.

INUJIMA ART HOUSE PROJECT

Inujima, Okayama, Japan, 2009–10

Area: F-Art House (114 m²); S-Art House (64 m²); I-Art House (40 m²);
Nakanotani Gazebo (62 m²). Client: Naoshima Fukutake Art Museum Foundation.

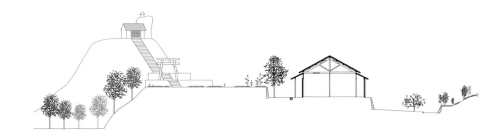

Like the Teshima Art Museum by Ryue Nishizawa, these structures were built on a small island in the Inland Sea of Japan for the same client as Tadao Ando's Naoshima projects. "Our project," says Sejima, "is designed to breathe new life into this village by making exhibition spaces in and around the existing townscape." The exhibition spaces are created by renovating abandoned houses and their surroundings. Some houses were rebuilt using translucent acrylic and aluminum because their structure was no longer viable. These art exhibition spaces are scattered around the village and are meant to blend into the existing landscape. Mirror-finish aluminum is used in the case of row houses "so that the surrounding houses and lives therein are reflected into the exhibition spaces." Sejima explains that the whole becomes "a new landscape including the various previous existing residences; architecture and art become one with the peaceful local scenery. We aimed to create a new type of museum where the whole village is a museum and the environment itself brings new scenery," she concludes.

Wie auch das Teshima Art Museum von Ryue Nishizawa wurden diese Bauten auf einer kleinen Insel in der Seto-Inlandsee in Auftrag gegeben – vom selben Bauherrn, der auch Tadao Andos Projekte in Naoshima beauftragt hatte. „Unser Projekt", so Sejima, „wurde konzipiert, um dem Dorf neues Leben einzuhauchen, indem es Ausstellungsflächen in und um die bestehende Dorflandschaft herum schafft." Die Ausstellungsräume entstanden durch die Sanierung verlassener Häuser und deren Umfeld. Manche Häuser wurden mithilfe von transparentem Acrylglas und Aluminium neu errichtet, weil ihr Tragwerk nicht mehr belastbar war. Die Ausstellungsräume sind im ganzen Dorf verstreut und sollen mit der Landschaft verschmelzen. Bei einigen Reihenhäusern arbeitete Sejima mit spiegelnd poliertem Aluminium, „sodass sich die Nachbarbauten und die darin Lebenden in den Ausstellungsräumen spiegeln". Sejima erklärt, das Ganze füge sich zu „einer neuen Landschaft, zu der auch viele ältere Wohnbauten gehören, Architektur und Kunst werden eins mit der friedlichen Umgebung. Wir wollten eine neue Form von Museum schaffen, bei der das gesamte Dorf zum Museum wird und die Umgebung selbst für eine stets neue Kulisse sorgt."

Comme le Musée d'art de Teshima de Ryue Nishizawa, ces constructions sont situées sur une petite île de la Mer intérieure du Japon et ont été réalisées pour le même client que celles de Tadao Ando à Naoshima. «Notre projet, explique Sejima, est conçu pour insuffler une vie nouvelle dans ce village par la présence de lieux d'exposition dans et autour de l'urbanisation existante.» Les espaces d'exposition occupent des maisons abandonnées rénovées, ainsi que leur environnement. Certaines ont été reconstruites en aluminium et panneaux d'acrylique transparents quand leur structure était trop vétuste. Ces petits espaces d'exposition se répartissent dans le village tout entier et se fondent dans le paysage. Pour certaines maisons alignées, l'architecte a utilisé des panneaux d'aluminium poli miroir «pour que les maisons voisines et leur vie se reflètent dans les espaces d'exposition». Sejima explique que l'ensemble devient «un nouveau paysage qui comprend diverses maisons existantes ; l'art et l'architecture ne forment plus qu'un avec ce cadre villageois paisible. Nous avons voulu créer un nouveau type de musée dans lequel le village tout entier devenait musée, et l'environnement lui-même un nouveau cadre».

The F-Art House has an unusual undulating garden gallery added on to
its rectangular volume. This element
is seen in the image below.

Das rechteckige Volumen des F-Art
House wurde um eine ungewöhnliche, geschwungene Gartengalerie
ergänzt. Unten ein Blick auf dieses
bauliche Element.

La maison F-Art de plan rectangulaire a reçu une étonnante galerie
de jardin de forme ondulée (photographie ci-dessous).

In the center, a section drawing of
the S-Art House in its site. Left and
below, a covered walkway runs near
the S-Art House.

*In der Mitte ein Querschnitt des
S-Art House in seinem Umfeld. Links
und unten ein überdachter Gang,
der unweit des S-Art House verläuft.*

*Au milieu, une coupe de la maison
S-Art sur son terrain. À gauche et
ci-dessous, une passerelle couverte
près de la maison.*

On this page an image and a section drawing of the gazebo structure designed for Inujima by Kazuyo Sejima.

Auf dieser Seite eine Ansicht und ein Querschnitt des Gartenpavillons, den Kazuyo Sejima für Inujima entwarf.

Photographie et dessin de coupe du belvédère conçu par Kazuyo Sejima pour Inujima.

SO-IL

FLORIAN IDENBURG was born in 1975 in Heemstede, The Netherlands. He received an M.Sc. degree in Architectural Engineering from the Technical University of Delft (1999), and worked with SANAA in Tokyo from 2000 to 2007. **JING LIU** was born in 1980 in Nanjing, China. She received her M.Arch. II degree from Tulane University in 2004 and worked from 2004 to 2007 with KPF in New York. Recent work includes Upto35, student housing (Athens, Greece, competition winner 2009); The Hague Dance and Music Center (The Netherlands, competition 2010); the Pole Dance installation (PS1, Long Island City, New York, USA, 2010); Park Pavilion (Amsterdam, The Netherlands, project 2010–11); Tri-Colonnade (Shenzhen, China, 2011, published here); Wedding Chapel (Nanjing, China, 2008–12); Kukje Art Gallery (Seoul, South Korea, 2009–12); Housing Block (Athens, Greece, project 2010–12); an installation for the *Frieze Art Fair* (New York, USA, 2012); and the installation Spiky for the *China International Architecture Biennial* (2013, Beijing, China). They are presently working on the Jan Shrem and Maria Manetti Shrem Museum of Art at the University of California (Davis, California, USA, 2016).

FLORIAN IDENBURG wurde 1975 in Heemstede, Niederlande, geboren. Er erwarb sein Diplom in Bauingenieurwesen an der Technischen Universität Delft (1999) und arbeitete dann von 2000 bis 2007 bei SANAA in Tokio. **JING LIU** wurde 1980 in Nanjing, China, geboren. Sie machte 2004 ihren M. Arch. II an der Tulane University und arbeitete von 2004 bis 2007 bei KPF in New York. Zu ihren jüngeren Arbeiten gehören Studentenwohnungen für den Wettbewerb Upto35 (Athen, Wettbewerbssieger, 2009), das Zentrum für Tanz und Musik in Den Haag (Niederlande, Wettbewerb, 2010), die Installation Pole Dance (PS1, Long Island City, New York, 2010), ein Parkpavillon (Amsterdam, Projekt 2010–11), Tri-Colonnade (Shenzhen, China, 2011, hier vorgestellt), eine Hochzeitskapelle (Nanjing, China, 2008–12), die Kunstgalerie Kukje (Seoul, Südkorea, 2009–12), ein Wohnbock (Athen, Projekt 2010–12), eine Installation für die Frieze Art Fair (New York, 2012) und die Installation Spiky für die Internationale Architektur-Biennale in China (Peking, 2013). Derzeit arbeiten sie an dem Jan Shrem and Maria Manetti Shrem Museum of Art an der University of California (Davis, Kalifornien, 2016).

FLORIAN IDENBURG est né en 1975 à Heemstede, aux Pays-Bas. Il est titulaire d'un M.Sc. en génie du bâtiment de l'Université technique de Delft (1999) et a travaillé avec SANAA à Tokyo de 2000 à 2007. **JING LIU** est née en 1980 à Nanjing, en Chine. Elle a obtenu son M.Arch. II à l'université Tulane en 2004 et a ensuite travaillé jusqu'en 2007 avec KPF à New York. Leurs réalisations récentes comprennent la résidence étudiante Upto35 (Athènes, vainqueur de la compétition 2009) ; le Centre de la danse et de la musique de La Haye (en compétition 2010) ; l'installation *Pole Dance* (PS1, Long Island City, New York, 2010) ; un pavillon de parc (Amsterdam, projet 2010–11) ; la *Tri-Colonnade* (Shenzhen, Chine, 2011, publié ici) ; une chapelle de mariage (Nanjing, Chine, 2008–12) ; la galerie d'art Kukje (Seoul, 2009–12) ; un bloc résidentiel (Athènes, projet 2010–12) ; une installation pour la Frieze Art Fair (New York, 2012) et l'installation *Spiky* pour la Biennale internationale d'architecture de Chine (Pékin, 2013). Ils travaillent actuellement au musée d'art Jan Shrem et Maria Manetti Shrem à l'université de Californie (Davis, 2016).

TRI-COLONNADE
Shenzhen, China, 2011

Area: 24 m².
Client: Shenzhen Hong Kong Bi-City Biennale.

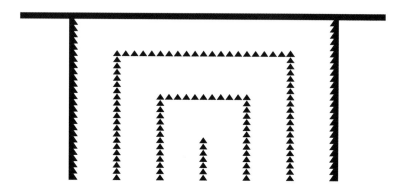

Tri-Colonnade was the architects' contribution to the exhibition *The Street* in the context of the *Shenzhen Hong Kong Bi-City Biennale*, curated by Terence Riley. Riley's concept was to recreate the "Strada Novissima," part of the 1980 *Venice Biennale* in which 20 architects—including Frank Gehry, Rem Koolhaas, and Aldo Rossi—designed parts of a façade in the central alley of the show. Florian Idenburg states: "As the historic 1980 exhibition has come to represent a moment of architecture's fixation on the symbolic façade, 2011 marks an anxiety that architecture itself has collapsed into nothing more than skin. The proposal, through a kind of reinvented colonnade, seeks to spatialize and instrumentalize what has become implicitly flat. The 'façade' unfolds, and becomes itself the space of occupation and exhibition." Fake marble (1 mm laminate with a marble print) marks the front of the columns with mirrors on the back, giving the impression that the marble expands as visitors approach it.

Tri-Colonnade war der Beitrag der Architekten zur Ausstellung „The Street", die, kuratiert von Terence Riley, im Rahmen der Shenzhen Hong Kong Bi-City Biennale stattfand. Rileys Idee war es, die „Strada Novissima", Teil der Biennale von 1980, für die 20 Architekten – unter ihnen Frank Gehry, Rem Koolhaas und Aldo Rossi – Teile einer Fassade im Hauptgang der Ausstellung entworfen hatten, neu zu interpretieren. Florian Idenburg dazu: „So wie die historische Ausstellung von 1980 mittlerweile für die Fixierung der Architektur auf die symbolische Fassade steht, ist 2011 die Angst prägend, dass von der Architektur nur noch die Oberfläche existiert. Der Entwurf in Form einer neu erfundenen Kolonnade versucht das, was fraglos flach geworden ist, wieder zu verräumlichen und zu instrumentalisieren. Die ‚Fassade' entfaltet sich, wird selbst zum besetzten Raum, zur Ausstellungsfläche." Die Säulen sind mit falschem Marmor (1 mm dicke Dekorfolie) verkleidet und von hinten verspiegelt, sodass, wenn sich der Betrachter nähert, der Eindruck entsteht, der Marmor dehne sich in die Tiefe aus.

La *Tri-Colonnade* était une contribution à l'exposition «The Street» à la Biennale de Shenzhen et de Hong Kong, dont le commissaire était Terence Riley. Son idée était de recréer la «Strada Novissima» de la Biennale de Venise 1980 où 20 architectes – parmi lesquels Frank Gehry, Rem Koolhaas et Aldo Rossi – avaient conçu des éléments de façade dans l'allée centrale de l'exposition. Florian Idenburg explique : «De même que l'exposition historique de 1980 incarne aujourd'hui un moment de fixation de l'architecture sur la façade symbolique, 2011 marque la peur que l'architecture ait déchu et en soit réduite à une simple enveloppe vide. Notre projet cherche, au moyen d'une colonnade pour ainsi dire réinventée, à spatialiser et instrumentaliser un élément devenu implicitement plan. La "façade" se déploie et devient elle-même lieu d'occupation et d'exposition.» Du faux marbre (imprimé plastifié marbré de 1 mm) est apposé à l'avant des colonnes, puis des miroirs par derrière afin de donner l'impression aux visiteurs que le «marbre» se dilate au fur et à mesure qu'ils s'en approchent.

More a piece of installation art
than actual architecture, this work
speculates about the tendency of
buildings to be about little more
than surface.

Diese Arbeit, eher eine Kunstinstallation als tatsächliche Architektur,
thematisiert die Tendenz vieler
Bauten, sich um nicht viel mehr als
die Oberfläche zu drehen.

Plus installation artistique que véritablement architecture, cette œuvre
spécule sur la tendance à construire
des bâtiments ne valant guère plus
que la surface.

JUAN AGUSTIN SOZA

JUAN AGUSTIN SOZA graduated in Architecture from the Central University of Chile (Santiago, 2001). He created his own firm, Agustin Soza Arquitectos, in 2004, and participated in the creation of the construction firm, Cubo Limitada, the same year. His recent work includes the Feuereisen House (Santa Sofia de Lo Cañas, Santiago, 2005, published here); Cozy Box (Santa Sofia de Lo Cañas, Santiago, 2010, also published here); the Zanetta House (El Arrayan, Santiago, 2011); and De Simone House (La Reina, Santiago, 2011), all in Chile.

JUAN AGUSTIN SOZA schloss sein Architekturstudium an der Central University of Chile (Santiago, 2001) ab. 2004 gründete er sein eigenes Büro, Agustin Soza Arquitectos, und war im selben Jahr an der Gründung der Baufirma Cubo Limitada beteiligt. Zu seinen jüngeren Arbeiten gehören das Haus Feuereisen (Santa Sofia de Lo Cañas, Santiago, 2005, hier vorgestellt), Cozy Box (Santa Sofia de Lo Cañas, Santiago, 2010, ebenfalls hier vorgestellt), das Haus Zanetta (El Arrayan, Santiago, 2011) und das Haus De Simone (La Reina, Santiago, 2011), alle in Chile.

JUAN AGUSTIN SOZA est diplômé en architecture de l'Université centrale du Chili (Santiago, 2001). Il a fondé son agence, Agustin Soza Arquitectos, en 2004 et a participé à la création de l'entreprise de construction Cubo Limitada la même année. Ses projets récents comprennent la maison Feuereisen (Santa Sofia de Lo Cañas, Santiago, 2005, publiée ici); Cozy Box (Santa Sofia de Lo Cañas, Santiago, 2010, également publié ici); la maison Zanetta (El Arrayan, Santiago, 2011) et la maison De Simone (La Reina, Santiago, 2011), tous au Chili.

FEUEREISEN HOUSE

Santa Sofia de Lo Cañas, Santiago, Chile, 2005

Area: 68 m².
Client: Fernando Feuereisen.

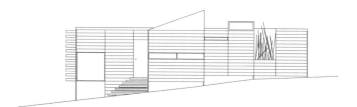

Using wooden ties from old railway tracks, the architect created this small cabin by lifting part of the structure off the ground and endowing it with a modern interior. Right page, below, site plan.

Der Architekt erschuf dieses kleine Bauwerk aus alten Bahnschwellen, wobei er einen Teil des Gebäudes aufständerte und es mit einer modernen Inneneinrichtung ausstattete. Auf der rechten Seite unten ist der Lageplan abgebildet.

Avec des traverses en bois d'anciennes voies de chemin de fer, l'architecte a créé cette petite maison en la surélevant en partie et en la dotant d'un intérieur moderne. Page de droite, en bas, plan du site.

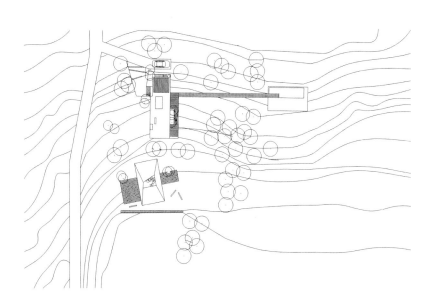

The architect employed old oak cross beams that had been part of a railway track for this house located at the foot of the Andes. These beams were split, with the aged external face forming the exterior surface of the house, and the more smoothly finished and modern looking inner face forming the interior walls. The house was built among existing trees, with a southern face that is closed and a northern face that is open to the light. Floor-to-ceiling glazing on the northern side gives the house a modern appearance, which is not the case of the rough wooden surfaces elsewhere. Skylights augment the presence of natural light. The bedroom faces east, while the living room, dining room, and kitchen are grouped facing west. A bathroom separates the two spaces. The architect explains: "The spaces change gradually by using different floor levels to separate them, ranging from 2.2 meters in height in the bedroom to 2.7 meters in the common area, integrating the special characteristics of each space and the slope of the site."

Für dieses Haus, am Fuße der Anden gelegen, verwendete der Architekt alte Bahnschwellen. Die Balken wurden gespalten und die verwitterten Seiten für die Außenwände des Hauses genutzt, aus den geglätteten und moderner anmutenden Innenflächen entstanden die Wände im Haus. Errichtet wurde es inmitten von Bäumen, die Südseite ist verschlossen, während die Nordseite Licht hineinlässt. Raumhohe Fenster auf dieser Seite verleihen dem Haus ein modernes Erscheinungsbild, das die rauen Holzoberflächen ansonsten nicht vermitteln. Oberlichter sorgen für zusätzliches Tageslicht. Das Schlafzimmer ist nach Osten ausgerichtet, Wohnzimmer, Esszimmer und Küche nach Westen. Ein Bad trennt die beiden Bereiche. Der Architekt dazu: „Die Räume verändern sich allmählich, da wir verschiedene Deckenhöhen verwendet haben, die von 2,20 m im Schlafzimmer bis zu 2,70 m im Wohnbereich reichen, um sie voneinander abzusetzen, wobei wir die speziellen Anforderungen jedes Raumes und die leichte Hanglage des Grundstücks mitberücksichtigt haben."

Pour cette maison au pied des Andes, l'architecte a utilisé de vieilles traverses de chêne récupérées sur une voie de chemin de fer. Elles ont été fendues, et la face externe vieillie a formé les murs extérieurs de la maison, tandis que la face interne, au fini plus lisse et d'apparence plus moderne, a donné les parois intérieures. La maison a été construite parmi des arbres, la façade sud fermée et la façade nord ouverte à la lumière avec un vitrage sur toute sa hauteur qui lui confère un aspect moderne, ce qui n'est pas le cas des surfaces de bois brut sur les autres côtés. Des lucarnes augmentent la présence de lumière naturelle. La chambre à coucher fait face à l'est, tandis que le salon, la salle à manger et la cuisine sont groupés vers l'ouest. Les deux espaces sont séparés par une salle de bains. Les architectes expliquent qu'« on passe progressivement d'un espace à l'autre grâce aux différences de niveau du sol, d'une hauteur de 2,2 m dans la chambre à 2,7 m dans les parties communes, prenant en compte les spécificités de chaque espace et la pente du terrain ».

Wood on the interior surfaces has a decidedly more polished or finished appearance than the railway ties seen in their natural state on the exterior (right). The space has numerous windows and, as seen on the left page, in the dining area, a skylight.

Die Holzoberflächen im Innern wirken um einiges glatter und bearbeiteter als die Bahnschwellen, die außen im ursprünglichen Zustand belassen sind (rechts). Das Gebäude hat zahlreiche Fenster und, wie auf der linken Seite zu sehen, im Essbereich ein Oberlicht.

Le bois des surfaces intérieures a un aspect beaucoup plus poli ou fini que les traverses de chemin de fer à l'état naturel de l'extérieur (à droite). Les fenêtres sont nombreuses avec, ci-contre, une lucarne dans la salle à manger.

COZY BOX

Santa Sofia de Lo Cañas, Santiago, Chile, 2010

Area: 63 m².

The Cozy Box actually looks rather strict from the exterior. Its black color and simple forms seen in these images showing the exterior and the two elevation drawings (left) give a rather minimalistic impression.

Von außen wirkt die Cozy Box recht streng. Das Schwarz und die schlichte Formensprache vermitteln einen eher minimalistischen Eindruck, wie diese Außenaufnahmen und die beiden Aufrisse (links) zeigen.

La Cozy Box semble plutôt austère de l'extérieur. Sa couleur noire et ses formes simples qu'on voit sur ces photos de l'extérieur et les plans en élévation (à gauche) donnent une impression plutôt minimaliste.

Built on a 1400-square-meter site, this house with brick and pigmented stucco walls includes a living room, kitchenette, bathroom, and bedroom. A preexisting house with an equally limited floor area could thus become a kitchen, study, guest bathroom, and living room, although the Cozy Box is independent from the earlier building. The project was marked by a close collaboration with the client. A light well brings daylight into the apparently dark box and forms an internal garden. Enameled ceramics with mineral pigments were used for the bath and kitchen counter. Essentially black on the exterior and surrounded by a wooden deck, the house is entirely painted white on the inside.

Dieses Haus aus Ziegel- und farbig verputzten Wänden steht auf einem 1400 m² großen Grundstück und verfügt über Wohnzimmer, Küchenzeile, Bad und Schlafraum. Küche, Arbeitszimmer, Gästebad und Wohnzimmer verblieben in einem bereits existierenden Haus mit ähnlich kleiner Grundfläche, obgleich die Cozy Box von dem älteren Gebäude völlig unabhängig ist. Das Projekt entstand in enger Zusammenarbeit mit dem Bauherrn. Ein Lichtschacht lässt Tageslicht in die vermeintlich dunkle Box und bildet einen kleinen Hofgarten. Im Bad und für die Küchenzeile wurden emaillierte Keramikplatten mit Mineralpigmenten verwendet. Das Haus, von außen vorwiegend schwarz und von einem Holzsteg umgeben, ist im Innern vollständig weiß gehalten.

Construite sur un terrain de 1400 m², cette maison de briques aux murs de stuc pigmenté comprend un salon, une kitchenette, une salle de bains et une chambre à coucher. Une maison précédente, à la surface tout aussi réduite, a ainsi pu accueillir une cuisine, un bureau, une salle de bains d'invités et un salon, même si la Cozy Box est un bâtiment indépendant. Le projet a fait l'objet d'une collaboration étroite avec le client. Un puits de lumière fait entrer le jour dans la «boîte» en apparence sombre et y crée un jardin intérieur. Des céramiques émaillées aux pigments minéraux ont été utilisées pour la baignoire et le bar de la cuisine. Presque complètement noire à l'extérieur et entourée d'un ponton en bois, la maison est entièrement peinte en blanc à l'intérieur.

The white interior, with its winter garden and skylight, brings to mind some contemporary Japanese architecture, although Santiago is obviously quite far from Tokyo.

Die weißen Innenräume mit Wintergarten und Oberlicht erinnern an Beispiele zeitgenössischer japanischer Architektur, auch wenn Santiago von Tokio natürlich weit entfernt ist.

L'intérieur en blanc avec son jardin d'hiver et sa lucarne fait penser à l'architecture japonaise contemporaine, même si Santiago est loin de Tokyo.

STUDIO MAKKINK & BEY

Designer Jurgen Bey and architect Rianne Makkink have operated Studio Makkink & Bey together in Rotterdam since 2002. The studio's projects include public spaces, product design, architecture, exhibition design, and applied arts. **JURGEN BEY** was born in 1965, studied at the Design Academy in Eindhoven (1984–89), and subsequently taught there for six years. Early in his career he was linked to the Dutch group Droog Design, for whom Makkink & Bey carried out the Blueprint project in New York (New York, USA, 2009). **RIANNE MAKKINK** was born in 1964 and studied Architecture at the Delft University of Technology (1983–90), and had her own office from 1991 until 2001. Their recent work includes the Ear Chair designed for Prooff (2001); the Education Space at the Boymans Van Beuningen Museum (*Haunting Boymans Van Beuningen*, Rotterdam, 2008); Brinta-House (Vijversburg, Tytsjerk, 2008, published here); the Pixelated Chair for the Galerie Pierre Bergé (2008); and the restaurant and shop of the Kunsthal Kade (Amersfoort, 2009). In 2012, they completed Camper Shoe Shops in Rome (Italy) and Lyon (France). Current work includes interior design for De Rotterdam, the 160 000-square-meter office building complex designed by OMA (Rotterdam, 2014), all in The Netherlands unless stated otherwise.

Der Designer Jurgen Bey und die Architektin Rianne Makkink betreiben seit 2002 gemeinsam das Studio Makkink & Bey in Rotterdam. Die Bandbreite ihrer Projekte reicht von der Gestaltung öffentlicher Räume, Produktdesign und Architektur über Ausstellungsdesign bis hin zu angewandeter Kunst. **JURGEN BEY** wurde 1965 geboren, studierte an der Design Academy in Eindhoven (1984–89) und unterrichtete im Anschluss daran sechs Jahre lang dort. Bereits früh in seiner Laufbahn unterhielt er Kontakt zur niederländischen Gruppe Droog Design, für die Makkink & Bey das Blueprint-Projekt in New York realisierten (2009). **RIANNE MAKKINK** wurde 1964 geboren, studierte an der Technischen Universität Delft Architektur (1983–90) und führte von 1991 bis 2001 ihr eigenes Büro. Zu ihren jüngeren Arbeiten gehören der Ear Chair, ein Entwurf für Prooff (2001), der museumspädagogische Bereich des Museums Boymans van Beunigen (Hautning Boymans van Beuningen, Rotterdam, 2008), das Brinta-House (Vijversburg, Tytsjerk, 2008, hier vorgestellt), der Pixelated Chair für die Galerie Pierre Bergé (2008) und das Restaurant und der Museumsshop der Kunsthalle Kade (Amersfoort, 2009). 2012 realisierten sie Camper-Schuhläden in Rom und Lyon. Derzeit arbeiten sie u. a. an der Innenarchitektur für De Rotterdam, einen 160 000 m² großen Bürokomplex, entworfen von OMA (Rotterdam, 2014), alle in den Niederlanden, soweit nicht anders angegeben.

Le designer Jurgen Bey et l'architecte Rianne Makkink dirigent ensemble Studio Makkink & Bey à Rotterdam depuis 2002. Leurs projets comptent des lieux publics, des designs de produits, des réalisations architecturales, des designs d'expositions et arts appliqués. **JURGEN BEY** est né en 1965, a fait ses études à l'Académie de design d'Eindhoven (1984–89) avant d'y enseigner pendant six ans. Dès le début de sa carrière, il s'est lié au groupe néerlandais Droog Design pour lequel Makkink & Bey ont réalisé le projet Blueprint à New York (2009). **RIANNE MAKKINK** est née en 1964 et a fait des études d'architecture à l'Université de technologie de Delft (1983–90). Elle a exploité sa propre agence de 1991 à 2001. Leurs réalisations récentes comprennent le fauteuil Ear Chair conçu pour Prooff (2001) ; l'espace pédagogique du musée Boymans van Beuningen (Haunting Boymans van Beuningen, Rotterdam, 2008) ; la Brinta-House (Vijversburg, Tytsjerk, 2008, publié ici) ; la chaise pixélisée pour la galerie Pierre Bergé (2008) et le restaurant et boutique de la galerie Kunsthal Kade (Amersfoort, 2009). En 2012, ils ont achevé les magasins de chaussures Camper de Rome et Lyon. Leurs projets en cours comprennent l'architecture intérieure de De Rotterdam, un complexe d'immeubles de bureaux de 160 000 m² créé par OMA (Rotterdam, 2014). Tous sont aux Pays-Bas sauf mention contraire.

BRINTA-HOUSE

Vijversburg, Tytsjerk, The Netherlands, 2008

Area: 6.5 m².
Client: Stichting Beeldenpark Vijversburg.

As the drawing above shows, the designers chose to make this small structure with some of the most basic, and yet rarely used elements of farming—crates of hay that are stacked together and made to resemble a house.

Wie die Zeichnung oben zeigt, entschieden sich die Designer bei diesem kleinen Bauwerk für eines der grundlegendsten und doch selten genutzten Elemente der Landwirtschaft – Stroh wurde in Kisten gepackt, die zu einem hausähnlichen Bau gestapelt wurden.

Comme on le voit sur le plan ci-dessus, les designers ont choisi de réaliser cette petite structure avec des éléments agricoles parmi les plus basiques, mais pourtant rarement utilisés – des meules de foin empilées pour ressembler à une maison.

The designers decided in this instance to work with the raw materials of farming, employing straw that was stored in crates, that were piled up to make the house. Though the effect is similar to that of timber framing, the structure was built out of modules that can be easily transported. Makkink & Bey compare the structure to "follies" that can be used as a place of repose. They write: "Every solution already exists in the world surrounding us. It is only a matter of recognizing it and converting it to something useful. This principle was put into practice by the Studio at Vijversburg VI. They worked the land, plowed it, and sowed the wheat." The idea of a structure that is intimately related to the land, but also to its products is emphasized by the designer's conclusion in the description of the Vijversburg project: "A view on the pasture offers a surprise, in the field of grain the letters 'Brinta' can be seen. The circle is closed: the wheat gives an oath to the well-known breakfast product with which generations have grown up."

Die Designer entschieden sich bei diesem Projekt, mit den Rohmaterialien der Landwirtschaft zu arbeiten, und verwendeten mit Stroh gefüllte Kästen, die zu einem Gebäude gestapelt wurden. Obwohl nach den Prinzipien des Fachwerks gearbeitet wurde, besteht das Bauwerk aus leicht transportablen Modulen. Makkink & Bey vergleichen es mit einem Zierbau, der als Rückzugsort genutzt werden kann. Sie schreiben: „Jede Lösung existiert bereits in der uns umgebenden Welt. Es geht nur darum, sie zu erkennen und sie sinnvoll zu nutzen. Dieses Prinzip hat das Büro in Vijversburg VI in die Tat umgesetzt. Das Land wurde bestellt, gepflügt und der Weizen gesät." In der Beschreibung des Vijversburg-Projekts heben die Designer die Idee eines eng mit dem Land und seinen Früchten verbundenen Gebäudes noch einmal hervor: „Ein Blick über das Gelände hält eine Überraschung bereit, im Weizenfeld ist das Wort ‚Brinta' zu erkennen. Der Kreis hat sich geschlossen: Der Weizen schwört dem allseits bekannten Frühstücksprodukt (einem Weizengrießbrei), mit dem Generationen groß geworden sind, einen Eid."

Les designers ont ici voulu travailler avec des matériaux agricoles bruts et ont empilé des caisses de paille pour construire la maison. Le résultat est semblable à celui d'une charpente en bois d'œuvre, mais la structure est faite de modules faciles à transporter. Makkink & Bey la comparent à ces « folies » propices au repos. Ils écrivent : « Toutes les solutions existent déjà dans le monde qui nous entoure. Il faut simplement les identifier et en faire quelque chose d'utile. Ce principe a été mis en pratique par le Studio à Vijversburg VI. Ils ont travaillé la terre, l'ont labourée et ont semé du blé. » L'idée d'une structure intimement liée à la terre, mais aussi à ses produits, est reprise dans la conclusion du designer à la description du projet de Vijversburg : « La vue du pré réserve une surprise : on peut lire les lettres de "Brinta" dans le champ de céréales. La boucle est bouclée : le blé rend allégeance à l'aliment de petit-déjeuner bien connu avec lequel plusieurs générations ont grandi. »

The rough surface of the structure is fully echoed in the interior, seen in the two images below, where a kind of caricature of furniture (a table on the right) is employed.

Die raue Oberfläche des Gebäudes wiederholt sich im Innern, wie auf den beiden Bildern unten zu sehen, wo eine Art Karikatur von Möbeln (rechts ein Tisch) zum Einsatz kommt.

La surface rude de la construction fait écho à l'intérieur que l'on voit sur les deux photos ci-dessous avec une caricature de mobilier (une table à droite).

STUDIO MUMBAI

BIJOY JAIN was born in Mumbai, India, in 1965 and received his M.Arch. degree from Washington University in Saint Louis in 1990. He worked in Los Angeles and London between 1989 and 1995, and returned to India in 1995 to found his practice. Recent projects of the firm include the Reading Room (Nagaon, Maharashtra, 2003); Tara House (Kashid, Maharashtra, 2005); Palmyra House (Nandgaon, Maharashtra, 2007); Leti 360 Resort (Leti, Uttaranchal, 2007); House on Pali Hill (Bandra, Mumbai, 2008); Utsav House (Satirje, Maharashtra, 2008); Belavali House (Belavali, Maharashtra, 2008); Copper House II (Chondi, Maharashtra, 2010); In-Between Architecture, Victoria and Albert Museum (London, UK, 2010, published here); and the exhibition *Work-Place*, *Venice Biennale* (Venice, Italy, 2010), all in India unless stated otherwise.

BIJOY JAIN wurde 1965 in Mumbai, Indien, geboren und schloss sein Studium an der Washington University in St. Louis 1990 mit einem M. Arch. ab. Von 1989 bis 1995 arbeitete er in Los Angeles und London und kehrte 1995 nach Indien zurück, wo er sein Büro gründete. Jüngere Projekte der Firma sind u. a. der Reading Room (Nagaon, Maharashtra, 2003), das Tara House (Kashid, Maharashtra, 2005), das Palmyra House (Nandgaon, Maharashtra, 2007), die Hotelanlage Leti 360 (Leti, Uttaranchal, 2007), ein Haus auf Pali Hill (Bandra, Mumbai, 2008), das Utsav House (Satirje, Maharashtra, 2008), das Belavali House (Belavali, Maharashtra, 2008), das Copper House II (Chondi, Maharashtra, 2010), „In-Between Architecture" im Victoria and Albert Museum (London, 2010, hier vorgestellt) sowie die Ausstellung „Work-Place", Biennale Venedig (2010).

BIJOY JAIN est né à Mumbai en 1965, a obtenu son M.Arch à l'université Washington de Saint Louis (1990). Il a travaillé à Los Angeles et Londres de 1989 à 1995, puis est revenu en Inde en 1995 pour y fonder son agence. Parmi ses projets récents figurent : une salle de lecture (Nagaon, Maharashtra, 2003) ; la maison Tara (Kashid, Maharashtra, 2005) ; la maison Palmyra (Nandgaon, Maharashtra, 2007) ; la station touristique Leti 360 (Leti, Uttaranchal, 2007) ; une maison sur la colline de Pali (Bandra, Mumbai, 2008), la maison Utsav (Satirje, Maharashtra, 2008) ; la maison Belavali (Belavali, Maharashtra, 2008) ; la maison Copper II (Chondi, Maharashtra, 2010) ; « In-Between Architecture » au Victoria and Albert Museum (Londres, 2010, publiée ici) et l'exposition « Work-Place » à la Biennale de Venise (2010), tous en Inde sauf mention contraire.

IN-BETWEEN ARCHITECTURE

Victoria and Albert Museum, London, UK, 2010

Area: 33 m². Client: Victoria and Albert Museum.
Cost: $35 000. Collaboration: Michael Anastassiades, Dr. Murien Kate Dinen.

This project was part of the exhibition *1:1 Architects Build Small Spaces 2010* held at the Victoria and Albert Museum in London from June 15 to August 30, 2010. The architects stated: "Our proposal explores architectural spaces formed between the boundaries of existing buildings. The structure is a slice from a series of dwellings sandwiched between our current studio and the adjacent warehouse. Although it is inspired by a real condition, our aim is not to produce an exact copy within a museum environment." Standing next to works such as a replica of Michelangelo's *David* in the museum, the structure, clearly inspired by a very different environment, shows the work of Studio Mumbai as "an abstraction of the relationship between artificiality and nature," as they put it. The architects conclude: "Our purpose is to show a genuine possibility; to create refuge from a constricted spatial condition that emerges from imagination, intimacy, and modesty."

Dieses Projekt war Teil der Ausstellung „1:1 Architects Build Small Spaces", die vom 15. Juni bis 30. August 2010 im Londoner Victoria and Albert Museum stattfand. Die Architekten dazu: „Unser Beitrag lotet architektonische Räume zwischen bestehenden Gebäuden aus. Bei dem Gebilde handelt es sich um einen Teil einer Reihe von Wohnhäusern, die zwischen unser derzeitiges Studio und das angrenzende Lagerhaus gepfercht wurden. Obgleich es von realen Verhältnissen inspiriert ist, geht es uns nicht darum, eine exakte Kopie für den musealen Kontext zu erzeugen." In direkter Nachbarschaft etwa zu einer Replik des „David" von Michelangelo lässt der Bau, offenkundig von einer doch sehr anderen Umgebung inspiriert, die Arbeit von Studio Mumbai als „eine Abstraktion der Beziehung zwischen Künstlichkeit und Natur" erscheinen, so wie die Architekten es formulieren. Sie fassen zusammen: „Unser Anliegen ist es, eine einmalige Möglichkeit sichtbar zu machen, nämlich aus einem beschränkten räumlichen Zustand eine Zuflucht entstehen zu lassen, die der Vorstellungskraft, Vertrautheit und Bescheidenheit entspringt."

Le projet est l'un de ceux qui a été présenté à l'exposition « 1:1 Architects Build Small Spaces 2010 » au Victoria and Albert Museum du 15 juin au 30 août 2010. Les architectes ont déclaré : « Nous nous proposons d'explorer les espaces architecturaux qui se forment entre les limites de bâtiments existants. La structure fait partie d'une série d'habitations prises en sandwich entre notre studio actuel et l'entrepôt adjacent. Bien qu'inspirée par une situation réelle, notre but n'est pas de réaliser une copie exacte dans un environnement muséal. » Placée à proximité d'œuvres comme une copie du *David* de Michel-Ange, la construction, inspirée par un environnement très différent, montre le travail de Studio Mumbai comme « une abstraction de la relation entre artificiel et naturel » selon les auteurs. Ils concluent : « Notre objectif est de montrer une possibilité réelle ; de créer un refuge pour échapper à une situation trop à l'étroit produite par l'imagination, l'intimité et la modestie. »

Part of the 2010 exhibition at the Victoria and Albert Museum that permitted a few architects to realize small structures inside the museum itself, this pavilion makes use of a kind of reproduction of the area near the architects' studio in Mumbai.

Der Pavillon, Teil der Ausstellung im Victoria and Albert Museum 2010, bei der einige wenige Architekten die Möglichkeit hatten, kleine Bauten im Museum selbst zu realisieren, spielt mit einer Art Reproduktion der Büroumgebung der Architekten in Mumbai.

Contribution à l'exposition de 2010 au Victoria and Albert Museum où quelques architectes ont pu réaliser des petites structures à l'intérieur. Le pavillon reprend en quelque sorte l'emplacement qui jouxte le cabinet des architectes à Mumbai.

The architects state: "This is a distilled architectural study of a dwelling, a home of multifunctional spaces consisting of communal living environments, places of refuge, contemplation, and worship."

Die Architekten erklären: „Diese Studie ist das architektonische Destillat eines Wohnhauses, ein Hort von Multifunktionsbereichen, Orten gemeinschaftlichen Lebens, aber auch des Rückzugs, der Einkehr und der Andacht."

Les architectes déclarent : « C'est une étude architecturale distillée d'un habitat, un chez-soi d'espaces multifonctions consistant en des environnements de vie communs, lieux de refuge, de contemplation et de culte. »

"The structure," says Studio Mumbai, "is ambiguous, creating an abstraction of the relationship between artificiality and nature."

„Das Bauwerk", so Studio Mumbai, „hat etwas Doppelbödiges, indem es eine Abstraktion der Beziehung zwischen Künstlichkeit und Natur erzeugt."

« La structure, explique Studio Mumbai, est ambiguë, créant une abstraction de la relation entre artificialité et nature. »

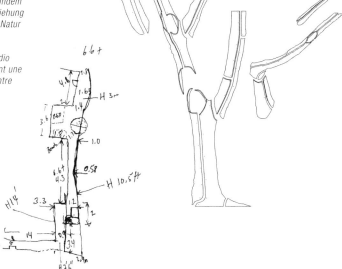

STUDIO ROLF.FR AND ZECC ARCHITECTS

ROLF BRUGGINK was born in 1969 in Hoogeveen, The Netherlands. He obtained his diplomas in Architecture and in Urban Planning from Delft University of Technology in 1997. He was a cofounder of Zecc Architects in 2003 in Utrecht with Marnix van der Meer. He created Studio Rolf.fr in 2009 with the aim of designing products and furniture. Bruggink's work in architecture includes Laboratory of Living, a house in Utrecht (2003–05); his own Black Pearl House and Studio (in collaboration with Zecc, Rotterdam, 2008–10, published here) and the Birdhouse House and Studio (Utrecht, 2010–13), all in The Netherlands. **MARNIX VAN DER MEER** was born in 1972 in Benschop, The Netherlands, and was educated at the University of Applied Sciences in Utrecht (1991–95), and the Amsterdam Academy of Architecture (1996–2002, M.Arch.). Zecc's work includes a design for 24 apartments (Vathorst, Amersfoort, 2005); remodeling of offices in Utrecht (Herenstraat 12, 2006); and apartment projects in Almere (Homeruskwartier, 2007). The firm has converted churches into offices (Dieren, 2005); and into a residence, Stairway to Heaven (Utrecht, 2007). More recently, they completed the renovation of the Drents Public Archives (Assen, 2010–12); and they are working on the Tower Apartments in Utrecht (2011–).

ROLF BRUGGINK wurde 1969 in Hoogeveen geboren. Seine Diplome in Architektur und Stadtplanung erwarb er 1997 an der Technischen Universität Delft. Zusammen mit Marnix van der Meer gründete er 2003 Zecc Architects in Utrecht. Mit dem Ziel, Produkte und Möbel zu entwerfen, gründete er 2009 Studio Rolf.fr. Zu Brugginks architektonischen Arbeiten gehören das Haus Laboratory of Living (Utrecht, 2003–05), sein eigenes Black Pearl House mit Studio (in Zusammenarbeit mit Zecc, Rotterdam, 2008–10, hier vorgestellt) und das Birdhouse House mit Studio (Utrecht, 2010–13). **MARNIX VAN DER MEER** wurde 1972 in Benschop, Niederlande, geboren, studierte an der Fachhochschule Utrecht (1991–95) sowie der Amsterdam Academy of Architecture (1996–2002, M. Arch.). Zu den Projekten von Zecc gehören der Entwurf von 24 Apartments (Vathorst, Amersfoort, 2005), Büroumbauten in Utrecht (Herenstraat 12, 2006) und Apartmentprojekte in Almere (Homeruskwartier, 2007). Das Büro hat Kirchen in Büros (Dieren, 2005) und in ein Wohnhaus verwandelt (Stairway to Heaven, Utrecht, 2007). In jüngerer Zeit wurde die Renovierung des Drenther Regionalarchivs (Assen, 2010–12) abgeschlossen; derzeit arbeiten die Architekten an den Tower Apartments in Utrecht (seit 2011).

ROLF BRUGGINK est né en 1969 à Hoogeveen, aux Pays-Bas. Il est diplômé en architecture et urbanisme de l'Université de technologie de Delft (1997). Il a fondé Zecc Architects en 2003 à Utrecht avec Marnix van der Meer. Il a également créé Studio Rolf.fr en 2009 dont l'objet est de créer des produits et des meubles. Ses réalisations architecturales comprennent une maison dite Laboratory of Living (Utrecht, 2003–05) ; sa maison personnelle et studio Black Pearl (en collaboration avec Zecc, Rotterdam, 2008–10, publiée ici) et la maison et studio Birdhouse (Utrecht, 2010–13). **MARNIX VAN DER MEER** est né en 1972 à Benschop, aux Pays-Bas, et a fait ses études à l'Université de sciences appliquées d'Utrecht (1991–95) et à l'Académie d'architecture d'Amsterdam (1996–2002, M.Arch). Parmi les projets de Zecc figurent le design de 24 appartements (Vathorst, Amersfoort, 2005) ; la reconfiguration de bureaux à Utrecht (Herenstraat 12, 2006) et des projets d'appartements à Almere (Homeruskwartier, 2007). L'agence a également converti des églises en bureaux (Dieren, 2005) et en résidence : Stairway to Heaven (Utrecht, 2007). Plus récemment, ils ont achevé la rénovation des archives publiques de la Drenthe (Assen, 2010–12) et ils travaillent aux appartements Tower à Utrecht (2011–).

THE BLACK PEARL

Rotterdam, The Netherlands, 2008–10

Area: 100 m². Client: Rolf and Yffi Bruggink.
Cost: €200 000. Collaboration: Yffi van den Berg.

Located in an area that has seen the renovation of older, neglected residences, this 100-year-old *métier* house is notable because of its entirely black façade. Some new windows were added, but, on the whole, Rolf Bruggink sought to give an impression of a "shadow" of the original façade. The interior plan of the structure was completely changed, with the original small rooms being replaced by a continuous space on four floors. The architects state: "This creates living spaces that are connected by voids, large stairwells, and long sightlines. All redundant banisters, railings, and doors are left out, causing a high degree of spatial abstraction. Floors, walls, stairs, and ceilings blend together and seem to recall an 'Escher-like' impossibility." A workroom occupies the lower part of the house with "semi-open living functions" located above. The old roof tiles of the house were removed on the roof where a greenhouse and hot tub were placed. The architect explains the importance of color: "In the house, five colors are used: black, white, and three gray scales. An existing side wall is painted totally white. The traces of construction, including the old railings and pipes, are all painted white. The other building wall is left untreated. The different faces of the object are painted in three gray scales."

Dieses 100 Jahre alte ehemalige Ständehaus steht in einem Areal, in dem weit ältere verlassene Gebäude renoviert worden sind, und fällt wegen seiner komplett schwarzen Fassade auf. Ein paar neue Fenster wurden hinzugefügt, insgesamt versuchte Rolf Bruggink aber. den „Schatten" der Originalfassade zu erhalten. Das Innere wurde vollständig verändert, wobei die früheren kleinen Zimmer durch einen durchgehenden offenen Raum über vier Stockwerke ersetzt wurden. Die Architekten dazu: „So entstehen Lebensbereiche, die durch Leerstellen, lange Treppen und weite Sichtachsen verbunden sind. Überflüssige Geländer, Brüstungen und Türen werden weggelassen, was für ein hohes Maß an räumlicher Abstraktion sorgt. Böden, Wände, Treppen und Decken gehen ineinander über und evozieren ein Gefühl der Unmöglichkeit à la Escher." Eine Werkstatt nimmt den unteren Teil des Hauses ein, darüber liegt ein „halb offener Wohnbereich". Das alte Ziegeldach wurde entfernt und durch ein Gewächshaus samt Whirlpool ersetzt. Die Architekten erläutern die Bedeutung der Farbgebung: „Im Haus werden fünf Farben verwendet: Schwarz, Weiß und drei Grautöne. Eine Seitenwand ist vollständig weiß gestrichen. Bauliche Spuren, einschließlich der alten Handläufe und Rohre, sind ebenfalls weiß gestrichen. Die Seitenwand zum angrenzenden Gebäude blieb unangetastet. Die unterschiedlichen Oberflächen des Objekts sind in drei verschiedenen Grautönen gehalten."

Située dans un quartier où plusieurs résidences anciennes et mal entretenues ont été rénovées, cette maison de métier vieille d'un siècle frappe par sa façade tout en noir. Quelques fenêtres ont été ajoutées, mais Rolf Bruggink a cherché à garder l'« ombre » de la façade d'origine. Le plan intérieur a été entièrement modifié, les petites pièces d'origine remplacées par un espace continu sur quatre niveaux. Les architectes expliquent : « Cela ouvre des espaces à vivre reliés par des vides, de larges escaliers et d'immenses panoramas. Toutes les rampes, balustrades et portes superflues ont été mises à l'écart, créant un degré élevé d'abstraction spatiale. Les sols, murs, escaliers et plafonds fusionnent comme pour évoquer une impossibilité de "type Escher". » Une pièce de travail occupe la partie la plus basse de la maison, avec des « fonctions séjour semi-ouvertes » au-dessus. Les anciennes tuiles ont été retirées du toit où une serre et un jacuzzi ont été aménagés. Les architectes insistent sur l'importance de la couleur : « Dans la maison, cinq couleurs ont été utilisées : noir, blanc et trois nuances de gris. Un mur latéral d'origine a été entièrement peint en blanc. De même, les traces de construction, notamment les anciennes balustrades et canalisations, ont été peintes en blanc. L'autre mur d'origine est resté non traité. Les différentes faces de l'objet sont peintes dans trois nuances de gris. »

Although it stands in a row of similarly proportioned houses, the Black Pearl stands out because of its color and also because of the modern approach to the interior. Right, section drawings.

Auch wenn es in einer Reihe ähnlich proportionierter Häuser steht, sticht das Black Pearl doch aufgrund seiner Farbe und des modernen Inneren heraus. Rechts Querschnitte.

Bien qu'appartenant à une série de demeures aux proportions similaires, la Black Pearl se distingue par sa couleur et l'approche moderne adoptée pour l'intérieur. À droite, schémas en coupe.

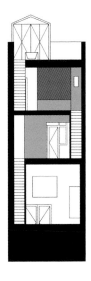
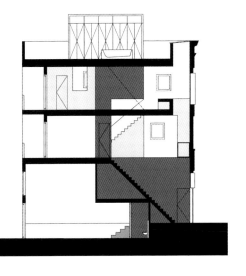

Some exposed surfaces, such as the brick wall above, reveal the history of the building, which has otherwise been totally redesigned. Below, floor plans.

Certaines surfaces apparentes comme le mur de briques ci-dessus révèlent l'histoire du bâtiment qui a sinon été entièrement redessiné. Ci-dessous, plans des étages.

Einige freiliegende Flächen, so wie die Backsteinwand oben, offenbaren die Geschichte des Gebäudes, das ansonsten vollständig umgestaltet wurde. Unten Grundrisse.

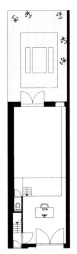
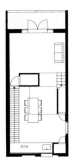
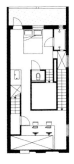
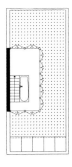

Rough brick walls neighbor smooth white, gray, and black surfaces creating a tactile interplay as well as an aesthetic one.

Grobe Backsteinmauern gleich neben glatten Oberflächen in Weiß, Grau oder Schwarz sorgen sowohl für eine taktile als auch eine ästhetische Wechselwirkung.

Les murs de briques brutes voisinent avec les surfaces lisses blanches, grises et noires, créant une interaction tactile autant qu'esthétique.

A courtyard (seen below) allows only the wooden table and benches and some greenery to deviate from the generally black color scheme.

Im Innenhof (unten) weichen nur ein Holztisch, Bänke und etwas Grün von der allgemeinen schwarzen Farbgebung ab.

Une cour (ci-dessous) tolère uniquement la table de bois, les bancs et un peu de verdure comme écarts de l'ensemble en noir.

STUDIO WG3

WG3 describe themselves as "a group of furniture designers and architects." The partners are Albert Erjavec, Matthias Gumhalter, Christian Reschreiter, and Jan Ries. **ALBERT ERJAVEC** was born in 1982 in Villach. He studied Architecture at the Technical University (TU) of Graz (2000–12), before being involved in the creation of WG3 in 2011. **MATTHIAS GUMHALTER** was born in 1980 in Vienna. He also studied at the TU in Graz. **CHRISTIAN RESCHREITER** was born in 1982 in Salzburg, also studying at the TU Graz (2003–10). Finally, **JAN RIES** was born in 1981 in the Czech Republic, with studies at the TU Graz between 2003 and 2009. Their work includes the Hypercubus (Graz, 2010, published here), and the HGO 15 House (Ollersdorf, Burgenland, 2011), both in Austria.

WG3 beschreiben sich selbst als „eine Gruppe von Möbeldesignern und Architekten". Sie besteht aus den Partnern Albert Erjavec, Matthias Gumhalter, Christian Reschreiter und Jan Ries. **ALBERT ERJAVEC** wurde 1982 in Villach geboren. Er studierte Architektur an der Technischen Universität (TU) Graz (2000–12) und war 2011 Mitbegründer von WG3. **MATTHIAS GUMHALTER** wurde 1980 in Wien geboren, auch er studierte an der TU Graz. **CHRISTIAN RESCHREITER** wurde 1982 in Salzburg geboren und studierte ebenfalls an der TU Graz (2010–13). Der Letzte, **JAN RIES**, wurde 1981 in der Tschechischen Republik geboren und studierte von 2003 bis 2009 auch an der TU Graz. Zu den Werken der Gruppe zählen der Hypercubus (Graz, 2010, hier veröffentlicht) und das Haus HGO 15 (Ollersdorf, Burgenland, 2011), beide in Österreich.

Les partenaires de WG3 se décrivent eux-mêmes comme « un groupe de designers de meubles et d'architectes ». Ce sont Albert Erjavec, Matthias Gumhalter, Christan Reschreiter et Jan Ries. **ALBERT ERJAVEC** est né en 1982 à Villach. Il a étudié l'architecture à l'Université technique (TU) de Graz (2000–12) avant de participer à la création de WG3 en 2011. **MATTHIAS GUMHALTER** est né en 1980 à Vienne. Il a aussi fait ses études à la TU de Graz. **CHRISTIAN RESCHREITER** est né en 1982 à Salzbourg et a également fait ses études à la TU de Graz (2003–10). Enfin **JAN RIES** est né en 1981 en République tchèque et a étudié à la TU de Graz de 2003 à 2009. Leurs projets comprennent l'Hypercubus (Graz, 2010, publié ici) et la maison HGO 15 (Ollersdorf, Burgenland, 2011), tous les deux en Autriche.

HYPERCUBUS

Graz, Austria, 2010

Area: 19 m². Client: Studio WG3.
Cost: € 63 500.

The base of this mobile structure is a reinforced-concrete foundation. The box or framework on the concrete foundation is made of glued laminated timber, and the main material employed is plywood. The Hypercubus is a research project that is related to a thesis. The intention of WG3 was "to develop a minimal apartment intended for two people. Aimed at the area of tourism, the scheme entails industrial manufacturing, transport capability, interior space optimization, self-sufficiency, memorable and recognizable architecture, and economic efficiency." They began their work on this project in January 2010 and completed the prototype in May 2010. The prototype envisaged a module that can be vertically stacked to create a "hotel-like structure."

Das Fundament dieser mobilen Einheit besteht aus Stahlbeton, auf dem ein Rahmentragwerk aus Schichtholz ruht. Zum Einsatz kam vornehmlich Sperrholz. Bei dem Hypercubus handelt es sich um ein Forschungsprojekt im Rahmen einer Abschlussarbeit. Es war die Absicht von WG3, „ein kleines Apartment für zwei Personen zu entwickeln. Auf den Tourismus ausgerichtet, schließt der Entwurf industrielle Fertigung, Transportmöglichkeit, die Optimierung des Innenraums, Selbstversorgung, eine wiedererkennbare Architektur und ökonomische Effizienz ein." WG3 arbeiteten ab Januar 2010 an dem Projekt und stellten im Mai 2010 den Prototypen fertig, der vertikal angeordnet werden kann, um eine „hotelähnliche Anlage" entstehen zu lassen.

Des fondations en béton armé forment la base de cette structure mobile, surmontées du cube, ou ossature, en bois de charpente lamellé collé, le contreplaqué étant le principal matériau utilisé. L'Hypercubus est au départ un projet de recherche dans le cadre d'une thèse. L'intention de WG3 était « de développer un logement minimal pour deux personnes. Destiné au secteur touristique, l'ensemble associe la fabrication industrielle, la transportabilité, l'optimisation de l'espace intérieur, l'auto-suffisance, une architecture originale et facilement reconnaissable et l'efficacité économique ». Les architectes ont commencé à travailler sur ce projet en janvier 2010, et le prototype a été achevé en mai 2010. Il prévoyait un module qui peut être empilé verticalement afin de créer une « structure de type hôtel ».

This project is based on a 3-D model created on a computer. The wood structure is then created on a CNC milling machine.

Das Projekt basiert auf einem 3D-Computermodell. Der Holzbau entstand mithilfe einer CNC-Fräse.

Le projet est basé sur un modèle 3D créé sur ordinateur. La structure de bois a ensuite été réalisée sur une fraiseuse à commande numérique.

Interior floors are carpeted. Medium-density fiberboard is used for the kitchen furniture. The bathroom has a movable mirror box.

Die Böden sind mit Teppich ausgelegt, das Küchenmobiliar besteht aus Hartfaserplatten mittlerer Dichte, und das Bad verfügt über eine bewegliche Spiegelbox.

À l'intérieur, les sols sont recouverts de moquette. Le mobilier de la cuisine est en panneaux de fibres de densité moyenne. La salle de bains est dotée d'un cube à miroirs mobile.

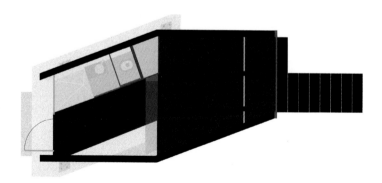

TACKLEBOX

JEREMY BARBOUR was born in Roanoke, Virginia, in 1976. He obtained his B.Arch. degree from Virginia Tech (Blacksburg, Virginia, 2001) and his M.Arch. degree from Columbia University GSAPP (New York, 2006). He is an Adjunct Professor at Parson's the New School of Design and an Adjunct Assistant Professor in the Columbia GSAPP Summer Studio program. He is the owner and principal of Tacklebox, which he founded in 2006. Prior to that date, he worked with Daniel Rowen Architects (New York, 2001–02), and with Andrew Bartle (ABA Studio, New York, 2002–06). His work includes the 3.1 Phillip Lim Boutique (New York, 2007); and Saipua (Brooklyn, New York, 2009, published here), both in the USA.

JEREMY BARBOUR wurde 1976 in Roanoke, Virginia, geboren. Er absolvierte seinen B. Arch. an der Virginia Tech (Blacksburg, Virginia, 2001) und seinen M. Arch. an der Columbia University GSAPP (New York, 2006). Er ist Lehrbeauftragter am Parson's, The New School of Design, und am Summer-Studio-Programm der Columbia GSAPP. Barbour ist Inhaber und Direktor seines Büros Tacklebox, das er 2006 gründete. Zuvor hatte er für Daniel Rowen Architects (New York, 2001–02) und Andrew Bartle (ABA Studio, New York, 2002–06) gearbeitet. Zu seinen Projekten zählen die 3.1 Phillip Lim Boutique (New York, 2007) und Saipua (Brooklyn, New York, 2009, hier vorgestellt).

JEREMY BARBOUR, né à Roanoke (Virginie) en 1976 a obtenu son B.Arch. de la Virginia Tech (Blacksburg, Virginie, 2001) et son M.Arch. de l'université de Columbia GSAPP (New York, 2006). Il est professeur adjoint à Parson's The New School of Design et professeur assistant adjoint pour le programme d'ateliers d'été de la Columbia GSAPP. Il a créé Tacklebox en 2006, qu'il dirige. Auparavant, il avait travaillé chez Daniel Rowen Architects (New York, 2001–02) et Andrew Bartle (ABA Studio, New York, 2002–06). Il a réalisé, entre autres, le magasin 3.1 Phillip Lim (New York, 2007) et la boutique Saipua (Brooklyn, 2009, publiée ici).

SAIPUA

Brooklyn, New York, USA, 2009

Area: 65 m².
Client: Saipua.

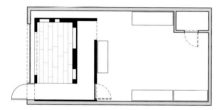
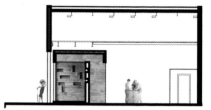

The designers made Saipua look as rugged and rural as possible. In such items as the alcoves destined to contain merchandise, the sophistication of their efforts becomes apparent.

Die Architekten gestalteten die Räume von Saipua so rustikal und ländlich wie möglich. Dennoch zeigt sich an Elementen wie den Wandnischen für die Waren, wie durchdacht das Konzept ist.

Les designers ont donné à la boutique Saipua un style aussi rustique que possible, même si dans les niches destinées à certains articles la sophistication du projet s'exprime clairement.

The main material used in this project was 167 square meters of reclaimed barn siding from a Shaker barn built in the 1890s in Michigan. Saipua is a family-run business that sells handmade soaps and floral arrangements. The shop is located in the industrial Red Hook area of Brooklyn. The architect states that the goal was to "create a new timeless space that simultaneously serves as a quiet backdrop and as an active participant in the ongoing act of making that defines Saipua." Located in an existing warehouse, Saipua was imagined as a "freestanding inhabitable box" made with the weathered wood brought from Michigan. The interior is made up of two small rooms, one nested within the other. The outer space dialogues with the street much like the front porch of a house, "serving as a place of gathering and performance: a stage where visitors take on the interchanging roles of performer and audience set against an ever-changing backdrop provided by both the interior life of the shop and the life of the street."

Bei diesem Projekt wurden als Material in erster Linie 167 m² altes Bauholz verwendet, das von der Seitenverkleidung einer alten Shaker-Scheune stammte, die in den 1890er-Jahren in Michigan erbaut worden war. Saipua ist ein Familienunternehmen, das handgemachte Seife und Blumen verkauft. Das Ladenlokal liegt im industriell geprägten Stadtviertel Red Hook in Brooklyn. Der Architekt betont, Ziel sei es gewesen, „einen neuen, zeitlosen Raum zu schaffen, der stille Kulisse und zugleich aktiver Darsteller in der Entstehungsgeschichte von Saipua ist". Der in einem alten Lagerhaus gelegene Laden wurde als „frei stehende, bewohnbare Box" konzipiert und aus dem verwitterten Holz aus Michigan gebaut. Das Interieur besteht aus zwei ineinandergeschachtelten Räumen. Der äußere Raum kommuniziert mit der Straße wie die Veranda eines Hauses und „dient als Treffpunkt und Bühne: eine Bühne, auf der die Besucher wechselseitig die Rollen von Darsteller und Publikum übernehmen, vor einer sich ständig wandelnden Kulisse – einerseits dem Interieur des Ladens, andererseits dem Treiben auf der Straße".

Le principal matériau utilisé dans ce projet est un bardage de bois de 167 m², récupéré d'une grange Shaker du Michigan datant des années 1890. Saipua est une entreprise familiale qui vend des savons artisanaux et des compositions florales. La boutique se trouve dans la zone industrielle de Red Hook à Brooklyn. Pour l'architecte, l'objectif était de « créer un nouvel espace intemporel qui soit en même temps un cadre tranquille et un participant actif à ce qui fait la spécificité de Saipua ». Installé dans un entrepôt existant, le magasin a été pensé comme « une boîte habitable autonome » faite du bois patiné rapporté du Michigan. L'intérieur se compose de deux petites pièces nichées l'une dans l'autre. L'espace extérieur dialogue avec la rue un peu comme le porche d'une maison « servant de lieu de rencontre et de performance, à la manière d'une scène sur laquelle les visiteurs peuvent emprunter le rôle à la fois de l'acteur et du public devant le décor en changement permanent de l'activité intérieure de la boutique et du spectacle de la rue ».

Weathered wood, and objects casually placed, as though in an inhabited environment, give Saipua a distinctive flavor that is not obviously modern.

Durch verwittertes Holz und die scheinbar spontan, wie in einem Wohnumfeld platzierten Objekte gewinnt Saipua ein ganz eigenes Flair, das auf den ersten Blick alles andere als modern wirkt.

Le bois patiné et des objets disposés de manière très libre, un peu comme dans une pièce inhabitée, confèrent à Saipua une personnalité très spécifique qui, à l'évidence, ne se veut pas moderne.

KOJI TSUTSUI

Born in Tokyo, Japan, in 1972, **KOJI TSUTSUI** graduated from the University of Tokyo (B.Arch., 1995). He then worked in the office of Tadao Ando (Osaka, 1995–2001). He went on to obtain an M.Arch. degree (The Bartlett, University College, London, 2004). In 2004, he founded his own firm, Koji Tsutsui & Associates, in Tokyo, and an office in San Francisco in 2010. He was selected for the Architectural Design Vanguard (2011). His work includes the InBetween House (Karuizawa, Nagano, Japan, 2010); Bent House (Tokyo, Japan, 2011–12, published here); Yutenji House (Tokyo, Japan, 2012); Mill Valley House (California, USA, 2012); a Hotel and Convention Center in India (2014); and Tohoku Village (northeast Japan, 2011–).

KOJI TSUTSUI, geboren 1972 in Tokio, absolvierte sein Studium an der Universität Tokio (B. Arch., 1995). Dann arbeitete er im Büro von Tadao Ando (Osaka, 1995–2001) und absolvierte 2004 seinen M. Arch. (The Bartlett, University College, London). Im selben Jahr gründete er sein eigenes Büro, Koji Tsutsui & Associates, in Tokio und eröffnete 2010 eine Zweigstelle in San Francisco. Er gehörte zur Auswahl des Architectural Design Vanguard 2011. Zu seinen Arbeiten zählen das InBetween House (Karuizawa, Nagano, Japan, 2010), das Bent House (Tokio, 2011–12, hier vorgestellt), das Yutenji House (Tokio, 2012), das Mill Valley House (Kalifornien, 2012), ein Hotel und Kongresszentrum in Indien (2014) und das Tohoku Village (im Nordosten Japans, seit 2011).

Né à Tokyo en 1972, **KOJI TSUTSUI** est diplômé de l'université de Tokyo (B.Arch, 1995). Il a ensuite travaillé dans l'agence de Tadao Ando (Osaka, 1995–2001) avant de poursuivre ses études et d'obtenir un M.Arch (The Bartlett University College, Londres, 2004). Il a créé son agence, Koji Tsutsui & Associates, à Tokyo en 2004, puis une agence à San Francisco en 2010. Il a été sélectionné pour le prix d'architecture Design Vanguard (2011). Ses réalisations comprennent l'InBetween House (Karuizawa, Nagano, Japon, 2010) ; la Bent House (Tokyo, 2011–12, publiée ici) ; la Yutenji House (Tokyo, 2012) ; la Mill Valley House (Californie, 2012) ; un hôtel et centre de congrès en Inde (2014) et le village de Tohoku (nord-est du Japon, 2011–).

BENT HOUSE

Tokyo, Japan, 2011–12

Area: 74 m².
Collaboration: Satoshi Ohkami (Project Manager).

A COR-TEN-steel entrance door opens into the narrow alley-like approach that leads to this house located in the dense urban fabric of Tokyo, on an 87-square-meter site. The architect conceived a structure made up of "three bent boxes" constituted by an entry, study, and a main living box. Each box is provided with a skylight. The architect explains: "The large main living box is bent to conform to the roof slope restriction of building code and to cover the terrace. The smaller boxes are bent to stretch out beyond the overhang of the larger box to harvest sunlight, while providing rain protection for the entrance. They also serve as guardrails for the second floor terrace and bring precious daylight to the first floor, which gets hardly any sun due to the proximity of neighboring houses." The forms of the house are in part determined by local building regulations. Koji Tsutsui states: "Our design engages light and spaces on the limited site to create a unique experience within the city."

Eine Eingangstür aus Cortenstahl öffnet den schmalen, gassenartigen Zugang, der zu diesem Haus führt, das im dichten urbanen Gewebe von Tokio auf einem 87 m² großen Grundstück steht. Der Architekt hat ein Gebäude aus „drei geknickten Schachteln" konzipiert, je eine enthält den Eingangsbereich, das Arbeitszimmer und den zentralen Wohnbereich. Jede Schachtel ist mit einem Oberlicht versehen. Der Architekt erläutert: „Die große Wohnbereichsschachtel ist geknickt, um den Baurichtlinien für Dachneigungen zu entsprechen und die Terrasse abzudecken. Die kleineren Schachteln sind geknickt, um über den Überhang der größeren Schachtel hinauszuragen und Sonne zu bekommen, gleichzeitig aber dem Eingang Regenschutz zu bieten. Sie fungieren außerdem als Schutzgeländer für die Terrasse im zweiten Stock und verhelfen dem ersten Stock zu kostbarem Tageslicht, der wegen der angrenzenden Häuser kaum Sonne bekommt." Die Gestalt des Hauses ist aber teilweise auch den lokalen Bauvorschriften geschuldet. Koji Tsutsui: „Unser Entwurf experimentiert mit Licht und Räumen und sorgt so für ein unverwechselbares Wohnerlebnis in der Stadt."

Une porte d'entrée en acier Corten ouvre sur l'étroite allée d'accès à cette maison construite sur un terrain de 87 m² dans le tissu urbain dense de Tokyo. L'architecte a imaginé une structure faite de « trois boîtes pliées » constituées par une entrée, un bureau et un salon dans la boîte principale. Chaque cube possède une lucarne. L'architecte explique : « La vaste boîte salon est repliée pour respecter la limitation de la pente du toit imposée par les réglementations de construction et couvrir la terrasse. Les deux autres boîtes plus petites sont repliées pour s'étendre au-delà du surplomb de la grande boîte afin de capter les rayons du soleil tout en protégeant l'entrée de la pluie. Elles servent également de balustrade à la terrasse du premier étage et font entrer la précieuse lumière du jour au rez-de-chaussée où la proximité avec les maisons avoisinantes empêche presque le soleil de pénétrer. » Les formes de la maison sont déterminées en partie par les réglementations locales des constructions. Koji Tsutsui constate que « notre idée associe la lumière et les espaces sur une surface réduite pour créer une expérience d'habitat unique au cœur de la ville ».

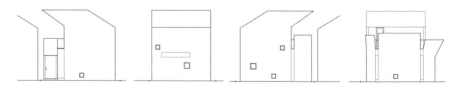

The design of the Bent House creates intimate, well-lit space in a very dense urban setting. This effect is achieved with a design that is "bent" to admit the light, as seen in the drawings above.

Das Bent House bietet intime, helle Räumlichkeiten in dicht besiedelter urbaner Umgebung. Den Effekt erzielt der Entwurf durch eine „abgeknickte" Formgebung, um den Lichteinfall zu gewährleisten, wie die Zeichnungen oben zeigen.

Le design de la Bent House crée un espace d'intimité bien éclairé dans un environnement urbain très dense. Cet effet est obtenu avec une conception « pliée » pour laisser entrer la lumière, comme on le voit sur les plans ci-dessus.

Interiors are bright and modern with such features as the stairway that emerges directly from a wall, seen above.

Die Innenräume sind hell und hochmodern ausgestattet, etwa mit einer Treppe, die direkt aus der Wand ragt, wie oben zu sehen.

L'intérieur est clair et moderne avec des éléments insolites, comme l'escalier qui émerge directement d'un mur (ci-dessus).

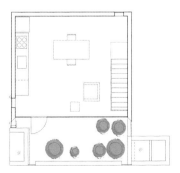

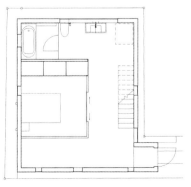

TYIN TEGNESTUE ARCHITECTS

TYIN tegnestue Architects was established in 2008. The office has completed several projects in poor and underdeveloped areas of Thailand, Burma, Haiti, and Uganda. TYIN is currently run by **M. ANDREAS G. GJERTSEN** and **YASHAR HANSTAD**, and has its headquarters in Trondheim, Norway. Their projects include the Safe Haven Library, Tak Province (Thailand, 2009); Old Market Library (Bangkok, Thailand, 2009); a Boathouse (Aure, Møre og Romsdal, Norway, 2010–11, published here); Klong Toey Community Lantern (Bangkok, Thailand, 2011); and the Cassia Co-Op Training Center (Sumatra, Indonesia, 2011).

TYIN tegnestue Architects wurde 2008 gegründet. Das Büro hat mehrere Projekte in armen und unterentwickelten Gebieten von Thailand, Burma, Haiti und Uganda ausgeführt. Gegenwärtig wird TYIN von **M. ANDREAS G. GJERTSEN** und **YASHAR HANSTAD** geleitet mit Sitz in Trondheim, Norwegen. Zu ihren Werken zählen die Safe Haven Library in der Provinz Tak (Thailand, 2009); die Old Market Library (Bangkok, Thailand, 2009); ein Bootshaus (Aure, Møre og Romsdal, Norwegen, 2010–11, hier veröffentlicht); Klong Toey Community Lantern (Bangkok, Thailand, 2011) und das Training Center Cassia Co-Op (Sumatra, Indonesien, 2011).

TYIN tegnestue Architects a été fondé en 2008. L'agence a depuis réalisé plusieurs projets dans des régions pauvres et sous-développées de Thaïlande, Birmanie, Haïti et Ouganda. Elle est actuellement dirigée par **M. ANDREAS G. GJERTSEN** et **YASHAR HANSTAD,** et son siège est situé à Trondheim, en Norvège. Leurs projets comprennent la bibliothèque de Safe Haven, dans la province de Tak (Thaïlande, 2009) ; la bibliothèque du Vieux Marché (Bangkok, Thaïlande, 2009) ; un hangar pour bateaux (Aure, Møre og Romsdal, Norvège, 2010–11, publié ici) ; Klong Toey Community Lantern (Bangkok, Thaïlande, 2011) et le centre de formation Cassia Co-Op (Sumatra, Indonésie, 2011).

BOATHOUSE

Aure, Møre og Romsdal, Norway, 2010–11

Area: 77 m². Client: Stein Erik Sørstrøm, Cost: €4 634.
Collaboration: Marianne Løbersli Sørstrøm.

This boathouse was built on the site of an 18th-century structure having the same function. The architects state: "It was in such a bad state that the owner decided to tear it down and build it anew. The simplicity of the old building, its good placement, and honest use of materials, would become key sources of inspiration for the design of the new building." Old windows from a nearby farmhouse were incorporated into the building, which is made of Norwegian pine, with materials from the old boathouse used to clad some interior surfaces. The architects explain: "Rational choices with regard to material use, method of construction, and detailing have given this boathouse its distinguished architectural features. The building remains true to the historical and cultural heritage of Norway's coastal regions, while catering to new modes of usage."

Dieses Bootshaus wurde anstelle eines Vorgängers aus dem 18. Jahrhundert errichtet. Die Architekten: „Das alte Boots-haus war in einem derart schlechten Zustand, dass sich der Eigentümer für Abriss und Neubau entschied. Die Einfachheit des alten Gebäudes, sein günstiger Standort und der ehrliche Materialeinsatz sollten zu einer wesentlichen Inspirationsquelle für den Neubau werden." Für das Projekt aus Norwegischer Kiefer kamen Fenster eines in der Nähe gelegenen Bauernhauses zum Einsatz und für einen Teil der Verkleidung im Inneren Materialien des alten Bootshauses. Die Architekten: „Den ausge-zeichneten architektonischen Eigenschaften des Bootshauses liegen rationale Entscheidungen im Hinblick auf verwendete Materialien, Baumethoden und Gestaltungsdetails zugrunde. Das Gebäude bleibt dem historischen und kulturellen Erbe der norwegischen Küstenregion treu und eröffnet gleichzeitig neue Nutzungsmöglichkeiten."

Ce hangar à bateaux a été construit sur le site d'une structure du XVIIIᵉ siècle qui avait déjà cette fonction. Les architectes ont expliqué qu'« elle était dans un état tellement mauvais que le propriétaire a préféré la raser et reconstruire. La simplicité de l'ancienne construction, son orientation favorable et l'usage sans fioritures des matériaux sont devenus des sources d'inspi-ration essentielles pour le nouveau bâtiment ». Des fenêtres d'une ferme voisine ont été réutilisées, les murs sont en épicéa et des éléments de l'ancien hangar à bateaux ont été repris pour revêtir certaines surfaces intérieures. Les architectes constatent : « Des choix rationnels en ce qui concerne l'emploi des matériaux, les méthodes de construction et les détails confèrent son caractère architectural distingué au hangar à bateaux. Il reste fidèle à l'héritage historique et culturel des régions côtières norvégiennes, tout en apportant de nouveaux usages. »

Sitting flush with the earth on the inland side, the Boathouse has a comfortable wooden terrace and appears quite closed from most angles, despite its large opening facing the water on the south façade.

Das Bootshaus steht auf der see-abgewandten Seite direkt auf dem Erdboden, hat eine bequeme Holz-terrasse und wirkt aus fast allen Blickwinkeln relativ geschlossen, trotz der großen wasserseitigen Öffnung in der Südfassade.

Posée de plain-pied avec le sol vers l'intérieur des terres, la Boathouse dispose d'une agréable terrasse de bois et montre une apparence plutôt fermée sous la plupart des angles, malgré la vaste ouverture face à l'eau dans le mur sud.

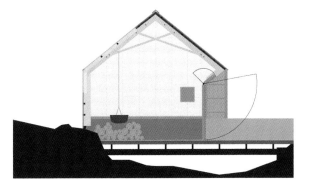

Above, band windows running down the roof and walls bring natural light into the structure. Below: the cladding is made from Norwegian pine, which was pressure-treated using a product based on environmentally friendly biological waste derived from the production of sugar (Kebony).

Oben die Bandfenster, die sich über Dach und Wände ziehen und natürliches Licht ins Gebäude lassen. Unten: Die Verschalung besteht aus dem Holz der Norwegischen Kiefer, das mit umweltfreundlichem, organischem Abfallmaterial aus der Zuckerherstellung (Kebony) druckimprägniert wurde.

Ci-dessus, des fenêtres en bande descendent du toit le long des murs et font pénétrer la lumière du jour à l'intérieur. Ci-dessous : le bardage des murs est en épicéa imprégné sous pression d'un produit à base de déchets biologiques de la production écologique de sucre (Kebony).

The façades of the house, lined with back-lit cotton canvas, open vertically, leaving only the supports of the house between the interior and the terrace.

Die mit hinterleuchtetem Baumwollstoff bespannten Wände lassen sich vertikal öffnen, sodass nur noch Stützpfeiler den Innenraum von der Terrasse trennen.

Les façades, doublées de toile de coton rétroéclairée, s'ouvrent verticalement, l'intérieur n'est alors plus séparé de la terrasse que par les appuis de la maison.

UNSTUDIO

BEN VAN BERKEL was born in Utrecht, The Netherlands, in 1957 and studied at the Rietveld Academy in Amsterdam and at the Architectural Association (AA) in London, receiving the AA Diploma with honors in 1987. After working briefly in the office of Santiago Calatrava in 1988, he set up his practice in Amsterdam with Caroline Bos, under the name United Network Studio (UNStudio). Their work include the Möbius House (Naarden, 1993–98); Het Valkhof Museum (Nijmegen, 1995–99); and NMR Laboratory (Utrecht, 1997–2000), all in The Netherlands; VilLA NM (upstate New York, USA, 2000–06); and the Mercedes-Benz Museum (Stuttgart, Germany, 2001–06). More recent work includes the Music Theater (Graz, Austria, 1998–2008); Burnham Pavilion (Chicago, Illinois, USA, 2009); New Amsterdam Pavilion (New York, USA, 2009, published here); Haus am Weinberg (Stuttgart, Germany, 2008–11); the Center for Virtual Engineering (ZVE), Fraunhofer Institute (Stuttgart, Germany, 2006–12); I'Park City (Suwon, South Korea, 2008–12); the King David the Builder International Airport in Kutaisi (Georgia, 2011–12); and Arnhem Station (The Netherlands, 1996–2014). Ongoing work includes Raffles City (Hangzhou, China, 2008–14); Singapore University of Technology and Design (Singapore, 2010–14); and the Dance Palace in St. Petersburg (Russia, 2009–).

BEN VAN BERKEL wurde 1957 in Utrecht geboren und studierte an der Rietveld-Akademie in Amsterdam sowie an der Architectural Association (AA) in London, wo er 1987 das Diplom mit Auszeichnung erhielt. Nach einer kurzen Tätigkeit bei Santiago Calatrava 1988 gründete er mit Caroline Bos unter dem Namen United Network Studio (UNStudio) sein eigenes Büro im Amsterdam. Zu den Arbeiten der beiden gehören das Haus Möbius (Naarden, 1993–98), das Museum Het Valkhof (Nimwegen, 1995–99), das Labor NMR (Utrecht, 1997–2000), die VilLA NM (bei New York, 2000–06) und das Mercedes-Benz-Museum (Stuttgart, 2001–06). Jüngere Arbeiten umfassen u.a. ein Musiktheater in Graz (1998–2008), den Burnham Pavilion (Chicago, Illinois, 2009), den New Amsterdam Pavilion (New York, 2009, hier vorgestellt), das Haus am Weinberg (Stuttgart, 2008–11), das Zentrum für Virtuelles Engineering (ZVE), das Fraunhofer-Institut (Stuttgart, 2006–12), I'Park City (Suwon, Südkorea, 2008–12), den internationalen Flughafen König David der Erbauer in Kutaisi (Georgien, 2011–12) und den Bahnhof Arnheim (1996–2014). Zu den aktuellen Projekten gehören Raffles City (Hangzhou, China, 2008–14), die Universität für Technologie und Design in Singapur (2010–14) und der Tanzpalast in St. Petersburg (seit 2009).

BEN VAN BERKEL, né à Utrecht, Pays-Bas, en 1957, a étudié à l'Académie Rietveld à Amsterdam et à l'Architectural Association (AA) de Londres dont il est sorti diplômé avec mention en 1987. Après avoir brièvement travaillé pour Santiago Calatrava en 1988, il a créé avec Caroline Bos son agence United Network Studio (UNStudio) à Amsterdam. Leurs projets comprennent: la maison Möbius (Naarden, 1993–98); le musée Het Valkhof (Nimègue, 1995–99) et le laboratoire NMR (Utrecht, 1997–2000), toutes aux Pays-Bas; la VilLA NM (Upstate New York, 2000–06) et le musée Mercedes-Benz (Stuttgart, 2001–06). Les projets récents comprennent le Théâtre musical (Graz, Autriche, 1998–2008); le pavillon Burnham (Chicago, 2009); le pavillon de la Nouvelle-Amsterdam (New York, 2009, publié ici); la Haus am Weinberg (Stuttgart, 2008–11); le Centre d'ingénierie virtuelle (ZVE) de l'Institut Fraunhofer (Stuttgart, 2006–12); I'Park City (Suwon, Corée du Sud, 2008–12); l'aéroport international David le Bâtisseur de Koutaïssi (Géorgie, 2011–12) et la gare d'Arnhem (Pays-Bas, 1996–2014). Les travaux en cours sont Raffles City (Hangzhou, Chine, 2008–14); l'Université de technologie et design de Singapour (2010–14) et le Palais de la danse à Saint-Pétersbourg (2009–).

NEW AMSTERDAM PAVILION

New York, USA, 2009

Area: 37 m². Client: The Battery Conservancy, New York.
Collaboration: Wouter de Jonge, Christian Veddeler, Handel Architects (Executive Architects).

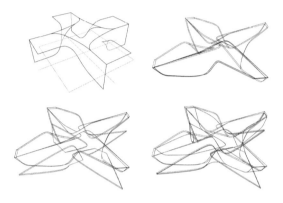

Commissioned by the Battery Conservancy, this structure was presented as a gift from the Dutch government to the people of New York. The pavilion is intended to introduce an opportunity for visitors to pause and learn more at this historically important location. The center of the installation was designed for "more permanent, enclosed functions." Long interested in computer-oriented design and complex forms in his architecture, Ben van Berkel created four wings for this pavilion, where "the contrast between the inside and the outside is blurred through the expression of continuous geometry." This also results in the fact that the structure has neither a front nor a back, but is meant to be viewed and approached from all angles. Alternating art and video installations also contribute to the interest of the structure. The envelope of the structure is made of polyurethane-coated plywood.

Das Gebäude, in Auftrag gegeben von der Battery Conservancy, war ein Geschenk der niederländischen Regierung an die Bürger von New York. Der Pavillon soll Besuchern die Möglichkeit geben, innezuhalten und mehr über diesen historisch bedeutsamen Ort zu erfahren. Der Innenraum der Installation soll als „eher dauerhafter, in sich geschlossener Funktionsbereich" fungieren. Ben van Berkel, der sich in seiner Architektur bereits seit Langem für computerorientierte Entwürfe und komplexe Formen interessiert, gestaltete vier Flügel für diesen Pavillon, bei dem „der Kontrast zwischen innen und außen durch die Unendlichkeit seiner Geometrie" verschwimmt – was zur Folge hat, dass das Gebäude keine Vorder- oder Rückseite hat, man es von allen Seiten betrachten und sich ihm nähern kann. Wechselnde Video- und Kunstinstallationen verstärken den Reiz des Bauwerks zusätzlich. Die Außenhülle der Konstruktion besteht aus mit Polyurethan beschichtetem Sperrholz.

Commandé par l'administration du Battery Park, le pavillon a été présenté comme un don du gouvernement néerlandais à la population de New York. Il vise à fournir aux visiteurs l'occasion de faire une pause et d'en apprendre plus sur l'importance historique du lieu. Le centre de l'installation a été conçu pour «des fonctions fermées plus permanentes». Intéressé depuis longtemps par le design informatisé et les formes complexes en architecture, Ben van Berkel a donné quatre ailes à son pavillon où «le contraste entre intérieur et extérieur est effacé par l'expression de géométrie continue». C'est aussi ce qui explique que le pavillon ne possède ni avant, ni arrière, mais puisse être vu et approché de tous les côtés. L'alternance des installations artistiques et vidéo contribuent également à son intérêt. L'enveloppe du bâtiment est en contreplaqué recouvert de polyuréthane.

Giving free rein to his interest in
computer-generated forms, Ben van
Berkel creates a form whose interior
and exterior are made of continuous
surfaces. Right, a site plan shows
the pavilion in Battery Park.

Ben van Berkel hat seiner Begeis-
terung für computergeneriertes
Entwerfen freien Lauf gelassen und
ein Gebilde geschaffen, dessen
Innen und Außen eine durchgehende
Oberfläche bilden. Rechts zeigt
ein Lageplan den Pavillon im
Battery Park.

Laissant libre cours à son intérêt
pour les formes générées par
ordinateur, Ben van Berkel crée une
forme dont l'intérieur et l'extérieur
sont des surfaces continues.
À droite, un plan du site montre le
pavillon dans le Battery Park.

VAILLO + IRIGARAY ARCHITECTS

ANTONIO VAILLO I DANIEL was born in Barcelona, Spain, in 1960 and studied Architecture at the ETSA of Navarre (1979–85). **JUAN LUIS IRIGARAY HUARTE** was born in Navarre, Spain, in 1956 and also studied at the ETSA of Navarre (1974–80). Their most significant recent projects are an Office Silo + Container (Tajonar, Navarre, 2005); B2 House (Pamplona, Navarre, 2005); D Jewelry (Pamplona, 2006–07, published here); Hotel and Office Tower (Vitoria, Álava, 2008); El Mercao Restaurant (Pamplona, 2008); Lounge ms (Cadreita, Navarre, 2009); Audenasa Office Building (Noain, Navarre, 2009); and the CIB Biomedical Research Center, Hospital of Navarre (Pamplona, 2011), all in Spain.

ANTONIO VAILLO I DANIEL wurde 1960 in Barcelona geboren und studierte Architektur an der ETSA in Navarra (1979–85). **JUAN LUIS IRIGARAY HUARTE** wurde 1956 in Navarra, Spanien, geboren und studierte ebenfalls an der ETSA in Navarra (1974–80). Ihre wichtigsten neueren Projekte sind ein Büro-Silo + Container (Tajonar, Navarre, 2005), das B2 House (Pamplona, Navarre, 2005), D Jewelry (Pamplona, 2006–07, hier vorgestellt), ein Hotel- und Bürohochhaus (Vitoria, Álava, 2008), das Restaurant El Mercao (Pamplona, 2008), Lounge ms (Cadreita, Navarre, 2009), das Audenasa-Bürohaus (Noain, Navarre, 2009) und das Biomedizinische Forschungszentrum CIB am Krankenhaus von Navarra (Pamplona, 2011), alle in Spanien.

ANTONIO VAILLO I DANIEL, né à Barcelone en 1960, a étudié l'architecture à l'ETSA de Navarre (1979–85). **JUAN LUIS IRIGARAY HUARTE**, né en Navarre en 1956, a suivi les mêmes études (1974–80). Leurs projets récents les plus significatifs sont un silo-bureaux + conteneurs (Tajonar, Navarre, 2005) ; la Maison B2 (Pampelune, Navarre, 2005) ; la joaillerie D (Pampelune, 2006–07, publiée ici) ; une tour pour un hôtel et des bureaux (Vitoria, Álava, 2008) ; le restaurant El Mercao (Pampelune, 2008) ; le Lounge ms (Cadreita, Navarre, 2009) ; l'immeuble de bureaux Audenasa (Noain, Navarre, 2009) et le Centre de recherches biomédicales CIB de l'Hôpital de Navarre (Pampelune, 2011).

D JEWELRY
Pamplona, Spain, 2006–07

Area: 50 m². Client: Danieli Joyeros. Cost: €267 000.
Collaboration: Daniel Galar (Project Manager).

The architects explain: "The project intends to create an atmosphere—and, therefore, a universe—(not a shop) in these little premises in the city center, whose rectangular, deep and narrow geometry has to contain the elements of jewelry." They further describe the sought-after atmosphere as "mysterious, strange, hollow, and weightless, while Oriental and Baroque." Inspired by a jewelry chest or box holding unique objects, the décor uses theatrical elements inspired by dark curtains and stage lighting. The upper section is dark and matt, while the lower one is "silver, bright, heavy, and rigid." The floor, some wall coverings, and doors to the jewelry boxes are made of thick aluminum plates measuring 100 x 60 centimeters that show the imperfections in their smelting, lending an air of age to recently fabricated elements.

Die Architekten erklären: „In diesem kleinen Ladenlokal im Stadtzentrum, dessen rechteckige, tiefe und schmale Form etwas von einem Schmuckstück hat, will das Projekt eine eigene Atmosphäre schaffen – und damit ein Universum – keinen Laden." Darüber hinaus beschreibt das Team die exklusive Atmosphäre als „geheimnisvoll, fremdartig, hohl und schwerelos, dabei zugleich orientalisch und barock". Das Interieur, inspiriert von einem Schmuckkästchen oder einer Schatulle für wertvolle Objekte, arbeitet mit theaterhaften Elementen wie dunklen Vorhängen und Bühnenscheinwerfern. Der obere Bereich ist dunkel und matt, der untere „silbern, hell, schwer und streng". Der Boden, einige der Deckenpaneele und die Türen zu den „Schmuck- kästchen" sind aus massiven, 100 x 60 cm großen Aluminiumplatten gefertigt. Durch Unregelmäßigkeiten im Schmelzprozess gewinnen die erst kürzlich gegossenen Paneele an Patina.

Selon le descriptif des architectes, « ce projet veut créer une atmosphère et donc un univers – pas une boutique – dans ce petit espace au centre de la ville dont le plan étroit, profond et rectangulaire doit recevoir des pièces de joaillerie ». Ils parlent également d'une atmosphère « mystérieuse, étrange, en creux, impondérable, orientale et baroque ». Inspiré d'une boîte à bijoux, le décor fait appel à des éléments théâtraux comme des rideaux sombres et un éclairage de scène. L'étage est traité dans des tonalités sombres et mates, tandis que le rez-de-chaussée est « argenté, lumineux, pesant et rigide ». Le sol, certains revêtements des murs et les portes sont en épaisses plaques d'aluminium de 100 x 60 cm qui laissent voir les imperfections de leur fabrication, imposant d'une certaine façon le poids du temps à des éléments qui viennent d'être fabriqués.

The small store is both austere and powerful, seeming to be carved out of solid aluminum, forming what the designers compare to a jewelry box.

Der kleine Laden ist ebenso streng wie eindrucksvoll und wirkt fast, als wäre er aus massivem Aluminium geschnitten, um ein – so die Architekten – Schmuckkästchen zu bilden.

Ce petit magasin au style d'une austère puissance semble creusé dans l'aluminium massif pour former ce que ses concepteurs ont appelé une boîte à bijoux.

The arrangement of spaces and displays appears from some angles to be part of an archaic machine.

Die Anordnung der Raumzonen und Vitrinen wirkt aus manchen Blickwinkeln wie das Innere einer archaischen Maschine.

La disposition des vitrines évoque sous certains angles une machinerie archaïque.

To the right, the roughly finished aluminum panels that are used in the lower section of the boutique.

Rechts: Aluminiumpaneele mit rauer Oberfläche, die im unteren Bereich des Ladens zum Einsatz kommen.

À droite, les panneaux d'aluminium brut de fonderie utilisés au rez-de-chaussée de la boutique.

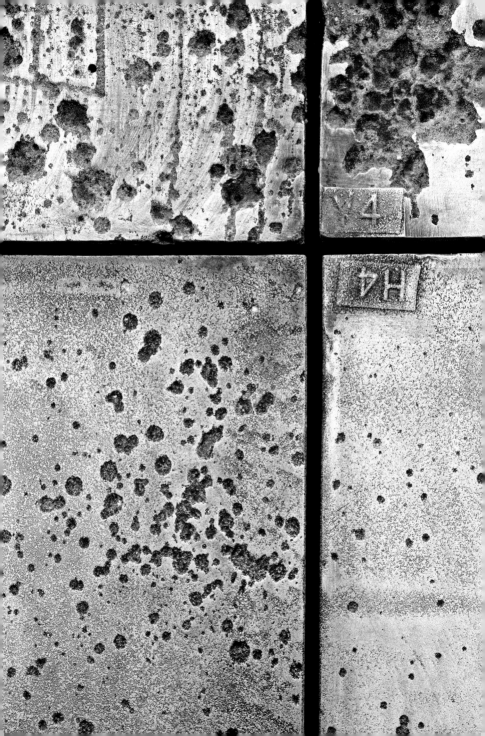

540

VO TRONG NGHIA

VO TRONG NGHIA, the founding partner of the company, was born in Quang Binh Province, Vietnam, in 1976. He attended Hanoi Architecture University (1994) and received a B.Arch. degree from the Nagoya Institute of Technology (Japan, 2002), followed by a Master of Civil Engineering from the University of Tokyo (2004). **MASAAKI IWAMOTO** was born in Tokyo in 1982. He studied Architecture at the University of Tokyo (2008) and the Institute of Lightweight Structures and Conceptual Design, Stuttgart University, Germany. In 2011 he joined Vo Trong Nghia Architects as a partner and Director of the Ho Chi Minh City office. The company's major works are wNw Café (Binh Duong, 2006); wNw Bar (Binh Duong, 2008); Bamboo Wing (Vinh Phuc, 2009); the Vietnam Pavilion for Shanghai Expo (Shanghai, China, 2010); Stacking Green (Ho Chi Minh City, 2011); Binh Duong School (Binh Duong, 2011); the Stone House (Quangninh, 2012); Dailai Conference Hall (Vinh Phuc, 2012); and Low-Cost House (Dongnai, 2012, published here), all in Vietnam unless stated otherwise.

VO TRONG NGHIA, Gründungspartner des Büros, wurde in der Provinz Quang Binh, Vietnam, geboren. Er studierte an der Architekturhochschule Hanoi (1994) und absolvierte einen B. Arch. am Nagoya Institut für Technik (Japan, 2002) sowie einen Master in Bauingenieurwesen an der Universität Tokio (2004). **MASAAKI IWAMOTO** wurde 1982 in Tokio geboren. Er studierte Architektur an der Universität Tokio (2008) und am Institut für Leichtbau, Entwerfen und Konstruieren der Universität Stuttgart. 2011 stieß er als Partner zu Vo Trong Nghia Architects und übernahm die Leitung des Büros in Ho-Chi-Minh-Stadt. Zu ihren wichtigsten Arbeiten zählen das Café wNw (Binh Duong, 2006), die Bar wNw (Binh Duong, 2008), Bamboo Wing (Vinh Phuc, 2009), der Vietnamesische Pavillon für die Expo in Schanghai (China, 2010), Stacking Green (Ho-Chi-Minh-Stadt, 2011), die Schule in Binh Duong (2011), das Steinhaus (Quangninh, 2012), der Konferenzsaal Dailai (Vinh Phuc, 2012) und das Niedrigpreishaus (Dongnai, 2012, hier vorgestellt), alle in Vietnam, sofern nicht anders angegeben.

VO TRONG NGHIA, partenaire fondateur de l'agence, est né dans la province de Quang Binh (Viêtnam) en 1976. Il a étudié à l'Université d'architecture d'Hanoï (1994). Il a obtenu un B.Arch à l'Institut de technologie de Nagoya (Japon, 2002) et un master en ingénierie civile à l'université de Tokyo (2004). **MASAAKI IWAMOTO** est né à Tokyo en 1982. Il a fait des études d'architecture à l'université de Tokyo (2008) et à l'Institut des structures légères et du design conceptuel de l'université de Stuttgart. Il a rejoint Vo Trong Nghia Architects en 2011, en est partenaire et directeur de l'agence d'Hô-Chi-Minh-Ville. Les réalisations les plus importantes de l'agence sont le café wNw (Binh Duong, 2006) ; le bar wNw (Binh Duong, 2008) ; Bamboo Wing (Vinh Phuc, 2009) ; le pavillon du Viêtnam pour l'Expo de Shanghai (2010) ; la maison Stacking Green (Hô-Chi-Minh-Ville, 2011) ; l'école de Binh Duong (2011) ; la Villa de pierre (Quangninh, 2012) ; la salle de conférences Dailai (Vinh Phuc, 2012) et la Maison à bas prix (Dong Nai, 2012, publiée ici), toutes au Viêtnam sauf mention contraire.

LOW-COST HOUSE

Dongnai, Vietnam, 2012

Area: 22 m² (House A), 18 m² (House B). Client: Wind and Water House JSC.
Cost: $3200 per house. Collaboration: Kosuke Nishijima (Team Manager).

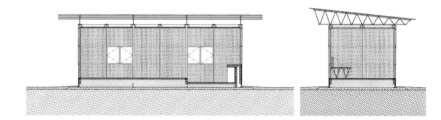

The simple, rectangular houses are made with bamboo screens and polycarbonate sheeting supported by a light metal frame. The interior (plan below) is an open space divided by curtains.

Die schlichten, rechteckigen Häuser bestehen aus Bambusblenden und Polycarbonatplatten, gehalten von einem leichten Metallrahmen. Das Innere (Grundriss unten) ist ein offener, von Vorhängen unterteilter Raum.

Les maisons rectangulaires très simples sont faites d'écrans de bambou et de feuilles de polycarbonate portés par une charpente métallique légère. L'intérieur (plan ci-dessous) est un espace ouvert divisé par des rideaux.

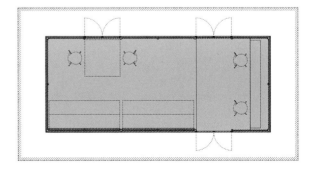

Although the amount of available low-cost housing in Vietnam has increased greatly in the past decade, many families still live in houses that are smaller than 10 square meters. The aim of this project is to propose a prototype house for low-income families in Vietnam. Two prototypes were built on an experimental basis in Dongnai province, on the construction site of a kindergarten project designed by the architects. The first house, with a floor area of 22.5 square meters, was designed as a model home; the second, measuring 18 square meters, was designed as a site office for the kindergarten, showing the flexibility of this prototype. On the assumption that the bathroom and kitchen are placed outside and shared by several families, the house has a minimum amount of space for living, eating, and sleeping. The plan was designed to be adjustable in the longitudinal direction, allowing for future expansion for family members and functions. The interior is a one-room space, articulated by curtains and differences in floor level. The floor rises higher, creating minimal pieces of furniture such as a desk. The other distinctive feature is the folding beds that allow the residents to sit on the floor during the day. These beds can also be transformed into sofas if required. The future residents participated in the construction in order to further reduce costs. A polycarbonate panel wall, corrugated FRP panel roof, and bamboo louvers are the main materials.

Auch wenn sich das Angebot an preisgünstigem Wohnraum in Vietnam in den letzten zehn Jahren entschieden verbessert hat, so leben doch noch immer viele Familien in Häusern mit weniger als 10 m² Wohnraum. Ziel des Projektes war es, einen Hausprototypen für einkommensschwache Schichten zu entwickeln. Auf dem Gelände eines Kindergartenprojektes der Architekten in der Provinz Dongnai wurden zwei experimentelle Häuser errichtet. Das erste, mit einer Grundfläche von 22,5 m², wurde als Musterhaus entworfen, das andere, 18 m² groß, als Baubüro für den Kindergarten, was die Flexibilität des Prototypen unter Beweis stellte. Unter der Voraussetzung, dass Bad und Küche sich außerhalb befinden und mit anderen Familien geteilt werden, bietet das Haus ein Mindestmaß an Platz zum Leben, Essen und Schlafen. Der Entwurf sieht eine mögliche Anpassung in Längsrichtung vor, was eine Erweiterung für weitere Familienmitglieder oder Nutzungen erlaubt. Das Innere besteht aus einem Raum, der durch Vorhänge und Unterschiede im Bodenniveau strukturiert wird. Dort, wo der Boden höher ist, entsteht eine minimalistische Möblierung, etwa ein Schreibtisch. Ein weiteres markantes Merkmal der Innenarchitektur sind die Faltbetten, die es den Bewohnern erlauben, tagsüber auf dem Boden zu sitzen. Bei Bedarf können die Betten auch in Sofas verwandelt werden. Um die Kosten noch weiter zu senken, halfen die zukünftigen Bewohner beim Bau mit. An Materialien wurden im Wesentlichen Polycarbonatplatten für die Wände, GFK-Platten (glasfaserverstärkter Kunststoff) für das Dach und Bambus für die Verblendungen verwendet.

Malgré une forte augmentation du nombre de logements à bas prix disponibles au Viêtnam depuis dix ans, de nombreuses familles habitent encore des maisons de moins de 10 m². Le but de ce projet est de fournir un prototype d'habitat pour les couches sociales à faible revenu du Viêtnam. Deux exemplaires ont été construits à titre expérimental dans la province de Dong Nai. La première maison, avec une surface au sol de 22,5 m², a été conçue comme une habitation modèle ; la deuxième, de 18 m², a été créée pour accueillir un bureau du jardin d'enfants, démontrant la souplesse et la polyvalence du prototype. La salle de bains et la cuisine étant extérieures et communes à plusieurs familles, la maison présente un espace minimal pour vivre, manger et dormir. Le plan a été conçu pour pouvoir être complété dans le sens de la longueur et permettre de futures extensions pour les différents membres de la famille et les différentes fonctions. L'intérieur est une pièce unique articulée par des rideaux et des différences du niveau du sol. Le sol s'élève pour créer des éléments de mobilier minimalistes, notamment un pupitre. L'autre caractéristique est constituée par les lits pliants qui permettent aux habitants de s'asseoir par terre pendant la journée ou peuvent au besoin être transformés en canapés. Afin de réduire encore plus les coûts, les futurs habitants ont participé à la construction. Les matériaux utilisés consistent essentiellement en un mur de panneaux polycarbonates, un toit en panneaux de FRP ondulé et des persiennes en bambou.

Although rustic in its ultimate simplicity, the house has a generous open space that can be used for various purposes, with white curtains available to create some privacy.

Rustikal in seiner radikalen Schlichtheit bietet das Haus doch reichlich Platz für unterschiedliche Zwecke. Mittels weißer Vorhänge kann etwas Privatsphäre geschaffen werden.

Bien que rustique dans sa simplicité extrême, la maison dispose d'un espace ouvert généreux qui peut avoir plusieurs usages, des rideaux blancs pouvant permettre un peu d'intimité.

JOHN WARDLE

JOHN WARDLE received his B.Arch. degree from RMIT University (Melbourne, 1980). He did postgraduate studies at Burnley Horticultural College (Melbourne, 1983) and obtained his M.Arch. degree from RMIT (Melbourne, 2001). The office has two Principals, John Wardle and Stefan Mee. Their work includes the Nigel Peck Centre for Learning and Leadership Building, Melbourne Grammar School (Melbourne, 2007); Hawke Building, University of South Australia (Adelaide, 2008; in association with Hassell Architects); Shearers Quarters (North Bruny Island, Tasmania, 2011, published here); UNISA Minerals and Materials Building and the Plasso, University of South Australia (Adelaide, 2011; in association with Swanbury Penglase, and Wilson Architects); Fairhaven House (Victoria, 2012); Westfield Sydney City Redevelopment (Sydney, 2012; in association with Westfield Design & Construction); New John Wardle Architects Studio (Collingwood, 2012); UTS Institute for Marine and Antarctic Studies, University of Tasmania (Tasmania, 2012; in association with Terroir Architects); and the Faculty of Architecture, Building and Planning Building, University of Melbourne (Melbourne, 2014–; in collaboration with NADAAA), all in Australia.

JOHN WARDLE absolvierte seinen B. Arch. an der RMIT University (Melbourne, 1980), machte ein Aufbaustudium am Burnley Horticultural College (Melbourne, 1983) und absolvierte dann seinen M. Arch. an der RMIT (Melbourne, 2001). Das Büro hat zwei Teilhaber, John Wardle und Stefan Mee. Zu ihren Arbeiten gehören das Nigel Peck Centre for Learning and Leadership Building der Melbourne Grammar School (Melbourne, 2007), das Hawke Building, University of South Australia (Adelaide, 2008, in Zusammenarbeit mit Hassell Architects), Shearers Quarters (North Bruny Island, Tasmanien, 2011, hier vorgestellt), das UNISA Minerals and Materials Building and the Plasso, University of South Australia (Adelaide, 2011, in Zusammenarbeit mit Swanbury Penglase und Wilson Architects), das Fairhaven House (Victoria, 2012), Westfield Sydney City Redevelopment (Sydney, 2012, in Zusammenarbeit mit Westfield Design & Construction), das neue Büro von John Wardle Architects (Collingwood, 2012), das UTS Institute for Marine and Antarctic Studies, University of Tasmania (Tasmanien, 2012, in Zusammenarbeit mit Terroir Architects), und das Building and Planning Building der Architekturfakultät der Universität Melbourne (Melbourne, 2014–, in Zusammenarbeit mit NADAAA), alle in Australien.

JOHN WARDLE a obtenu son B.Arch à l'université RMIT (Melbourne, 1980). Il a ensuite fait des études de troisième cycle au collège horticole Burnley (Melbourne, 1983) et a obtenu son M.Arch à la RMIT (Melbourne, 2001). Il est responsable de l'agence avec Stefan Mee. Leurs réalisations comprennent le Nigel Peck Centre for Learning and Leadership Building du lycée de Melbourne (Melbourne, 2007) ; le bâtiment Hawke, université d'Australie-Méridionale (Adelaïde, 2008 ; en association avec Hassell Architects) ; Shearers Quarters (île de North Bruny, Tasmanie, 2011, publié ici) ; le bâtiment UNISA Minerals and Materials and the Plasso, université d'Australie-Méridionale (Adelaïde, 2011 ; en association avec Swanbury Penglase et Wilson Architects) ; la Fairhaven House (Victoria, 2012) ; le réaménagement de Westfield Sydney (Sydney, 2012 ; en association avec Westfield Design & Construction) ; le nouveau cabinet de John Wardle Architects (Collingwood, 2012) ; l'UTS Institute for Marine and Antarctic Studies, université de Tasmanie (Tasmanie, 2012 ; en association avec Terroir Architects) et la faculté d'architecture, bâtiment, construction et planification, de l'université de Melbourne (Melbourne, 2014– ; en collaboration avec NADAAA), toutes en Australie.

SHEARERS QUARTERS

North Bruny Island, Tasmania, Australia, 2011

Area: 120 m². Client: Susan and John Wardle.
Collaboration: Andy Wong, Chloe Lanser.

Like a simple shed with a single-slanted roof, the Shearers Quarters structure is clad in corrugated galvanized iron.

Shearers Quarters ist mit verzinktem Wellblech verkleidet wie ein schlichter Schuppen mit Pultdach.

Tel un simple abri avec un toit à une seule pente, la structure du Shearers Quarters est revêtue de fer galvanisé ondulé.

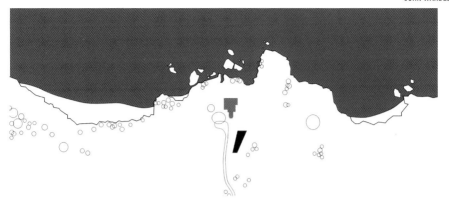

Located on a 440-hectare working sheep farm on North Bruny Island off the southeastern coast of Tasmania, Shearers Quarters was built on the site of an old shearing shed destroyed by fire in the 1980s. It is set near a historic cottage and contains a living/dining/kitchen area, a small bathroom, two bedrooms, and a bunk-room. Corrugated, galvanized iron was used for the exterior surfaces and timber for the interiors (locally sourced *Pinus Macrocarpa*). The architects explain that the "bedrooms are lined in recycled applebox crates, sourced from the many old orchards of the Huon Valley where the timber has remained stacked but unused since the late 1960s." Shearers Quarters won the World's Best Villa Award at the World Architecture Festival (WAF) Awards 2012.

Shearers Quarters steht auf dem 440 ha großen Gelände einer in Betrieb stehenden Schaffarm auf North Bruny Island vor der Südostküste Tasmaniens und wurde anstelle eines Schuppens für die Schafschur errichtet, der in den 1980er-Jahren einem Feuer zum Opfer fiel. Das Haus steht unweit eines historischen Cottages und verfügt über einen Wohn-/Ess-/Küchenbereich, ein kleines Bad, zwei Schlafzimmer und im Innern Holz (*Pinus Macrocarpa*, aus lokalen Beständen). Für die Außenverkleidung wurden verzinkte Wellbleche verwendet und im Innern Holz (*Pinus Macrocarpa*, aus lokalen Beständen). Die „Schlafzimmer sind mit dem Holz alter Apfelkisten ausgekleidet", erläutert der Architekt, „die von den vielen alten Obstplantagen des Huon Valley stammen, wo es seit den 1960er-Jahren ungenutzt lagert". Shearers Quarters gewann den World's Best Villa Award beim World Architecture Festival (WAF) 2012.

Shearers Quarters a été construit à l'emplacement d'un ancien hangar de tonte détruit par un incendie dans les années 1980, sur les 440 hectares d'un élevage de moutons en activité sur l'île de North Bruny, au large de la côte sud-est de la Tasmanie. L'ensemble jouxte un cottage historique et comporte un espace séjour/salle à manger/cuisine, une petite salle de bains, deux chambres à coucher et un dortoir. Les surfaces extérieures sont en fer galvanisé ondulé, et les intérieurs en bois (*Pinus Macrocarpa* d'origine locale). Les architectes expliquent que les « chambres sont garnies de cageots de pommes recyclés, récupérés dans les nombreux vergers anciens de la vallée de l'Huon où le bois était resté empilé sans être utilisé depuis la fin des années 1960 ». Shearers Quarters a remporté le prix international de la villa au World Architecture Festival (WAF) 2012.

Right, a site plan. Above, an image of the structure seen from the side with slat openings allowing in light and air.

À droite, un plan de l'ensemble. En haut, vue de la structure depuis le côté, les ouvertures des lattes laissant entrer air et lumière.

Rechts ein Lageplan. Oben eine Seitenansicht des Gebäudes, wo die Verkleidung sich lamellenartig öffnen lässt, um Licht und Luft hineinzulassen.

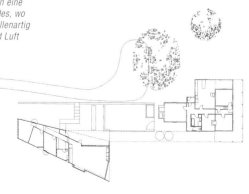

The spectacular interior seems quite distant in its spirit from the farm vocabulary used for the outside of the building. A vast glazed opening allows residents to view the water in comfortable surroundings.

Die spektakulären Innenräume sind offenkundig weit vom bäuerlichen Vokabular des Gebäudeäußeren entfernt. Eine enorme Glaswand ermöglicht den Bewohnern in komfortablem Ambiente den Blick zum Wasser.

L'extraordinaire intérieur semble bien loin du vocabulaire fermier utilisé pour l'extérieur. Une large ouverture vitrée permet aux habitants de regarder l'eau, confortablement installés.

Wood is the main visible material aside from the metal-framed windows. Some openings are triangular in shape at the top, allowing the sky to be seen as well as the sea.

Bis auf die Metallfassungen der Fenster ist Holz das vorwiegend sichtbare Material. Durch einige der Fenster, die oben durch eine Dreiecksfläche erweitert sind, kann man sowohl den Himmel als auch das Meer sehen.

Le bois est le principal matériau visible avec les cadres de fenêtres en métal. Des ouvertures triangulaires en haut permettent d'admirer le ciel autant que la mer.

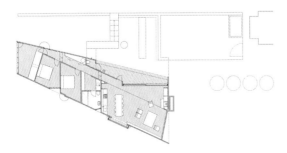

The bedrooms are lined in recycled apple crates, sourced from orchards in the Huon Valley where the wood had remained stacked but unused since the late 1960s. Below, elevation drawings.

Die Verkleidung der Schlafzimmer besteht aus recycelten Apfelkisten, die von Plantagen im Huon Valley stammen, wo das Holz seit den späten 1960er-Jahren ungenutzt lagerte. Unten Aufrisse.

Les chambres sont garnies de cageots de pommes recyclés, récupérés dans les nombreux vergers anciens de la vallée de l'Huon où le bois était resté empilé sans être utilisé depuis la fin des années 1960. Ci-dessous, plans en élévation.

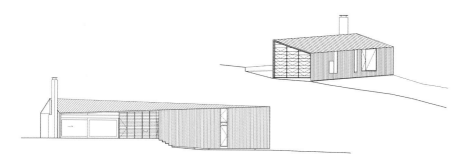

HELENA WILLEMEIT

HELENA WILLEMEIT was born in 1975 in Lilongwe, Malawi. She was raised in Malawi, Zimbabwe, and Germany and studied Architecture at the Universität der Künste (Berlin, 1994–2001) and at the University of New South Wales (Sydney, 1999–2000). She worked in several offices, including those of Daniel Libeskind (Berlin, 2003) and Graft (Berlin and Los Angeles, 2004). In 2004, she participated in the creation of a firm called NYANGA (conception, design, and construction of architecture, surfaces, and furniture from concrete and wood) and, in 2008, the company Airscape, dedicated to "nomadic living," temporary architecture, and furniture: see the project published here, Airscape (Berlin, Germany, 2008).

HELENA WILLEMEIT wurde 1975 in Lilongwe, Malawi, geboren. Sie wuchs in Malawi, Simbabwe und Deutschland auf und studierte Architektur an der Universität der Künste Berlin (1994–2001) und der Universität von New South Wales (Sydney, 1999–2000). Sie war in verschiedenen Büros tätig, darunter für Daniel Libeskind (Berlin, 2003) und Graft (Berlin und Los Angeles, 2004). 2004 war sie an der Gründung des Büros NYANGA beteiligt (Konzeption, Entwurf und bauliche Realisierung von Architektur, Oberflächen und Möbeln aus Beton und Holz) sowie 2008 an der Gründung von Airscape, einem Büro, das sich „nomadischen Wohnformen", temporärer Architektur und dem Möbeldesign verschrieben hat, siehe auch das hier vorgestellte Projekt Airscape (Berlin, 2008).

HELENA WILLEMEIT, née en 1975 à Lilongwe (Malawi), a été élevée au Malawi, au Zimbabwe et en Allemagne. Elle a fait ses études d'architecture à l'Université des arts (Universität der Künste, Berlin, 1994–2001) et à l'université de la Nouvelle-Galles du Sud (Sydney, 1999–2000). Elle a travaillé dans plusieurs agences, dont celle de Daniel Libeskind (Berlin, 2003) et Graft (Berlin et Los Angeles, 2004). En 2004, elle a participé à la création de l'agence NYANGA (conception, design et construction d'architectures, surfaces et mobiliers en bois et béton) et, en 2008, à celle de la société Airscape qui se consacre à la « vie nomade », l'architecture temporaire et le mobilier – voir son projet publié ici, Airscape (Berlin, 2008).

AIRSCAPE

Berlin, Germany, 2008

Area: 70 m².
Client: Helena Willemeit.

Airscape is essentially an inflatable arch that can serve as a shelter. The structure can be articulated in different ways and combined with other Airscape elements.

Airscape, ein aufblasbarer Bogen, lässt sich als schützender Unterstand nutzen. Die Struktur kann zu verschiedenen Formen konfiguriert und mit weiteren Airscape-Elementen kombiniert werden.

Airscape est tout simplement un arc gonflable qui peut servir d'abri. Il peut s'articuler de différentes façons et se combiner avec d'autres éléments identiques.

Airscape tents are "amorphous and mobile architectural spaces" that can be inflated within a few minutes. "With their sensual arched roofs," says Helena Willemeit, "the structures can enclose a floor space of 70 square meters to over 300 square meters. The outstanding characteristic of the modular system is its creative potential: whether a solitary sculpture is presented as a distinct, eye-catching structure, or tents are combined in groups to create a landscape of flowing spaces—the range of applications is wide open." She suggests that the tents can be used for private or corporate events and emphasizes the correspondence between this initiative and the increasingly "nomadic" lifestyle of developed countries. In this sense she seems to be returning in a more modern way to her African upbringing. Airscape tents were used for the 2010 Nintendo Wii City summer tour (Potsdam).

Die Airscape-Zelte sind „amorphe und mobile architektonische Räume", die sich innerhalb weniger Minuten aufblasen lassen. „Mit ihren sinnlich geschwungenen Dächern", so Helena Willemeit, „können die Konstruktionen eine Grundfläche von 70 bis zu über 300 m² haben. Das hervorstechendste Merkmal des modularen Systems ist sein kreatives Potenzial: Ob nun eine einzelne Skulptur als individuelle, plakative Struktur präsentiert wird oder Zelte zu Gruppen und damit zu einer Landschaft aus fließenden Räumen kombiniert werden – das Spektrum der Anwendungsmöglichkeiten ist denkbar breit." Willemeit weist darauf hin, dass die Zelte sowohl für private als auch für Firmenveranstaltungen eingesetzt werden können, und hebt insbesondere die Ähnlichkeiten zwischen ihrer Aktion und dem zunehmend „nomadenhaften" Lebensstil entwickelter Länder hervor. In diesem Sinne scheint sie auf zeitgenössische Weise an ihre Kindheit in Afrika anzuknüpfen. Die Airscape-Zelte kamen unter anderem bei der Nintendo-Wii-Sommertour City 2010 zum Einsatz (Potsdam).

Les tentes Airscape sont des « espaces amorphes et mobiles » gonflables en quelques minutes. « Sous leur forme arquée, sensuelle, explique Helena Willemeit, ces structures peuvent recouvrir un espace de 70 à plus de 300 m². La caractéristique la plus remarquable de ce système modulaire est son potentiel créatif : d'une sculpture surprenante et solitaire à des combinaisons en groupe pour créer un paysage d'espaces en flux, la gamme de ses applications est grande ouverte. » Elle suggère des utilisations pour des manifestations privées ou d'entreprise et insiste sur la correspondance entre cette initiative et le style de vie de plus en plus « nomade » dans les pays développés. En ce sens, elle semble revenir, mais de façon moderne, à ses racines africaines. Les tentes Airscape ont été utilisées pour la tournée 2010 du Nintendo Wii City (Potsdam).

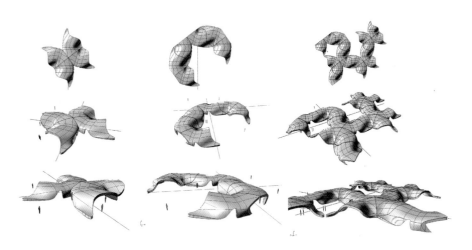

Drawings show the relative scale of the inflatable arches and a number of the ways in which they might be combined to form more complex structures.

Zeichnungen veranschaulichen die Größenverhältnisse der aufblasbaren Bögen und verschiedene Kombinationsmöglichkeiten zu komplexeren Strukturen.

Les dessins montrent des arcs gonflables à différentes échelles et un certain nombre de combinaisons permettant de constituer des structures plus complexes.

In these images, children give some sense of the way in which users can appropriate the structures themselves, going beyond the immediate intentions of the architect.

Diese Aufnahmen mit Kindern vermitteln, wie sich Nutzer die Strukturen aneignen und dabei durchaus von den ursprünglichen Absichten der Architektin lösen können.

Ici, des enfants montrent certaines utilisations d'Airscape, qui dépassent peut-être les intentions de l'architecte.

Configured as a simple, low arch, the Airscape can readily be installed or moved according to needs.

In seiner Konfiguration als einfacher niedriger Bogen lässt sich Airscape problemlos aufbauen und nach Bedarf bewegen.

En forme d'arc simple surbaissé, Airscape s'installe et se déplace aisément, selon les besoins.

INDEX OF ARCHITECTS, BUILDINGS, AND PLACES

#
2by4-architects   38–43

A
Alabama Silo,
Greensboro, Alabama, USA   11, 21, 31, 223–225
Airscape, Berlin, Germany   561–565
Aisslinger, Werner   44–49
AND Market, Tokyo, Japan   201–205
Ark Booktower, Victoria and Albert Museum,
London, UK   10, 20, 30, 424–427
Atelier Bow-Wow   50–61
Atelier de Lyon   392–395
Aula Abierta / La Araña,
Seville, Spain   13, 24, 33, 403–407
Australia
North Bruny Island, Tasmania,
Shearers Quarters   549–559
Austria
Graz, Hpyercubus   505–509
Laterns, Mountain Cabin   327–331
Stubai Glacier, Tyrol,
Top of Tyrol Mountain Platform   287–291

B
Ban, Shigeru   13, 24, 34, 62–77
Barkow Leibinger Architects   78–83
baumraum   12, 23, 33, 84–97
BCMF   98–103
Beetle's House, Victoria and Albert Museum,
London, UK   10, 20, 30, 163–167
Belgium
Berloon, Reading between the Lines 9, 19, 29, 179–185
Brussels, RDF181   439–443
Hechtel-Eksel, The Tree House   85–91
Bent House, Tokyo, Japan   517–521
The Black Pearl,
Rotterdam, The Netherlands   14, 25, 35, 497–503
Blackwell, Marlon   15, 26, 36, 104–107
BMW Guggenheim Lab
New York, USA; Berlin, Germany; Mumbai, India   51–57
Boathouse, Aure, Møre og Romsdal, Norway   523–527
Brazil
Belo Horizonte, Inhotim,
Vegetation Room Inhotim   10, 20, 30, 227–231

Belo Horizonte, Minas Gerais,
Casa Cor Bar   99–103
Brinta House,
Vijversburg, Tytsjerk, The Netherlands   483–487
Bunker 599,
Zijderveld, The Netherlands   9, 19, 29, 393–395
Burnham Pavilion, Chicago, USA 15, 26, 35, 195–199

C
Cadilhe, José   15, 26, 36, 108–113
Camper Pavilion,
Alicante, Spain; Sanya, China; Miami, USA;
Lorient, France   70–73
Camper Store, Barcelona, Spain   333–335
Canada
Gulf Islands, British Columbia,
Gulf Islands Cabin   374–379
Verdun, Montreal, The Tire Shop Project   319–325
Cave for Children,
Trondheim, Norway   14, 24, 34, 207–211
Casa Cor Bar,
Belo Horizonte, Minas Gerais, Brazil   99–103
Children's Room, Mexico City, Mexico   433–437
Chile
Santa Sofia de Lo Cañas, Santiago, Cozy Box 476–481
Santa Sofia de Lo Cañas, Santiago,
Feuereisen House   471–475
China
Beijing, Red+Housing: Architecture on the
Edge of Survival   355–359
Sanya, Camper Pavilion   70–73
Shenzhen, Tri-Colonnade   11, 21, 31, 465–469
Clavel-Rojo, Manuel   114–119
Cloud Pantheon, Espinardo, Murcia, Spain 115–119
Coelacanth and Associates   120–125
Container GuestHouse, San Antonio, USA   389–391
Corvalán, Javier   126–129
Cozy Box, Santa Sofia de Lo Cañas,
Santiago, Chile   476–481
Crosson Clarke Carnachan   12, 22, 32, 130–139

D
D Jewelry, Pamplona, Spain 535–539
design neuob 15, 25, 35, 140–145
Discovering Columbus, New York, USA 345–347
Dovecote Studio, Snape, Suffolk, UK 217–221

E
Endémico Resguardo Silvestre, Valle de Guadalupe,
Ensenada, Mexico 12, 22, 32, 187–193
Endo, Shuhei 146–153
Endoh, Masaki 154–157

F
Falck, Robin 158–161
Feuereisen House, Santa Sofia de Lo Cañas,
Santiago, Chile 471–475
Fincube, Winterinn, Ritten, South Tyrol, Italy 45–49
Finland
Sipoo, Nido 159–161
Fireplace for Children,
Trondheim, Norway 14, 24, 34, 212–215
France
Lorient, Camper Pavilion 70–73
Paris, Pink Bar 260–263
Fujimori, Terunobu 10, 20, 30, 162–167
Fujimoto, Sou 168–177
Fukita Pavilion,
Shodoshima, Kagawa, Japan 9, 20, 30, 349–353

G
Germany
Bad Zwischenahn,
Tree Whisper Tree-House Hotel 12, 23, 33, 92–97
Berlin, Airscape 561–565
Berlin, BMW Guggenheim Lab 51–57
Gijs Van Vaerenbergh 9, 19, 29, 178–185
Gracia García, Jorge 12, 22, 32, 186–193
Greenhouses, Japanese Pavilion,
Venice, Italy 10, 20, 30, 233–237
Gulf Islands Cabin,
Gulf Islands, British Columbia, Canada 374–379

H
Hadid, Zaha 15, 26, 35, 194–199
Haiti
Port-au-Prince,
Paper Temporary Shelters in Haiti 13, 24, 34, 74–77
Hakuhodo 200–205
Hamaca House, Luque, Paraguay 127–129
Haugen/Zohar 14, 24, 34, 206–215
Haus der Hoffnung, Natori, Miyagi, Japan 313–317
Haworth Tompkins 216–221
Hojo-an, Kyoto, Japan 277–279
Home-for-All in Rikuzentakata,
Rikuzentakata, Iwate, Japan 13, 23, 33, 247–251
House 77, Póvoa de Varzim, Portugal 15, 26, 36, 109–113
House in Chayagasaka,
Nagoya, Aichi, Japan 12, 22, 32, 269–275
House K, Nishinomiya-shi, Hyogo, Japan 169–173
House of Stone, Milan, Italy 385–387
Hursley, Timothy 11, 21, 31, 222–225
Hut on Sleds,
Whangapoua, New Zealand 12, 22, 32, 131–139
Hut to Hut, Kagala, Karnataka, India 10, 21, 31, 415–419
Hypercubus, Graz, Austria 505–509

I
Iglesias, Cristina 10, 20, 30, 226–231
Illy Push Button House, Venice, Italy 265–267
In-Between Architecture,
Victoria and Albert Museum, London, UK 489–495
India
Kagala, Karnataka, Hut to Hut 10, 21, 31, 415–419
Mumbai, BMW Guggenheim Lab 51–57
Inside In, Tokyo, Japan 252–257
Inujima Art House Project,
Inujima, Okayama, Japan 460–463
Isozaki, Arata 238–245
Ishigami, Junya 10, 20, 30, 232–237
Island House, Breukelen, The Netherlands 39–43
Italy
Milan, House of Stone 385–387
South Tyrol, Winterinn, Ritten, Fincube 45–49
Venice, Greenhouses,
Japanese Pavilion 10, 20, 30, 233–237
Venice, Illy Push Button House 265–267
Ito, Toyo 13, 23, 33, 246–257

J
Jakob+MacFarlane   258–263
Japan
Hiroshima, Peanuts   14, 24, 34, 306–311
Hokkaido, Même Experimental House   280–285
Ichihara City, Chiba, Public Toilet in Ichihara   174–177
Inujima, Okayama,
Inujima Art House Projekt   460–463
Kumamoto City,
Shirakawa Public Toilet   15, 25, 35, 141–145
Kyoto, Hojo-an   277–279
Nagoya, Aichi,
House in Chayagasaka   12, 22, 32, 269–275
Natori, Miyagi, Haus der Hoffnung   313–317
Nishinomiya-shi, Hyogo, House K   169–173
Odawara, Kanagawa, Sunken House   121–125
Osaka, Rooftecture OT2   147–153
Rikuzentakata, Iwate,
Home-for-All in Rikuzentakata   13, 23, 33, 247–251
Shodoshima, Kagawa,
Fukita Pavilion   9, 20, 30, 349–353
Tokyo, AND Market   201–205
Tokyo, Bent House   517–521
Tokyo, Inside In   252–257
Tokyo, Natural Illuminance II   155–157
Tokyo, Rendez-Vous   58–61
Tokyo, Suginami, Riverside House   337–343
Tokyo, Tsuchihashi House   11, 22, 32, 455–459

K
Kalkin, Adam   264–267
Kondo, Tetsuo   12, 22, 32, 268–275
Kuma, Kengo   276–285

L
LAAC   286–291
LOT-EK   292–303
Low-Cost House, Dongnai, Vietnam   13, 24, 34, 541–547

M
Madison Avenue (Doll)House,
New York, USA   12, 22, 32, 409–413
Maeda, Keisuke   14, 24, 34, 304–311
Maki, Fumihiko   312–317

Marcus Prize Pavilion
Menomonee Valley, Milwaukee, USA   79–83
MARK+VIVI   318–325
Marte.Marte   326–331
Même Experimental House, Hokkaido, Japan   280–285
Mexico
Mexico City, Children's Room   433–437
Mexico City, Portal of Awareness   11, 21, 31, 429–431
Valle de Guadalupe, Ensenada,
Endémico Resguardo Silvestre   12, 22, 32, 187–193
Miralles Tagliabue EMBT   332–335
Mizuishi, Kota   336–343
Mountain Cabin, Laterns, Austria   327–331

N
Natural Illuminance II, Tokyo, Japan   155–157
The Netherlands
Breukelen, Island House   39–43
Zijderveld, Bunker 599   9, 19, 29, 393–395
Vijversburg, Tytsjerk, Brinta House   483–487
Rotterdam, The Black Pearl   14, 25, 35, 497–503
New Amsterdam Pavilion,
New York, USA   15, 26, 35, 529–533
New Zealand
Whangapoua, Hut on Sleds   12, 22, 32, 131–139
Nido, Sipoo, Finland   159–161
Nishi, Tatzu   344–347
Nishizawa, Ryue   9, 20, 30, 348–353
Norway
Aure, Møre og Romsdal, Boathouse   523–527
Rysjedalsvika,
Sogn og Fjordane Summer Cabin   451–453
Seljord, Telemark,
Seljord Watchtower   10, 21, 31, 420–423
Trondheim, Cave for Children   14, 24, 34, 207–211
Trondheim, Fireplace for Children   14, 24, 34, 212–215

O
Obscured Horizon, Pioneertown, California, USA   239–245
OBRA Architects   354–359
Office of Mobile Design   360–367
Olson Cabin, Longbranch, Washington, USA   380–383
Olson Kundig   12, 23, 33, 368–383
OMD Prefab Show House,
Joshua Tree, California, USA   361–365

P

Paraguay
  Luque, Hamaca House   127–129
Pawson, John   384–387
Peanuts, Hiroshima, Japan   14, 24, 34, 306–311
Paper Temporary Shelters in Haiti,
  Port-au-Prince, Haiti   13, 24, 34, 74–77
Pink Bar, Paris, France   260–263
Portal of Awareness,
  Mexico City, Mexico   11, 21, 31, 429–431
Portugal
  Algarve, Quinta Botanica   63–69
  Póvoa de Varzim, House 77   15, 26, 36, 109–113
Poteet, Jim   388–391
Public Toilet in Ichihara,
  Ichihara City, Chiba, Japan   174–177

Q

Quinta Botanica, Algarve, Portugal   63–69

R

RAAAF   9, 19, 29, 392–395
Raumlaborberlin   396–401
RDF181, Brussels, Belgium   439–443
Reading between the Lines,
  Bergloon, Belgium   9, 19, 29, 179–185
Recetas Urbanas   13, 23, 33, 402–407
Red+Housing: Architecture on the Edge of Survival,
  Beijing, China   355–359
Rendez-Vous, Tokyo, Japan   58–61
REX   12, 22, 32, 408–413
Rintala Eggertsson   10, 20, 30, 414–427
Riverside House, Suginami, Tokyo, Japan   337–343
Rojkind Arquitectos   11, 21, 31, 428–431
Romero, Fernando   432–437
Rooftecture OT2, Osaka, Japan   147–153
Rotor   438–443

S

Saint Nicholas Eastern Orthodox Church,
  Springdale, Arkansas, USA   15, 26, 36, 105–107
Saipua, Brooklyn, New York, USA   511–515
Salmela, David   444–449
Saunders, Todd   450–453

Sejima, Kazuyo   11, 22, 32, 454–463
Seljord Watchtower,
  Seljord, Telemark, Norway   10, 21, 31, 420–423
Shearers Quarters, North Bruny Island,
  Tasmania, Australia   549–559
Shirakawa Public Toilet,
  Kumamoto City, Japan   15, 25, 35, 141–145
SO – IL   11, 21, 31, 464–469
Sogn og Fjordane Summer Cabin,
  Rysjedalsvika, Norway   451–453
Sol Duc Cabin, Olympic Peninsula,
  Washington, USA   12, 23, 33, 369–373
Soza, Juan Agustin   470–481
Spain
  Alicante, Camper Pavilion   70–73
  Barcelona, Camper Store   333–335
  Espinardo, Murcia, Cloud Pantheon   115–119
  Pamplona, D Jewelry   535–539
  Seville, Aula Abierta / La Araña 13, 24, 33, 403–407
Spacebuster, New York, USA   397–401
Studio Makkink & Bey   482–487
Studio Mumbai   488–495
Studio Rolf.fr   14, 25, 35, 496–503
Studio WG3   504–509
Sunken House, Odawara, Kanagawa, Japan   121–125

T

Tacklebox   510–515
Taliesin Mod.Fab, Scottsdale, Arizona, USA   366–367
The Tire Shop Project,
  Verdun, Montreal, Canada   319–325
The Tree House, Hechtel-Eksel, Belgium   85–91
Top of Tyrol Mountain Platform,
  Stubai Glacier, Tyrol, Austria   287–291
Tree Whisper Tree-House Hotel,
  Bad Zwischenahn, Germany   12, 23, 33, 92–97
Tri-Colonnade, Shenzhen, China 11, 21, 31, 465–469
Tsuchihashi House, Tokyo, Japan 11, 22, 32, 455–459
Tsutsui, Koji   516–521
TYIN tegnestue Architects   522–527

Crosson Clarke Carnachan, ▶
Hut on Sleds, Whangapoua,
New Zealand, 2011 (page 132)

U
UID architects   14, 24, 34, 304–311
UK
London, Victoria and Albert Museum,
Ark Booktower   10, 20, 30, 424–427
London, Victoria and Albert Museum,
Beetle's House   10, 20, 30, 163–167
London, Victoria and Albert Museum,
In-Between Architecture   489–495
Snape, Suffolk, Dovecote Studio   217–221
UNStudio   15, 26, 35, 528–533
USA
Brooklyn, New York, Saipua   511–515
Chicago, Burnham Pavilion   15, 26, 35, 195–199
Greensboro, Alabama,
Alabama Silo   11, 21, 31, 223–225
Joshua Tree, California,
OMD Prefab Show House   361–365
Longbranch, Washington, Olson Cabin   380–383
Menomonee Valley, Milwaukee, USA,
Marcus Prize Pavilion   79–83
Miami, Camper Pavilion   70–73
New York, BMW Guggenheim Lab   51–57
New York,
Madison Avenue (Doll)House   12, 22, 32, 409–413
New York, Discovering Columbus   345–347
New York, New Amsterdam Pavilion   15, 26, 35, 529–533
New York, Spacebuster   399–401
New York, Van Alen Books   300–303
New York, Whitney Studio   293–299
Olympic Peninsula, Washington,
Sol Duc Cabin   12, 23, 33, 369–373
Pioneertown, California, Obscured Horizon   239–245
San Antonio, Container GuestHouse   389–391
Scottsdale, Arizona, Taliesin Mod.Fab   366–367
Springdale, Arkansas, Saint Nicholas Eastern
Orthodox Church   15, 26, 36, 105–107
Traverse City, Michigan,
Yingst Pavilion and Sauna   445–449

V
Vaillo + Irigaray Architects   534–539
Van Alen Books, New York, USA   300–303
Vegetation Room Inhotim,
Inhotim, Belo Horizonte, Brazil   10, 20, 30, 227–231

Vietnam
Dongnai, Low-Cost House   13, 24, 34, 541–547
Vo Trong Nghia   13, 24, 34, 540–547

W
Wardle, John   548–559
Whitney Studio, New York, USA   293–299
Willemeit, Helena   560–565

Y
Yingst Pavilion and Sauna,
Traverse City, Michigan, USA   445–449

Z
Zecc Architects   14, 25, 35, 496–503

CREDITS

CREDITS FOR PLANS / DRAWINGS / CAD DOCUMENTS — **40** © 2by4-architects / **49** © Studio Aisslinger / **52, 54, 56** © Atelier Bow-Wow / **67, 69, 72, 74** © Shigeru Ban Architects Europe / **81–82** © Barkow Leibinger Architects / **86, 90, 92** © baumraum Andreas Wenning / **100** © BCMF Arquitetos / **107** © Marlon Blackwell Architect / **110, 112–113** © dIONISO LAB / **123, 125** © CAt / **129** © Laboratorio de Arquitectura / **134–136** © Crosson Clarke Carnachan Architects / **143–144** © design neuob / **150, 153** © Endo Shuhei Architect Insitute Inc. / **156–157** © Endoh Design House / **160** © Robin Falck / **165** © Terunobu Fujimori / **170–171** © Sou Fujimoti Architects / **183–184** © Gijs Van Vaerenbergh / **189, 191–193** © Studio Odile Decq / **198** © Zaha Hadid Architects / **203** © Hakuhodo Inc. / **210, 212, 215** © Haugen/Zohar Architekter / **218** © Haworth Tompkins / **229, 231** © Cristina Iglesias / **237** © junya.ishigami+associates, courtesy of Gallery Koyanagi / **254** © Toyo Ito / **263** © Jakob+MacFarlane / **270, 274–275** © Tetsuo Kondo Architects / **279, 281** © Kengo Kuma & Associates / **290** © LAAC Architects / **294–295, 298, 302** © Courtesy of LOT-EK / **309–310** © UID Architects / **314–315** © Maki and Associates / **325** © MARK+VIVI / **329** © Stefan Marte / **334** © Miralles Tagliabue EMBT / **338, 342** © Mizuishi Architect Atelier / **356, 359** © OBRA Architects / **364–365** © Office of Mobile Design / **371, 373, 375–377, 381–382** © Olson Kundig Architects / **391** © Poteet Architects / **396, 398** © Raumlaborberlin / **405–407** © Recetas Urbanas S.L. / **419** © Rintala Eggertson Architects / **436** © FR-EE/Fernando Romero Enterprise / **440, 443** © Rotor vzw-asbl / **446–447** © Salmela Architect / **460, 462–463** © Kazuyo Sejima & Associates / **466** © SO – IL / **472–473, 476** © Agustin Soza Arquitectos Asociados / **485** © Studio Makkink & Bey / **490, 495** © Studio Mumbai / **499, 501** © Rolf.fr & Zecc Architects / **508** © Studio WG3 and Karin Lernbeiß/Lupi Spuma / **512** © Tacklebox LLC / **518, 521** © Koji Tsutsui & Associates / **524** © TYIN tegnestue Architects / **532–533** © UNStudio / **542–543** © Vo Trong Nghia Architects / **551, 553, 556, 559** © John Wardle Architects / **564** © Helena Willemeit

100 Illustrators

The Package Design
Book

Logo Design.
Global Brands

D&AD.
The Copy Book

Modern Art

**Bookworm's delight:
never bore, always excite!**

TASCHEN
Bibliotheca Universalis

Design of the 20th Century

1000 Chairs

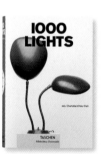

1000 Lights

Industrial Design A–Z

Bauhaus

1000 Record Covers

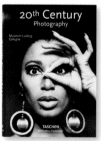

20th Century Photography

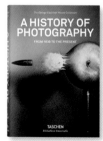

A History of Photography

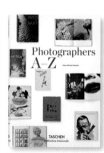

Photographers A–Z

Eugène Atget. Paris

Photo Icons

New Deal Photography

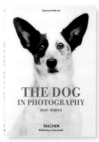

The Dog in Photography

Curtis. The North American Indian

Stieglitz. Camera Work

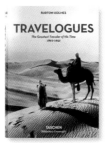

Burton Holmes. Travelogues

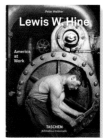

Lewis W. Hine

Film Noir

Horror Cinema

100 All-Time Favorite Movies

The Stanley Kubrick Archives

20th Century Fashion

Fashion History

1000 Tattoos

Tiki Pop

Domestic bliss

Innovative, intimate architecture from China to Chile

Designing private residences has its own very special challenges and nuances for the architect. The scale may be more modest than public projects, the technical fittings less complex than an industrial site, but the preferences, requirements and vision of particular personalities becomes priority. The delicate task is to translate all the emotive associations and practical requirements of "home" into a workable, constructed reality. This publication rounds up 100 of the world's most interesting and pioneering homes designed in the past two decades, featuring a host of talents both new and established, including John Pawson, Richard Meier, Shigeru Ban, Tadao Ando, Zaha Hadid, Herzog & de Meuron, Daniel Libeskind, Alvaro Siza, and Peter Zumthor.

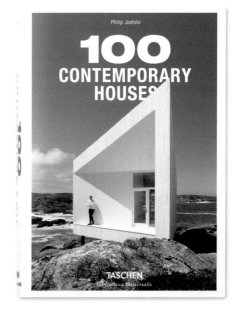

"Take a ride around the world's best new houses with TASCHEN ... From timber shacks to glazed pavilions, there's a weird and wonderful inspiration for all."

— *Grand Designs*, London

100 Contemporary Houses
Philip Jodidio
688 pages

TRILINGUAL EDITIONS IN:
ENGLISH / DEUTSCH / FRANÇAIS &
ESPAÑOL / ITALIANO / PORTUGUÊS

Space shapers

An encyclopedia of modern architecture

Explore the A–Z of modern space. From Gio Ponti's colored geometries
to Zaha Hadid's free-flowing futurism, this comprehensive overview features
more than 280 profiles of architects, styles, movements, and trends
that have shaped structures from the 19th to the 21st century.

"A splendid record of
architecture from
the nineteenth century
to the present day."

— *Architectural Review*, London

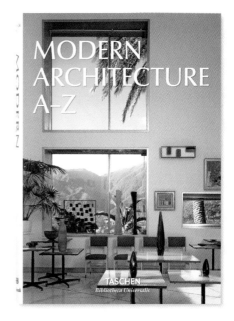

Modern Architecture A–Z
696 pages
EDITIONS IN: ENGLISH / DEUTSCH /
FRANÇAIS / ESPAÑOL

Form meets function

The industrial designs that shape our lives

If you take even the slightest interest in the design of your toothbrush, the history behind your washing machine, or the evolution of the telephone, you'll take an even greater interest in this completely updated edition of *Industrial Design A–Z*. Tracing the evolution of industrial design from the Industrial Revolution to the present day, the book bursts with synergies of form and function that transform our daily experience. From cameras to kitchenware, Lego to Lamborghini, we meet the individual designers, the global businesses, and above all the genius products, that become integrated into even the smallest details of our lives.

"This invaluable bible will tell you all about the origin of the objects around you."

—*Elle Décoration*, Paris

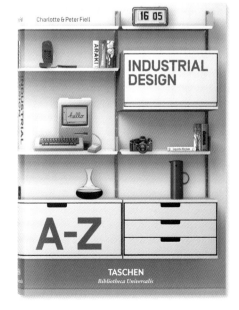

Industrial Design A-Z
Charlotte & Peter Fiell
616 pages
EDITIONS IN: ENGLISH / DEUTSCH /
FRANÇAIS / ESPAÑOL / ITALIANO

YOU CAN FIND TASCHEN STORES IN

Berlin
Schlüterstr. 39

Beverly Hills
354 N. Beverly Drive

Brussels
Place du Grand Sablon /
Grote Zavel 35

Cologne
Neumarkt 3

Hollywood
Farmers Market,
6333 W. 3rd Street, CT-10

Hong Kong
Shop 01-G02 Tai Kwun,
10 Hollywood Road,
Central

London
12 Duke of York Square

Madrid
Calle del Barquillo, 30

Miami
1111 Lincoln Rd.

Milan
Via Meravigli 17

"If browsing is considered an art form, the TASCHEN store is a masterpiece."
— *Dwell*

New York
60 Gansevoort St

Paris
2 rue de Buci

EACH AND EVERY TASCHEN BOOK PLANTS A SEED!
TASCHEN is a carbon neutral publisher. Each year, we off-
set our annual carbon emissions with carbon credits at the
Instituto Terra, a reforestation program in Minas Gerais,
Brazil, founded by Lélia and Sebastião Salgado. To find out
more about this ecological partnership, please check:
www.taschen.com/zerocarbon
INSPIRATION: UNLIMITED. CARBON FOOTPRINT: ZERO.

To stay informed about TASCHEN and our upcoming titles,
please subscribe to our free magazine at *www.taschen.com/
magazine*, follow us on Instagram and Facebook, or e-mail
your questions to *contact@taschen.com*.

Illustration page 2: Studio Rolf.fr and Zecc Architects,
The Black Pearl, Rotterdam, The Netherlands, 2008–10
(page 498)

GERMAN TRANSLATION
Johann Christoph Maass, Kristina Brigitta Köper,
Holger Wölfle & Gregor Runge, Berlin;
Nora von Mühlendahl, Ludwigsburg

FRENCH TRANSLATION
Blandine Pélissier & Jacques Bosser, Paris;
Claire Debard, Freiburg

PRINTED IN BOSNIA-HERZEGOVINA
ISBN 978–3–8365–4790–1